THE BLACKBIRDERS

Also by E. W. Docker
SIMPLY HUMAN BEINGS

THE BLACKBIRDERS

*The Recruiting of South Seas Labour
for Queensland, 1863-1907*

_____

EDWARD WYBERGH DOCKER

ANGUS AND ROBERTSON

First published in 1970 by

ANGUS & ROBERTSON LTD

221 George Street, Sydney

54 Bartholomew Close, London

107 Elizabeth Street, Melbourne

89 Anson Road, Singapore

National Library of Australia card number and
ISBN 0 207 12038 2

Registered in Australia for transmission by post as a book
PRINTED IN AUSTRALIA BY HALSTEAD PRESS, SYDNEY

TO MY MOTHER AND FATHER

Acknowledgments

I wish firstly to thank Mrs Faith Bandler of Sydney for asking me to write this book. As a result of her initial help and encouragement I was able to meet and talk to many members of the Melanesian community in Australia, including especially the Mussing family of Tweed Heads and Mr Arthur Corrowa of Bowen and members of his family. I should also like to thank the staffs of the Mitchell and Dixson libraries, Sydney, of the Archives Section of the Public Library of Queensland, of the Public Library of Vila, New Hebrides, of the South Pacific Commission Library, Noumea, of the Commonwealth Archives Office, Canberra, and National Library of Australia. Members of the British Office in Vila were of great help to me during my stay in the New Hebrides. Dr M. R. Allen of the Anthropology Department, Sydney University, kindly permitted me to read his thesis on the Nduindui of Oba. My thanks are due also to Mrs Yvonne Besant and Miss Lucy Breen, who typed the manuscript.

The photographs are reproduced by kind permission of the Trustees of the Mitchell Library. The maps were drawn by Beverley Docker.

E.W.D.

"They were not going pearl-fishing, but blackbird-hunting. It is said you should have evidence as to what blackbird-hunting meant. I think it is a grievous mistake to pretend to ignorance of things passing before our eyes every day. We may know the meaning of slang words, though we do not use them. Is there not a wide distinction between blackbird-hunting and a legitimate labour-trade, if such a thing is to be carried on? What did he allude to? To get labourers honestly if they could, but, if not, any way?"

> The Melbourne *Argus*, 21st December 1872, reporting Chief Justice Sir William Stawell's charge in the case of the *"Carl* Outrage"

If you at last must have a word to say,
Say neither in their way,
"It is a deadly magic and accursed"
Nor "It is blest." But only "It is here."

> Stephen Vincent Benét, *John Brown's Body*

Contents

1   The Old Plantation   1

2   The Homeland   18

3   The Recruiters Become Established, 1864-9   42

4   The Recruiting Booms, 1870-1   68

5   The Sugar Industry Booms, 1864-80   95

6   Changing Melanesia   115

7   Recruiting, 1871-83   139

8   Blackbirding in New Guinea   169

9   The Reaction in Queensland   203

10   Recruiting—the Last Phase   227

11   Deportation   258

12   Epilogue   275

     Select Bibliography   277

     Index   283

Illustrations

Robert Towns	36
James Burns	36
An elaborate canoe at Pileni	37
Native shrine and men's club-house on Vella Lavella	37
Natives of Ada Gege, one of Malaita's artificial islands	52
A Malekula chief	52
A Malekulan	52
Taki, a chief of Wango, San Cristobal	53
Trading with the natives	53
Plantation workers in the islands husking coconuts	100
A planter's home in the islands	100
A bachelor planter?	101
Bishop Patteson	101
The Reverend Alfred Lombu	116
A young recruit for the Church at Vella Lavella	116
Patteson's grave at Nukapu	117
Bishop Cecil Wilson at steer oar	117
Residence of the Reverend J. Geddie at Aneityum	164
The Reverend J. Goldie with his henchmen	164
Recruited. On the way to Queensland c. 1890	165
Three members of a boat-crew	165
Samuel Griffith	180
William Brookes	180
A planter's home in the Bundaberg district	181
A communal dwelling-house built by plantation labourers in Queensland	181
The C.S.R.'s Childers mill in the Bundaberg district	244
A home built by a time-expired labourer	244
The overseer with a chipping gang in Queensland	244
Kanakas cutting cane on a Queensland plantation	245
The recruiter *Fearless* with recruits on their way home	245
Returns with their boxes	260
A victim of the Deportation Act	260
Aoban girls	261

ONE

The Old Plantation

FORTY miles south of Brisbane on the Logan River, Townsvale in 1864 was the cotton plantation of the prosperous Sydney businessman and shipowner, Robert Towns. Yet "plantation", although it was used of Townsvale almost for the first time in Australia to describe any such establishment, is a misleading term. Black field hands toiled, bent between the hot rows, watched over by men on horseback. Otherwise the atmosphere that one tends to associate with the Old South, of cool porticoes fragrant with orange blossom, of dusky retainers stooping to proffer, with exquisite tact, the mint julep, was quite starkly absent. This was still the pioneering stage.

At the foot of a thickly timbered ridge, adjacent to several large lagoons, lay the weatherboard homestead—plain, practical, indomitably Australian. Other buildings, fronting in different directions as though suddenly called into being according to the inspiration of the moment, were scattered beyond—a machine shed, blacksmith's shop, carpenter's shop, a very large structure known as the cotton chamber, packing and loading sheds, sawmill, flour mill, stables, butcher's shop, stockyards. All were kept very whitewashed and neat, nevertheless. Towns had invested £6,000 in the property to make it the show-piece of Queensland's burgeoning cotton industry.

The pride of the whole place, however, was the steam plough. It was not the very latest thing of its kind compared with certain American inventions. It was a solidly British achievement with ingenious local improvisations to suit the uncompromisingly Australian conditions. Drawn behind a horse, a portable 12-horsepower engine proceeded by degrees, a few yards at a time, down the middle of a 40-acre paddock. Two revolving drums were attached to opposite sides of this engine, one paying out, the other winding in a continuous length of wire rope. The whole process had an almost hypnotic quality as one watched the rope in action, lolloping out into the clumps of swamp-grass, ceaselessly disappearing towards one distant margin of the field. There, out of sight, it passed around a couple of corner blocks before setting out on its journey across the field, via the drum in the middle to keep it taut, to the far side. At first one drum revolving in a certain direction drew the rope one way, and then the other went into action to reverse the process, two sets of ploughs shuttlecocked back and forth between the engine and one side of the field.

The beauty of the system was that it kept constantly employed, in the slack season between picking and planting, sixty-odd Kanakas. When one set of ploughs arrived at the outward end of its journey a black signalman signalled the engineer to stop the engine. Whereupon three more assisted the plough-driver to raise one frame of plough-wheels and lower into position a second frame with the wheels set at an opposite angle—so that on the return journey along the same furrow the earth would be turned the other way and the ground left uniform. Meanwhile six men would be moving the corner-blocks systematically downfield parallel with the engine; another three attending the little sets of wheels that kept the rope travelling clear of obstructions on the ground; another three wandering around oiling the pulleys. Finally there was a man to follow each set of ploughs armed with a handspike to free them if they stuck; a man to water the horse and feed the engine; water the engine and feed the horse; cut the firewood, cart the firewood, and so on—up to sixty.

There was thus a feast of activity to contemplate during the ploughing, a state of affairs that gave intense satisfaction to every Kanaka present. Simple souls they appeared to many, larking around the engine, shouting and gleeful, chiacking each other, brandishing a weapon as if about to strike, lying in wait and springing out. Some of them were only boys, fourteen or fifteen, but there were others full grown, all with the same unselfconscious air of thoroughly enjoying themselves. By August 1864 they had been in Queensland twelve months and so far been fully and happily occupied the whole time. After the ploughing, bullock- and horse-teams harrowed and drilled, escorted by gangs of boys to remove stone and weeds, adjust the harrows and shout encouragement to the driver. Then the seed was planted; cartloads of seed would be dumped in the field each morning and the sowers with large bags slung over their backs would advance in long lines, dashing the seed around until the furrows were quite white.

Engendering a spirit of rivalry, making one group of islanders compete with another, keeping up their interest by providing as much variety as possible, was the recipe which got the most out of them.

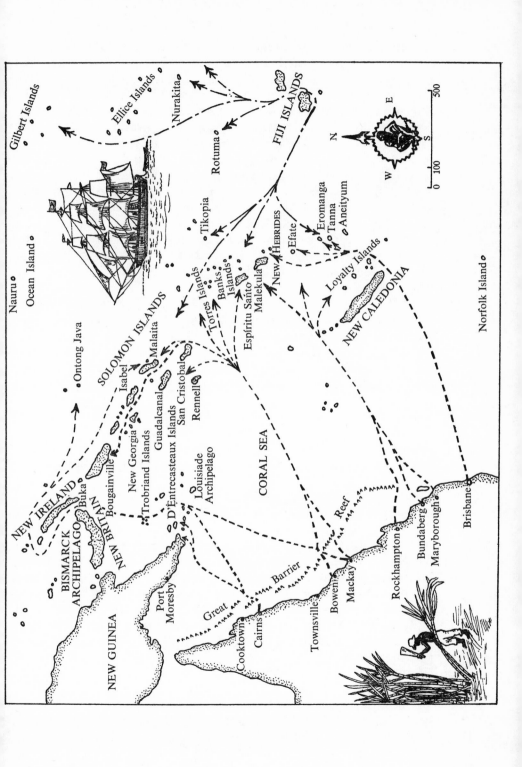

One lot, however, from the island of Tanna, seemed to have made themselves especially at home. Strikingly handsome after their own wild fashion, with long hair twisted into hundreds of tight ringlets, the Tannamen were generally taller and better-muscled than the rest and therefore reserved for the heavier tasks. On the whole the islanders did not take particularly to the axe-work. They were apt to plunge the blade into a stout trunk when nobody was looking and break off the handle by pulling it sideways. But the Tannese revelled in their superior stamina. Attacking each tree as they would an enemy, grunting and moaning with the strain of every blow, they kept at it until the tree began to give way under the onslaught. Finally as it creaked and toppled they leapt aside turning with wild cries of exultation to contemplate the slain. When Towns visited the plantation at Christmas 1864 and saw how well the experiment with Kanaka labour was going, he wondered why he had delayed so long before attempting it.

Eastern Australia, in common with other European colonies all over the world, had been plagued by the lack of a reliable labour supply ever since the territory had been originally settled in 1788. Also at this time, in South America, in North America, in South Africa, in New Zealand, in Western as well as eastern Australia, large tracts of the earth's surface were being opened up to the enterprise of the white races, and yet the native inhabitants of these places, out of sheer stubbornness it seemed, or some innate indisposition to labour, refused to be employed. Reason was useless with them. The idle brutes simply could not be made to see that this opportunity of being steadily occupied and earning regular wages was their one-and-only chance of escaping from their primitive ignorance.

Never before in their European experience had the colonizers encountered people so unaccustomed to the notion of service. In former centuries they had had no compunction in enslaving the population of one continent and carrying it off to work in another. It was but a law of nature surely that the weak should serve the strong. Besides, people argued, was it not obvious from the very thickness of their hides, from the impervious quality of the skull into which no light had ever been known to penetrate, that this was the purpose for which the Creator had intended them, to be mere hewers of wood and drawers of water? But then, in the nineteenth century, Great Britain, foremost of the nations, had led the way in discrediting and finally outlawing the institution of slavery, making it appear an anachronism in an age when machines were being created to do the labour of slaves. The other nations had been reluctantly obliged to follow suit.

By freeing the slaves throughout the Empire, however, the British had not intended to ruin the slave-owners, not even seriously to inconvenience them. The former slaves, it thought, would be compelled to continue in the same employment through economic necessity. What other regular employments, in the exclusively sugar-producing colonies of Mauritius, Demerara (British Guiana), Jamaica, Barbados, and other West Indian Islands, could they hope to find? And yet, and it was very surprising and upsetting to economic theory to discover, the liberated ones chose not to go on labouring in the plantation. They preferred to eke out a bare existence farming, or affecting to be thus engaged, in the surrounding hills and forests. Centuries of slavery had apparently taught them nothing about the dignity of labour. So the disappointed planters, after several frustrating years of casting about for some alternative means of enforcing African labour against its will and not finding any satisfactory substitute, turned to an altogether different source of supply in Asia. In British India, they discovered, there were large native populations habituated to toil, trained to obedience. China too, seemed to be filled to overflowing, though the Chinese were not as yet so amenable to the European influence.

The Indian coolie trade began only twelve months after the great emancipation: to Mauritius in 1834; to the more distant West Indies in 1844. The Imperial Government chartered the ships in the case of the West Indies; a local immigration authority in the case of Mauritius. The Indian Government had to approve the selections. The idea was that the emigration and employment of coolies should be Government-controlled at all stages, from supervision of the emigrants in their depots at Madras and Calcutta awaiting embarkation to the moment five years later at the end of their indentures when they should be free to return to India or serve another term on the plantation.

It was still a system very much open to abuse, it appeared, though not for one minute threatening to degenerate into another slave trade. Already around the coasts of Africa the Admiralty was spending too much money putting down other illegal slave trades to tolerate the possibility of that. If a better parallel be sought, it might be found in the still-continuing transportation of convicts to Western Australia. Like the convicts, the coolies had temporarily forfeited whatever rights they might have enjoyed as free citizens, yet could look forward to eventual release and perhaps a better way of life in a new country. And thus it happened. All the cruelties and indignities inflicted on them in the meantime notwithstanding, few of these convicts or coolies would ever wish to return home. It was as though after a period of intense trial and suffering they had reached the

B

Promised Land, had graduated to the plane of the elect and could best derive some meaning from all their experiences by enjoying the sufferings of those who came after. Anyway, the coolie seemed to prosper wherever he emigrated, and by the late 1850s the trade bore a sufficiently respectable character for the British Colonial Secretary to plead with the Indian Government to approve its extension to the young colony of Natal.

Natal in 1858 was in much the same situation as Western Australia had been in 1849 and as Queensland was shortly to be—possessing land by the hundreds of square miles, capitalists waiting to invest, and the native population, for some inscrutable reason of its own, unwilling to work. Cotton had been the staple originally envisaged for Natal, and the Zulu locations had been spaced so that each planter should be able to draw upon an adequate supply of labour from its immediate vicinity. But the labour refused to be drawn.

It seems strange, after the example of the past, that the British rulers of South Africa should have failed to appreciate that the African was not interested in working for wages, even in the relatively light tasks of picking and tending cotton, while he had land to subsist on and his own seemingly shiftless employments. The colonists quickly learned from their mistake, however, and in 1859 passed a law enabling the Government to obtain coolies from India. There was some minor opposition in the Legislative Council—chiefly from men who owned land in the interior and seemed to think there were enough natives in Natal already—but the Act was acclaimed in the colony at large ". . . essential to our prosperity . . . a revitalizing principle . . . to give wider scope for the employment of our own skilled countrymen". The first shiploads arrived in November 1860. By the turn of the century there were nearly a hundred thousand coolies in the colony.

The practice of drawing upon British India was thus well established by the time Queensland came into existence. And some of the leading pastoralists of the Darling Downs, as well as certain Sydney merchants—Robert Towns, Thomas Mort, Flower, Salting & Co.—having substantial interests in the north, wasted no time approaching Sir George Bowen, the new Governor, in the matter. They pointed out the importance of Asiatic labour in the development of tropical countries and prayed that his Government take immediate steps towards importing such labour.

Obtaining sanction for such a traffic was thought to be mainly a question of bringing pressure to bear on the Indian Government through the Secretary of State for India. In Britain, lobbyists such as the Peel River Co., the North British Australian Co., and others had appealed directly to members of the Imperial Cabinet on the same behalf. They understood the need for keeping Queensland primarily a field for free European emigration, the petitioners emphasized. They sought for their purpose no appropriation of the public revenues of the colony as in Natal, but were content that all the expense of bringing in the coolies should rest upon themselves.

The Duke of Newcastle, Secretary of State for the Colonies, proved to be highly receptive to the idea. So did Bowen in Queensland, though he was inclined to take a broader view of the question, arguing that there were not only the interests of pastoralists to think of, but those of agriculturists as well. He was in fact very closely in touch with the Cotton Supply Association of Manchester. His immediate object, he wrote to Newcastle on 6th January 1860, was "to solicit the attention of Her Majesty's Government to projects now on foot for the cultivation of cotton."

Bowen's plan for the promotion of cotton-growing was twofold. In the temperate regions around Brisbane and Maryborough he saw it being carried on by small farmers assisted by the entire family at harvest time. In the tropics, "where the climate is unfavourable to European field-work", he envisaged large plantations worked by Asiatic labour. Why, he asked, should not British capital and Indian labour do for cotton in north Australia what it had done for sugar in Mauritius? And quoting from a recent speech in the House of Commons, he added that the introduction of Asiatic labour would assuredly produce the same effect on Queensland as once the invention of the machine had produced in England. "It will elevate the European labourer to the rank of mechanic; the mechanic to employer. It will work wonders for our whole society."

But Bowen's proposals were never to come to anything, although for the next two years it seemed quite likely that they would. For encouraged by the outbreak of the American Civil War and the temporary cutting off of cotton supplies from the South, British capital invested in land on the Caboolture River just to the north of Brisbane, and Robert Towns started Townsvale to the south. Experiments suggested that Queensland was capable of growing a very superior type of cotton with a higher yield to the acre than the average American plantation. When in July 1862 the Queensland Legislature passed a law (The "Coolie Act") making provision for the introduction of labourers from British India it seemed that Bowen would achieve his object.

A hitch developed, however: the Indian Government would permit the emigration of coolies only if Queensland paid the expenses of an Emigration Officer to supervise the operation at the Indian end. Bowen had to reply that funds for such a person were restricted to the emigration of Europeans. Then followed great correspondence to and fro, but still the position was by no means clear. Robert Towns, who was an impetuous sort of person and had recently dismissed all the German emigrants on his plantation because their families were too large and ate too much, suddenly arrived at the decision to import islanders. It was certainly an impetuous decision. The first and, up till then, the last attempt to introduce South Sea Islanders to Australia, by Benjamin Boyd in 1847, had ended in complete disaster.

But Towns was no fool. He was a Northumbrian of exceptional shrewdness and determination, a seaman who had been apprentice aboard a collier out of Newcastle at the age of eleven; mate at sixteen; skipper at seventeen. By the time he was twenty-six he was commander of his own vessel, a 355-ton clipper, the *Brothers*, which he was to sail all round the world. On one occasion, when somebody had suggested that surely he would not risk such a splendid craft on the China coast, he had replied, "I'd sail her to Hades and back, if there was a profit in it." That was the Northumbrian in him speaking, both in the language and the true merchant instinct. He had at least one other very north of England characteristic, too: a stern Puritan conscience. No drinking at sea, no alcohol even to be carried aboard was the rule on Captain Towns's ships. It was a rule that often made it very hard for him to get crews, and sometimes even cost him a profit, since liquor was a very lucrative sideline with skippers and shipowners trading in the islands.

There was more to this attitude than a mere obsession about drink; he was, in fact, a very conscientious employer, and did not want to see people drinking themselves stupid and "going to the devil" generally while he was in any way responsible for their moral welfare. Thus, while engaged in the emigration trade to Australia in the twenties and thirties he would ensure that every cabin was supplied with a Bible, a prayer book, several Temperance tracts, and a small volume of cottage maxims. The mere lives of these people were not so important to him (or he would not have sent men to sea in such rotten ships) as their immortal souls.

This, then, was the former sea-captain who settled down in Sydney in 1842. It turned out to be a most propitious time, as so many small shipowners were on the point of bankruptcy, and he very quickly began to make his fortune in the sandalwood trade. But he would have been successful at any time, being such an enterprising business-man, ready to venture into almost any kind of commerce—whaling, coconut oil, turtle shell, the export of horses to India, the import of Chinese indentured labour to the goldfields. Normally he was quite merciless in business, yet he had one noticeable softness, a predilection for the merry-hearted islanders who for twenty years and more had formed the crews of his sandalwooding vessels.

When dealing with *them*, he could be considerate, even tender, and would take infinite pains to please. "We have great difficulty in hitting on the article to suit the fancy of the natives," he wrote once. Beads, however, they liked, particularly "the small dust beads in bright blue and green colours, also the middle and smaller sizes of the same colours". Quite apart from its being good business to study their tastes, it gave him great pleasure to indulge them in this way.

Again, it was important to have the natives on one's side in collecting sandalwood, and Towns cultivated their friendship. He met Bwaxat, a chief of New Caledonia, when he was brought to Sydney in one of Towns's vessels. Towns would refer to Bwaxat as "my friend, Mr Bassett". "You'd better take young Bassett with you," he instructed one particular captain, "if he will go willingly, and call your ship Bassett's ship. It appears Bassett is liked amongst them." In fact he had *carte blanche* apparently to travel on any of Towns's ships, anywhere, at any time. The merchant loaded him with favours and presents and liked to tell the story of the time when H.M.S. *Pelorus* visited New Caledonia in 1862. Bassett was invited aboard, to wander all over the man-o'-war, running his fingers over the brasswork and fittings, and at length to exclaim wonderingly "Bobby Towns. All Bobby Towns." While Towns certainly did not own all the ships that sailed the South Seas he did own a great number. And when the New Caledonians came to Sydney and were landed at Miller's Point, they would find that he owned the land there and all the adjacent wharves and warehouses also.

Thus, personally, his relationships with the islanders were very good. Yet he had shrunk, when first considering it, from the idea of employing them in any large-scale way in Australia. His own observations led him to suppose only that they were a cheerful, good-natured people longing for a firm hand to guide them. But the dark and terrible incidents in which so many of his ships had been involved, and the "inherently treacherous" nature universally attributed to them by his crews, gave him pause.

If what his captains had occasionally hinted at—hideous unmentionable practices, cannibalism, orgiastic ceremonies—were only half true, what would be the effect, he wondered, of bringing such creatures into close contact with the white race, especially with innocent women and children? People seemed to feel that a lurking animality pervaded the islands, and might possibly be contagious.

However, Towns had an urgent problem to solve in 1863—the declining health of Townsvale, starved of reliable labour, was faced with its second bad season in succession. He made his decision early in 1863, and although he never doubted its rightness, he was at pains very often to explain that he was driven to it. On 29th May, while the schooner *Don Juan* lay in the Brisbane River awaiting his further instructions, he wrote a final letter to Captain Grueber.

DEAR SIR,

Your vessel now ready and victualled with supplies sufficient for the voyage and return with natives, you will at once proceed to sea and make the best of your way to the Isle of Leefoo [*sic*] for the purpose of pro-curing natives for the cotton field. . . .

I have put on board two suits of shirts and trousers each for 100 natives, you will please serve out one suit when they first embark, keeping one for their landing. If you can procure 100 natives in all, you may do so, but half the number will do if you find much difficulty in getting them. On no account attempt force or take the people against their own free will and consent. . . .

If you find any missionaries at the islands, make their acquaintance and tell them from me what your object is in engaging the natives to leave the island they belong to, and engage for a short season to serve me in cultivating cotton; the labour will be light in weeding and cleaning and picking cotton, and I engage to provide them comfortable huts and regular rations of rice, meat, pumpkins, potatoes, and yams, if they will grow. . . .

And you may also explain to the missionaries that it is my intention to bring over their wives with them next year, if they like the place and answer my purpose to do so. . . .

I have now shadowed forth my views and intentions and leave you to carry them out. I again repeat, on no account allow the natives to be ill-used; they are a poor, timid, unoffending race, and require all the kindness you can show them; you may lead them to anything and I will not allow them to be driven.

It was nothing to Towns to write half a dozen long letters in the course of one day. His next letter was to Ross Lewin, the man who was to do the actual recruiting and be directly responsible for the recruits' welfare on the voyage:

MR ROSS LEWIN,
SIR,

Referring to our verbal agreement for your present employment in the *Don Juan*. In engaging or persuading these people, you must tell them exactly what they will have to do; that is, their chief work will be in the cotton fields, that they will have a kind master to protect them; that you will take them back in twelve months, if not six, and that you will be on the station to explain and interpret for them; that they will be paid at the rate of ten shillings a month (over and above their rations) for the able men, and the others according to their worth and value. . . .

You must endeavour to keep the natives in good humour and friendly with each other; on no account allow them to quarrel or have any of their national disputes on board; keep all such quarrelling from them; if you find such unfortunately to take place, at once separate them, and put up bulkheads between them. Take care none of the old beachcombers [European sailors] smuggle themselves on board with the natives. . . .

Finally he turned to the missionaries, who had so persistently misunderstood his motives in the past, and whose work had already been disrupted by the activities of his sandalwooders. He addressed an open letter to them, dashing it off, it seems, a trifle impatiently:

To any missionary into whose hands this may come
REVEREND SIR,
Should this meet the eye of any gentleman in that sacred calling I beg to explain the nature of the voyage on which I am about to dispatch the bearer, Captain Grueber. . . . I have embarked considerable capital in Queensland, in the cultivation of cotton, and as so much depends on the rate of labour, I am endeavouring to try our natives from the immediate adjacent islands whose habits, though not strictly industrious, may be rendered most serviceable in the light work of weeding and picking cotton. Such being my views on the subject I have sent this, my pioneer vessel, to enlist and supply and will be much obliged if you will kindly assist us in this our worldly mission, and as I have told your worthy brotherhood, Messrs Inglis and Geddes [*sic*] that I with my cotton emigration will do more towards civilizing the natives in one year than you can possibly in ten!

When, at a later date, Towns had cause to have these letters published in pamphlet form, it was immediately assumed that they were some sort of pious fraud, since they made him sound too scrupulous to be true. But they were quite authentic, merely Towns, bombastic and long-winded as usual, pointing out to each man his duty. If it sometimes occurred to him that he had omitted some small point after he had waxed and sealed the envelope he would instantly begin a second letter, even a third. Failing his own presence on the spot, it was the least a conscientious employer could do.

Anyway the *Don Juan*'s voyage was without incident; one of Towns's agents in the islands helped Lewin gather the recruits, and on 15th August 1863 Queensland's first consignment of Kanakas was landed at Redbank, near Brisbane. Here they remained a day or two, the marvel of the populace, while arrangements were made to transport them on to Townsvale. It was a simple, touching occasion by all accounts, with everybody anxious to be friendly, to find some point of contact, to comprehend even the idea of their all belonging to the same human race. Articles were exchanged: bows and arrows for hats and boots; comparisons made of such things as eating habits.

It was considered remarkable, for instance, that the islanders should find the bread, meat, and tea offered to them positively distasteful. Yet it was impossible to take offence. They had such an agreeable way of grinning and giggling in embarrassment to indicate their refusal. Then they were on their way and the outcry started.

Cheap coloured labour was being introduced into Queensland, accused the Brisbane *Courier*, in the cold-blooded certainty that it could only lead to the degradation and demoralization of the working class. "Can the free immigrant be expected to survive if his labour is to be put in the scale against that of the savage hired at ten shillings a month with rations? Are the industrious poor of the mother country together with their English ideas, English principles, English customs to be swamped by the barbarian?"

Bowen had perhaps expected some trouble of this sort. A local branch of the British and Foreign Anti-Slavery Society had spoken up, and indeed had first drawn attention to its existence in Brisbane when the "Coolie Act" had been passed thirteen months previously. For the Society generally had never really accepted the idea of coolie emigration, since that day in 1834 when the first indentured Indian had arrived in Mauritius to take the place of the African slave. Despite the Indian Government's protective regulations; despite the respectability of the European shippers involved in the traffic; despite whatever further safeguard one could think of, the impression given by reports in the Calcutta Press between 1834 and 1838 was that the so called voluntary recruitment of emigrants was little other than plain kidnapping.

The shipper employed whomever he liked, unlicensed, to crimp for him, and the methods such people used, those of the press gang, were only what one might have expected in that impoverished and over-populated city. More regulations were issued, reforms instituted, but the Society eventually tired of complaining to the India Office and having its complaints tardily investigated, and turned its attention to the other aspect of the problem—the treatment of the coolie in the land of his indentures.

The period of engagement, the Society noted, grew longer and longer—from one year originally to five years in many cases. Moreover, the expense of bringing labour all the way from India was wasted if the immigrants should take to the jungle, as some did, soon after their arrival. To counter this, penal legislation had to be passed enabling the planters, through a system of fines and punishments, to deter potential deserters. However, this seemed to open a possible avenue of exploitation: armed with his penal powers, the planter might be tempted to turn blackmailer; to give his man no choice but to offer his services for a further five years or be turned over to a magistrate to suffer punishment for some offence. The whole object of discipline, as the Society pointed out with reference to Trinidad in 1850, was being subordinated to one end: to induce the coolie to reindenture.

This complaint was ignored altogether; the brave days of the 1820s and 1830s, when the great figures of the humanitarian movement had commanded the conscience of an entire House, belonged to the distant past. In these more comfortable times there were no Wilberforces to contend with; the Society had become an old bore, and Earl Grey, the Colonial Secretary, writing to the Governor of Trinidad in connection with some correspondence he had been having with the Society's secretary, felt constrained to tell him quite frankly: "You are fully entitled to every protection which I can give you against the unfounded and unjustifiable imputations such as those contained in the Society's letter."

More pertinent in the circumstances were the facts that the coolie had saved the West Indies, the Government of India was only too glad to be relieved of part of its surplus population, and the picture of the humble Indian squatting passively beside his bowl of rice simply had not the same power to compel a public outcry as that of the African in chains. The position had not greatly changed by the time Towns brought his first Kanakas to Townsvale in 1863. Perhaps because the Imperial Government felt that it had disposed of the question of slavery and slave-dealing many years before, it—or at least the Colonial Office, the only department actually required to know what was going on—would think of the recruitment of Pacific Islanders in the same terms as it regarded the indenture of coolies.

However, if Governor Bowen at least seemed unconcerned about what was being said in certain Brisbane newspapers, Robert Towns was not. He never dreamed that what was in his eyes the innocent voyage of the *Don Juan* would be likened to the beginnings of a new slave trade; that the outrageous remarks of the radical Press would be taken up in the House. "I was represented as a perfect monster," Towns complained afterwards. "My proceedings were scandalous. Every vile epithet was applied to me and I thought something should be done by me to expose the fallacy of these people's statements." So he embarked on yet another long letter, this time to Robert Herbert, Premier of Queensland.

Sir,

My attention has been called to the report of certain proceedings in the Assembly, in reference to the introduction of a number of natives from the South Sea Islands for special service at my cotton plantation on the Logan. The remarks in some of the newspapers to which this matter has given rise, I would, as I usually do, have treated with the silent contempt they merit; but the proceedings in this case, in which you have been called upon in your official place in Parliament to answer questions on a subject in which I alone am responsible, seem to me to be out of the ordinary course and compel me, in justice to you, to state clearly the principle on which I have acted.

It will be in your recollection that at the time when so much anxiety prevailed for the growth of cotton in Queensland with the view to the development of a new industrial resource in the colony, as well as to supply the want of raw material under which the Lancashire operatives were suffering so much, I applied for and took up a maximum grant of cotton land upon which speculation I have spent upwards of £6,000 without as yet any return.

It is true that the season has been much against the experiment, but the question of labour has had much more to do with this result and has induced me to embark in the present South Sea Island immigration. . . . For the greater part of the work on a cotton plantation, I believe these islanders will be well suited; and instead of being attacked and branded as I have been, I think I deserve the thanks of the community for the introduction of that kind of labour which is suited to our wants and which may save us from the inhumanity of driving to the exposed labour of field work the least tropically hardy European women and children; for I suppose the most thorough advocate for European labour will admit that in cotton clearing and picking, they, as well as the men, must take part in the labour. I feel confident I have the good wishes of the employers of labour, by substituting this native labour for the generous palefaces who have been brought out at the expense of the country, who delight in scheming about rather than in honest working, and who feel insulted if you offer them, for a day's work, that which they have been accustomed to receive at home for a week's labour.

It is these drones in the hive of industry, whom I call the "breeches pocket patriots", who first drove me to the employment of native labour; and it is these men, or others pandering to their feelings who after putting the colony to so much expense for their own passage now seek to raise an outcry against those who cost the colony nothing for their passage and who, I venture to predict, will leave a lasting benefit behind them. As to the danger expressed by some of the newspaper scribblers lest the Government be put to enormous expense in the additional police requisite to keep these "barbarians" in order, I venture to predict there will be less crime among them, if not interfered with by these agitators, than among an equal number of European labourers from whatever country they may have been drawn at the public expense. I have, etc.,

R. TOWNS

Sydney, 31st August 1963

However, the agitation had already died again by the time Towns's letter had been passed on to Bowen and he was ready to communicate the full story to London. In the meantime the sixty-seven Kanakas were out of the way at Townsvale, gradually acclimatizing themselves, being gently inducted into the routine of regular hours. Work was from 6.00 a.m. till 6.00 p.m., with an hour for breakfast at 8.00 a.m. and another hour for lunch at noon—extended in the heat of midsummer to two hours, in compensation for which they started an hour earlier in the morning.

They were long hours, Towns admitted on a later occasion, for a people not used to continuous labour. But the value of it, he claimed, was proved by the fact that their physiques were unquestionably improved at the end of twelve months. The important thing, he declared, was that they led healthy lives in healthy surroundings. They had a large new building to themselves, sixty feet by forty, surrounded by a veranda and containing two rooms, with bunks around the walls broad enough for two sleepers apiece. In winter two thick blankets were provided.

Apparently there was some early trouble over food: the tea which Towns had intended to be their principal beverage, stimulating and economical, they declined to drink. It was wanton waste, the manager told him: they smoked the tea and mixed the sugar and water to drink. Another mistake, too, which Towns came to regret, was serving them three meals a day when they had been accustomed to only two at home. But by the time the "error" was discovered, they had grown to depend on the three and would not change back. These meals were prepared in six different huts, scattered over the three miles of the plantation, each gang having its own cook. The times of eating must have been staggered to some extent because Towns, normally a stickler for regularity, had laid it down that all programmes of work be subordinated to the requirements of the steam plough, which was to be kept constantly at work during the day. After all, it had cost a lot of money; one didn't want it to stand idle.

The last important item of rations—in fact not just an item, but the one indispensable commodity—was tobacco. Tobacco was the reward, the bribe for the "boy" who picked the greatest daily amount of cotton in the gang; for the one who remembered to pull on a shirt and a pair of pants when he approached the homestead; for the one who obediently stayed behind for the weekend and went fishing and hunting locally instead of going into town or spending his wages with some travelling hawker of cheap grog.

In this way it became customary for the islanders to receive little or no cash during their period of employment. Mostly they started out during the first few months to accumulate small articles of trade —yards of cloth, strings of beads, pipes and so on—while reserving the balance of their steadily accruing wages for a big splurge at the finish. These things they stored in little red-painted, imitation-cedar boxes, the great attraction of which was that they possessed locks and needed to be opened and locked again with a set of keys. As the years passed and their desire for possessions increased, the little boxes tended to be replaced by massive, imitation-oak chests which, for large numbers of Queenslanders at least were to be their most enduring memory of the Kanaka days: the departing islander gaudily dressed, lugging his outsize chest through the streets on his way to the ship. In fact recruiting would have been impossible, sneered the cynics, had the islanders not been such a nicely undiscriminating market; had there not already existed in the South Seas a thriving business in cheap calico, bad rice, Brummagem pots and pans—anything that was peddled around the Pacific in the sacred name of trade.

Towns, as one might guess, looked at it another way. He thought their trustfulness, their readiness to please and be pleased, one of their most charming attributes. They did not behave like white labour, as though expecting their employer to cheat them all the time. And if anybody were disposed to think that employing the islanders in this state of innocence was taking advantage of them it was open to such a person to go and have a look, as for instance Governor Bowen did on two or three occasions, to see for himself that the islanders were well content to be taken advantage of. Not only did they seem to love their employment, they seemed to love their employer also, proud merely to be associated with him, like Bassett.

On that first Christmastide when Towns paid what became his annual visit to Townsvale, they killed half a dozen bullocks and feasted and the islanders sang and danced and celebrated the labour they performed for Bobby Towns. One incident Towns always remembered: as the dancers slowly worked themselves up into the spirit of the occasion and the ground began to tremble under the insistent thudding of their stamping feet, one man seized up a little white child about two years old and carried it around on his shoulders as he danced. The child, Towns remarked, showed not the slightest fear. It seemed to symbolize the union which had been achieved between black and white.

Some months afterwards, however, when there was no longer the same need to demonstrate how elaborately the islanders were being cared for, gangs of Kanakas began to be drafted off all over the countryside. The pick of them, the Tannamen, went with John Melton Black, Towns's dynamic chief manager, to build the port of Townsville. The Tannamen, as already noted, were exceptional. In the vanguard of whatever was happening, they blasted away the rocks at the entrance to Ross Creek, drained the mangrove swamps around the river delta, and drove in the piles for the first wharf.

At one point in the middle of the excitement of creating a new settlement it was discovered that they had forgotten to comply with certain provisions of the Coffee and Sugar Cultivation Act, which alone had enabled Towns to acquire his lease of Cleveland Bay in the first place. Thus when Black learnt that a Government man was on his way to inspect the non-existent but formally necessary coffee plantations, he set the Kanakas to plough up a couple of acres of Ross Island and sow two rows of roasted coffee beans which had been sent up as stores. The Government man apparently took it in the right spirit: the beans were accepted as evidence of a genuine attempt to plant, and Towns got his way with the Queensland Government in the end and had the settlement officially proclaimed a port of entry.

Northern developers, pastoralists and all those who would shortly be employing Kanakas in a variety of tasks, had good cause to feel grateful to Robert Towns. He had made the breakthrough; he had assumed all the responsibility; borne the brunt of the initial objections and shown that the introduction of cheap island labour was easier than anyone had dared think. At the same time, in the hearts of many thousands of young Pacific Islanders, he had awakened a sudden, consuming interest in the "island" of Queensland.

TWO

The Homeland

In all this time throughout several hundreds of small islands to the
east and north-east of Australia an older and wiser generation was
engaged in a constant battle to preserve an ancient and cherished
way of life. It was a general problem: keeping some check on the
young people in the interests of all, though the circumstances of the
problem differed widely from island to island. For centuries the
inhabitants of dark-green Melanesia had had to adapt themselves to
changes introduced from outside Melanesia, but never so much as in
the nineteenth century.

Early in the century some of the islands of the western Solomons
—the Shortlands, the Treasurys, Eddystone, New Georgia, and others
—became the regular resort of European whaling crews. During the
season, from October to January, ships were particularly attracted to
New Georgia's Rubiana Lagoon—a twenty-mile stretch of water
protected by a large coral reef and dotted with many populous islets.
It was a superb anchorage and the site of perhaps the most luxuriant
coconut groves in the entire Pacific. The fact that the men of
Rubiana were notable head-hunters did not deter the whalers;
danger was a part of their everyday lives. In the event the natives
proved to be extremely friendly. They were not interested in
European heads, at this stage, only in European trade. With iron
tomahawks and iron tools they could get their garden work done in
half the time and spend the extra days fishing and idling. Basically
they were an easygoing, good-natured people who liked to relax as
much as anyone else.

They enjoyed particularly the visits of the whalers because the
strange white people, coming from an island evidently without
women, brought with them the breath of adventure, the hint of a
wider world than they had ever dreamed of. At first they tended to
be slightly stunned by the visitors' technology but not overwhelmed

by it. They were accustomed to being held in some awe themselves, especially when they went adventuring towards Choiseul and Isabel in search of women and slaves. Or heads. At villages along the lagoon there were canoe-houses that contained more than three hundred heads.

For in the eternal struggle to win the esteem of their fellow men, the lagoon-dwellers had certain advantages. Both Choiseul and Isabel, fifty to a hundred miles away, possessed a long, exposed shoreline with numerous coastal villages where it was possible to land unobserved and attack overland. It could be hard going, paddling a seventy-foot canoe across the straits when the prevailing south-east trades were blowing. On the other hand it meant having wind and waves behind them in that desperate half-hour after their victims had been secured and the enemy was still struggling to launch his canoes and set out in pursuit.

For the same reason it was all the more difficult for their opponents to stage retaliatory raids. Finding the entrance to Rubiana Lagoon was not easy in the dark, nor was getting out again in a hurry with hostile villages on either side. Even so, the New Georgians did not have things all their own way. In any case they had no wish to liquidate the tribes of Choiseul and Isabel, with whom they also had important trading relationships. Their real object was to out-score their rivals across the lagoon, to spread the fame of their name in Kolombangara, Simbo, Vella Lavella, even to Fauro and Short-land.

In the lives of these Solomon Islanders, to take a man's head was the supreme adventure. A European trader witnessed such a raid in the year 1870. He looked on unseen while a fleet of six large war canoes, fifty men in each, paddled stealthily towards a sleeping village in the Floridas. As they grounded silently on a narrow strip of beach close by, the paddlers jumped out and stood around for several minutes until every warrior had chosen either a tomahawk or a handful of spears from the weapons piled amidships.

Then they advanced in a line, fanning out to approach their prey on three sides. After a while a dog started barking, and with a terrible "Wah-wah-wah" the warriors charged. A shower of spears hurtled into the midst of long rows of huts, piercing the bamboo-thatched roofs and hanging outwards at crazy angles, while the axemen streaked in behind. The barely awakened villagers were mostly too paralysed to move. Clinging to one another in the darkness of their huts, they could only pray that the invaders had not come to burn them out. Some of the bravest, however, attempted to crawl out only to find two axemen stationed by the door. They struck swiftly with their modern steel axes, cleanly severing head from shoulders with a

single blow. Ten minutes later they were away again with two or
three women and half a dozen bloody trophies, bundling the lot into
the canoes and paddling for their lives.

The New Georgians were pre-eminent at this sort of thing. Yet
there had been little danger in pre-European days of the practice
getting out of hand; of the head-hunter succumbing to an insatiable
lust for more and more heads. A successful warrior, after he had
returned home and had his deed proclaimed before the whole
village, could henceforth consider his own head an object of great
value to other young aspirants for fame. Moreover, it was the
responsibility of the elders in the tribe to see that the whole community did not advance too far ahead of its jealous neighbours and
thereby invite a massive retaliation from all sides.

Yet few if any of the European skippers who put in at Rubiana
during the forties and fifties guessed that native life was so complicated. They were only aware that the natives were head-hunters, and
so, presumably, lost to moral feeling. The old men would invite the
seamen to look at the village's collection of heads, some with the
flesh still in the process of rotting away from the grinning teeth and
sunken eye-sockets, and seem proud of themselves. A head was
necessary, the Europeans were led to understand, as a sort of sacrifice
to the ancestors, to consecrate the installing of a new chief perhaps,
or the launching of a new war canoe. But they did not believe it.
They thought it was because of the savage's innate bloodthirstiness.

The natives of New Georgia, Captain Andrew Cheyne wrote in
1849, are extremely ferocious and treacherous, void of affection,
truly wretches. These were the usual adjectives. Together with
revengeful, cruel, faithless, licentious, degraded, etc. There was
scarcely a tribe anywhere which had not been described at some
time or other as the most ferocious, the most cannibalistic in the
Pacific.

What had happened was that after the first, brief, usually friendly
contacts, misunderstandings had arisen. The matter could be quite
trivial perhaps, but enough to lay bare certain basic attitudes. The
New Georgians could not read what the white people said about
them in their books, but they could read it in their manner and tone
of voice, in the way they reacted to the most harmless souveniring.
While most of the whalers were ashore enjoying the amenities the
natives would be all over the ship, prying into cabins, carrying off
sundry articles, prising nails out of the wood, perhaps emerging
again with a sailor's pipe stuck through the perforation of one ear-
lobe. It was not that they had no respect for property; they respected
one another's. But it was just inconceivable that this multitude of
new things scattered in such profusion could be anything but

NEW HEBRIDES

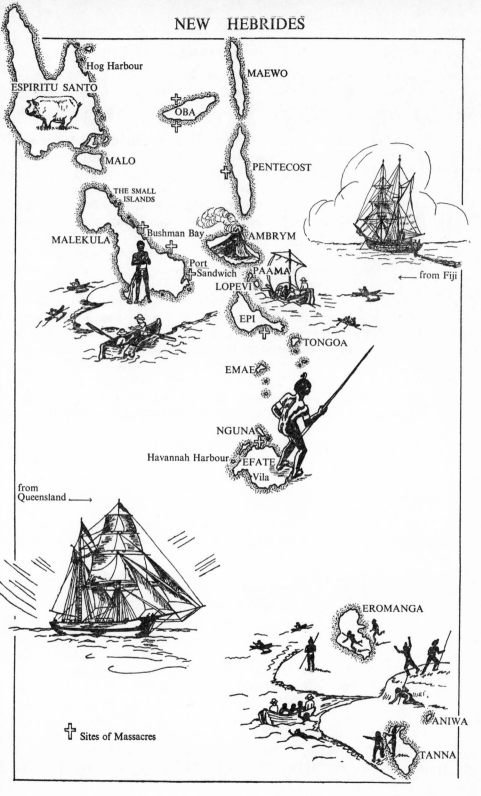

Hog Harbour

ESPIRITU SANTO

MAEWO

OBA

MALO

PENTECOST

THE SMALL ISLANDS

MALEKULA

Bushman Bay

AMBRYM

Port Sandwich

PAAMA

LOPEVI

EPI

TONGOA

EMAE

NGUNA

Havannah Harbour

EFATE

Vila

from Queensland

← from Fiji

EROMANGA

ANEITYUM

ANIWA

TANNA

✝ Sites of Massacres

C

Nature's bounty intended for the good of all. The Europeans retaliated with threats and blows, sometimes even with the lash, and the islanders sensed in their anger and violence an underlying irresponsibility towards native lives.

And at the same time as they began to understand the white man they saw how to incorporate him and use him within their system. They certainly did not want to antagonize their visitors and make them go away, perhaps to a rival tribe or island. Also they had come to need the white man's tobacco, and most of the chiefs were greedy for the gaudy calicoes, for by the 1850s status in many of the islands was measured in fathoms of cloth.

By this time, too, seekers after tortoise-shell and bêche-de-mer for the Chinese trade were regularly visiting Rubiana, and many skippers found it possible to buy heads from the New Georgia people in exchange for cloth, then sail over to the Floridas and trade the heads for tortoise-shell. The opportunity was too good to be missed: if the white men were heading for the Floridas and the new canoe was ready from the builders, only waiting to be formally dedicated by making its first voyage in search of heads, why should it not be towed along behind. The Floridas were well out of Rubiana's normal zone of operation, but that did not seem to matter. With a few muskets to fire and frighten the locals out of their wits and with their latest steel axes, the head-hunters were completely irresistible.

The old sanctions were ceasing to operate. There was no possibility of the Florida men being able to strike back. Their warriors rarely made the long hazardous journey to Rubiana. They knew the Rubiana people were head-hunters of awesome reputation, protected by powerful gods, but the spectacle of their fellow islanders in alliance with the white men, borrowing his strength, simply made their own strength drain from them.

An English naturalist, Henry Guppy, travelling through the Solomons in 1881 noted this in the natives more than once. He described one occasion when he was seated on the second bow thwart of a native war canoe, alongside the local chief. Suddenly the canoe rounded a point and they came upon a number of natives fishing from a little beach. Their faces were familiar even to the Englishman, and he was surprised when the fishermen did not shout out salutations but only continued to squat motionless, eyes downcast, until the canoe had passed. The incident must have seemed to need some explanation, for the chief turned to Guppy after a while and spoke. "They too much fright," he said, and smiled.

The white stranger and the black chief in close communion. It was like the gods siding with men. With such power at their back, the people of Rubiana drove their war canoes wherever they wanted and took what they chose. The balance of power had been destroyed. The old arrangements whereby Rubiana visited this island for its beautiful mats, that one for its collection of shells patiently strung together by its incomparable local craftswomen, were tacitly dissolved. Rubiana was no longer dependent on its neighbours, nor those neighbours upon Rubiana. And in the breakdown of the old balance the inhabitants of the Treasury Islands and the Shortlands harried the coast of Bougainville. Kolombangara and Vella Lavella devastated southern Choiseul. Rendova and Simbo joined with New Georgia in raiding Isabel. Isabel preyed upon Malaita. Islanders who had once regarded the practice with abhorrence became ardent head-hunters almost overnight.

Near the end of the century when the head-hunters were still as active as ever, despite the fact that the British had declared a protectorate over that part of the Solomons, a deputy resident commissioner described what the situation was like. "The perpetual and elaborate watch kept on Simbo through the nights, where sentry answers sentry with a strange regularity; where the midnight rumour of the arrival of five men in a strange canoe is sufficient to set the whole island in an uproar of panic . . . speak volumes as to the general state of uncertainty and insecurity felt by the natives of these islands." By this time, of course, the outward lives of the islanders bore little resemblance to pre-European times. The coast of Isabel, probably the worst affected of all the Solomons because of its vulnerable central position, seemed to be practically uninhabited. The populations of its former numerous villages were either dead or had fled to inland lagoons or were living almost out of sight in extraordinary aerial villages in the trees. Bridges of logs resting in the forks of great branches allowed the tree-dwellers to move as freely about these elevated villages as once they had on the ground. By day they descended to fish and hunt and tend their gardens. At night they pulled up their vine-ladders after them to be safe from the head-hunters.

More typical, however, of what had been happening everywhere was the capital of "King Berry", near Cape Prieto at the southernmost tip of the island. North from Cape Prieto, all up and down Isabel's east and west coasts, were ruined, abandoned villages, but this one village was overcrowded. It was really a fortress, a collection of large huts built up on piles at the end of a rocky peninsula. The place resembled an old-fashioned Maori *pah* more than anything previously seen in Melanesia, and Berry, like the great Maori chiefs of old, led out his warriors on expedition after expedition until he literally ran out of enemies. From all parts of Isabel and from surrounding islands, people had joined him, some drawn by hopes of booty; most out of fear.

Considering that the bulk of the Solomons were little visited by whites before the 1870s it is not surprising that they should have regarded men like King Berry as the model of the Melanesian native chief. They spoke disparagingly of chiefs elsewhere who appeared to have little or no control over their subjects. Yet helpful as it was to have somebody capable and intelligent to deal with, the average European regarded Berry with abhorrence. Like all natives, they said, he could be charming when it suited him, but at heart he was a savage lusting after your blood.

Every island seemed to have its own King Berry, each on the lookout for plunder. One particularly notorious character in the late seventies was Chief Hailey of Kolombangara. On one occasion, after ordering the massacre of a certain ship's crew, he sent out the following message to Captain Ferguson of the *Ripple*. "Me, Hailey. King belong Kolombangara, big fella fighting-man; me speak you; me kai-kai [eat] ten-one [eleven] feller man belong *Esperanza*; me take him altogether trade, musket powder, tobacco, bead, plenty, me take everything, me make big fire, ship he finish. . . . White man allasame woman. He no savee fight; s'pose woman plenty cross, she make plenty noise. He allasame woman." In native eyes of course Hailey was only performing a vital function: he was telling the white man, "Beware. We are not afraid of you. We will eat you." And this was one way of telling one another they had nothing to fear. For in their terror and confusion they had turned to these maverick adventurers, these fierce, bold leaders of war expeditions, putting up with their arrogance and greed in return for this feeling of security.

Not every chief was so personally objectionable or disgusting in his habits as the fat Chief Hailey. King Ghorai of the Shortlands, by way of contrast, could be quite charming. He sometimes remarked, "White man, he savvy too much. Poor black man, he savvy nothing." See him then as he waits, in his admiral's uniform (British Navy belt and sword, silk topper, and seaman's jumper) to receive a European guest. Behind him is the palace, a large rather dingy-looking hut, where meals are served European style, eaten around a dinner table with a white cloth, where now the white man is seated in the place of honour and food brought until the visitor cannot swallow another mouthful.

Later they are settled down with pipes discussing business when a slight misunderstanding occurs and Ghorai chuckles and has to explain. He does not want to buy just the cargo his guest has brought. He wants to buy his entire schooner. His intention is to

arm it with some of his surplus cannon and sail it round his domains
with the white man as skipper. For already by 1870 Ghorai had a
considerable dominion throughout the Shortlands, across the Bougainville Strait to parts of northern Choiseul, then via Fauro along
much of the south-west coast of Bougainville as far as Buka. Once
when a trader was murdered over on Bougainville, he very quickly
mustered a punitive expedition, sent it off to the scene of the killing
under the command of his eldest son, and took twenty heads—
"Allasame man-o'-war," said his admiring subjects.

While certain islands of the western Solomons had thus been able
to take the measure of the white man, to hold their own, and more,
against him, the opposite, south-easternmost end of Melanesia was
faring less well. There are many possible explanations of why this
was so, but one feels that what was happening to people like the
Eromangans and the Aneityumese was destined to happen anyway.
"Small, mean-looking, dirty, unfriendly" was the average visitor's
first impression of the population of Eromanga. The writings of the
early navigators from Cook onwards show that the Eromangans
affected all of them in the same distasteful way.

Had it been possible for these occasional European visitors to have
enquired first how a community stood in the eyes of all its neighbours before they visited, it might have saved a lot of trouble. They
might have adjusted their approach accordingly. If the islanders
were a self-confident people, aggressively sure of themselves in any
surroundings, as, for example, the Tannese were, they would greet
the Europeans in a hearty, back-slapping manner, glad of the
opportunity to show off their island and do a bit of boasting about
themselves. If on the other hand they were always getting the bad
side of a bargain, as the Eromangans were, their first reaction would
be to see that the strangers did not somehow get the better of them.
It was remarked by almost every passing trader that the Eromangans
showed no interest in European goods, almost the only people in the
Pacific to display utter indifference. In fact they were just as anxious
to get trade as anybody else, as their later behaviour abundantly
proved. The point was that they did not wish the white man to see
that they were pleased and thus place him at an advantage.

Given this general attitude, their worst suspicions were almost
certain to be realized. In 1839 the first missionaries landed on the
island, and to the trials of this long-suffering people was added a
brand new crop of afflictions. Dysentery swept the island in 1842,
for which the Eromangans blamed their Samoan Christian teachers,
the disease-makers as they called them. So they murdered the
teachers, and for a little while they were left mostly to themselves—

until the fatal discovery, by one of Captain Towns's sandalwooding skippers in the year 1845, of the island's potentiality as a sandalwood-producer.

The sandal tree was another of the curses of the place, being a useless parasite on the roots of more valuable trees. It was not of the slightest value to the Eromangans themselves but was a precious commodity in the eyes of many a Sydney merchant who sold it to China for incense-burning. Although 1845 was not the first year the sandalwooders had come to Eromanga it was the first time that Eromangans had had to deal with an adversary of the calibre of Robert Towns.

When Towns's vessel, the *Elizabeth*, anchored in Cook's Bay in September 1845 the natives welcomed a boat's party ashore, the way they usually treated visitors, and then murdered them at the first opportunity. This should have deterred the sandalwooders from coming back, as it had most of the earlier ones. But it did not stop Towns. Sandalwood was bringing fifty pounds a ton in China in 1845. Six days after the *Elizabeth* arrived back in Sydney minus one boat-crew, it set out again for Eromanga with a new crew to collect the pile of sandalwood previously cut but not loaded. Again one party was treacherously attacked while ashore; two more white men were killed this time, but the *Elizabeth* was able to load its cargo and leave. A few months later Captain Jones, formerly of the *Elizabeth*, was back again in the *Isabella Anna* and procured for Towns another hundred or more tons.

If the Eromangans had been steadfast and had stuck to their determination to expel the white man and his diseases at any price, they might well have succeeded. No small group of Europeans could have lasted a week on Eromanga in the face of united resistance. In contrast stood the natives of Rubiana Lagoon: fifty years hence they would still be in a position to paddle out in their canoes in order to look over the European visitors and decide for themselves whether they wanted to trade with them or not. Even if they did decide to trade, they would not allow Europeans to land unless they knew them. "S'pose missionary come," they said, "we die." The Eromangans, on the other hand, being the people they were, wavered.

There were naturally other considerations. Sooner or later they would want to have everything their neighbours, the Tannese, had. So one party of Eromangans at least, who saw an opportunity to use the whites against their enemies on the opposite side of the island, turned to a policy of welcoming the newcomers, with due caution naturally. At Dillon's Bay in the west it was arranged with certain skippers that they should call there regularly bringing various goods, whereupon the locals would swim out with logs of sandalwood to

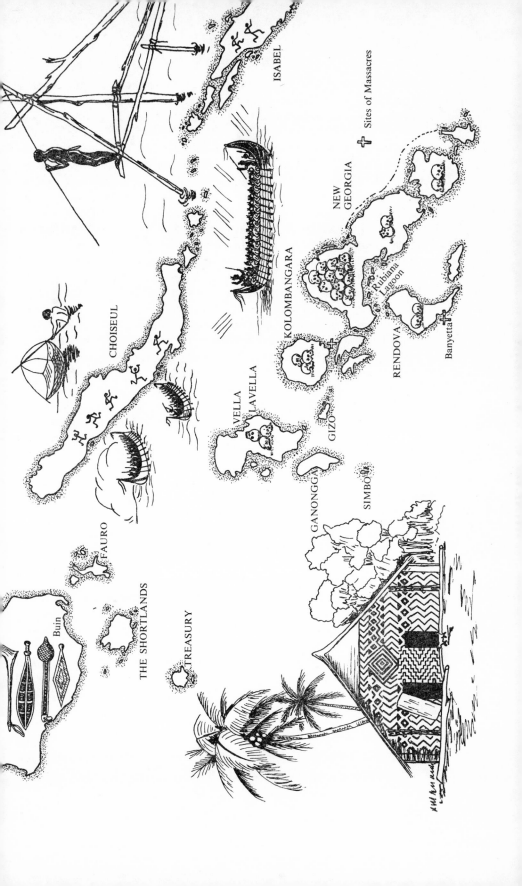

ISABEL

Sites of Massacres

NEW
GEORGIA

KOLOMBANGARA

Rubiana
Lagoon

CHOISEUL

RENDOVA

Banyetta

VELLA
LAVELLA

GIZO

GANONGA

SIMBO

FAURO

Buin

THE SHORTLANDS

TREASURY

exchange for them. At Eromanga, wrote the missionary, George Turner, "the sandalwooder spends most of his day in his longboat armed to the teeth. Wherever he sees some natives collected with wood, he pulls in, buys from them from the rocks, with the pistol in one hand and his beads or fish-hooks in the other."

Trading with the Eromangans was certainly a hazardous business. One trick they had learnt by 1848 was to swim out to the trader's boat with a billet of sandalwood as bait, and suddenly dive underneath the boat and capsize it. The whites usually could not swim.

It was obvious that the sandalwooders would not tolerate that sort of treatment for very long. Starting from 1848 they began transporting raiding parties of Tannese to Eromanga, using them as shock troops in what was the beginning of a regular European invasion; the white men had discovered that the best way to collect sandalwood was to ignore the local population, recruit cutters and cleaners from some other island, and establish a depot on the spot.

The Eromangans fought back, forming a great league of districts, pledging themselves in the ritual eating of slain sandalwooders and their Tannese allies to destroy the invaders and chase them from their island forever. But it was too late. The white men were far too strong, far too clever. Playing off one tribe against the other, they were soon buying up land everywhere, building roads and importing donkeys, careless of the dangers, intent only on reaching the best stands of sandalwood in the far interior. Once a visitor happened to call in at Dillon's Bay just as the manager of Towns's sandalwood depot was setting off to inspect one of the gangs working inland. "Suddenly the great gates of the stockade were swung back and Captain V. galloped through, a big cavalry sabre flapping against the horse's flanks, a double-barrelled gun over his right shoulder, a magazine around his waist."

In fairness, the sandalwooders were not entirely the brutal rogues the missionaries made them out to be, but they did some terrible things. One man boasted of how he and a companion had held up an Eromangan at gun-point and forced him to look on while they raped his wife. A few days later, however, he heard that the Eromangans were planning vengeance and, suddenly afraid, he fled from the island, selling his share in the profits of that season for £25. But such incidents were only typical of the white man's behaviour all over the Pacific. And what drove the sandalwooders to deeds that shocked even themselves sometimes was jealousy of one another.

The mate of a Sydney vessel, the *Daniel Watson*, described how having loaded his cargo and got safely away, he had then sailed close inshore down the coast firing at every little village on the way. His intention was to spoil the market for those who came later. And for those later the struggle only seemed to grow more ruthless. In the 1860s, by which time the lesser operators were all gone and the crews of Robert Towns were left to battle it out with those of his rival, Henry Burns, the following is alleged to have happened: In January 1861 a schooner belonging to Towns's partner, James Paddon, deliberately embarked a party of Tannamen knowing them to be infected with measles and landed them on Eromanga. How many died on Eromanga is sheer guesswork, but five thousand were supposed dead as a result of the great measles epidemic on Tanna in 1861.

By 1864, when the contest between the sandalwooders began to subside, Eromanga was in a fearful state. There were 340 foreigners living on the island in that year, and it can be safely presumed that the local population would have cheerfully murdered the lot of them, had they been able to get away with it. But they were by now too suspicious of one another and too afraid of the consequences to do much more than hang about the settlements waiting for a job or the chance to sneak off with something. It was not likely to be an article of great value. If it were, some Eromangan would come creeping in a day or two later, probably bearing in one hand a stalk of wild sugar-cane as a peace offering, pleading to be allowed to make restitution.

It was in 1864 also that the labour-recruiting vessels began to set off for the islands—just the opportunity, one might have supposed, for some of the younger Eromangans to migrate to Queensland. But the early recruiters, prejudiced against Eromanga by the stories of the sandalwooders, called there infrequently. When they did, the local people for their part were not specially inclined to go. For the time being the two races had just about had enough of one another.

Approximately the same distance south of Tanna as Eromanga lies to the north is the island of Aneityum. Thus the Aneityumese, too, have suffered from having to grow up in the shadow of the terrible Tannese. In certain physical respects they are very like the Tannese, being closely related to them in blood, and they twist their hair into the same long cords, sometimes several hundreds after many years assiduous plaiting. But they are quite different in character. The Aneityumese are gentler, milder, less demanding of life and therefore not so much inclined as the Eromangans to resent their inferior status.

Possibly the reason is that Aneityum is situated at the extreme southern end of the New Hebridean chain, and the people had little or no contact with other island groups and so less compulsion to compete with their neighbours. Tanna was their main point of contact with the outside world, the place to which an adventurous young Aneityumese might gravitate if he were bored. Otherwise the Aneityumese tended to be the country cousins. The pace was slower on Aneityum, the people less lively; houses, canoes, and the vital implements of war a little drab in comparison—precisely the sort of things, however, that would make the island attractive to Europeans. In 1834 James Paddon built the first sandalwood establishment on Aneityum, having decided that it would be safer there than anywhere else. He was followed in 1848 by the first white missionaries to settle permanently in that part of Melanesia, the Reverend and Mrs John Geddie, Presbyterians from Nova Scotia.

It would be impossible to exaggerate the dangers and discomforts endured by these early missionaries. Not that they ever complained; it was a privilege and a pleasure to serve their God, no matter how trying the circumstances. But the New Hebrideans could be very exasperating, as this extract from the diary of a missionary wife shows:

Just when my bread was in the oven, a lot of bushmen came to barter. They brought sugar-cane, coconuts, bananas, and a very few yams, for the most of which they wanted red beads. . . . When I had bought all they brought, as usual they wished to hear the harmonium. I played two hymns and then suddenly remembered that the bread was burning in the oven. So I had to run as fast as I could, turn it over and come back to the music. And all this while some arrowroot for dinner was half mixed up. All this was bad enough at the time, although I can laugh at them afterwards. But the thing that comes nearest the end of my enduring power is to see a great, dirty, and next-to-naked fellow seated right on top of the table.

That extract actually referred to Eromanga, but the dirt, the heat, the apathy and stupidity of the people were the same. Yet the missionaries felt somehow they were wanted.

After worship on Sabbaths the poor women and children crowd around me to see the pictures. They seem to be fond of me and say "Asurum iko" (I love you). I can only answer "Asurum iko" and wish oh so much that I could speak to them and tell of Jesus' love. But the natives do not sit with lips apart and tear-stained cheeks listening in wonder at the glorious Gospel—that is rather the romantic idea of Mission life. The reality is that they sit with their backs to you, or look at you with a most incredible or indifferent expression on their countenances and when you finish speaking burst out laughing and think you have been telling them some foolish fable.

The men were the same:

They would scarcely listen to anything said about Jehovah and the worship. Some of them talked and laughed just to keep from hearing, and the chief said they did not want to know anything about Jehovah or the Book. Tell them of Jesus dying for sinners and they laugh outright. It is very sad and disheartening.

John Geddie did not admit such feelings in *his* diary. He was not worried about teaching much at this stage, being totally concerned with the task to which he believed God had called him above all others—the defeat of the Devil and all his works. For he had perceived on the very first day of landing in July 1848 that the enemy had preceded him. Priests of the Marist Brotherhood were in temporary occupation when he arrived, and he wrote:

By the aid of a spyglass we noticed some persons walking in front of an iron house, dressed in long priestly robes. In this we recognized at once the mark of the beast. . . . The battle is no longer to be fought with paganism alone but with paganism and popery combined.

But God smote them, even in the midst of their lying abominations. The Marists suddenly left the island, having succumbed to amoebic dysentery, and Geddie was left to carry on his work unimpeded by popery at least. He concentrated first on kava, that pleasant native drink brewed from the root of *Piper methysticum,* which inebriates but leaves no hangover. A most diabolical invention. What he could do in the way of breaking up certain kava-drinking ceremonies he did—which was unfortunate, since it was also an excellent cure for gonorrhoea—and his attention was soon to be distracted by the activities of the sandalwooders on the other side of the harbour.

He wrote early in 1849, "I have been obliged to condemn the conduct of my own countrymen before the natives. And also of the miserable native women who were sharers in their guilt." Another evil brought in by the sandalwooders was tobacco, which he accordingly denounced in his Sunday sermons—and complained about to Paddon. Geddie and Paddon were soon indulging in regular shouting-matches. He was deliberately inciting the natives against him, shouted Geddie; he was a liar and a hypocrite, Paddon shouted back. And Mrs Geddie was a good deal worse.

The Aneityumese had come to regard angry outbursts like this as typical of the white men. As long as the anger was not directed against themselves, as long as the trade continued to flow at both ends of the harbour so that opposing villages could exchange tobacco for print dresses and red shirts, they did not mind in the least. But then in November 1851 there was a rumour that Geddie intended to cut off the supply of tobacco on his side. In anger the village burned down his house. The Geddies with their two baby daughters got out only just in time.

That night turned out to be one of the most decisive moments in the island's history. Amid all the doubt and contrition of the following morning, nothing stood out so firmly as the way in which the Geddies went about their daily tasks, undaunted in the midst of their enemies, calmly preparing to build anew. It was a wonderful advertisement for the Christian religion, a piece of personal bravura which the impressionable Aneityumese were to talk about for many a day. And thus it came about in the following year with the visit of the missionary vessel *John Williams* and in the presence of various dignitaries of the church, that the first converts, thirteen in number, were baptized and the Lord's Supper observed. Every year the numbers grew: so many baptized; so many admitted to Communion; so many teachers; so many out-churches; so many Christian marriages; so many elders and deacons created. And all this time John Geddie was carrying the war deep into the heart of the enemy's territory, stamping out "amid of one the most savage tribes on earth, some of the most debasing superstitions and vices of heathenism".

Geddie was not, in fact, so intolerant a fellow as he sounded. He knew that there was some point behind certain of their customs, which was why he had proceeded so cautiously at first. But there were other customs, the strangulation of widows for instance, so horrible, so repugnant to every decent Christian feeling, that they simply had to be eliminated at the earliest opportunity. On the death of a husband, particularly if he were a leading member of the community, it was the practice of various New Hebridean peoples, not only the Aneityumese, to kill one or more of the surviving wives. Strangling was the favoured method, carried out by some relative of the deceased. How could the missionaries tolerate such a barbarity? Geddie lectured them about it, raved against it, reasoned with them, pleaded. But it was nine years before he had finally crushed it out, or thought he had. With wooden faces they agreed that it was utterly bad, but still it went on behind his back.

It turned out in the end that he had been lecturing the wrong people. The section of society most strongly in favour of the strangulation of widows were the women themselves. One old wife repeatedly told the Geddies, with tears streaming down her face every time she mentioned the subject, that she had no desire to survive her ailing husband. Her only wish was to die also so that she could go on being his wife and serving him in the next world. But the missionaries could not understand this. When the old chief died, they brought the widow into their own household to keep a protective eye on her. They managed to foil her first attempt to commit suicide, but failed to prevent her hanging herself at a second attempt.

On the whole it required quite exceptional determination of a kind the Aneityumese did not possess to hold out against a man like Geddie. It was really extraordinary the way these missionaries stuck to their tasks in spite of all else. Dysentery and malaria did not shake them, nor the death of their first children and the subsequent loneliness, nor hurricanes and earthquakes, nor occasional savage demonstrations and threats to kill them. The last crisis was in 1861 when the measles arrived from Tanna and everywhere it was said that the people were dying of the new religion. The Eromangans murdered their missionaries, the Reverend George Gordon and his wife, in revenge, but the Geddies survived, suffering no worse treatment than the burning down of the church and adjacent school-house. John Geddie instantly retaliated, sentencing one elderly offender to thirty lashes, followed by six months banishment. He was "thankful to say that the events of the past year seem to have had a solemnizing influence on many of the natives and there is a more than usual attention to religion. . . . I have reason to hope that not a few are now in heaven."

Yet how did they do it? Work, it seems, was the great opiate, enabling them to forget their disappointments and not to recognize their failures. Fencing, stone-gathering, wood-sawing, well-sinking, house-building, boat-repairing, grass-cutting, tree-felling, lime-burning were just some of the jobs Geddie had to do in the early days, mostly on his own. Together with preparing sermons, organizing services, translating the Bible into Aneityumese, fighting the good fight in sundry other directions, it did not leave much time to consider how the rest of the world was faring. (A colleague of Geddie's working on the island of Nguna failed to notice until one 26th December that Christmas had come and gone—even though he kept a diary of each day's events.)

Geddie's own preoccupation was the new church, being built of coral rocks, in which he hoped eventually to seat a thousand. It did not matter that the last great epidemic of 1861 had reduced the numbers on his side of the island to about only seven hundred; this resolution did not falter. The building continued to grow and the population to decline. And when after fifteen years continuous service his colleagues persuaded him he needed a change he took their proposition to heart and drew up his plans. He would spend the first week visiting the congregations of Cape Breton, the next week visiting . . .

Aneityum was the first island in Melanesia to be proclaimed fully Christianized. Actually there were still many backsliders, many pockets of heathenism never satisfactorily cleaned up. But the tone of the island was predominantly Christian. The greatest sin was nakedness. The greatest deprivation was to be cut off from the white man's favour. At the bottom of the social scale were the heathen, the despised "man o' bush". At the top was the chief Lathella, the son of Geddie's first important convert, whom a visiting missionary, meeting him for the first time, described thus: "He came nearer, holding himself erect, looking grave and dignified, stopped as he reached us, raised his black hat, gave a most stately bow and presented us with his card on which was inscribed 'Lathella, High-Chief of Aneityum'."

So Geddie had wrought a great triumph: heathenism practically crushed out; his authority supreme; the whole community respectfully aware of the superior virtues of the Christian way of life. Yet Aneityum was not at peace because John Geddie was not at peace with himself and less so as the years passed. He should not have been always shouting at them, but he knew they had a reputation for being a miserable, lazy, good-for-nothing lot of people. He was constantly at them to get rid of their filthy, slothful habits, to live cleanly, actively, cheerfully. The response was fearfully discouraging. At one stage he tried to imitate his old enemy, Robert Towns, and start a cotton plantation. But no Aneityum native could maintain a pitch of performance necessary to keep a plantation going. The man's methods were all wrong. What he needed to do, as we know from the example of the sandalwooders, was to import labour from outside. But he could not very well do that.

Still he had no need to despair while there were the sandalwooders, Towns and Paddon, and later the labour recruiters, to blame. "All the sandalwood vessels I know are floating brothels," he wrote in his diary. All the outrages and murders of missionaries were due to the malignant influence of the traders. There was not much he could do about this, but he could at least see to it that the sandalwooders got no encouragement by not letting his natives sell them food nor serve as crew in their ships. The ungodly could rage as they liked, but Geddie managed to keep most of his men at home, sending them on working parties into the interior to fetch beams for his cathedral whenever a trader appeared in port. He punished them with the lock-up if they were disobedient. Later, when the recruiters came with their bribes and solicitations, Geddie taught his people to turn on the heel and walk deliberately away. On the island they might enjoy only a second-class status in comparison with the white missionaries, but it was a great comfort to know that they were a good deal purer and holier than the rest of the world.

As for the remarkable Tannese themselves, it is impossible to understand them as they once were without understanding the Melanesian concept of death, from which they have contrived somehow to remove the sting. Thus they regard all human faculties other than the merely corporeal as being not extinguished but enhanced by death. Many of the ceremonies which the missionaries found so degrading—the weird, wild music, the beating of the drums, the naked, glistening, sweating bodies—were merely their familiar friends from around the mission transporting themselves into a communion with the long line of the immortal dead.

Thus too an old man, feeling death come near, makes his final preparations, disposes of his worldly possessions and waits calmly for the end. When he dies, his relatives, even the whole community, may indulge in noisy lamentations. But it is the loss to their society they are mourning, not the decease of one human life. Man grows old and changes his skin like the crab and is reborn. Even for those who suffer on the way to the grave, there is no particular sympathy. Suffering on the journey into immortality is but the price of the fare. Like childbirth it might be painful, but it is pain with a purpose and therefore different.

The Rubiana head-hunters felt no compunction about taking human life. The Tannese seemed to be completely irresponsible about it. For some reason or other Tanna was the first island in the Hebrides to receive the musket, and very soon the entire island was utterly and deliriously trigger-happy. A trader reporting the arrival back to their homes of his Tannese boat-crew described them recklessly firing off muskets merely to announce their return. All day the firing went on, in a purely light-hearted way and with a terrible waste of ammunition, at fish and fowl. The Tannese would kill a person just as off-handedly, it was said; they might kill someone out of some temporary annoyance even though they still generally liked him and sincerely regretted his death afterwards. Yet on one famous occasion when they had the boat-crew of a sandalwooder absolutely at their mercy far upstream, they let the intruders escape unharmed, seeming to derive more pleasure from contemplating their looks of mingled terror and astonishment than from killing them.

In fact, it was not mere wanton disregard for human life that was responsible for their uncertain behaviour so much as the example shown them by the kind of European trader who happened to settle on the island in those early days. For, with its active volcano and unusually fertile soil, Tanna was able to grow quite outstanding varieties of yam, bananas, coconut, and breadfruit. A white man with a small store might buy these from the natives for next to nothing and then pass them on to the crews of visiting ships at a very reasonable profit. But what an assortment of white men! One, a "Captain Winchester", lived aboard a lugger anchored well out in the bay, only coming ashore, and then escorted by a powerful armed body-guard, to deal with the natives at his beach store. There was nothing particularly wrong with his manner of doing business. His methods were basically the conventional ones: pitting village against village, promising certain advantages to one if it would concentrate exclusively on the production of, say, coconut oil. Such a village would then turn furiously to producing coconut oil, probably to the detriment of more important activities, and thus become even more dependent upon the white man than before.

Winchester carried this basic strategy to extremes, however. He would pass on or invent remarks made by one chieftain about another, calculating that by keeping the entire district in a state of constant unrest he would increase the demand for his muskets and powder. At one stage the price of a small wineglass of powder had gone as high as one large hog, which was utterly exorbitant. His yards were all crammed with poultry and pigs and he was just about to fly, it was rumoured, when the Tannese broke in and burned the store to the ground.

There were also planters. In the region of a place called Black Beach there was a wonderful belt of rich volcanic country which three or four daring pioneers in the 1860s began clearing for maize and cotton. Gangs of labourers from Efate and Malekula did the work, hacking at the jungle, and always with their muskets constantly beside them. The Tannese meanwhile hovered around taking occasional pot-shots. Most of the planters were in fact killed, but some managed to survive. One who survived rather longer than most was another Nova Scotian, Donald McLeod. Apparently his technique for survival was to ensure that the great majority of his imported field hands were women. So long as he was able to bring in fresh batches of women to replace those who systematically disappeared into the jungle, he was safe.

But just how unsafe Tanna was for white people generally is indicated by the fact that for fifteen years no attempt was made to settle a missionary on the island after the last mission teachers had died there in 1843. Geddie had been longing to establish a permanent outstation on Tanna, but his Aneityumese advisers were opposed to the idea. However, they took courage when a fresh group of missionaries arrived in 1858—a certain John Paton and his wife from Scotland, the Reverend Mr Mathieson and his wife from Nova Scotia, and the Reverend Joseph Copeland. In the comforting presence of the white people, the Aneityumese now agreed to go off to Tanna to see whether they could not quell the island by Christianity.

Robert Towns.

James Burns.

An elaborate canoe at Pileni in the Reef Islands.

The islet on the left is the site of a native shrine on Vella Lavella. At right is a men's club-house.

In the knowledge of the troubled times that lay ahead of the little party, it is clear that for their safety they should have paid attention to what certain Tannese had been so earnestly trying to tell them at their first arrival. Though personally glad to know you, the people of Port Resolution had said in effect, we cannot guarantee your protection against the fierce tribes of the inland. This meant that had the missionaries brought gifts of muskets to help guard their hosts against the jealousy which their presence must inevitably arouse in others, the situation might have been different. But, being missionaries, they did not bring muskets, so there was no saying whether they would be able to survive or not. In the circumstances nobody particularly wanted the responsibility of having them.

John Paton was hardly a man to heed the advice of savages, especially since his first impressions of the Tannese were highly unfavourable. "Had I given up my beloved work and my dear people in Glasgow, with so many delightful associations, to consecrate my life to these degraded creatures?" he reflected. But it really was a disconcerting time to arrive, with Winchester hard at work fomenting discord, and feuds going on all round them. "The discharge of muskets in the adjoining bush, and the horrid yells of the savages, soon informed us that they were engaged in deadly fights. Excitement and terror were on every countenance; armed men rushed about in every direction. . . . Some of the women ran with their children to places of safety; but even then we saw other girls and women on the shore close by, chewing sugar-cane and chaffering and laughing, as if their fathers and brothers had been engaged in a country dance instead of a bloody war." The reaction of his supposedly civilized Aneityum helpers was hardly reassuring. Six men had been killed in the war, and his boy told him indignantly: "At the boiling spring they have cooked and feasted upon the slain. They have washed the blood into the stream. They have bathed there until all the waters are red. I cannot get water to make your tea. What shall I do?"

A primitive, bloodthirsty people to deal with. An appalling climate for Europeans. Mrs Paton died after giving birth to a baby, which also died soon after. Mr and Mrs Mathieson fell ill and never recovered from their experience. Another missionary came and took Mathieson's place and died also. John Paton, however, endured—until, on New Year's Day 1861, the first of a new decade, the measles came to Tanna.

There were different ways of looking at the great measles epidemic. On neighbouring Eromanga the Reverend George Gordon had warned the people shortly before they murdered him that a pestilence from Heaven was about to descend, to punish them for their sinful ways. And subsequently the murdered man's brother, the

D

Reverend James Gordon, who followed him to Eromanga, wrote also, "Were I to give you a catalogue of the crimes these people have committed . . . you will not be surprised to learn that God has cut off two-thirds of them in some settlements, if not in all. This terrible judgment will, I trust, open up Tanna and Eromanga to the Gospel which have hitherto been so obstinately shut against it."

Further north, however, in the Banks Group and Solomon Islands, missionaries belonging to the Church of England, the Melanesian Mission, were concerned less with the long-term spiritual gains and more with the immediate human suffering; concerned, but powerless to do anything much about it. For as their little missionary vessel, the *Southern Cross*, cruised here and there, distributing gifts of clothes, making contact with new peoples, opening the Way, so did it spread infection. Apparently the clothes, being great repositories of bacteria, were largely responsible, particularly the way the natives wore them. They did not so much change their clothes, as superimpose one layer upon another until the whole rotting mass simply disintegrated. Terrible lung infections, tuberculosis and pneumonia, followed the *Southern Cross* in its Christianizing mission. Babies were being jogged along on their mothers' hips, racked with coughing.

Not all these Banks and Solomon Islanders, making almost their first acquaintance with the white people in many cases, seemed to connect the new sickness with the arrival of the missionaries. But the sophisticated Tannese knew better. While Paton was blaming it on the sandalwooders and traders, and they on him, the Tannese blamed the white people generally. Two sandalwooders arrived shortly after that fatal New Year's Day. Said Paton, "They had letters for me. But on landing they were instantly surrounded by the chiefs and people who formed a ring about them on the beach and called for me to come. The two white men stood in the midst with many weapons pointed at them and death if they dared to move. The natives shouted to me, 'This is one of the vessels which brought the measles. You and they made the sickness and destroyed our people. If you do not leave with this vessel, we will kill you all.' "

Paton managed to talk his way out of it temporarily, but his days on Tanna were obviously numbered. He mentions large numbers of armed men coming to curse and threaten him; a chief following him around for four hours with a musket levelled at his back. When he had to depart it was in ignominious haste, accepting rescue by a sandalwooder, of all possible vessels, urgently sent over from Aneityum at John Geddie's special request to pick him up.

Why had they not killed him as they had killed a hundred white men before on Tanna? Because they feared him as a mighty caster of spells, someone whose ghost would return after his death to plague them? Or did they still feel, in spite of the friendly warning they had given him three years before, a certain responsibility for his well-being? The Tannese were a strange, erratic people, but evidently not completely devoid of feelings. Paton would have been astonished to hear that after his flight, chief Nowar, one of the few Tannese to have remained consistently friendly to the missionaries, had immediately nailed up his house in an endeavour to prevent its being looted.

The fact remained, however, that the Presbyterian cause had received a severe setback. John Geddie was furious. He had never looked very kindly upon Paton, feeling he was not the type to have been sent to Tanna in the first place. In Geddie's view at least, Paton had brought about his own downfall by being completely tactless and pig-headed, so it was now arranged that he should spend the next eighteen months among the good folk back at home in Scotland, employing his undoubted powers of imagination and vivid description to publicize the New Hebridean mission and perhaps raise some funds.

He proved in fact to be a highly successful fund-raiser. When he had finished in Scotland, he started in Australia, until the "wails of the cannibal heathen", as one of his biographers said, "could be heard across the land". But he did not spend all his time addressing meetings and making speeches. He was also busy in private convincing the Governor of New South Wales and various influential politicians that the missionaries in the New Hebrides needed improved naval protection. More exactly, as he put it in a petition he had drawn up on behalf of those natives of Tanna who were friendly, he wanted "the Chief of Sydney to send quickly a man-o'-war to punish our enemies and to revenge all their bad conduct towards Missi".

So it happened that when the annual New Hebridean Presbyterian Synod opened at Aneityum in 1865 the steam frigate H.M.S. *Curacoa*, with Commodore Sir William Wiseman, commander of the Australia station, was present in the bay. It was apparently one of those stormy sessions, the kind that had once moved a critic of the Kirk to remark that where two or three Presbyterian divines are gathered together, there is raging discord in the midst of them. For whereas it was admitted on all sides that this was the missionaries' opportunity to register their many long-standing grievances, there was strong disagreement about how they should be remedied. Geddie declared he was firmly against warships in the islands, loosing off great bursts of gunnery to the indiscriminate danger of everybody, friend and enemy alike. But Paton, it appeared, was bent on vengeance, emphasizing the treacherous behaviour of the Tannese after originally seeming to welcome his party.

The final decision of synod was, however, unanimous. A memorial was to be presented to Sir William containing a list of all the outrages suffered by the missionaries over the years, leaving it to him to act as he thought fit. The Commodore agreed to this next day, asking only that several missionaries should accompany him as interpreters.

In the event, Wiseman's actions were determined largely by what took place after the warship reached Tanna and dropped anchor in Port Resolution Bay. The Commodore was astonished evidently by the spirit and address of a lot of near-naked savages. To his demand that the chiefs appear instantly on board, there was no reply. So he sent another message which produced only insults. J. L. Brenchley, an English naturalist travelling in the *Curacoa*, reported that the Commodore was very angry and felt that the honour of the Navy was at stake.

Three hundred yards offshore, the warship's 112-pound Armstrong mounted on the fo'c'sle opened up on the nearest native village, followed by a broadside from the port guns, the three 40-pounders on the quarter-deck, and the eight 8-inch guns on the main deck. Wiseman must have thought he was still in New Zealand, helping to bring the Waikato to their knees: first the heavy artillery to soften them up; then raiding-parties to either flank to destroy all canoes and cut off their means of retreat; finally the major part of his force, a hundred and seventy men of the Naval Brigade, to land under the ship's guns and begin the assault on the enemy's main position. Unfortunately the enemy did not have a main position like some easily recognizable hilltop *pah*. But there was a dancing-ground located near the top of one particular hill, Paton pointed out, surrounded by a number of heathen idols. This was where they hatched all their devilish schemes against the white people.

After the best part of two years in New Zealand, the brigade was thoroughly familiar with the tactics. No enemy was in sight when they hit the beach. So they fixed bayonets and dashed across an open space, scattering hand-grenades into a couple of likely-looking spots for an ambush. There was still no response, so the bluejackets gripped their rifles and charged on up the hill. Actually they had carried the hilltop and were in victorious occupation long before any fighting began. Then it was only a brief scuffle: a few shots fired out of the jungle killed a sailor V.C. and were replied to by a volley from the brigade which killed a prominent inland chief. After that the bluejackets scouted around, burning several villages, cutting down a few coconut-trees. According to Brenchley, who was against the whole operation from the beginning, they returned to the ship rather shamefaced.

What had the Tannese done to deserve such a hammering? They had, after all, only expelled Paton. White men had been murdered from time to time in the Pacific for which natives had suffered no worse retaliation than a little light shelling! The Tannese had no idea why they were being punished but they had a delightful time running out on to the beach during every lull in the bombardment, jumping up and down, inviting the white men to hit them. The game was to track the shells through the air, determine where they would land, then fly in the opposite direction. When the seamen landed they disappeared into the jungle to watch.

Wiseman, also, was vague about what they had done, but fortunately Paton very shortly produced the justification designed to please all parties. That master of putting words into other peoples' mouths went ashore after all was quiet and eventually returned with a sort of declaration which he said had been agreed to by various chiefs. It was addressed to himself:

Formerly we had been guilty of so many murders that we feared a man-o'-war would come and punish us; we all thought and said they durst not try, and so we delighted in our bad conduct. Then we had no idea of the multitude of fighting men in a man-o'-war and of her awful power to destroy us and our lands. We never saw anything like this before. Now we are all weeping for our evil conduct. Go and plead with the chief of the man-o'-war not to punish us any more. . . . Tell him to inform your good Queen Victoria that we will kill no more of her people and learn to obey the will of Jehovah.

It was a most misleading document and in the event it pleased nobody. Brenchley, who made no apologies for being violently prejudiced against Paton, says that the so-called declaration was only part of a deep plot to get Paton back on Tanna. If so, it failed. Geddie and his supporters made sure he did not get the chance. Much more important than that, however, was the impression of the New Hebrideans it helped to create in Australia and elsewhere. One might have supposed listening to Paton that the people were mere donkeys to be so led by the nose, biting viciously when the leader turned his back, cringing when they felt the whip. If such were the case, then the cruelties said to have been committed by the labour traders upon a defenceless race were abominable. It would behove us to mount a platform like John Paton and rain down curses upon their ungodly heads. But it was not even remotely like that. At Aneityum the people turned their backs and walked away. At Eromanga you landed at your peril. Call at Tanna when the mood was upon them and they might shoot you. At Rubiana you dare not call at all; in the Shortlands only with the permission of King Ghorai. Pity the poor recruiter when he went a-blackbirding.

THREE

The Recruiters Become Established, 1864-9

ROBERT TOWNS, however, had no time to be aware of any of this. As far as he was concerned the battle concerning the islanders had been fought and won. He had fought it and he had won it. It was he, was it not, who had originally conceived the idea of using Pacific Islanders to cure the labour problems; he who had had to endure all the personal unpopularity associated with first bringing them into the country. That was all over now. The Kanaka had arrived and been accepted. In June 1864 another old Towns vessel, the brigantine *Uncle Tom*, returned to Queensland with sixty-seven more islanders, then set out again with the original recruits (two of whom had died), who had by this time completed their twelve months' engagements. This work of actual recruitment and repatriation Towns left entirely to his man Lewin.

How much, though, did he know about Lewin? It is an interesting question, impossible to answer. His only direct contact with him had been in the sandalwood trade. He may not have heard that this former Royal Navy seaman and deserter was popularly supposed to have engaged in the Peruvian guano trade, in the carrying off of thousands of Pacific Islanders to labour in Peru's offshore guano deposits. Or he may have disbelieved the rumour. It had been a most bloody, violent business by all accounts, conducted mainly in remote places where the only European witnesses were a rather lawless breed themselves. But since the Peruvian Government had abolished slavery in 1855 there had seemed no other labour available to help gather up the millions of tons of valuable bird-droppings that must have otherwise gone unexploited. The Anti-Slavery Society had been among the most active of those opposing this traffic, being successful in persuading the British Government to make representations to Lima about it. But it was not really the result of British protests that brought the trade to an end in 1863 so much as the fact that half the islanders died in Peru, and the whole operation became untenable.

Whether this was where Ross Lewin had gained his first experience of large-scale recruiting cannot be proved. In any case he must have been a hard man, a valuable employee for those Sydney merchants and shipowners intent upon opening up a trade with the unpromising New Hebrideans. For instance, given the task of discovering if there were stands of sandalwood on the island of Malekula in 1864, he had simply landed his gang of Tannese cutthroats at the south end of the place and slogged north with them until he reached the opposite end. The journey took a week. At night the party camped behind earthworks and fought many bloody battles with the Malekulans, but it proved to be the only reliable method of finding out whether there was sandalwood growing on Malekula. There was not.

Now his job was to seek out the best islands for recruiting Townsvale plantation hands. Again it seems very important to know how the man went about his recruiting, whether he was required to give any detailed account of his doings to his employer in Sydney. It was, after all, the birth of a very important industry. But such records simply do not exist. Early in 1865 there was a rumour in Brisbane's *North Australian* that the *Uncle Tom* was a blatant kidnapper equipped with handcuffs, leg-irons, whips and knouts, harpoon-guns for firing into the sides of canoes and reeling them in, nooses for hauling the occupants aboard, and so on. Towns was so incensed about the article that he applied to the Queensland Supreme Court for permission to proceed against the publishers. He was refused and that was the end of the matter at the time.

It was apparently the *Uncle Tom*'s second voyage of 1864 to which the *North Australian* had been referring. Lewin had recruited yet another batch of 67 on this journey, so that the total Kanaka workforce on Townsvale now amounted to 134. Cotton was evidently booming. There had been in fact a good deal of progress in tropical agriculture in Queensland by this time, particularly since the beginning of the Civil War in the U.S.A. and the subsequent sharp rise in world cotton and sugar prices. At his property, Ormiston, near Cleveland, Captain Louis Hope had begun growing sugar-cane as early as 1862, employing the services of a former Barbadian, John Buhot, to help him in his first sugar-making experiments. Robert Philp, then a young office boy, later a founder of Burns, Philp & Co. and Premier of Queensland, saw Hope's sugar put up for auction in Brisbane in January 1866. "It was as black as my hat," he recalled. But Hope persevered with fair success and stimulated one or two more to follow suit.

Another pioneer was Captain Claudius Whish, who came out from India in 1862 with the vague intention of joining Hope in Ormiston. The partnership did not come off, however, and Whish established Oaklands plantation on the Caboolture River instead. He planned originally to go into cotton, but, on Hope's advice, converted to sugar.

Louis Hope was a younger son of the fourth Earl of Hopetoun and the uncle of that future Earl who was to become Australia's first Governor-General. Whish, formerly of the 14th Light Dragoons, had a niece who was married to Lord Napier. So the beginnings of the Queensland sugar industry had quite aristocratic connections. Possibly seeing in it a suitable occupation for a gentleman, more settled than squatting, more steadily profitable than sheep, one or two squatters beside Hope, and a number of Brisbane merchants and professional men, began to invest in agricultural blocks. The whole of the available river lands along the Caboolture were quickly occupied, then along the banks of the Albert, the Logan, the Pimpama, the Coomera, to a point as far south as the Nerang, and as far north as Maryborough. At the same time established small farmers of the Moreton Bay district generally, unable to make much of a living out of maize and potatoes, were going over to sugar in large numbers.

Yet sugar, tempting though it sounds, is the very devil of a crop. Taking longer to mature than almost any other, requiring a messy and complicated process of manufacture before it can be turned into a marketable commodity, it drove many of these early experimenters hopelessly into debt while they were still learning from their original mistakes. It is, moreover, a very vulnerable crop: a strike in the mill, an absence of labour at the moment when the stalk has reached its sweetest, when the cane is standing in the field all ripe for the harvest, can ruin the sugar grower completely.

This was partly why the planters of Mauritius and the West Indies had fought so doggedly to retain slavery. Lazy and inefficient as the slave may have been in theory, he was nevertheless a constant and permanent factor in the plantation economy, a patient beast of burden capable of being goaded into sudden spurts of activity. On 18th August 1865, courting the displeasure of several neighbouring growers whom he well knew to be opposed to the idea, Claudius Whish visited Towns's place on the Logan to look into the prospects of obtaining a regular supply of island labour.

Shortly afterwards the *Black Dog*, another of Towns's former sandalwooders, followed in the path of the *Don Juan* and *Uncle Tom*. The *Black Dog* in its hey-day had been a noted opium-runner; now at the end of its career the old schooner had been fitted out to carry Kanakas, not all of whom were destined for Townsvale. Whish took thirty-three of them, and there were probably other orders as well. Also in 1865 the registered pearler *Telegraph* arrived in Bowen with sixty-five islanders for various inland employers, followed in 1866 by the *Spec*, the *Percy*, and the *Heather Bell*, in the same behalf. It is impossible to say how many more labour traders there were, since a vessel might clear from Brisbane or Maryborough, even Sydney and Melbourne, ostensibly to collect bêche-de-mer or coconut oil, but really, it was rumoured, to sneak labour into Burke-town or one of the Gulf ports.

The pearl-shellers of Torres Strait certainly used the back-door entrance on occasions. They had long been in the habit of running over to New Caledonia and the Loyalties when they needed divers, so it was a relatively simple business to switch from pearl-shelling to full-scale recruiting and back again, according to the demand. Between 1866 and 1868 a Sydney businessman, John Crossley, evi-dently made a good deal of money out of chartering various pearl-shellers and other vessels from their Sydney owners and sending them over to the Loyalties or the New Hebrides for a speculative cargo. The most successful entrepreneur of them all, however, was Ross Lewin.

After four years with Towns, Lewin set up business on his own account. On 26th April 1867 he published the following advertise-ment in Brisbane:

Sugar Planters. Cotton Growers. And Others. Henry Ross Lewin, for many years engaged in trade in the South Sea Islands and practically acquainted with the language and habits of the natives and for the last four years in the employment of Captain Towns, having brought the natives now on Townsvale plantation and superintended them during that time, begs to inform his friends and the public that he intends immediately visiting the South Seas and will be happy to receive orders for the importation of South Sea natives to work on the cotton and sugar plantations now rapidly springing up in this colony. Parties favouring H.R.L. with orders may rely on having the best and most serviceable natives to be had among the islands. . . . Terms £7 each man.

A pretty high figure, £7 a man, but one felt that this big, burly, bluntly spoken seaman would stand on his word; would provide only the best and most serviceable. He was rushed with orders, not only from sugar-planters and cotton-growers, but also from pastoral-ists, town employers, and ordinary householders. Others, like John Crossley, could have used Lewin's experience in their own business and wanted to join him in his enterprise.

Lewin was in demand; Crossley would have to wait. Lewin's first partner was a Captain Gibbins, skipper and owner of the 248-ton barque, *King Oscar*, once a Swedish gunboat, later prominently employed in the coal trade between Newcastle and Adelaide. But in May 1867 Gibbins turned aside from all other enterprises and, having loaded a good cargo of fire-arms and gunpowder, sailed down the Brisbane River bound for the New Hebrides. First, at the Loyalties, Lewin, the supercargo, spent some time selecting two or three capable boat-crews. Then they set out for the island of Epi.

It is worth following the voyage of the *King Oscar* in some detail, as it was the first by a Queensland blackbirder about which there is any information at all—even if that very little is piecemeal and supplied by the recruiter's sworn enemy, the missionary. At Epi, it appeared, a large party of Europeans, assisted by a number of Loyalty Islanders, had landed from four boats very early one morning. They crept through thick bush until directly behind a sleeping village, when a fire was started which drove the panic-stricken villagers straight into an ambush prepared on the far side. By such means twenty men and women were "recruited".

Was this how Lewin had collected his recruits when he was recruiter for Towns aboard the *Don Juan* (1863), *Uncle Tom* (1864), *Black Dog* (1865), and *Spec* (1866)? The only piece of evidence to suggest that this may have been so is contained in a report by Captain William Blake, commander of H.M.S. *Falcon*, which returned from a visit to the New Hebrides shortly before the *King Oscar* set out. At Efate, Blake said an English-speaking native told him how a white man in Queensland (Lewin, apparently?) had battered one of the recruits to death with a stick. At another island a chiefly looking person waded out to meet them when the man-o'-war dropped anchor in the bay. He came forward out of an unusually large gathering of natives on the beach and bore a stick of sugar-cane as if wanting to speak with the white men on a serious matter. A boat's party put off for the shore only to be greeted by the levelling of muskets and a sudden angry outcry from the crowd on the beach. The chief waded further out and all at once struck the head off the piece of sugar-cane with a blow of his tomahawk. Blake took it to mean that he was expressing their general feelings about the cane fields. It was in fact a declaration of war.

It certainly appears from other evidence, e.g. Blake of the *Falcon*, that Lewin's activities had provoked this demonstration. He was addicted to violence, and yet like many other violent men, also proud of his cunning, of his ability to undo his enemies by sheer guile.

The *King Oscar* next visited Aniwa, a tiny island about fifteen miles east of Tanna, where Lewin used quite different tactics. His old enemy, John Paton, had settled here after being refused Synod's permission to return to Tanna, and under the eye of that terrible man of God, the bold Mr Lewin was not so bold. He scouted around cautiously among the villages a little removed from the mission and discovered that some Aniwan canoes had recently gone to Tanna to trade. The recruiters followed the canoes across, found the Aniwans ready to return again, and persuaded them that they had been engaged by Paton to convey them home.

It was not, in fact, a clear-cut case of kidnapping, however much Paton raged about the affair at the 1867 Synod. No force was employed at any stage. The Aniwans were asked if they would prefer to go to Queensland instead of going home, and they immediately chose Queensland, though they had no idea how long they would be expected to stay and did not even ask. According to another Presbyterian missionary who visited them twelve months later on Louis Hope's plantation near Cleveland, they had laboured cheerfully for six moons until they learned to their dismay that their agreement was for thirty-nine months.

The *King Oscar* is recorded to have brought 225 recruits back to Brisbane on its return from this first voyage, and another 282 on 11th November 1867 after a second voyage. They were disposed of at an average £9 a head. The gross proceeds from the second expedition, shared between Lewin, Gibbins, and the charterers W. D. Whyte and Graham Mylne, M.P., was said to amount to £2,430. This profit had been obtained, the missionaries alleged, by deliberately ramming canoes; by enticing islanders aboard with gifts and then clapping them under hatches; by enticing canoes under the stern where lengths of jagged iron would be poised overhead and allowed to crash down—a device known as the eye-drop.

One cannot, however, just accept everything the missionaries would have the world believe about these early recruiters. If such stratagems were employed by Lewin in the *King Oscar*, they were only standard practice in Melanesia at the time, having originated with the sandalwooders, possibly even with the whalers. There were many such tricks. For example, if you had plenty of sea-room, you went to windward of the canoe steering as if you intended to pass to leeward. Suddenly you hauled in the main sheet, let go the headsail, and with the helm hard over the ship came into the wind within its own length. The canoe was shattered.

More original, more ingenious and definitely attributable to Lewin, was the "missionary" trick. The idea originated from the fact that the *Spunkie*, Lewin's next vessel, after Gibbins and the *King Oscar* had quickly retired from the trade, rather resembled the missionary schooner *Southern Cross*. The technique was roughly this: the moment the *Spunkie* dropped anchor, members of the crew would grab a book each and stand round singing hymns, while a figure clothed in white mackintosh, white bell-topper, spectacles, and umbrella, gravely descended into a boat and permitted himself to be rowed ashore. Very likely it was Lewin himself, who had a smattering of the language, or else the mate, John Coath. As missionaries were generally popular visitors in the Banks group, quite a crowd would be sure to assemble on the beach within a very short time. Lewin or Coath would then hand round leaves from some nautical almanac as if they were religious tracts, explaining that Bishop Patteson was at the moment indisposed, but looking forward to seeing all his old friends in his cabin aboard.

There were many variations to this: one of the boat-crew might be sent ashore extravagantly rigged out and claim that Patteson had made him a bishop or Governor of Sydney and wanted to honour other natives in the same way. It was not so far-fetched as all that when one considers some of the stories the genuine missionaries asked the natives to accept. To succeed, it only needed a little tact and the hint that other islands might be stealing a march on them. For the Banks Islanders were really rather timid and would not approach the ship if they saw any sail set. But sooner or later some braver fellow would offer to accompany the stranger back to the vessel and so inspire the rest. The missionary trick was really an extraordinarily clever piece of deception, still being successfully practised in other parts of Melanesia years afterwards.

The success of the *King Oscar* and the *Spunkie* gave a tremendous fillip to recruiting in the years 1867-8. Approximately 1,237 Kanakas were introduced into Queensland in 1867, almost ten times the number of those introduced in any previous year. The rapid opening up of vast areas of central and northern Queensland accounted for the sudden surge in demand, together with the knowledge that orders for South Sea Islanders could be promptly and smoothly fulfilled. No trouble need be expected in connection with them.

It was noted in most Brisbane newspapers at the time that given the angry accusations by the missionaries it was strange that a representative of the Immigration Department was able to visit the *King Oscar* on its second return to Brisbane and find everything in order. There was no evidence of kidnapping, and asked had they come to Queensland quite voluntarily, or had they in fact been stolen, the islanders were much amused, reported the official. "They all laughed at the notion that Mr Lewin ran away with them and gave a decided negative to the question, which I put to them in various forms, with the same result."

But it was really not so strange when one considers that Queensland had a considerable stake in the recruiting trade by this time.

Throughout 1867 it was well known that the firm of John Fenwick & Co., auctioneers, stock, station, and commission agents of Queen Street, Brisbane was expanding its activities to include the placing of Kanakas and that this had become a sizeable part of the business. On 15th November 1867 the company advertised in the Brisbane *Courier*: "South Sea Islanders. Parties wishing to engage Kanakas for employment on stations, plantations etc. to apply immediately to agents, Fenwick & Co.", followed by regular such notices: "On behalf of H. Ross Lewin, Lissadale Cottage, Mary St. H.R.L. being about to proceed to the islands, parties desirous of engaging labourers please send in their orders before the 14th inst. to Fenwick & Co."

Robert Ramsay Mackenzie, one of the partners of Fenwicks, was Premier of Queensland at the time. George Raff, sugar-planter of the Caboolture, and William Henry Walsh, pastoralist of Maryborough, were two very prominent employers of Kanaka labour on behalf of whom Fenwick & Co. had been acting. One was a member of a previous Administration, the other of a later one. So the position of the Government officer suddenly summoned from official obscurity to express an opinion on the morality of the *King Oscar*'s proceedings was a ticklish one indeed.

Yet the Immigration Department's failure to condemn the recruiters in any way, despite their notorious reputation, could only encourage a host of imitators—ship-owners and ships' captains who might otherwise have been disposed to steer well clear of the labour trade. A case in point was that of the brig *Syren*, whose skipper, R. McEachern of Hobart, found himself in November 1867 stranded in Noumea harbour waiting for a return cargo. Carrying coals from Newcastle, copper from Adelaide, hides from New Caledonia—it was a precarious business to be engaged in. Noumea offered nothing at that time of year, so McEachern called his very motley crew together and told them that he "meant to proceed to some of the other islands and take on a cargo of islanders for Queensland".

According to Ishmael Williamson, the Negro cook, *he* was the only member of the lower-deck crew who had qualms about participating in something questionable, possibly downright illegal. The second mate resigned immediately when he saw what "taking on a cargo of islanders" was going to involve. The cook, however, managed to stifle his conscience for the time being and said nothing to anybody until the vessel reached Queensland and McEachern promptly discharged him for laziness. Thus the only account of the first recruiting voyage of the *Syren* is by the disgruntled Ishmael Williamson. It seems to be a fairly reliable one, however, allowing for the fact that illiterate sailors had to rely on their memories for what happened, and were apt to confuse the names of the islands and the sequence of events through visiting so many places that were so much alike. Most of the incidents mentioned were in fact later confirmed by the missionaries.

The recruiter's first landfall was the Loyalty Islands, where they immediately began trading with the natives, attracting great interest with a display of curiously shaped pipes and twists of tobacco. In one instance a chief and three others were induced to come aboard under the impression that the *Syren* was proceeding directly to Sydney where wages were two to three pounds a month. The Loyalties—Maré, Lifu, Uvéa—three small island dependencies of French New Caledonia, were out of bounds, strictly speaking, to the recruiters, but the French Navy was notoriously slack in the matter of patrols. The more daring poachers would sail right into Noumea harbour at night and pick up recruits under the very noses of the Administration. The New Caledonians were generally only too glad to have the opportunity to work in Australia for so much a month instead of doing forced labour on the roads at home for nothing.

Thus the *Syren* was able to do fairly well around the Loyalties before sailing for Malekula in the New Hebrides. Later in the century, after various sinister and strange events, Malekula was to become a name of menacing import for the white man, a "mountain of impenetrable green jungle where death trembled behind every shining leaf, and innocent men dreaded to set foot lest the Evil Eye turned them to stone". But this was in the future. Greeting the *Syren* as she dropped anchor off Malekula in December 1867 a bunch of natives came swimming out, cheerful and laughing, pushing before them pieces of stick bearing yams and coconuts. More followed in canoes, and finally twenty-one in all were taken below to view the mysteries of the hold. According to Malekulan tradition, when the wives of the kidnapped men saw the canoes adrift and the brig sliding away towards the horizon, they swam three miles out to sea calling on the *Syren* to return. It was too far for them to swim back, but when it appeared that they would never see their menfolk again, they wished for nothing more, it was said, except to drown.

The *Syren* continued northwards to little Mota in the Banks Group. On the face of it Mota should have been proof against the kidnappers; sheer cliffs protected the islanders at almost every vulnerable point. But the Anglicans had been to Mota first, more or less reassuring the Motans with their hearty cheerful ways about white men, and as soon as the *Syren* arrived a number of canoes paddled out. About fifteen or sixteen men subsequently offered to go off with McEachern to Queensland. Williamson, the Negro cook, does not say what made them change their minds afterwards, but when the brig called at the next island for water, all the Banks

Islanders escaped during the night. Raging that the carelessness of the watch had cost him £100, the captain punished them by stopping their coffee allowance for two days; an oddly mild punishment considering £100 was involved.

Generally they did very well in the Banks Group, however, and McEachern was soon able to turn for home with his quota complete. But at an unspecified island somewhere along the homeward journey he decided to recruit a few more. Six natives were lured aboard and persuaded to sign on for Queensland. The *Syren* was now filled to capacity, and McEachern planned to sail with the next tide. But early the following morning an alarming situation developed: the brig was still not ready for sea when suddenly it seemed to be surrounded with canoes. An angry mob was also demonstrating on the beach. It was dangerously obvious that the village wanted its six men back.

It was infuriating for the recruiters to have to back down before natives, but McEachern was still sensible enough to see that there was no point in risking the fruits of an entire voyage merely on this issue. The six were returned after an interval, along with a final gesture of spite from the Europeans. As the ship got under way, a ship's boat swept round its bows from the seaward side and made straight for the nearest canoe. Its crew had just time to reach the shore and dive into the bush before the white men landed. They fired a few shots in the direction of a nearby village and kicked the canoes to pieces as they tramped back to the boat.

The *Syren*'s trials were still not over. The last stage of the journey home, across a thousand miles of open ocean to Australia, was always the worst. Half the islanders were seriously seasick and could not eat; half the rest would not eat, claiming that they found the food unpalatable. Not sure whether or not they were malingering, McEachern stood over them with a thick stick and threatened to thrash the next man who refused. After that dysentery developed, spreading rapidly among people already weakened by undernourishment and exposure to cold and unsanitary conditions. One died one day and was thrown overboard. Two went the next day. A total of twelve were dead before the *Syren* dropped anchor in the Brisbane River on 2nd January 1868; another twelve succumbed at the quarantine station after they had all been taken off and the vessel disinfected. In the end McEachern made a profit on fewer than a hundred recruits, none of them properly healthy and fit. At an average of £7 a head, it represented a gross of something under £700 earned in less than two months.

The *Syren* case was the first serious recruiting scandal the Government had to deal with. There had already been letters to the Press

from various missionary organizations, and a good deal of waterfront
gossip, about kidnapping on the earlier voyage of the *King Oscar*.
In the face of it, the Government was obliged to do more than call
for a report from the relevant department. McEachern's voyage on
the other hand had been a purely personal speculation, entered into
without prior knowledge of any parties in Queensland. It could not
compromise the Immigration Department at all, nor involve any
member of the Administration. In the circumstances the Government was free to take a decisive stand over the *Syren*, declaring that
it would no longer tolerate the colony's being swamped with un-
authorized immigrants in this blatant manner. "Immense numbers
of Polynesians are coming in," Arthur Hunter Palmer, the Colonial
Secretary, told the Lower House on 17th January 1868. "In the
present state of the law the Government is absolutely helpless, except
so far as sending the health officer to visit the ship on her arrival,
and prevent the passengers from landing if they were not in a healthy
state."

In fact, pressure on the Government to enact controlling legislation of some kind had been coming from many quarters. The
attitude of the Colonial Office itself, for instance, was that Government supervision of the trade would have to come eventually. It had
always considered this the case, but for four years had refrained from
offering any advice on the subject as it had been informed by the
Admiralty as early as 1863 that regulations would be useless while
there remained no one to police the actual recruiting in the unad-
ministered islands.

The Admiralty held very stern views about the absence of any
firm European authority in the area, and it had never wavered in its
opinion formed during the sandalwooding era that what was happening in Melanesia was outright slave-hunting. If it was empowered
under the anti-slavery laws to suppress the traffic in Negroes between
Zanzibar and the coast of Arabia, it should also, the Admiralty
considered, be empowered to act more effectively against the slave
traders of the Pacific. However, unlike Africa, the Pacific was of
slight significance in Britain's global strategy, and successive Governments had declined to vote the necessary funds for bases and patrol
ships. Thus the Navy had had to be content with sending an occasional solitary warship from Sydney.

But slowly the situation was changing: more and more the Pacific
was beginning to enter into imperial calculations. First, in 1865,
then more strongly in 1867, the French ambassador in London had
cause to complain to the Foreign Office about the activities of British
vessels off the coast of New Caledonia. At Lifu on 8th July 1867, he
charged, John Crossley's *Fanny Nicholson*, after stealing off half a

Natives of Ada Gege, one of Malaita's artificial islands.

A Malekula chief.

A Malekulan.

Taki, a chief of Wango, San Cristobal.

Trading with the natives. Note the loaded musket held at the ready in the background.

village, had been fired on and nearly captured by French soldiers. It was clear that this sort of thing should not continue, and in October the Duke of Buckingham, the new Colonial Secretary, wrote to Bowen explaining that while he heartily endorsed the Queensland Government's immigration policy in principle, he suggested that it should be more closely controlled for the sake of the French and the islanders themselves. He did not believe any special legislation would be necessary, but thought the Legislature might be willing to entrust the Governor with the power to regulate the trade in some way.

Before the dispatch actually arrived the Queensland Government had already decided to legislate along much the same lines and had sketched out the rudiments of a bill. In the event the various regulations proposed by the Colonial Secretary conveniently became the basis of a Polynesian* Labourers Act designed to give not the Governor, but the Immigration Department itself, the power of control. Matters had already been evolving slowly, then, along these lines; it merely needed the arrival of the *Syren* with a cargo of dead and dying to precipitate positive legislative action. The bill rapidly passed both Houses, received the Governor's assent on 4th March 1868, and was sent on to London for approval.

Briefly what the Act of 1868 sought to do was to limit the recruiters' freedom to recruit where, how, and whomsoever they liked. To the average merchant trading in the South Seas a speculation in Kanakas was no different from a speculation in pork, coconuts, or shrunken heads. He sold them for what he could get wherever there was a market. Now, the Act stated, the recruiter would be merely an agent. The first move could only be initiated by the prospective employer, applying to the Immigration Office in advance, stating how many Kanakas he wanted, and how he intended to employ them and where. Not until his application had been approved would he be free to engage a licensed recruiter to act as his recruiting agent. Then, the shipmaster, having collected a sufficient number of successful applications to make the expedition worthwhile, would set out, being bound to engage only a specific number of recruits and to deliver them at a particular port. Furthermore, before his own licence to recruit was granted, the recruiter would be required to lodge a bond with two sureties that his voyage was not intended as a commercial speculation; that he would engage nobody against his will.

* "Polynesian" was in the nineteenth century the Queensland Government's official designation for all Pacific Islanders. Elsewhere, however, the term "Melanesian", as in the Church of England's Melanesian Mission, was coming into favour to distinguish the generally blacker-skinned inhabitants of the New Hebrides, the Solomons, New Caledonia, and neighbouring groups.

There was still no way of policing what went on in the islands, but on the vessel's return to Queensland, the Act went on, the local Immigration Agent would be waiting to go aboard and no recruit could be landed until the ship's master had received a certificate from the agent stating that he had inspected and found correct the following documents: the vessel's licence; a register showing the number of recruits engaged at each island, with their names and the names of the employers to whom they were indented; and a signed statement by some missionary or responsible island resident that the recruit knew the full meaning and effect of what he was doing and had had the text of the agreement explained to him through an interpreter. At this stage a medical officer would inspect the recruits to make sure they were all in good health and physically capable of doing the work. Following this the agent himself would interrogate them, checking that the recruits had no complaints about the voyage and satisfying himself that they understood their contract.

It looked very comprehensive on paper, as if a genuine effort had been made to seek out whatever was wrong or unjust in the present unregulated state of the trade and to remedy such defects. And yet there were still people who remained dissatisfied. The missionaries in the islands, for instance, did not seem very impressed by the Act, despite its regulations, appendixes, and attached schedules, forms of agreement to be filled out with provision for the signature of witnesses and so on. Such legal apparatus would only serve "to legalize slavery", the missionaries thought, "to confirm skippers in the practice of kidnapping". It was hard to imagine the Act affording great protection to the unfortunate native.

The body most indignant about it was the Anti-Slavery Society in London. The agreements, it noted, had been laid down in the Act as being for three years. But the period which it had always associated with the indenturing of Kanakas for the Queensland plantations was twelve months, the period for which Robert Towns had engaged the original batch of sixty-seven for Townsvale in 1863. In the meantime, by the same mysterious process that had formerly operated in Mauritius, in the West Indies, and in Natal, it had grown to three years. The Society wrote to one of its correspondents in Brisbane, Robert Short, seeking to discover just how this had happened. But Short, despite diligent enquiries, could not really enlighten it. He discovered that the recruits by the *Uncle Tom* had been the first group detained beyond the previously understood twelve months, after which it had simply become standard practice.

In fact, three years was the period now legally embodied and it did not seem to have any adverse effect on the volume of recruiting after March 1868, except that there was a marked falling-off of volunteers from Efate, which together with Tanna and the Loyalties had once furnished the majority of recruits. According to the Presbyterian missionaries on Efate, the Efatese were reacting against the white man through having been deceived by the recruiters over the length of the period of engagement. There had been no trouble, they said, until the *Uncle Tom*'s recruits failed to return after thirteen or fourteen moons. But there were innumerable other islands still untouched, hundreds more volunteers only too anxious to take the place of the reluctant Efatese.

The labour traffic was becoming quite profitable in 1868-9. For the Sydney merchants and shipowners who carried on the great bulk of Australia's trade with the South Seas it was particularly attractive since it solved the problem of finding a return cargo from the islands. There were planters, traders, and missionaries to be supplied in the New Hebrides and the Solomons and at Norfolk and Lord Howe Islands, as well as the entire convict and military establishment of New Caledonia. Yet all these island groups between them yielded hardly a single, reliable item for export, which meant that a ship often had to go on to Tonga, Samoa, or even Tahiti to find a cargo.

Now, this was no longer so. Early in 1868 two Sydney businessmen, Eldred and Spence, had formed the South Seas Trading Co. at an address on Church Hill, engaged the services of Captain Albert Hovell, an experienced South Seas trading skipper, and chartered the schooner *Young Australia*. They had planned originally to obtain contracts for supplying labour to various cotton and sugar plantations in southern Queensland, but when the news arrived of the Queensland Government's legislation they decided to recruit for Fiji instead.

It was increasingly the practice, Hovell assured them, to clear from Sydney with a small general cargo as if nothing more than an ordinary trading voyage were intended; then to change the vessel's name and have it re-registered and provided with new papers by the British consul at Levuka, the Fijian capital. It was a simple matter, for instance, to convert a barque into a brig by just unshipping the mizzen mast. He instanced the case of the barque *Australasian Packet*, so well-known in the Sydney–Hobart trade, which he had seen operating in the Solomons dressed out as a brig. So the *Young Australia* set out for Fiji to become the *Young Australian* in Levuka, and then journey to secure recruits for certain Fijian cotton planters. Hovell was captain; Hugo Levinger, a German national lately of Melbourne, was supercargo; Robert Lennie, a Frenchman, second mate. The boat-crews were Eromangan.

One cargo of recruits from the New Hebrides was successfully landed and disposed of at Levuka and the *Young Australian* returned to Port Resolution, Tanna, which was to be its temporary head-quarters in the New Hebrides. Then while quietly trading the outwards cargo of muskets, powder, and tobacco for pigs and coco-nuts, Charlie Hyde, a resident recruiting agent originally established by Lewin, set out around the coast to engage labour. For several days the recruits continued to come in steadily to the ship. There was no trouble until the Reverend Thomas Neilson intervened.

Neilson was the first Presbyterian missionary to become estab-lished on Tanna after the expulsion of John Paton, and only then after repeated efforts. He, like all his brethren in the islands, had come to take a proprietary interest in whatever was happening in his neighbourhood. On and off, mainly off, he had been there for nearly two years, and in Neilson's opinion, Levinger's sale of guns and ammunition to the Tannese would keep the district in a state of continuous upheaval. This he had in mind to tell Hovell and Levinger when he boarded the *Young Australian* in September 1868.

Levinger was busy melting down the lining of tea-chests to cast into bullets when he arrived, and affected not to take the missionary's stern words very seriously. They still had three hundred pounds weight of bullets to get rid of, he answered, and could not very well stop selling the natives ammunition at this stage. How would *he* like it, Hovell joined in, if they were to walk up to him and tell him to stop banging his Bible at the islanders.

It was fine mockery indeed, but inopportune in the circumstances. The Greeks had a word for it, *hubris*, the presumptuous pride of mortal man wantonly provoking the Fates, heedlessly working his own destruction. Neilson, as it happened, was in close touch with John Paton at Aniwa, and Paton was in touch with Sydney and Melbourne, Glasgow, Edinburgh, and Westminster.

Unaware then of how the gods were preparing vengeance, the reckless pair sailed out of Port Resolution with sixty Tannese at large about the ship—in the hold, on deck, practising their balancing tricks on the boom, scampering through the rigging. It was unwise to take such little precaution against the islanders' suddenly seizing the ship. But most skippers allowed it. What bold recruiter of the Levuka waterfront wanted it bruited about that he was afraid of a few Kanakas. The *Young Australian* went on to Efate, Epi, Paama.

Here Lennie, the mate and recruiter, intercepted three men in a canoe and dragged them into the boat. One managed to dive over-board only to be immediately retrieved by Sam, the Rotuman bos'n, using a boathook skewered through one cheek to haul him back. When the Paamans were brought aboard, the Tannese jeered at them as silly, witless creatures, so isolated from the realities of the modern world, it appeared, so innocently unaware of the white man's real intentions, as to permit themselves to be caught. The Tannese in fact became so abusive and threatening that Lennie shouted to them to shut up. "You look out, Tom Tannaman. You make plenty of fight presently." "Orright mate," they answered, "Me make no fight."

But it started again a few minutes later. The Paamans, neither so cowed nor so stupid as they had first appeared, had got possession of a pile of bows and arrows and stones in one corner of the hold. They were now using these against a group of Tannese and apparently having the best of it. Pieces of iron ballast, billets of wood, stones and coconuts flew round the hold. At least one man was badly wounded, judging by his cries.

The Tannese on deck, powerless to help their fellow islanders because the hatches were battened down, called to the Europeans to set afire so that the Paamans might be smoked out. Instead Hovell went forward with a handful of green leaves, supposedly a peace offering on occasions like this, hoping to negotiate with them. However, when one of the hatches was cautiously lifted, an arrow almost knocked the skipper's cap off.

It is difficult to know exactly what happened then; everyone was so anxious to blame everybody else afterwards. But it is probable, and also logical, that it was Hovell and Levinger who were the more concerned to see that nobody was hurt, and Lennie, who had least to lose, the more inclined to drastic measures. Hovell finally surrendered to the mate's insistence when it appeared that the Paamans were heaping up coconut husks against the main hatchway, intending to fire the ship. "Shoot them then," he told Lennie. "But for God's sake aim low and hit them only in the legs."

Lennie and his two French offsiders in the crew then proceeded to deal with the situation according to a definite plan. A ball of cotton steeped in kerosene was wrapped round the end of a long rod, ignited and lowered down into the hold. All at once the noise stopped. Faces glistening with sweat looked up startled while Lennie, from a door opening into the hold, looked down. Soon the figures of the three Paama men danced in the flickering light and abruptly like sharp bursts of thunder, methodical and sure as fate, the cracks of the rifles filled the hold. It was all over in about two minutes; the three bodies, one of them still twitching, were quickly located with the aid of a lamp, tomahawked and thrown into the sea.

That brutal episode seemed to quieten the Tannese considerably; they were not nearly so fussy about who was to be put in with them. Nor were they as vocal as usual when the hold began to get uncomfortably full. Fortunately the ship encountered better weather than might have been expected for the rest of the journey, and they were able to spend most of their time on deck. It was thus a remarkably healthy voyage. Nobody died, apart from the three Paamans. Two hundred and thirty men and six women were sold in Levuka for £1,200.

The first details of the Paama incident leaked out on 22nd December 1868, when a Wesleyan mission-educated Fijian, Daniel Afu, made a statement before John Thurston, the British acting consul. He apparently had heard the story from one of the Tannese recruits. The consul encouraged the Fijians to bring him reports of this kind, as he wanted to know what was going on, although he was aware that native accounts of such occurrences often amounted to very little. If a quarter of the testimony passionately sworn to by the Tannese, patiently vouched for by the solemn-faced Fijians, could have stood up in a court of law, Thurston would have been justified in handing over the entire planter community to the captain of the next man-o'-war. And Thurston was the sort of man who would have done just that if he had conceived it to be his duty. But in this case he did nothing because he and Captain Hovell had once spent several months together shipwrecked on a coral island; he simply did not believe the allegations against him. Also, it was he who had originally given his consul's approval to the voyage and inspected the ship before it set out.

In Sydney, however, the Reverend Robert Steel, agent of the Presbyterian's New Hebridean mission, and its very active and enthusiastic publicist throughout Australia, had no such doubts nor inhibitions. For almost eighteen months John Paton had been assiduously assembling evidence against the labour trade and sending it on to Steel. And the evidence was mounting pretty high in February 1869: first, the *King Oscar*; then the *Syren*; now the *Young Australian*.

Advised by Paton, Steel went to the police and procured the holding in custody of three members of the schooner's recently returned crew. Once again it was the ship's cook who broke the case. McMaster, the newly promoted mate, said nothing at first. Young Johnson, the cabin boy, remained stolidly loyal. But then Henry Heath, the cook, broke down and confessed everything. As a result of their combined depositions, Albert Ross Hovell was arrested at his home in Pyrmont, Sydney, and charged with the wilful murder of three South Sea Islanders, names unknown. However, Hovell's trial for murder, originally set down for April, was postponed until late May upon rumours that events had occurred in Fiji which might have a vital bearing on the case.

Ross Lewin was back in the news again. This time he had teamed with a South Australian, Thomas Pritchard, to become partner in a tired old tub called the *Daphne* purchased from the South Australian Government. Teak-built at Bombay of the very finest materials, it was said, the *Daphne* had done good service in its day, but was now thoroughly worn out. Lewin, however, had no hesitation in ripping out half the old fittings and refurbishing it for the labour trade. It was ironical in the light of what was to follow, but the *Daphne* actually became the first labour trader to be licensed under the new Queensland regulations. Despite its vermin-infested condition and the fact that the shelves running round the hold were in no sense the bunks prescribed in the Act, it passed muster. It was generally accepted in those days that one passenger per ton was a fair ratio; the 56-ton *Daphne* was licensed to carry fifty-eight recruits.

Nor, evidently, did Lewin have very much trouble in securing his own licence to import labour on behalf of three different employers, although he and Pritchard had no firm plans at this stage about their future movements. It seemed they might have to settle down permanently in the Hebrides—the partnership had incurred quite a few debts in Australia—in which case the *Daphne* would be needed to recruit for their own plantations. It was common enough to set out with such vague plans. There was the *Young Australian* and any number of such itinerants around the islands in those early months of 1868. To discover exactly what they were up to was only possible when, as in the case of the *Young Australian*, something went amiss.

There was the case of the schooner *Reliance*, registered in Auckland, skippered by John Austin of Sydney, which had cleared Port Jackson in February 1868, allegedly in pursuit of tortoise-shell. Yet when it ran aground on Indispensable Reef in the Solomons on 2nd April there were no less than seventy Kanakas in the hold. They attempted to rush the boats, and the crews' muskets kept them at bay, enabling the white men to get safely away with twenty-eight pounds of bread, a tin of water, and all the fire-arms and ammunition.

The ship, however, remained intact on the reef, and for the next four days the white men beat about within sight of it, waiting for the time when thirst or starvation drove the islanders over the side, whereupon they would reboard. Eventually fourteen put off on a raft which drifted away to the north-west. Captain Austin suddenly decided to follow them, thinking that the islanders might somehow have some scraps of food with them. But the two boats lost the raft in the night and Austin led them vaguely on in the direction of New Guinea. One of the boats disappeared altogether, but the other party was rescued after thirty-five days of dreadful suffering and privations, and then landed at Townsville. Upon his recovery, Austin gave a graphic description of their adventures to the newspapers, without, naturally, making mention of the Kanaka passengers. Their fate remains unknown.

The *Daphne* was more fortunate. For several months Lewin seems to have just cruised about, casually trading, trying out boat-crews, and generally attending to the affairs of the island recruiting businesses he had set up at Tanna and in the Loyalties. One day, quite by chance, he came across the very spot, that little piece of Melanesian paradise, he had spent half a lifetime searching for. At a small bay on south-west Tanna, out of the way of prying eyes, he landed with his partner, wife, wife's family, livestock, retainers, and all his worldly goods and took formal possession.

Coral blocks, four feet thick, were cut on the beach and dragged more than a mile up a steep, winding track to the site Lewin had marked out—on top of a hill more or less, and yet invisible from the sea behind some luxuriant tropical foliage. The owner, however, had merely to descend his veranda steps and stroll across the front lawn in order to see everything that was happening in the bay below. Not that the place was in any sense a retreat. He still had a great deal to do, planting, trading, building, always adding to his empire, while continuing to keep a tight hold over the recruiting business.

It was not until 15th November 1868, seven months after originally setting out, that the *Daphne* was able to return to Brisbane with its first cargo of Queensland recruits. There was some trouble at first, but all were ultimately passed satisfactorily at the Immigration Office. Lewin was deep in preparations to commence a regular traffic, when word reached him that he was wanted at the police office. This time it was over the most trifling matter. At Tanna he had arranged to accept the very charming, thirteen-year-old daughter of Chief Kiki in exchange for certain presents that Lewin had previously made the chief. The girl had actually been his concubine for some time, until tiring of her he passed her on to one of his Loyalty Island crew boys. When the *Daphne* had reached Brisbane, she had been sold to a planter for £20, and now some disgruntled member of the ship's company was impudently accusing him of rape. Assault was the charge he finally had to face at Brisbane Police Court, and he was quickly acquitted, the original witnesses against him having withdrawn part of their evidence.

Lewin was furious, none the less. That was the end of Queensland for him, he raged, as he sailed off to the islands again at the end of January 1869. He never wanted to see the place again. However, as he still had undischarged commitments to various employers in Queensland, it is by no means certain that this was the real reason for his decision to send the *Daphne* on to Fiji under Pritchard instead of back to Queensland. It seems at least just as likely that he had been frightened off by the presence of Captain George Palmer in the Pacific.

Palmer belonged to the regular, fire-eating breed of British naval commander, the kind whose erratic, high-pressure progress from one crisis point to another, and arbitrary intrusion into everybody else's maritime affairs, suggest that he was probably suffering from an ulcer. Thus when in March 1869 it was rumoured that Captain Palmer in H.M. Sloop *Rosario* had been sent to New Caledonia to enquire into the whole question of illegal recruiting by "British subjects in British registered ships", that was virtually the end of the recruiting in the Loyalties. But the *Rosario* did not catch any of the poachers. Warned of its approach, they had all scuttled off in time, and Palmer had to bridle his impatience a little longer.

In the meantime the *Daphne* had collected another load of recruits and was en route to Fiji. Kanakas were currently bringing only £5 a head in Levuka market compared with £9 in Queensland, Lewin had calculated. But against this there were no Government regulations to worry about in Fiji; no trade-consuming requirements to be met regarding food and clothing: £5 unclothed in Fiji was possibly as good a proposition as £9 clothed in Queensland. Unfortunately for Pritchard, however, his first voyage in charge of the *Daphne* proved an exceptionally trying one. For three weeks the ship beat laboriously to windward, battling head winds and heavy seas, leaking heavily the whole time. The recruits had to be confined below for most of the trip. Here they talked and smoked or slept, stark naked without mats upon the iron ballast. Finally the trades let up a little and in calmer waters and hot sunshine the little vessel sailed into Levuka harbour. Pritchard had calculated that out of 108 recruits only 9 would be unfit for auction. Excellent! But the ship sailed straight into the arms of H.M.S. *Rosario*! John Daggett, the *Daphne*'s captain, had seen the *Rosario*'s masts sticking up above the headland before he entered the harbour, but by that time it was too late to turn and run.

Here was Captain George Palmer, the fire-eater, hero of the West African slave trade naval patrol, snorting like a warhorse on the bit because the authorities in Sydney had assured him that the Kanaka recruiting business was not at all like the slave trade, despite all the evidence he had seen and heard to the contrary. And *there* was the *Daphne*, with a cargo of naked islanders battened below decks, licensed to carry 58 but carrying 108, looking for all the world exactly like any African slaver. A message was conveyed to Pritchard and Daggett that Captain Palmer would like to see them at the consul's office.

It was exactly what the captain might have expected: pages in the log smudged and missing; entries crossed out and rewritten; dates failing to tally with those in the recruiting journal. The ship, owned by South Australians, registered in Melbourne, cleared out of Brisbane for the New Hebrides, arriving in Fiji—altogether a most interesting set of papers. A man called Ross Lewin had a licence to import Kanakas into Queensland and here was a document deputing Thomas Pritchard to act as his agent in this matter, with another purporting to show that the recruits had in fact been consigned to Ross Lewin and were now willing to be transferred to Fiji. The present position apparently was that Lewin owned the major interest in the merchandise and had appointed Pritchard to dispose of it on his behalf to the highest bidder. To this Pritchard's only answer was that the *Daphne* had been originally bound for Queensland when, chancing to fall in with a Fijian recruiter, they had been so traduced by its crew's description of conditions there that one and all, recruiters and recruited, had decided to forget about Queensland and go to Fiji instead.

Now that he seemed to have all the evidence he could possibly require, Palmer went energetically to work in the manner prescribed for Her Majesty's commanders under the anti-slavery regulations. The recruits were taken ashore and handed over to the British consul and the *Daphne* was detained (given in charge of a lieutenant and a prize crew) "on the ground of grave suspicion that the schooner master, supercargo, and crew have been engaged either in actual slavery or at least in a most irregular traffic tending to promote and encourage the slave trade".

Seizing a vessel in these circumstances might have been all right had one been dealing with a crew of shifty Arabs off the coast of Zanzibar. But it was quite another thing to do so in face of a community of freeborn British subjects, one or two of whom had been in the Navy themselves and retired with a rank higher than Palmer's. The planters had been relying on those Kanakas, and they did not care to have their own and their island's good name openly associated with the slave trade. But the protest meetings and petitions to the consul in Levuka were nothing compared with the furore aroused in Sydney when the news arrived that the *Daphne* had been seized and was on the way to Sydney under a prize crew.

The *Daphne* was in no way connected with Sydney, but the *Young Australian* was. And it was an open secret that some of the leading shipowners in the harbour had been dabbling in the recruiting business and had ships engaged in the islands at that moment. It was awkward, indeed, given that Sydney was the headquarters of the Australian Station, and that the Navy generally had been getting such fine publicity for its work suppressing slavery in East Africa. It was particularly awkward since the trade's clerical enemies were being supplied with all sorts of mischievous tales by John Paton, now being maintained in the New Hebrides by the Presbyterian Church of Victoria—the first missionary representative there of any church group in Australia. Little wonder that the missionaries seemed to be ignoring Brisbane and concentrating their anti-Kanaka campaign in Sydney. Little wonder Robert Towns in publicly vindicating his own part in starting the labour traffic was so bitter about the missionaries.

The lawyers even then were being called in to consider whether or not the cruise of the *Daphne* was in any way cognizable under the Imperial Passenger Act, the Merchant Shipping Act, or one of the many statutes abolishing slavery and the slave trade. And meanwhile Albert Hovell was being tried before the Central Criminal Court for murder on the high seas. It was certainly very unfortunate for Hovell that his long-delayed trial on the *Young Australian*'s voyage should take place only four days after the *Rosario* had arrived in port. No juryman could have read the unsavoury story of the *Daphne* in all the Sydney papers and failed to be prejudiced in one direction or another. In past cases of this nature the alleged events had been considered just too fantastic, too far removed from the experience of the ordinary man and woman in the courtroom, to be believed. But now the world, it seemed, was watching, waiting for an answer, looking to the judge and jury to pronounce a judgment on this sort of thing. Close attention was required.

The utmost care was taken, in fact, to foster an atmosphere of impartiality. Islanders as well as Europeans were allowed to give evidence. Members of the crew testified to the intentions of the owners and to the whole character of the voyage upon setting out from Fiji. Evidence was taken from recruits about the inducements held out to them to recruit, and about their treatment on board. All this tended to blacken the case against Hovell, but then the defence dealt with his former stainless record, stressing the fact that on this occasion he had first tried to reason with the rioters; that he had commanded the mate to shoot, but most positively not to kill; that finally he had lost all control over the actions of these three rascally Frenchmen.

The jury did its conscientious best. When it retired at the end of the long day to consider its verdict, it spent another ninety-five minutes deliberating and getting nowhere and was locked up for the night. Next morning it was still undecided. But later it reached a decision: the prisoner was found guilty of murder with a recommendation of mercy. The judge had little alternative but to pronounce sentence of death.

The waterfront was stunned by the news; nobody could remember when a respectable ship's captain had been convicted of an offence against mere natives. It is no exaggeration to say that the outcome of the trial created dismay in shipping circles—dismay, anger, and dark hints of foul play. The arrival of the *Rosario* four days beforehand could have been mere coincidence. Or was it? Anybody disposed to be cynical had only to consult back issues of the *Sydney Morning Herald* to have his worst suspicions confirmed: between February and May, in the months during which Hovell had lain in Darlinghurst Gaol awaiting trial, when the whole case was presumably *sub judice*, the *Herald* had given no fewer than twelve columns of newsprint, letters, editorials, and general articles to denunciations of the labour trade. Two letters in particular, from the missionary at Port Resolution referring to the activities of the *Young Australian* at Tanna, were plainly calculated to influence the course of the trial.

At the same time the prisoner's counsel, James Martin, had been digging up further interesting facts. One of the witnesses for the prosecution, an islander named Hau, had been allowed to swear on the Bible and give testimony on the understanding that he was a recent convert to Christianity. (His evidence, in fact, had been quite damning.) But Hau, Martin had since discovered, nominal Christian though he might be, could not comprehend a single word of the Scriptures, let alone understand the meaning of an oath.

It was beginning to be made plain—the missionaries again! Less than four weeks after Hovell's trial and conviction, the Reverend Robert Steel together with the proprietors of the *Sydney Morning Herald* were called upon to show whether in "conspiring to publish material reflecting on the character of the accused", they had not committed contempt of court. It was one occasion at least when the three judges composing the Supreme Court Bench were prepared to shed not a little of their traditional air of lofty impartiality. "If people were to thrust their proofs piecemeal into the newspaper," they told Steel, "with all the abusive misrepresentations of partisans scattering their slanders . . . if they were to be allowed to use the Press to circulate all their infamous insinuations, propagated, multiplied, and exaggerated by every venal scribe of every mendacious newspaper", etc., etc., well, nobody would have any character left at all.

Steel was fined £100 for his actions in forwarding two letters to the *Herald*, and henceforth, it seemed, the law was bent on making amends for any possible miscarriage of justice that may have occurred earlier. Hovell's sentence was commuted to life imprisonment (he was released some years later).

Next came the trial of Daggett and Pritchard, captain and super-cargo of the *Daphne*, accused before the Sydney Water Police Court of having "knowingly, wilfully, feloniously, and piratically received and conveyed certain persons . . . with a view to their being dealt with as slaves". But there was no sting in the charge. The man who should, it seems, have been in the dock instead was Captain George Palmer. Now he sat in the back of the courtroom, and was made to feel pretty uncomfortable as William Bede Dalley, counsel for the defence, treated the court to some very cutting remarks about the impetuosity of certain naval officers. "It was a charming sight," Palmer remembered afterwards, "to see this dapper little barrister with his well-cut coat and white waistcoat stand up to deliver his harangue with hat, lavender kid gloves, and cane before him". The case was quickly dismissed after that. There was absolutely no evidence, the magistrate found, to show first, either that the natives had been illegally obtained, or secondly, dealt with as slaves.

Finally came the last episode in the *Daphne* affair, the hearing before the New South Wales Supreme Court in its Vice-Admiralty jurisdiction to decide whether the little schooner had been justly seized. The Court ruled that it had not. And the Chief Justice, Sir Alfred Stephen, had more to say while on that subject: people had a right to import this labour, he thought; it was a lawful trade, notwithstanding the injuries which might arise from it. Moreover, "the Queensland Government has done all in its power to see it so managed that as little injury as possible would result". Rather than censure for not having done enough, it deserved high credit for already having done so much. That was that: case dismissed; *Daphne* to be released; costs against Captain Palmer.

The Admiralty paid, but Palmer was so aggrieved about the whole affair that he wrote a book about it. If the principles applied by the courts of New South Wales, he reflected, were applied by law courts all over the world, the Afro-American slave trade might still be in a most flourishing state of business and profitable new slave trades would soon be coming into existence. And one result of the *Daphne* case was quite obviously to give comfort and encouragement to all the fugitive groups of Pacific *banditti*. These were mostly Americans —pirates, kidnappers, and blackbirders—usually to be found in the Marianas, the Carolines, the Gilberts, the Line Islands, or wherever they considered themselves safe from a patrolling man-o'-war. They only needed one hint that the Navy's guns were spiked, that it was nothing but a toothless bulldog, to be down like a pack of wolves.

It was not quite so drastic as Palmer predicted. But in 1870 and 1871 they were being sighted around the Solomons for the first time: "Bully" Hayes in his famous black brig, the *Waterlily*; Ben Pease, formerly of the U.S. Navy, and several others of the same brutal and sinister kind. Having deserted their island harems for the time, they had come probing around to see what might be picked up in the recruiting business.

These men helped coin a new expression in Melanesian pidgin: instead of being "thief-ships" or "snatch-snatches" they were "kill-kills". The method was roughly as follows. On 29th August 1871 Charles Brooke, an Anglican missionary at Ngela in the Floridas was standing on the beach at Mboli when an unidentified vessel anchored about a mile and a half offshore. Immediately five young village men, who must have known what risks they were taking because they had been warned repeatedly by Chief Dikea, paddled out to trade. The entire village assembled to watch. Just as Dikea had predicted, a boat with four white men in it (possibly they were light-haired islanders) swept under the ship's bow and crashed straight into the canoe. An oar was then seen to smash down on the head of one of the swimmers and the body hauled out of the water until the neck lay athwart the gunwale. A tomahawk flashed, once and twice; the head rolled into the boat and the trunk slid back into the water. Brooke felt too sick to look. "But I have not the least doubt," he wrote, "that my companions saw everything plainly. At each successive act in the murder of their fellow islanders they raised a large cry and at length launched a war fleet."

They were too late to do anything, and when they returned empty-handed Dikea jumped out and strode grimly towards Brooke, who was certain he was going to be struck down on the spot. But he was not; Dikea only shouted and waved his arms angrily and extracted a promise from the missionary that he would do all in his power to revenge them.

The visitors were after skulls to exchange for women; the heads would be carried back to one of the head-hunting islands in the west, and King Ghorai or some lesser potentate with his own ample collection of women and female slaves to draw upon would buy the heads for so many young women. These women were a very valuable commodity in Queensland, being generally pretty hard to obtain; planters would pay up to £20 each for them.

The ironical thing about it all was that had the recruiters been less impatient and greedy; had there been less pressure on them to grab a cargo and return, cramming in as many voyages as possible before the hurricane season started, they would have seen that there was no real need to use force at all: the recruits were there for the patient taking. They would have to be paid for, certainly, but they did not cost very much. For instance, if a group were in the middle of an important communal task, like building a canoe, when the recruiter happened to arrive, a recruit could not simply abandon the task and leave his fellow-builders in the lurch. Compensation was in order. So the practice had grown up whereby some close relative, some representative of the group that stood to suffer most by the loss of a potential recruit, waited at the recruit's side at the moment when he actually stepped into the boat and thereby signified his willingness to go. The recruiter would then hand the recruit a "present" which he would immediately pass back to the "friend" hovering in the background.

Naturally there were always disputes about how much a particular person's services were worth. And as the natives had much more time to haggle over the terms than the recruiter, it seemed to the recruiter that the cheapest and quickest way of all was to just snatch up your man or woman and run. One could not expect the whole world to slow down to the Melanesian pace; in Queensland an important new South Pacific industry was waiting to grow.

Such activities as skull-hunting must, it seems, be viewed in the proper perspectives of the time. Perhaps poor Brooke in the emotion of the moment had tended to magnify the enormity of what he saw? In the event, his account of the skull-hunters received scant credence, even from the Governor of New South Wales. What about those other representatives of responsible society, members of the Anti-Slavery Society, the Aborigines Protection Society and so on, gathered in Westminster Hall in July 1871 to discuss the perennial problem of slavery in the world? How did these faraway proceedings appear to them from their position of comfortable rectitude? "We may despise the Negro in his native barbarism," they had been reminded by the chairman in his usual elegant address, "feel contempt for the too submissive Chinaman, look down with haughty superiority upon Papuan Negroes, Malayans, and Polynesian Islanders. The fact remains that we cannot solve the multifarious problems of human destiny without their active co-operation." One must be capable of taking the broad view, in other words, the world view, and must not judge too narrowly.

FOUR

The Recruiting Booms, 1870-1

THERE was now no way that the Navy could effectively intervene after the legal decisions of 1869; the recruiters were engaged in a perfectly legitimate traffic, the law had stated, and were perfectly entitled to carry on their own concerns in their own way. Yet bloody affrays with the islanders continued to be reported in the newspapers, and the bitterness with which the early planting communities would suddenly turn and revile one another makes one think that they themselves must have felt uneasy about the way in which their labour was being recruited. As the *Fiji Times* pointed out in December 1869, Queensland's *Maryborough Chronicle* had never ceased to attack the Fijian labour trade from its very beginning. Was it, the *Times* hinted, because the good people of Maryborough themselves felt guilty about the town's former association with the notorious Queensland Black Police: about one incident in particular in which scores of innocent Aborigines had been shot down in cold blood under the very eyes of its citizens, who had attempted to hush the matter up?

The *Chronicle* would then retaliate by highlighting unsavoury incidents in which Fijian boats had been involved, remarking how much these were helping to give the whole trade a bad name. In contrast, the paper might refer to the career of the *Jason*, Maryborough's own, locally based recruiter, whose record in respect of such incidents was spotless. Under its skipper, John William Coath, the schooner had become a regular visitor to the New Hebrides since early in 1869 and not once had Coath needed to resort to trickery or violence. On the one occasion when no recruits were immediately available he had simply sailed home again with a practically empty hold. Naturally the voyage had resulted in a serious loss, but the ship's master had scorned to use other than simple persuasion. Such was the implication. And the islanders themselves recognized the fact, as proved by the several very successful voyages made subsequently.

There was, however, another aspect of the matter of which the owners of the *Jason*, and, incidentally, of half the newspaper also, may not have been aware: the skipper of the *Jason* had once been Ross Lewin's right-hand man, and what he knew about recruiting he had learnt under Lewin. Lewin, the master, had originally conceived the notion of disguising his recruiter in the robes of the great missionary bishop; Coath, the disciple, had developed the slightly more subtle variation of dressing one of the native boatmen in that costume. It immediately implied that the islanders too could become bishops. In fact the *Jason* was no different from the average recruiter, as the following account of the voyage on which it set out from Maryborough in early December 1870 will show.

As usual the ship called first at Tanna, where two islanders were recruited, one of whom had already spent five years in Fiji and spoke good English. It was quite normal for Queensland recruiters to do this. By 1870 returned labourers throughout the New Hebrides were comparing notes and in the process of deciding that Queensland was a markedly better proposition than Fiji. Queensland wages were higher, to start with, £6 a year compared with £3 a year in Fiji, and the food was generally superior. "You likee come work Fiji?" the recruiter would wheedle. "Me no savvy [haven't decided]." "Fiji very good. Plenty kai kai bullamacow [beef]. Big fella yam. Big fella coconut." A shrug of the shoulders. "Too muchee work, Fiji. No good. Suppos'm you come by'm by. Small fellow ship a ship no likee; me go next time."

But it was not just the money or the fact that the Queensland recruiting vessels were generally larger and more imposing. Queensland was a more glamorous prospect altogether—bigger, busier, noisier, with easily the better shops. Along the straggling waterfront at Levuka the store-keepers would lie in wait for the returning labourer, waiting to exploit his ignorance of current money values after the recruit's three to five years spent at some bush plantation in the interior. In Queensland on the other hand an official of the Immigration Department was sometimes available to accompany the returns on their last-minute shopping excursions just to make sure they were not cheated. They would buy saws, adzes, hatchets, files for themselves, then something for their wives, perhaps a blue scarf or a mushroom hat. A few made a particular point of keeping their last £2 or so to be able to pay their own fare back to Queensland at some future date and thus, they hoped, be in a position to re-engage on their own terms.

So the Fijian recruiter, in a very inferior bargaining position, had

F

to resort to all kinds of tricks. The obvious one was to pretend to be a Queenslander; to invite the islanders, "You go make sugar, Mally Bulla [Maryborough]?" If this were impossible because the vessel had already been recognized as Fijian (there were thirteen vessels regularly employed in the Fijian labour trade in 1870 and about twelve in the Queensland) it might put to sea again and return two days later with topsails furled and the hull painted a different colour. There was a good deal of confusion when rival recruiters chanced to meet, and many a willing battle was fought out on the beach between the two crews to decide the issue.

Something like this happened apparently at Havannah Harbour, Efate, on New Year's Day 1871, when the Queenslander *Jason* anchored not very far from the Fijian *Margaret Chessel*. In evidence taken down afterwards, the mate of the *Margaret Chessel* alleged that one of the *Jason*'s two Tannese recruits, startled when Coath had suddenly begun playing a music box at breakfast, dived overboard and swam across to the Fijian. Coath counter charged that the Fijian recruiter had deliberately enticed him over. Whatever the native's real motive for escaping, Coath called for a rifle and in full view of numerous witnesses aimed it at the head in the water. He missed four or five times, but the escapee was later brought back at the point of a revolver.

It was hardly a noteworthy event for Havannah Harbour. But it was an indiscreet action by the captain of the *Jason* in the presence of his Fijian rivals. After that, nothing went right for him. Soon after, at Nguna, the mate, J. C. Irving, was rowing back to the ship with two female recruits when the boat was fired on from the shore. Coath at once set off for the nearby Presbyterian mission station to lodge a complaint—only to learn to his stupefaction that the shots had been fired on the standing order of the white missionary in charge, the Reverend Peter Milne. At any rate this is what the Rarotongan teachers told him, Milne himself being then away on a journey. Milne's instructions, they claimed, were to shoot if necessary to prevent recruiters from taking their wives.

Coath had still not recovered from the shock of this when at first light several mornings later, sailing between Paama and Epi, they met a canoe containing nine men. The canoeists held up a pig as if anxious to trade but then, following some ineffective parleying with the interpreter, refused to take hold of the rope that was thrown down to them. Apparently they would have liked to come aboard, but were deterred by the sight of some familiar faces among the Efate Island boat-crew.

Irving quickly tired of their shilly-shallying and, armed with a revolver, jumped into the canoe and forced them to paddle right alongside. One dived into the water and set out to swim to Epi five miles away, but in the end all were secured and locked below where they caused considerable annoyance by their cries. Again it was only a small incident, but later at Maryborough a mutinous seaman made it seem much worse by abusing the skipper about it in the main street. All told it had been rather an unhappy voyage, but it was nothing to Coath's next experience.

It was now March 1871, and by this time, Coath discovered, an entirely new phenomenon had appeared upon the scene—the Government Agent. A Select Committee of the Queensland Legislative Assembly had originally recommended the appointment of such functionaries back in July 1869. The Committee reported that it had made diligent inquiries into the workings of the Polynesian Labourers Act and reached the conclusion that it was operating satisfactorily. However, it strongly urged that an agent be sent with each vessel licensed to engage in the labour traffic. It was as a precaution against possible wrongdoing. The Government had then considered the matter at some length and eventually, in December 1870, issued regulations to that effect: a good and separate cabin was to be provided on every ship for the accommodation of a Government Agent. Thus when the *Jason* sailed again in April 1871, Coath found himself saddled with a 54-year-old sugar planter, John Meiklejohn, who was to keep a close eye on all his doings and record them in a special Government Agent's log-book for the private information of the Immigration Department.

There were many, of whom the British consul in Fiji was one, who believed that this action by the Queensland Government was merely an empty gesture designed to appease widespread criticism of the trade. The agent's job, they scoffed, would be a great billet for retired officials and other favourites of the Administration in need of a sea change and a little rest. John Meiklejohn, however, appears not to have belonged to this class. A citizen of some standing in the community, as well as a planter who had become indirectly involved in the trade as a large-scale employer of Kanakas, he was conscientiously determined to find out just how they were being recruited; if necessary to suggest certain reforms.

Others had regarded the job as a mere sinecure, whereas Meiklejohn intended to take his duties seriously. For instance, had his instructions from the Department arrived when they were due, and not a few hours before the ship was due to sail, he would have acted immediately to detain it. Too late, he noted, after the ship was halfway down the Mary River and approaching the Heads, that the space supposedly reserved for the accommodation of one hundred islanders was occupied largely by sails and stores; that their provisions included neither tea nor sugar. There were many other deficiencies besides: only one boiler for cooking yams, rice, and meat for all the recruits and Kanaka crew; the shirts were cotton instead of the prescribed wool or flannel; and finally, the blankets were utterly inadequate for cold nights at sea, "being of a thin, very inferior quality".

In any case it was unlikely that two rough sailors like Coath and Irving would have paid him any heed. And it was apparent, after only a day or two at sea, that they had chosen to regard this first voyage under a Government Agent as something of a trial of strength. Sheer argument could not shift him, they discovered, but he could be frightened. And so by a campaign of calculated insult (obliging him to sit on deck for hours at a time without shade) and cruel gibes they were able to reduce him to submission.

By the time the *Jason* was ready to receive its first batch of recruits, the planter/agent had given up all pretence of imposing his authority; he was merely going through the motions. He would need an independent interpreter to ensure that they all understood their agreements, he hinted to Irving, as they stood watching the recruits embark. The mate answered with a sneering laugh. He would, would he? Then he would have to find one. Or he could have the ship's interpreter, who did only what he was told to by the captain.

Meiklejohn swallowed this, and then decided to speak up bravely. "In that case, all I can do is report the matter to the Government. You may find it very difficult to get another licence."

"That is, if the Government ever gets the report," replied Irving with a wink to Hawthorn, a passenger, standing near. "Sometimes I've known a Government Agent to get a lift overboard when nobody's looking."

After six weeks, off Ambrym, they had the good fortune to stand in with two Malekulan war-canoes. Two boat-crews with tow-ropes immediately put off, and one canoe was quickly hauled alongside. According to Meiklejohn:

Nine islanders and a boy of six or seven years old were forced on board the *Jason*, the last islander being hoisted up by a rope being passed under his arms. On seeing this plain kidnapping, I told the captain that these men did not wish to come with us. He was at this time in the canoe, stealing the pigs in her, and handing up arrows. He shouted out to me from the canoe in an insolent manner, "When you open your mouth, speak so as to be understood."

He came on deck very soon afterwards, and approaching where Mr Hawthorn and I were standing, said to me, "How do you like it?" I replied, "Not at all." And I went into the cabin. He immediately followed with a loaded revolver in his hand, called me a scoundrel, and threatened to shoot me through the head. I cautioned him, and he ordered me on deck, saying that the cabin was no place for me. He followed me with the loaded revolver still in his hand, and I called Mr Hawthorn to witness that I was chased from the cabin with a loaded pistol. The captain then threw the pistol violently down, and wanted to fight me. He said he did not know me as Government Agent; taunted me with not drinking; said that I was only Mr Travis's boy, and that Mr Travis would make a poor little man of me when I got to Maryborough if I reported anything unfavourable of the ship.

Five days later the *Jason* was close off Malekula again and the kidnapped islanders were clustered in the bow singing how a bad wind had sprung up on their voyage to Ambrym and they had been caught by a "thief-ship". Below the captain had insisted on Meiklejohn taking a glass of wine with him, to prove, he said, that the agent no longer bore him animosity. Meiklejohn's account continues:

I told him I would do so, but that I would still do my duty, and that he must not be deceived. He said, "If I thought you would report me, you would never see Maryborough, as it would be very easy to put you out of the way", and that I surely could not be so cruel, as it would completely ruin him and his family. I took about a wine-glassful of wine out of a tumbler, standing at the time in the cabin in front of the captain's berth. I do not recollect leaving the place where I was standing. I seem to recollect being seized and dragged on deck. The next thing I remember was finding myself in the ship's hold among the islanders, handcuffed and chained.

Incredibly, the 54-year-old planter/agent spent the rest of the voyage chained to a ring-bolt in the hold, sleeping along with the islanders, without bedding, on top of the ballast. More than three weeks later when the *Jason* arrived off Maryborough Heads, the port doctor found him released from his handcuffs, but in a state of gibbering idiocy, wasted to a skeleton, glassy-eyed, unable to give any coherent account of what had happened to him. He had gone raving mad, Coath explained, and he had had to chain him up for his own safety.

A few days later a police magistrate's board of enquiry hastily convened by the local Member and Minister for Works, William Walsh, took evidence from various recruits through Coath's interpreter and decided there was little point in pursuing the matter further. In the meantime the schooner and its crew had been sent off to Sydney on some urgent business in the south.

But that was not the end of the *Jason* case. As it happened Meiklejohn had a son-in-law, a Presbyterian clergyman, who happened to be connected with the small party within the Queensland Protestant

Church pressing for the total abolition of the labour trade. And that son-in-law was quickly in touch with the very ardent abolitionist and former Member for North Brisbane, William Brookes.

Whether or not Meiklejohn was still suffering from delusions may have been a debatable point. (He had in fact suffered from previous attacks of insanity and was later permanently confined in Gladesville Asylum, Sydney.) But he was here a living martyr in the cause, in full recovery of his wits, able to testify to the evils of the labour trade and the way he personally, the representative of the Queensland Government, had been treated by one of those brutal, blackbirding skippers. Meetings were held in Brisbane, letters sent to all the newspapers, a statement prepared in which Meiklejohn accused Walsh, the Minister, of urging him to hush the matter up in view of the approaching general elections.

For Maryborough, it was most unfortunate publicity. It was still some months before the fuss over the *Jason* obliged the Government to bring charges against Coath and his crew, but already it was clear (and useless for the *Chronicle* to continue to lament the fact) that Maryborough and, by implication, the Queensland labour trade as a whole had become identified in the public mind with the practices commonly alleged against the Fijian recruiters.

As for the Fijian trade, almost every month of 1871 brought news of some fresh outrage or calamity. On 9th July, four days before the *Jason* reached Maryborough, the schooner *Fanny*, with a batch of returned labourers from Kandavu, anchored near Nguna, the little island where shots had been fired at the *Jason*'s boat six months before. Peter Milne, the missionary who, according to the natives, encouraged them to fire on recruiters, was again absent.

The missionary's frequent trips abroad were disconcerting; in residence his formidable presence effectively deterred the fierce hill-tribes who boasted they were going to wipe out every mission native on the island. But this only made life even more uncomfortable for the Rarotongan teachers left in charge in his absence and forbidden as Christian converts to touch a weapon in their own defence. For in the prohibitive sense, Milne was the strictest of all the Presbyterians. He was against not only cowards who needed guns rather than their faith to protect them; he was against the recruiters and the casual traders; against the settlers at Havannah Harbour; against the Anglicans in the islands to the north; against even his own younger colleague on the Efate mainland whom he claimed was trying to poach potential converts rightfully his. The reason he sometimes refused to attend the annual missionary synod or attended only under protest ("a synagogue of Satan", he called it) was because some of the brethren were smokers and some occasional drinkers.

"All missionary smokers should be drawn and quartered and afterwards drowned in the great North American lakes," he would say. On Nguna he had founded "a teetotal and anti-tobacco club" even before the Ngunans had had a chance to become addicted to either vice.

Unfortunately, while all trembled and obeyed while the master was at home and there was perfect order, none knew how to act for himself while the master was gone. The crowd of islanders on the mission beach visible to those on board the *Fanny* were actually not mission natives at all but Niuta hill people who had come down to terrorize the mission natives. Unaware of this, however, Bartlett, skipper of the *Fanny*, had no reason to be suspicious when they signalled one of the ship's boats to go ashore.

Seven men jumped in as they beached, volunteering to recruit. Skipper Bartlett was still unsuspecting when the boat returned and they came aboard, each armed with a long-handled tomahawk. They would need to retain their weapons, they insisted, while the recruiter remained on the coast and they were still within reach of tribal enemies. Of the white men belonging to the *Fanny*, only one, named Jim, continued to be worried by something unusual in their manner. "Listen to their conversation," he whispered to the Emai interpreter, "and if you hear them speaking bad, mind you tell me." Jim however was soon sent ashore to fetch more recruits, and a little later only two whites remained aboard—Bartlett, below with a headache, and Alec, the mate, dozing on deck.

In such attacks, the natives would try first to separate their white enemies, then to strike in two places simultaneously. Thus the ship's boat was suddenly raked by a volley of musketry in the same moment as an islander on deck stole up behind the sleeping mate and aimed a blow at his chin. Bartlett was instantly awake at his companion's terrible cry and snatched up two loaded revolvers. He was half-way to the deck before the mate, hands clutched to his face, stumbled down the hatchway towards him, and both men staggered back into the cabin. By this time the rest of the crew were dead or mortally wounded and the natives were gathered round the cabin scuttle waiting for the last two white men to come out. Others had cut the chain cable and the ship was fast drifting ashore.

Meanwhile, not yet aware of this, Bartlett had laid the bleeding mate on the floor out of the way and was heaping canisters of powder on the cabin table preparing to blow the natives on the hatch above to Kingdom Come. But even while he was stooping, pistol in hand, to fire the mass of powder, the schooner grounded on the reef and heeled over. With wild shouts of jubilation the islanders now dived overboard and swam ashore knowing that they had the schooner at their mercy. It was Nguna's first major success in the war against the recruiters.

Victory was still not complete, however. Jim in the ship's boat had managed somehow to get away from the shore after the rest had been killed and was adrift in mid-channel, severely wounded in a boat leaking badly, never to be seen again. Bartlett and the mate had not yet been accounted for either. From concealed positions on a point of land a hundred yards away the natives kept up an irregular fire on the ship, aiming through the cabin scuttle. But they could not budge the trapped men. Occasionally they fired back, all through one afternoon and again the next day. The mate, with a bloody bandage round his head, was too weak from loss of blood to hold a rifle, but he could crawl round the sloping cabin deck, keeping all the guns loaded.

All this time Bartlett had been frantically wondering why the mission party had not yet come to their aid. He realized that something must be seriously wrong ashore, but still clung to the belief that if they could only get to the mission station they would be all right. At low tide on the second night the two men crept from the cabin, waded ashore and made their way quietly to the mission. The main house was deserted and locked, but they discovered the huts of the Rarotongan teachers. These unfortunates, terrified out of their wits at the thought of what the Niuta would do to them for giving the white people sanctuary, were even more terrified at the prospect of Peter Milne's sudden return to find that they had been too afraid to do so. Reluctantly they agreed to take them in.

For the next six days they managed to hide and feed the white men, moving the pair from their own huts to the mission cellar, thence to a place in the bush, while the Niuta prowled about everywhere seeking to finish the white men off. The wretched mate could neither eat nor drink without help, and twice a day two native women stole quietly to the place where he lay hidden to ease a little food and water down his throat. But their brave endeavours to save him just failed; less than twenty-four hours before rescue arrived at the hands of another Fijian recruiter, the mate became quite delirious and began wandering abroad until the Niuta found him and led him away to a small clearing in the jungle. Two executioners placed their muskets against his body and fired simultaneously. Then as he writhed on the ground in agony a tomahawk plunged into his neck.

There was an ironic sequel to the capture of the *Fanny*: by the time the forces of vengeance had organized themselves the Niuta had fled back to their hills, and only the innocent mission natives awaited the arrival of the punitive expedition from Havannah Harbour. In those days the distinction between hill peoples and coastal peoples, "man o' bush" and "man alonga saltwater", was still imperfectly understood by the average European. To the settlers of Havannah Harbour the thousand-odd inhabitants of little Nguna were all equally culpable—together with the missionary, Milne, sworn enemy of the recruiter, whom they saw as the real instigator of the massacre, and the Rarotongan teachers, his cut-throat accomplices. Even Bartlett, who was now guiding the expedition, had been too confused and overcome by all he had suffered to grasp that it was actually the Rarotongans who had saved his life.

On Sunday, 23rd July, a landing party came across the teachers and their wives and several other natives celebrating morning service under a tree and clapped the teachers in irons on the spot. Those with them were carried back to Havannah, to give evidence at the "trial". Not that a trial was really intended, for it had been made quite clear to the teachers that after some brief preliminaries it would be their fate to hang.

Thus it came about that in their terror the Rarotongans were to place the entire responsibility for the *Fanny* affair on Peter Milne. This was quite unnecessary as it turned out, for the missionary vessel *Dayspring* turned up just in time, to explain everything, and the Rarotongans were saved. But Milne was never forgiven; after that seamen and settlers alike were quite satisfied to believe that it was the missionaries once again who had turned the natives against them.

What with bloody-minded missionaries and crazed Government Agents, the labour trade had difficulties enough, it seemed. But now the recruiters had discovered a new enemy in the ferocious bushmen of the interior. The bushmen were not really more ferocious than they had ever been, but they were certainly behaving with more freedom and confidence than usual, encouraged by the fact that at various points along the coast the missionaries were slowly sapping their coastal enemies' capacity to resist them. Also the casual violence of various recruiters was provoking them to acts of retaliation against the white people generally. After the *Jason* had stolen two of their women, and other like incidents, the Niuta had been simply waiting for Milne to get out of the way before avenging themselves on the next European vessel to appear.

New factors were thus operating to disturb the old balance of power between inland and coast. The saltwater people generally had the initiative because of their readier access to European weapons and greater opportunity to build up an immunity to European diseases. But where the situation was complicated by the presence of missionaries able to interfere with the flow of arms from the traders, the advantage might pass temporarily to the bushmen. This had happened on Nguna, but on such a tiny island the hill people like the Niuta were still too exposed to European pressures to preserve their independence for very long. They accounted for at least one other European trader after the *Fanny*, but then disease ravaged them and they capitulated to Milne only a few years later. But it was very different on large, almost impenetrable islands like Malekula, where tribes such as the Big Nambas were to go on resisting every kind of European contact, repulsing even large-scale naval expeditions, until well into the twentieth century.

Meanwhile, despite all the risks, there was still a lot of money to be made in blackbirding, as the experiences of a certain Dr James Murray would prove. The doctor was an Irishman born and reared in New Zealand and subsequently sent home to Dublin to get his licentiate from Ireland's Royal College of Surgeons. He was a likable, amusing young scoundrel at this stage, always in trouble with the ladies or the grog, but able to talk his way out of every scrape with polished assurance. His appetite both for work and pleasure marked him out as one who would certainly go far in the world. On his return to New Zealand Murray was soon appointed Resident Surgeon at Otago Hospital with privileges of private practice far exceeding those enjoyed by his predecessor. He was also unusually young for the job, and his colleagues in the profession were jealous, even outraged. But the young surgeon disarmed criticism. He was bright and cheery with everyone, idolized by the patients, and obviously capable. Thus stories about him having been involved in various rather shocking escapades and cut off by his father with a shilling, and the like, were discounted.

In fact there was no particular evil in him. It was just that he had absolutely no real feeling for other people; their sufferings and tribulations amused him but no more. Once, after moving from New Zealand to Victoria, he left several of his patients at Melbourne's Benevolent Asylum heavily drugged with morphia so that he could enjoy the weekend without fear of interruption. There was a scandal about this when he returned, though no immediate harm seems to have been done.

There was another outrageous episode during the period that Murray was Resident Physician to Melbourne Hospital. He had previously been a member of Alfred Howitt's expedition in search of Burke and Wills and had proved such an excellent travelling companion and general life of the party that in 1865 he was the obvious choice as medical officer to accompany Duncan MacIntyre's expedition belatedly seeking for traces of Leichhardt.

Had all gone well on this second trip, the world would never have learned the disgraceful details. But it did not. After a seventy-five-

mile march from the Paroo to Cooper's Creek, MacIntyre found that
the particular water-hole he had been making for was quite dry. So
he pushed on with only one black boy to seek the next, leaving
Murray in charge of the rest of the expedition. The surgeon's job,
in circumstances that were grim though not yet desperate, was to
hold the party together, preserve discipline and push slowly ahead
until MacIntyre returned.

But almost his first act after his leader was out of sight was to rip
open a couple of flour-bags in which he had hidden brandy. Everybody got blind, raving drunk; the horses wandered away and
eventually died of thirst, and much equipment towards which the
people of Melbourne had subscribed £4,000, was recklessly lost.
Murray, however, with three others managed to find their way back
to civilization with a plausible story of what had happened, only to
discover that MacIntyre had subsequently died of fever near Burke-
town and that he was being held responsible. It appeared that the
medicine chest had been full of drugs with which the explorer could
possibly have dosed himself, but not being able to read Latin, and
thus not knowing which drug was which, he had used none and so
had perished.

Naturally there was another scandal; the most dishonourable episode in the annals of Australian exploration, it was said. But Murray
survived it all, and before long he was appointed medical officer at
the Government Sanatorium, Bendigo, where he earned much praise
for dealing energetically with an epidemic of smallpox, a subject
upon which he afterwards published a long paper.

This, then, was the notorious Dr James Patrick Murray who
bought the brig *Carl* and set off in June 1871 seeking adventure—
and whatever else—in the South Seas. Eleven people, not counting
the crew, comprised the expedition, most of them harum-scarum
young fellows of good family, with no particular objective except to see
some of the world and perhaps settle down for a time in some tropical
paradise. They had stock and seed with them and a vague arrangement with Murray whereby they would take up land in the New
Hebrides and start a cotton plantation. The plans were so indefinite,
however, that having arrived and found the climate of the New
Hebrides not to their liking they decided to go on to Fiji.

It was at this stage, it seems, that Murray brought up the subject
of blackbirding. Some of his companions thought it could be a great
lark, while others refused at first to have anything to do with it. The
doctor got his way, however, and when the *Carl* reached Fiji he
sacked the entire crew except the mate, Armstrong, whom he promoted to captain, and hired a fresh crew of experienced blackbirders

from the Levuka waterfront. Then they sailed for Tanna to begin operations.

Two of the partners, Bell and Grut, quarrelled with Murray at Tanna and left the ship, though not because they objected to recruiting. The whole party had already committed themselves to this, whatever private reservations they may have still retained. Indeed, to many men in Australia and the islands at the time, blackbirding appeared primarily a new kind of dangerous and exciting pastime, basically, if boyishly, all right since everybody in Fiji, it seemed, was daring one to attempt it; it was really rather a challenge to one's ingenuity in getting away with it as long as there remained the remote possibility of running foul of the law and ending up in jail.

There was an atmosphere of rare high spirits when the black-birders anchored off Paama. The ship was much bigger than the average recruiter, Murray joked, so they would pretend to be missionaries. Armstrong, the captain, turned the mate's monkey-jacket inside out and put it on with the red lining outside. Then Murray took a rug and fastened it over the shoulders of William Morris, one of the partners. Another, Henry Mount, dressed himself in a red dressing-gown, a smoking-cap, Chinese slippers, and a Chinese umbrella and walked about the deck with a book under his arm. Still there was no response from the Paamans, so the fancy-dress party went ashore, formed a group on the beach, and stood round listening to one another deliver sermons. Their play-acting was pretty juvenile and self-conscious, but they, as newcomers to Fiji, had been told extravagant stories of how simply the innocent savages could be beguiled. They were really quite hurt and disappointed when the natives only stared and giggled. Nobody seemed anxious to recruit or even approach.

Malekula was the next stop. There the behaviour of the islanders was even more inexplicable. One moment they were friendly and welcoming; the next, hostile and threatening. It went well past a joke, however, when one group came out in canoes and deliberately shot arrows at a ship's boat proceeding innocently shorewards to collect firewood. The schoolboy games were over now, and Murray's patience evaporated. "Get them," he ordered the crew. "Shoot them. Just get them."

The kidnapping started at Malekula, where about a dozen un-willing recruits were fetched aboard, the doctor quickly revealing that he was ready for any contingency and had devoted a lot of thought to likely problems. One innovation, which may have been Murray's own, was a cannon rigged in the shrouds so that it could be made to plunge downwards on top of some luckless canoe, then hauled back into position for another drop. For a while the game

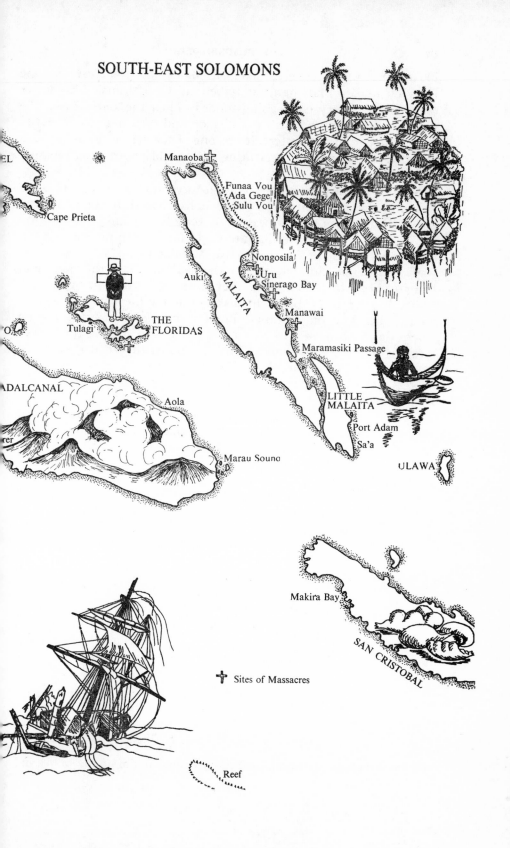

SOUTH-EAST SOLOMONS

EL

Cape Prieta

Manaoba

Funaa Vou
Ada Gege
Sulu Vou

Auki

MALAITA

Nongosila
Uru
Sinerago Bay

Manawai

Maramasiki Passage

LITTLE
MALAITA

Port Adam

Sa'a

ULAWA

Tulagi

THE
FLORIDAS

ADALCANAL

Aola

Marau Souno

Makira Bay

SAN CRISTOBAL

✝ Sites of Massacres

Reef

looked pretty easy: twelve taken at Malekula; twenty-five in one foray off Malaita; fair hauls at Isabel and Guadalcanal. Fifty-six in one week was very good going indeed. Then the *Carl* visited the regions of the dreaded Rubiana Lagoon and even here contrived to capture twenty head-hunters. It was one of the very rare instances in more than forty years of recruiting where a blackbirder successfully raided Rubiana.

Fortune might favour the bold, but to venture uninvited into the western Solomons, where the islanders had had thirty years' experience of white men's ships, was really blindly to court disaster. God knows what plans the head-hunters had for freeing themselves, but already in the hold the twenty-five Malaitamen had discovered a way of worming through one of the chain-holes in the bows and hanging there by a rope until they were ready to drop overboard. "Alas. We are to be killed to make meat for the papalag-i [white men]", they told one another. But for the moment, not knowing where they were, afraid of swimming ashore and finding themselves meat in the hands of some unknown enemy, they had decided to defer their plans. No experienced recruiter would for a moment have kept as many as twenty-five kidnapped Malaitamen together in one batch, but Murray of course would not have understood.

Meanwhile the *Carl* had sailed on to northern Bougainville and Buka Passage. Even King Ghorai of the Shortlands with his mighty war fleet never dared attack Buka, and with visiting ships the big, very black Bukamen paddled out in their twenty-man canoes prepared either to trade or fight as the mood suggested. They never had such a shock in their lives. Large lumps of pig-iron or cannon slung in ropes crashed down on the canoes; then immediately, as they struggled in the water, with many of them badly gashed and bruised, the boats were among them, hauling them in like tuna. The score was forty the first day; forty-five the next. The earlier captives were now stowed right forward and aft, with the eighty-five Bukamen under the main hatch. Not one was either handcuffed nor leg-ironed.

That evening there was much recrimination on deck among Murray's party about these methods of recruitment—with no attention being paid to what was happening below. Here the Bukamen had broken up their bunks and were using them as implements to force open the hatch. Before long the clamour from the hold drowned out all sounds of the dispute on deck and settled the argument among the white men, at least for the time being.

The best-corroborated version of the events of that evening are supplied by a seaman, Devescove. He later testified:

I was awakened about ten by the boy Fallon coming to my bunk, and asking me for God's sake to come on deck, as the ship was on fire, and they would be all dead men. I went on deck, and to the main hatch, where I found the passengers and others assembled, calling out to the natives to keep quiet. I saw no signs of fire, and went below to the cabin for a minute. While away I heard sounds of firing, and returned on deck, and saw William Scott, Dr Murray, Captain Armstrong, and others firing down into the hold. The natives were fighting amongst themselves, and trying to break open the hatchways, Mount and Morris were firing with revolvers.

After the natives had been fighting a bit they would stop, for a few minutes, and then the firing would cease, and be resumed when the row began again. I went to the cabin after the first row was quieted. I saw Morris there loading a rifle, and Dr Murray loading a revolver. There was firing off and on during the night. I fired myself, once or twice, before I saw Morris and Murray in the cabin. At one o'clock in the morning the mate raised a cry that the natives had charge of the deck, and Dr Murray called out, "Shoot them, shoot them, shoot every one of them."

When daylight broke, everything was quiet. The shooting continued, off and on, until about three o'clock, or half-past three, when we knocked off altogether. The firing was resumed at intervals of five, ten, and fifteen minutes, and sometimes half an hour elapsed between the rows. At four o'clock everything was quiet, and I went into the galley and served out some coffee to the men and passengers. After a bit Dr Murray came aft. Lewis, the second mate, said, "What would people say to my killing twelve niggers before breakfast?" Dr Murray replied, "My word, that's the proper way to pop them off."

Everything was then quiet, and breakfast was got ready. After breakfast the ladder was put down the hold by the passengers and crew, and the natives were told to come on deck. Some of the wounded natives came up; they were wounded in the back, arms, and legs. Those who had a narrow wound were put on one side, and those more dangerously wounded on the other. All the wounded natives who could come up, came up. Two of the good natives were sent down by Dr Murray with ropes, which they fixed round those who were dangerously wounded, so that they could be hauled up. The wounded were separated as I have described by Dr Murray's directions. The passengers were looking on all the time, and Mount and Morris told the natives to do their work. I heard them tell them to lay the wounded down, and make fast their hands.

Dr Murray went forward to the starboard side of the ship, and said, "Well, boys, what do you think of doing with these men?" Mount asked, "What do you think of doing?" "Well," said Murray, "I think that the best we can do is to go the leeward of the island and land them there." A man said, "How far are we from land?" Dr Murray answered, "I don't know, but not very far." Mount said, "You have been gaffer all this time, what are you going to do?" Dr Murray then took four or five of the friendly natives and went aft, and told them to pick up a man and throw him overboard. There was a boy with six fingers and six toes, who was wounded in the wrist, and he was the first thrown overboard. When Dr Murray told the friendly natives to pick up the boy, the other natives screamed out, "No, no, no!" He was lifted onto the rail, and Dr Murray pushed him overboard. He was the first who was thrown overboard. At this, all the Bougainville men who could do so, jumped overboard.

In the end the total of natives killed outright or tossed badly wounded into the sea amounted to seventy. Another fifteen or so of the unwounded may have swum safely ashore, which now left on board the seventy-six so-called "friendly" natives. One result of the abortive mutiny was that the Malaitamen had completely abandoned their former over-hasty ideas of escape.

In the MacIntyre expedition and the doctor's other adventures, and now with the *Carl*, run little touches of the macabre and absurd. Thus while the firing was at its height, Murray had been heard singing in a cheerful baritone, quite unconcernedly, as though he were at a concert instead of a massacre, the very popular "Marching Through Georgia".

Again a few weeks later, after the ship's hold had been thoroughly cleansed and white-washed, and only the bullet-holes remained as evidence, the brig ran into H.M.S. *Rosario* off Epi. There must have been missed heartbeats and thoughts of the *Daphne*'s being seized by the Navy in Levuka Harbour. But there was no need for alarm; George Palmer was no longer in command. He had been replaced by a much more circumspect officer, Lieutenant Albert Markham, who had been carefully warned by the Commodore before setting out from Sydney of just what was expected of him. Thus, while required to look into "the general question of the deportation of Kanakas from their homes", he was also to bear in mind that the labour traffic was closely connected with the cotton and sugar industries and various influential houses in Sydney, Melbourne, and Auckland.

In any case Markham had heard nothing of the Buka affair as yet; he was on his way to investigate an entirely different sort of incident in the eastern Solomons. It was not regarded as a particularly suspicious circumstance that the *Carl* ignored the warship's signal to heave-to and fled in the opposite direction until a cannon-ball brought the main topsail crashing down. All the slavers (as the Navy termed them) did this on sighting a man-o'-war. So a sub-lieutenant was sent aboard to make only a routine inspection. He returned and reported, "All correct, sir." "Her papers in order, Lieutenant?" "Yes, sir." "Any suggestion that her recruits are being held against their will?" "No, sir. They all looked to be happy and enjoying the voyage."

This deliberate massacre of seventy helpless islanders is undoubtedly the worst recorded case of its kind. But there may have been other horrors, equally revolting, which never came to light. Many of the recruiters of the time had a grim reputation, the *Nukulau* of Fiji; the *Mystery* of Sydney; the *Stormbird* of Brisbane; the *Margaret Chessel*, originally of Melbourne. So much is known about the *Carl* only because Murray happened to make a full confession, describing in great detail the events of the voyage from the time the brig sailed out of Port Phillip Bay. That was the doctor's way. To come out into the open, making an apparently clean breast of it, before the authorities approached him instead.

After Buka, said Murray, there had been nothing but fighting and ugly scenes among the white men aft. At Epi he and Scott disembarked with a dozen recruits to start work on the plantation. Mount, Morris, and Wilson went on to Fiji, with dark threats of revealing everything if they did not get their fair share of the profits. They did not, of course. And neither did they breathe a word. They simply returned quietly to Melbourne, burying themselves in various employments in the interior, until dramatically recalled to the centre of the stage fourteen months afterwards.

In the meantime Armstrong the skipper and Dowden the mate had negotiated the sale of sixty-odd labourers at an average £10 per head in Fiji and returned to Epi to pick up Murray and Scott before setting out on another expedition. Unfortunately the bad feeling among the white men aft persisted. Earlier, Murray had been accused of trying to poison one of his companions with arsenic. Now, the doctor believed, Armstrong and Dowden were trying to poison him.

The crucial moment to come out into the open with his story, before anybody else, had clearly arrived. Thus upon the *Carl*'s return to Fiji at the end of its second recruiting voyage the doctor went straight to the office of the British Consul and confessed everything. Armstrong and Dowden were then arrested and sent to Sydney by warship for trial and Murray went with them, though not as a prisoner. Perhaps as the result of a bargain he had struck with the authorities; perhaps because he had not yet been identified as the principal figure in the case, he was granted a safe conduct to Sydney where he was allowed to turn Queen's Evidence.

There, for the moment, the main outline of the story must be interrupted, since the climax, the outcome in the courts, was greatly affected by later events, and especially by the fate of the sixty and more survivors of the first voyage.

Invariably it was to prove, both in Queensland or Fiji, that men

G

taken by force were the most difficult to manage on the plantations, especially if they happened to be Solomon Islanders. A dozen of those originally disposed of in Levuka were later transhipped to the little cutter, *Meva*, for passage to the island of Taveuni. The planters in charge of *Meva* were a carefree, rather lackadaisical crowd; rarely did they take any great precautions. So the recruits, most of them Rubiana men at that, were left on deck unshackled and unwatched while the three white men went below for tea. The cutter was still only twenty miles from Levuka when the recruits suddenly fell on the Fijian crew with tomahawks and murdered the lot except for one man who dived overboard and swam fifteen miles to shore with the story. The three whites were picked off one by one as they emerged from the tiny hatch.

A short while later another little vessel, the 25-ton schooner, *Peri*, set out from Suva with a second shipload of recruits which included the twenty-five Malaitamen from the *Carl*. Twice before, aboard the *Carl*, the Malaitans' plans to escape had been frustrated and, though they had already discovered the way out of the hold they still were doubtful about casting themselves adrift on a cannibal shore. Then, on the late afternoon of 30th December a seaman, suddenly enraged at their request for more rice, rushed into the midst of one squatting group, seized a large pot of rice simmering quietly on the fire and hurled it, forty men's daily ration, into the sea. "You disgusting pigs," he shouted at them. That night the *Peri*'s part-white, part-Fijian crew shared exactly the same fate as their counterparts of the *Meva*. Every single man was systematically hacked to death except for one Fijian whom the Malaitamen had deliberately spared so that he could navigate their vessel to land. But he too dived overboard and escaped.

The *Peri* was now discovered to be almost destitute of food and fresh water. The sufferings faced as they drifted, sails set and helm lashed, at the mercy of the south-east trades, is best described in the words of a Fijian native clerk who pieced their story together years afterwards.

The next day it blew hard and they were smitten by a headwind and they lost themselves not knowing in what direction the land was to which they wished to go. They sailed on, their provisions failing them and their water running dry, and they ate boards and cases which were very bad.

Then the Leli [Malaita] men had a talk among themselves; what about eating some of the people? Some of them said that ought not be, as it is tabu in the Solomons to eat men. Then it was agreed that they should eat some, as it was so uncertain whether they would reach land safely again. That was the commencement of eating human beings, and that day they devoured two women, one in the morning and one in the evening. Those who remained in the hold wished their ship would sink and that they could all be drowned. When their water was done they drank sea water. Things were so until thirty had been devoured and twenty had died and only the Leli men remained. So they sailed on for a moon and then the Leli men commenced to die. When one of them died he was rolled up, weighted with stones, and thrown overboard.

Then the second moon came and they discovered land and some said: "It is the Solomons", but others: "It is a different country." That night heavy rain fell and they drank of it. Had it not been for that rain they would all have perished.

When the sun rose they knew they were in a strange land. Two of their number were dead in the hold and those they did not throw in the water, intending to bury them on shore. Then they saw a large ship draw near which put out four boats and pulled together to the Solomons' vessel.

The ship was H.M.S. *Basilisk* (Captain John Moresby); the strange land, Australia, in the region of Townsville; the date, 5th February 1872. The schooner had drifted eighteen hundred miles in five weeks, freakishly managing to avoid the countless coral reefs studding its path, finally to discover a rare opening in the Great Barrier Reef and pass through unscathed.

And the saga of the *Peri* was still not ended. For two of the Malaitamen had seen the man-o'-war and the approaching boats and resolved to die fighting rather than surrender. As the seamen drew to within twenty to thirty yards they were dismayed to see two wild-looking figures rise up in the stern; to see gun-barrels being poked unsteadily over the rails towards them. For a moment it looked as though the Navy had blundered into a trap. But then the *Peri* drifted on, the guns continued to point harmlessly past them in the same fixed direction, and the sailors clambered aboard and gently laid hold of the rusty, lockless muskets clutched to two wasted bodies. Thirteen out of the original eighty put aboard at Suva were found to be still alive.

It was an incredible story, a tiny Fijian schooner cast up on the shores of Queensland, a story of massacre and mutiny, of cannibalism finally in order to survive. Yet it made little impact in Australia. Probably the general public were no longer sensitive to South Seas horrors by that time. Every week brought news of some fresh atrocity; a boat-crew attacked, a European settler murdered, with more than an occasional hint of savage reprisals against the islanders. Once such incidents had been fairly rare. But now about two dozen regular recruiters, plus occasional outsiders like the *Carl*, were busily at work from March to December, extending their operations in every direction, visiting places where white men had never been seen before. It was depressing to travel from island to island and find the natives depleted in numbers, everywhere suspicious and hostile, even when the visiting white man, like Bishop John Coleridge Patteson, was an old friend.

In a last letter to a friend, the bishop wrote: "My afternoon ashore [at Emai] was one of the saddest for many a long day. I encountered in all about forty-eight people in the village when of old three hundred certainly were to be seen. Fighting going on and even the cannibalism for the most part unchecked. They have all guns and will shoot at any white man. How to act upon the people I am at a loss altogether to imagine." The writer instanced the case of Tivea, whom he had known as a boy, a laughing, sparkling-eyed youngster, devoted to the missionaries. Now he was not unfriendly, but his manner was casual, his language deliberately coarsened, his eyes preying everywhere as he spoke. "To see him as I saw him this afternoon is enough to break one's heart."

The Anglican Melanesian Mission had been founded by Bishop George Selwyn in 1848 to bring Christianity to the people of the Solomon Islands and New Hebrides. The Reverend John Geddie, for the Presbyterians, had also begun to do the same at Aneityum a little before this. But Selwyn's Christianity was of a quite different order, a more cheerful, frank and manly, Tom Brown's Schooldays type. Selwyn had been an Eton and Cambridge man, and you could not join his Mission at all unless you could swim, manage a boat, play cricket or rugger, and had been at Oxford or Cambridge. His successor was John Coleridge Patteson, captain of the Eton eleven, 1844, and a fine boatsman; to be followed by John Richardson Selwyn, stroke of the Cambridge eight in 1862, winner of the university pairs at Henley; then by Cecil Wilson, Tonbridge and Cambridge, a member of the Kent eleven that defeated the 1884 Australian team, the only county to do so. And so on, it was like joining a crack regiment.

This was the tradition. Selwyn did not settle anywhere and preach. He moved continually from island to island, swimming ashore alone at every strange place, various gifts tucked under his top hat, so that none other should have to share the danger or endure the discomfort of scrambling over the coral in bare feet. Patteson, consecrated first Bishop of Melanesia in 1861, did the same, so impressing the islanders that every year a steady number of the best young natives was carried off for training at the Mission headquarters at Norfolk Island. Patteson used to describe this work as "recruiting", and in effect, if not always in method, it closely resembled what the labour recruiters were doing. Even the Santa Cruz islanders, who inhabited the eastern extremity of this maritime diocese and were exceptionally distrustful of foreigners because of their isolation, would have let their young men go had they dared. As it was, they would allow various boys to take their places in the missionary boat, as evidence of their goodwill in the matter, only to pull them out again just before it cast off. They paid high honour to "Bisampe" when he visited them, but by 1871 Patteson had still not obtained a single scholar. "I'm not coming again," he would say in mock disgust. "It's a waste of time talking to you."

But Santa Cruz in not offering at all was not half so disappointing as other places where great strides had once been made. Patteson would now arrive to find that the resident teacher, some promising graduate of Norfolk Island perhaps, was unaccountably missing. He had died, he would eventually discover, after much probing of the uneasy villagers. Or he had defected; or turned head-hunter; or most probably, gone off to Queensland in a labour vessel.

It was not at all the world of his young Eton and Oxford imaginings, and the Bishop (who was still only forty-four) had become sick at heart and depressed at the inability of the Church to make progress against the powerful material interests massed against it. He set out on his last tour of the islands at the end of April 1871, and everywhere they went the labour traders had been first and all talk was of Queensland and Fiji, or else the subject was carefully avoided altogether. "Why don't you do something about it," the natives beseeched him once at San Cristobal, "or else let us do something?"

Near the end of the voyage, off Santa Cruz, he wrote in his diary: "Fully alive to the probability that some outrage has been committed here by one or more vessels. Atkin saw the master [of the *Emma Bell*] today who did not deny his intentions of taking any he could get." It might be a wise move, he went on to reflect, to avoid the main island of Santa Cruz for the moment; to visit first the Reef Islands, little Nukapu perhaps, where people were in constant communication with the north face of Santa Cruz. They would be sure to know if a labour vessel had been in the vicinity and thus left the inhabitants in a mood to murder the next white men who appeared. There was no sense, he thought, in simply inviting retaliation.

However, a labour vessel, very probably the *Margaret Chessel* of Fiji and formerly of Melbourne, had also discovered Nukapu. By the device of impersonating the Bishop (the trick still seemed to work when tried at a new place for the first time), the recruiter had kidnapped five boys. Now the uncle of one, Teandule, had been deputed to carry out the work of vengeance.

At 11.30 a.m. on 20th September 1871, the missionary vessel, *Southern Cross*, dropped anchor off Nukapu, approximately the same time, as it happened, as the *Carl* arrived at Buka. It was a glowingly hot morning, it is recorded; with the squat little island shimmering just ahead, blue waves breaking over the circling reef— where now, unless the glare were playing tricks, several canoes seemed to have gathered, hovering as though in some doubt about what to do next. When they made no move to come farther out, Patteson asked for a boat to be lowered, and four men rowed him across to where Moto and Taula, two chiefs, greeted him warmly and demanded he join them in their canoe. The bishop complied instantly, knowing that the slightest hesitation would be interpreted as a lack of confidence in them, even though the mission natives and the Reef islanders were continuing to eye one another rather warily. Soon the canoe carrying the bishop was on its way to shore while the boat remained at the reef with the other canoes, unable to cross because it was low tide.

For half an hour or more boat and canoes drifted around, the two parties making desultory conversation. Then suddenly, for no apparent reason, but presumably in response to some signal from land, the men in the canoes jumped to their feet and began shooting arrows into the boat, Atkin, a white missionary, was mortally wounded and two of the others were struck, before the boat could be pulled out of range and rowed hastily back to the ship. While the injured men were being treated, all eyes were fixed on the shore, though still there was no sign that anything untoward had occurred. Then at about four o'clock two canoes were seen to move out from the beach, one of them being detached after a time from the other and allowed to drift apparently unoccupied towards the ship. It came on, and on, until a bundle was visible in the bottom of the canoe, wrapped in a native mat, with a pair of the bishop's boots projecting from one end.

It was ironic that the Reef Islanders should have been so firm in resisting the Scriptures; their manner of taking revenge might have come straight out of the Old Testament. For when the mat was unrolled and the body revealed, the missionary's party saw a palm leaf fastened over the breast with five knots made in long leaflets, seemingly a strange and rather beautiful accounting for the five kidnapped boys. There were also just five wounds; first, a blow on the right side of the skull which must have killed instantly; then the work of some sharper weapon that had cloven the top of the head; a deep gash on the body; and finally two arrow wounds in the legs that could only have been made after death when the corpse lay stripped. An eye for an eye. And a tooth for a tooth. Five young men had been taken and presumably eaten. Here, in expiation, lay the body of one of the white men's very foremost chiefs. Honour was satisfied.

Perhaps it needed a good clean killing to purge the air, to let some of the blood; a martyr in the cause of humanity, to bring the authorities to their senses, to let them know that if they accepted a moral responsibility for the preservation of law and order in this part of the South Seas they ought to do something about it. For those far distant administrators, Secretaries of State in London and their underlings in the Admiralty, the Foreign Office, the Colonial Office, must have known in their hearts, even if they had always disclaimed any legal or political obligation, that they ought never to have allowed the plundering to go so long unchecked. They had been reminded often enough of what was happening and pretended it was not their business. But it was useless to expect the Australian colonists to do anything, or the French in New Caledonia. They would merely continue to reap what profits they could behind a front of legality, crying all the time that it was the British Government which should be in effective control of the area, should be curbing such lawlessness.

In fact, the pretence that Great Britain was genuinely concerned to put down the kidnapping was really laughable. Every year before 1872, barring accidents, one of the six ships of the Australian Station had been sent for a spell of police duties in the islands. This meant usually that some obsolete old tub like H.M.S. *Basilisk* would set off reluctantly for the New Hebrides, to spend several weeks investigating various accusations of white or black having broken the peace, finishing up in Fiji for a spot of leave. If the commander concerned was at all conscientious in his duties, he ran the risk, like Captain George Palmer, of being sued for false arrest; or like Commodore William Wiseman of being held up to public execration for being too mercilessly severe with the poor savages. Certainly after Palmer there was no naval commander resolved to see his man actually brought before the courts and punished with the full rigour of the law.

The fact that the Supreme Courts of the colonies had full powers to try "treasons, piracies, felonies, robberies, murders, conspiracies, and other offences of what nature or kind soever committed . . . in any island situate in the Pacific . . . and not subject to His Majesty . . ." did not help them. In practice the Crown's law officers simply refused to frame charges—knowing that however much the nature of the offence was watered down, from murder and kidnapping to simple assault and robbery of canoes, they had little hope of obtaining a conviction. Most of the seamen who lost their lives in the South Seas were Australians, and colonial juries did not seem to think the islanders needed the "special protection of British law". They thought it more important that the European should have an absolutely unfettered discretion to take whatever precautions seen as necessary to protect his own life.

Essentially there were only two lines of approach: either you thought the islander inherently treacherous, killing wantonly because it was his black nature to do so; or else, a rather gentle and helpless creature only responding to previous European outrages. At the sudden shock of Patteson's death, the "gentle and helpless" school of thought had the chance to seize the initiative, to get in first and insist that the bishop's murder was the work of revenge. In great public demonstrations throughout Australia and New Zealand, in speeches, pamphlets, and letters to the Press, the missionaries, the enemies of the planters and all those who wanted to see the labour trade abolished, hammered home their simple point that the present recruiting system was helping to turn the islanders into demons.

Very conveniently, they had the testimony of the martyred bishop himself to support their case. For various letters and diary jottings had come to light; his musings over the previous two or three years spoke more eloquently than a hundred speeches of impassioned denunciation, more telling than any number of signatures to a petition, of what a desperate pass island life had been brought to. To trade honestly with the natives, to communicate reasonably with them, had become impossible. Not only European recruiters, but the returned labourers themselves, for their own malicious purposes, would encourage people to recruit, these recruits often being mere boys with no idea of what they were doing, no notion of what was being said except they were being invited to some other place for a space of two or three moons. The dead bishop had known one fellow to volunteer for no other reason than to get a rifle to shoot his neighbour. And time and again the bishop would ask, "To whom ultimately was the benefit?" Was it in the interests of Australians, in their long-term trading interests, that the native races of the Pacific should die out altogether? Would God need to show His hand, to cause some tragedy to come to pass, before anything was done?

The letters made the most profound impression in London. In an astonishingly short time, considering the number of years that memoranda on the subject had been passing from one bored department to another, the outlines of a Pacific Islanders Protection Act was drawn up. It was designed to deal specifically for that portion of the Pacific. It began by defining exactly the crime of kidnapping; by stating what a kidnapping vessel was; by laying down for the guidance of naval commanders what they would be expected to do when they met one. It was drafted originally in March 1872, and finally made law by June.

Meanwhile out in the colonies, John Bramston, Attorney-General for Queensland, had been closely considering the papers in the Coath case and finally decided that the captain and crew of the *Jason* should be prosecuted. From September to December 1871 their trial dragged on at weary length, numerous adjournments to consider special points of law causing it to be unduly prolonged. All this time, in reaction to the bishop's murder, public attitudes to the islanders were undergoing a remarkable change. The final verdict of the jury was unequivocal. The crew members were acquitted, but John Coath, once the pride of Maryborough for his spotless recruiting record, was found guilty on the third of four separate counts of offences against natives and sentenced to five years' jail. He was later pardoned, only to return to the trade and lose his life in it shortly afterwards.

While the new Imperial legislation was still pending, a decision by the Queensland Supreme Court in the Coath case made the existing laws about kidnapping a little easier to follow. Originally, it pointed out, the Common Law misdemeanour of kidnapping was intended to apply only to Her Majesty's subjects suddenly deprived of the protection of British law. But, the judges thought, in the present circumstances in the Pacific, it could extend to a person of any nationality. The heat was now being turned on the recruiters. In November 1872, in Sydney, Armstrong and Dowden of the *Carl* were convicted of kidnapping on the evidence of Dr Murray and sentenced to death. Victoria was constrained to follow suit. The following month Henry Mount and William Morris of the same ship were arrested after months and charged with having committed wilful murder on the high seas. The damning testimony this time was supplied by a number of the *Carl*'s crew. There was also much evidence to show that they had entered only reluctantly and of necessity into the business of suppressing mutiny, but they too were found guilty and sentenced to fifteen years' hard labour.

By this time public opinion was crying aloud, in the name of suffering humanity and all the slaughtered populations of the Pacific, for the blood of that arch-scoundrel James Murray. In fact the man's own father wrote to a Sydney newspaper: "As regards Dr Murray, the celebrated *Carl* man-catching approver whom I have for years cut off as a disgrace to creed, country and family, I fully endorse your condemnation of that cruel, unhappy being and add that although opposed to capital punishment on principle, that if any of the *Carl* crew murderers ever ascend the gibbet for the seventy kidnapped and cruelly slaughtered poor Polynesians, Dr Murray should be the first, as head."

But the doctor must have been used to people calling him names; he never appeared to suffer remorse, to quake in terror at the thought of what must surely have been awaiting him in the next world. He was very adept, however, at expressing contrition, at gaining the good opinion of religious bodies content to believe that a man might suddenly be smitten in conscience for the crimes of a lifetime, see the light, and be reformed. Thus, early in 1873, full of penitence and pious sentiments, he left Australia for England, abandoning a wife and two children in the process. He sought an audience with Lord Kimberley, Secretary of State for the Colonies; not to explain nor extenuate, but to advise his Lordship upon a more effectual method of suppressing the rampant blackbirding that he claimed was still going on. How the Secretary of State, who had once had the task of describing his exploits to a shocked Upper House, dealt with him on this occasion is not recorded. But the Bishop of Oxford was supposed to have found the doctor a most charming person.

Even so, bloody, smiling villain or unspeakable hypocrite though he might have been, his crimes were little in comparison with those of Ross Lewin. The kidnapping age could never properly be considered at an end while Lewin himself was alive and flourishing· But his time too was near. It was the year 1874, one midday, and the lord of Tanna had just roused himself from a short siesta and was stretching his limbs and strolling across the front lawn to take a peek from his ocean look-out. With its great walls and underground cellars capable of storing provisions for a six months' siege, the castle was considered well-nigh impregnable. Yet a native had managed to penetrate his outer defences and was waiting in a nearby coconut-palm to avenge the death of a cousin whom Lewin had shot a week or two before for banana-stealing. The islander had been waiting for three whole days, he claimed afterwards, and now that the long-awaited moment had come was about to nod off to sleep. But some special sense must have prompted him, for he opened his eyes just in time, picked up the carbine and took careful aim. His victim, struck somewhere in the back, spun round completely, staggered a few yards to the veranda steps and collapsed. It was the end of the greatest old blackbirder of them all.

FIVE

The Sugar Industry Booms, 1864-80

A FEW Queenslanders in the earlier years of the colony argued that nothing of this fuss would have arisen, and no Ross Lewins would have been necessary, had the Government of the day not made the mistake of granting away large tracts of land for agricultural purposes at ridiculously low prices. A shipowner like Robert Towns might not otherwise have attempted to establish a cotton plantation; nor a typical cattle man like Captain Louis Hope been tempted into a risky experiment with sugar after sixteen years' ranching. Large holdings requiring large capital expenditure and devoted principally to growing crops immediately implied large quantities of cheap labour to work them. Thus, it was said, Queensland had missed the opportunity of following the example of northern New South Wales and building up a class of small cane-growers who did most of the work themselves. Experience showed that the farmer who worked his land himself would work all day and every day if necessary, irrespective of climate; while the farmer whose main occupation was to supervise the labour of others would very soon not be doing even that, but employing an overseer and driving into town in a buggy.

In the event Queensland had its plantations and the Ross Lewins. The bottom soon fell out of the cotton market, but sugar continued to do well among the swamps of the Pimpama and Coomera Creek, along the Brisbane, the Albert, the Logan. Today it seems amazing that anyone should have tried to grow sugar in such generally indifferent country, when they had the rest of the colony to choose from. But they persevered—so long as good yellow sugar sold at from £36 to £40 a ton—and learnt from their mistakes. On 1st June 1865 a Devonshireman named John Spiller planted the first cane at Mackay to the north. He lived in a grass humpy during the first few years, growing the original cane-plants in an enclosure forty yards square. He was much troubled by crocodiles which came right up to his front door to seize fowls and other livestock. But Spiller was a large, powerful man with a great spade of a beard. He got the better of the crocodiles by coolly lying in ambush for them behind a tree, waiting until they drew level and then firing at the vital point behind the jaw. He went on to master the techniques of sugar production in the same cool, imperturbable spirit and when he finally sold out of the sugar business in 1885 he was worth, it was said, a good quarter of a million.

Spiller had been fortunate in discovering more or less by accident the finest possible land for growing sugar. But everything in those days seemed to be conspiring to get the young industry off to a successful beginning. In the valleys of the Mary and Burnett, on the Pioneer and the Herbert, cheap and abundant land of the highest quality was coming on to the market at the same time as world sugar prices were rising to a record level and an apparently inexhaustible supply of cheap labour was being discovered in the nearby islands. It was possible for the ignorant beginner to make mistake after mistake—and yet survive in many cases. He would plant the wrong variety of cane that would succumb to disease if the season proved wetter than usual. Or he might plant in the wrong place, without proper drainage, and be destroyed by flood. Or else he might cut too soon, before the assurance of a good yield of sugar in the stem, not realizing that in Australia sugar-cane needed a much longer period to mature than that laid down in the textbooks. Even in 1875, after ten years' collective experience, few planters appreciated the necessity of constant cultivation between the cane rows, one of the reasons assigned by a Government committee of inquiry for the general failure of the crop that year. By that time the New South Wales farmer, hands to the plough in his own piddling fifteen to twenty acres under crop, had discovered that growing such things as carrots between the rows had much the same effect as cultivation and was a lucrative sideline as well. Alternatively, if he judged the season unsuitable, he might plough the whole crop in and let the land lie fallow for a time. Thus the New South Wales sugar industry was pretty solidly established in the early 1870s. Progress was slow and unspectacular, but at least nobody suddenly crashed as did the occasional big grower in Queensland at the end of a bad season.

The small farmer was also unburdened in another way. Having a limited capacity he was not likely to be tempted into investing capital in a mill. Instead he would take his cane to some more enterprising neighbour who would do the crushing for everybody in the district. In Queensland, on the other hand, a man starting in a big way would want to have his own mill. And thus money saved by having a cheap labour force to do the initial heavy clearing would tend to be swallowed up in expensive machinery. He needed first the crushing equipment—usually a set of three ironbark rollers mounted in an iron framework. Into these, Kanakas would feed the long stalks of cane while two horses, yoked to poles, plodded a circle round them, causing the great rollers to revolve, creaking and jerking. By 1870 horses had been generally replaced by twelve-horsepower steam engines, while at one stage planters in the vicinity of Brisbane combined to buy a small river steamer, the *Walrus*, equipped with its own cane-crushing machinery. This would visit the various waterside plantations and do the crushing for each in turn. However, the experiment came to nothing, as the steamer was constantly breaking down.

Altogether early manufacturing was messy, time-consuming, and inefficient. From the crushers a stream of yellowish juice would squirt out into several cast-iron pots, in which it was boiled and then allowed to cool. It was a clumsy and wasteful process. Whereas modern milling machinery extracts one ton of sugar from about six tons of cane, these early mills averaged only one ton from twenty. The cooked mixture was allowed a week to granulate before being transferred to V-shaped boxes perforated at the bottom and sides to let the molasses drain slowly away. The residue was a large-grained bright yellow sugar produced at the rate of about a ton a day.

Everybody perpetually moved about in sticky streams of molasses. Horses ate it instead of oats; builders mixed it with water to make a sort of cement. But the industry continued to make steady progress. There were fifteen sugar mills in the Maryborough district in 1876, turning out 3,400 tons of sugar a year plus 178,000 gallons of molasses. And all the time production methods were gradually improving. About 1870 for instance Messrs Tooth and Cran, of Yengarie plantation, Maryborough, inaugurated a new system of sugar manufacture whereby the ordinary planter did only the crushing, and conveyed the juice by way of tanks floated on punts, and later by pipes, to the new modern plant at Yengarie to await the latter stages of processing. Robert Tooth and Robert Cran were two very skilful and enterprising engineers, and Yengarie led the way with newer, more efficient techniques. Steam-jacketed copper pans instead of old-fashioned iron pots prevented the juice from burning during the important crystallizing stage. New centrifugal machines, replacing the crude old boxes with draining holes, spun off the syrupy molasses in a matter not of weeks but of hours.

Organization was Yengarie's success. Expensive new plants needed to be kept continuously in operation right through the crushing season if they were to be economic. So a method was worked out

whereby fifteen to twenty growers, subordinating their operations
to an overall plan, would each begin cutting at a prearranged time.
They would then crush with their local plant and convey the juice
to one of half a dozen "huge receptacles" provided by Yengarie
within a radius of five miles from the mill. A special lime solution
devised by Tooth was then added so that the juice could stand for
up to a month without risk of fermentation. Finally it was pumped
into a series of large open cisterns at the central factory where the
process of liming and treating would begin all over again. During
all this Yengarie would be cutting also; the mill swarmed like an
ant-heap as Kanakas unloaded the carts, carried heavy bundles into
the mill-house on their shoulders, and raked up the megass—the
mangled stalks that had been squeezed of their sugar and were now
to be dried in the sun before being used to fuel the boilers. It was
all becoming more and more systematic. The growers would lend
some of their labour for the unskilled tasks around the mill while
Yengarie would hire out to the grower its own gangs of skilled cane-
cutters whose rate of output could be estimated in advance.

Out of all Queensland's sugar-growing areas Maryborough was the
islanders' favourite district at this time. Probably the temperament
of individual overseers had something to do with the preference; or
the degree and kind of supervision exercised by the local Immigra-
tion Agent. Certainly in the 1870s Maryborough had a very zealous
official, R. B. Sheridan. But Maryborough was definitely preferred,
just as Mackay was universally detested. A recruiter, Captain William
Wawn of the *Stanley*, recorded the following conversation at Tanna:
Native: "What name ship?"
Recruiter: "*Stanley*."
Native: "Where you come from?"
Recruiter: "Maryborough."
"Mally Bulla very good. You buy boy?"
"Yes. You got boy? He like come?"
"P'raps by'm by. You buy yam?"
"Yes. We buy yam together. All you have."
A naval man, Captain James Goodenough, Commodore of the
Australian Station in 1875, confirmed this. One of his informants
also expressed a preference for Maryborough and added, "Porta
Mackay. Very bad man. He shoot. He kill blackfellow."

Possibly what they liked most about Maryborough was its atmosphere. For at the height of the crushing season there would be an
almost holiday spirit in the air, with Yengarie mill the focus of
most of the activity. During the day and well into the night the
grinding of the rollers and the beat of the engines could be heard
far away in the canefields, keeping the Kanaka out of his bed, causing

him to stamp out this same compulsive rhythm with his bare feet while the line of dancers went swaying and shuffling round the fire, remembering the steps of the great festival dances they had been taught when they were youths.

The celebrations would go on sometimes until dawn, but next day was just the same. For fourteen hours they would be hard at work, cutting, loading, carting, unloading. They did not care how hard they worked when they were happy, and they were usually happy when something was going on around them. The manufacturing held an endless fascination. All the natives awaited their turn in the mill or boiler-house to watch the pumps' ceaseless pounding, the steam rising up in clouds, the frothing rivers of juice coursing through the pipes, which abruptly changed direction, now shooting up to the roof, now plunging down again towards the rows of vacuum-pans standing like mighty kettle-drums, waiting to inaugurate the next stage. They found it all very exciting, reminiscent perhaps of those days in the islands after the harvest had been gathered in, when the yam-houses were filled to bursting with the earth's goodness, and the ceremonial season was about to begin.

The notion, so popularly held at the time, that the Kanaka was a mere unresisting object of exploitation was simply not true. When in the mood, they ran skylarking out into the fields to begin the day's work; raced one another to the end of the row and, at midday, flung themselves down, laughing and exhausted, to gobble some food. The planter could never really understand how the mere spectacle of Kanaka labourers working contentedly in the fields could rouse people to a state of passion.

This feeling apart, by the late 1870s the sugar industry had overcome most of its earlier problems and was entering a peaceful, prosperous period. Such improvement had taken place in manufacturing techniques that Queensland sugar was now regarded as good as the best Mauritius or West Indian.

In 1877, according to the statistics, Queensland produced 12,240 tons of sugar; which had risen to 18,200 in 1879, and to 21,000 tons in 1880. Mackay and Maryborough were still the main ports of export, but with the rich scrublands of the lower Burnett being hailed as the coming place. Already in 1878 the two Young brothers had come from New Zealand to establish Fairymead plantation near Bundaberg. In 1881 Robert Cran, formerly of Maryborough, moved there also, founding the Millaquin refinery. Finally by special Act of Parliament, the Colonial Sugar Refining Company of Sydney was permitted to take up great areas of land in various places, undertaking at the same time to spend £200,000 within five years on the clearing and cultivation of that land and erection of plant.

Only a fanatic surely would have wished to destroy an industry so young and promising, attracting so much healthy capital into the colony, so many keen and enterprising new colonists like the Youngs. However, it appeared that Queensland did possess such a person— William Brookes. Parliamentarian, publicist, pamphleteer, professional critic at large, he seemed the living embodiment of all the latent hatred in the community towards the planting interest. It was the Kanaka question apparently that chiefly aroused him: the state of affairs that quietly festered, in good times as in bad, like a cancer feeding on something malignant in human nature.

The image the planters had of their implacable enemy was that of an envenomed old man, white locks flying, foam flecking the corners of his mouth, leaping to his feet at the back of the Queensland Legislative Assembly to denounce them. It is 2nd September 1886, the complaint has just been made that the employer of coloured labour in Queensland has never had fair play, and William Brookes is on his feet in a flash: "I tell you, Mr Speaker, what fair play to these people means. It is this: that they shall have just entirely their own way. And nobody else shall have a voice in anything. The Governor has had large experience of coloured labour. He knows that when there are representative institutions, coloured labour and white men never did work, never will work and never can work together. It is utterly impossible to reconcile the two. Why sir, these employers of coloured labour would go through blood and bones and every obstacle to reach their selfish ends. . . . Coloured labour means ruin; ruin body and soul as a British colony; ruin to our trade. It means an entire suppression of . . . all our morals, our religion, our civil and constitutional liberties."

This was Brookes: the very picture of the rabid abolitionist, unstrung, unreasoning, and quite clearly unbalanced in some way. His cause was a compulsion; if it drove him into the grave he would stop the trade somehow. In fact at one stage it seemed as if his efforts had contributed towards stopping it. But then the devious politicians, manoeuvring shrewdly through the shifting winds of public opinion, recanted on the question. Brookes from his sick bed was carried into the Chamber to expose their shallow proceedings. He was too weak to stand, but he was given permission to speak sitting down, which he did for more than an hour, with the aid of a large stick that every now and again he would bang loudly on the floor, to emphasize a point. Finally as he stumbled and spluttered over the last few sentences, searching for the words to bring the tirade to a fitting conclusion, he suddenly collapsed on the floor. The members were genuinely spellbound.

Hailing originally from Manchester, England, Brookes had always

Plantation workers in the islands husking coconuts.

A planter's home in the islands.

A bachelor planter?

Bishop Patteson.

been an ardent young man, of fierce passions, encouraged in the lower middle class *milieu* in which he was raised to direct these passions towards the attainment of the Englishman's highest goal in life—a position of upper middle class respectability. Yet there was also this strain of waywardness in the family. His father, the owner of a shoe-shop, had actually eloped with the daughter of a cotton manufacturer, and young William, despite intense efforts towards self-improvement, seems not to have eradicated the same disposition suddenly to veer off the rails. He was working for a Manchester wholesale draper while in his early twenties, and was plunged also in the affairs of the local Wesleyan chapel, where "his employer's wife accused him of abusing their hospitality at Wesleyan singing by laying siege to the affections of their thirteen-year-old daughter". Brookes replied by emigrating to Australia, where ultimately he prospered and became the owner of a successful ironmongery business in the heart of Brisbane.

He could always be relied upon for "a few remarks at Church socials", he had once written in his journal, that intimate account of his long struggle to succeed and win recognition in Australia. He was too modest; he had in fact a most wonderful gift of oratory, of the scarifying phrase. Even in the privacy of his journal it was natural for him to refer to lawyers, for instance, in such terms as "sharks" and "cormorants"; to describe successful businessmen as "people who would cart the relics of their ancestors to the nearest bone mill if they thought they could get cash for them". It did not necessarily mean that he habitually felt like this about them; it was just that he possessed this very vivid imagination. Reflecting upon his private business fortunes, for instance, he would see himself "treading through dense scrubs of sharp and wounding brambles"; emerging safe "from a dark sea of angry, curling waves". He himself was always at the centre of every drama.

John Bright, that other great Manchester orator and enemy of the vested interest, was his model, it happened, so perhaps inevitably he was soon in politics, taking part in a great popular outcry against the squatters' threatened domination of the legislature when Queensland gained separation from New South Wales in 1859. It is hard to tell from his writings just how warm his feelings really were in a question like this. On the platform he had a tendency to start a free fight every time he opened his mouth; privately, he would express his opinions almost as forcibly. It was all part of his general approach to life. However, on the subject of whether Queensland should receive coloured labour, coolie, Chinese, or Polynesian, one can see at once his deepest convictions being challenged. In his time he would use all the arguments of the abolitionists, advance a hundred good

H

reasons why it was best that Queensland do without Kanakas. But the fact remains that there was but one basic reason why he would spend the next thirty years fighting the labour traffic: he did not like coloured people—at least not in Queensland. It was as instinctive as a dog barking at the front gate to warn off strangers.

On 22nd May 1863, for instance, when Robert Towns was still only considering the importation of Kanaka labour for his cotton plantation, Brookes wrote to the *Courier*: "With reference to who comes to this colony as immigrants, I am perfectly indifferent. The only exception I make are coolies and Chinamen, two races of the human family who are quite unable to contribute to the respectability and progress of the colony."

It was probably fortunate for the planters that Brookes was elected member for North Brisbane at a by-election in 1864. It meant that other political questions would divide his attention for the next three years. But then he was defeated at the general elections of 1867 and all his spare time after that was devoted to the fight. There was already a small abolitionist society in Brisbane led by a newspaperman and former resident of the West Indies, Robert Short, with whom Brookes now closely associated himself. He learnt a lot from Short about the West Indies: how the slave trade had held back the normal social and political development of the island; how it had caused the economy to slow down and finally become completely stagnant; how it had the inevitable effect of corrupting masters and men and eventually everybody who came into contact with it. It was not so much the humanitarian movement in England which had destroyed the plantation system, Short pointed out, as the plantations themselves going bankrupt through their own sheer inefficiency. So Brookes carefully studied all the available literature on the subject, all the tracts of the American abolitionists, and prepared his great series of articles for the Brisbane *Courier*.

Queensland debentures may be at a heavy discount, her railway administration corrupt; her commercial credit collapsed . . . these misfortunes were to be expected, to be endured, not to be compared in the same breath with that single stark, overwhelming fact that the colony had attempted to introduce slavery to her shores [he might have been on the platform again, instead of at his desk]. . . . The soil of Queensland should be a source of prosperity to the whole people. Not the means of perpetuating those deep divisions in society that have split the Southern whites of America into the slave-holding few and the non-slave-holding, poverty-stricken remainder.

These were sentiments calculated to provoke a lively discussion and yet the response was very disappointing; one or two letters in respectful support, some furious protests from the planters, but otherwise very little interest at all. In fact, his campaign to awaken the conscience of the British Empire fell completely flat in almost every respect. Articles he wrote for *Leisure Hours, Household Words*, and other important London papers were not even published. He wrote to the Anti-Slavery Society, pointing out that the distress of the Lancashire millers was no reason why Queensland should have to produce Kanaka-grown cotton. "Their reply displayed a grave deficiency of warmth and sympathy," he lamented.

Just at that time a delegation of visiting Quakers arrived in Brisbane, and Brookes appealed to them. "They listened to me," he said, "as they would listen to one who played fairly well on a musical instrument." In other words, "they had the Quaker acuteness in seeing how money was to be made; the Quaker aptitude for turning corners and walking in bypaths so that objectionable ways of making money might be made more presentable . . ." and of course they could not see what all the fuss was about. Like sensible businessfolk everywhere they thought that a ready supply of low-priced labour was just what a young colony needed.

The trouble was that hardly anybody was prepared to think really deeply about the subject, and to look beyond the immediate present. Periodically slumps occurred and jobs were scarce; then the various trade unions and working-class organizations would come together and petition the Government that "Polynesian immigration be stopped lest it make Queensland unpopular as a field for emigration with the poor but industrious classes of the 'mother country' ". But it was not an argument that they liked to press too far; the Government could use the unemployment situation to turn off the tap of European emigration altogether and devise some secret means of flooding the colony with coolies. But before his working-class audiences in North Brisbane Brookes hammered away about the insidious dangers that Polynesian immigration was storing up for the future. They heard him for the most part in silence. His campaign might even have contributed to his defeat in the 1867 election. In political terms he would have been better advised to concentrate on more immediate issues.

In fact, the only time it paid to introduce the coloured labour question directly into politics, he came to realize, was when the details of some recent enormity like the *Daphne* or *Jason* case were still fresh in the public memory. Then one could safely denounce it from the moral point of view, and clergymen and other well-meaning citizens would come forward and propose some possible mechanism of Government supervision to enable the worst abuses of the trade to be mitigated. But they could not conceivably mean what they said on these occasions, he reflected, or one would not be confronted with the spectacle of a leading Brisbane churchman riding about in a carriage, with a liveried Kanaka youth, clearly under age, to wait on him.

Brookes saw the problem in more fundamental terms. He would not have approved the labour trade even without the kidnapping and violence attached to it; even if recruits came entirely of their own free will and knew exactly what they were doing; and the arrangements for shipping and accommodating them were perfectly decent and comfortable. He would still have objected and gone on objecting if it had meant the ruination of the entire sugar industry. Because, more important than the sugar industry, he believed, was the future of Queensland as a British colony.

Thousands of good agricultural labourers were breaking stones on the roads in England, he would tell his audiences, when they could be opening up new land in central Queensland. Was the colony to continue to be a favoured place of emigration for enterprising young Englishmen? Or a slave state ruled over by a clique of squatter-planters? Because if such men got their way completely, he foresaw, it would not be very long before they had their runs all fenced in, and, with a supply of cheap labour ensured in perpetuity, be in a position to defy the colony at large. Each in his vast, thinly populated electorate, surrounded by a population of docile Kanaka slaves, would be politically unassailable.

The more he thought about it, the more enraged he became. Time and again since his election defeat he considered the position of a former parliamentary colleague, George Raff. Once merely a merchant like himself, Raff was now a sugar planter on intimate terms with all the gentry, sitting in Parliament by the grace of the working men and freeholders of East Moreton.

On and off during a busy year in 1868, at the same time as he was fighting to save his ironmongery business from a sudden threatened disaster, he worked out the details of a scheme to destroy the planters. Every incident, every rumour, every instance of cruelty towards Kanakas by planter or recruiter was to be followed up and exploited for all it was worth, he wrote. Not because he was a sensationalist, but because anything which helped to lift the labour question to the level of public consciousness was good. "My object is to injure the public standing and repute of any public man who approves of and assists towards establishing South Sea Islanders as a labouring class in Queensland."

There was only one way to do it: go down to the waterfront and find out for himself. The newspapers had ceased to be of any assistance. They would merely record the arrival of, say, the *Lyttona*, "with 700 coconuts, from the South Seas", making no mention of her one hundred or so recruits. So Brookes would keep a close watch on the movements of the various recruiters, waiting for the opportunity to present himself at the quayside, perhaps even to bluff his way aboard. There was always the possibility of finding some disaffected member of the crew, and of persuading him to talk.

His first success was in the *Syren* affair in January 1868. The allegations of the Negro cook, Williamson, against the skipper, McEachern, had been printed originally in the *Mercury* of Hobart, McEachern's home port. Brookes saw to it that the article was reprinted in the Brisbane *Courier*. And later on when McEachern publicly denied the allegations and it seemed that the cook was about to retract his statements, it was Brookes who got hold of him when the *Syren* returned to Brisbane and persuaded him to sign an affidavit on the subject.

However, his most notable achievement in this line was to take up the case of the Immigration Office's agent, John Meiklejohn, after the latter had been sent to him, claiming to have been most barbarously ill-used by the captain of the *Jason*, John Coath. Brookes then proceeded to make such a nuisance of himself at the Colonial Secretary's Office that the exasperated Minister finally promised to send on all the papers in the case to the Attorney General's Department. Thus, in due course, charges were laid, witnesses summoned, the trial initiated that was to culminate in the disgrace and imprisonment of Captain John Coath. Maryborough was most aggrieved about it all, attributing the whole proceedings to the malignity of Brisbane people in general, and of Brookes in particular.

Finally then, the persistent intervention of one busy, conscientious citizen, deliberately drawing the fire of the planters and the big battalions every time he moved into the fray, was having some effect. Brookes's tenacity seemed to be achieving something. Once, however, he interfered rather too precipitately and landed himself in an embarrassing situation instead. According to a report in the *Courier*, the crew of the Brisbane recruiter *May Queen* had been suddenly set upon by treacherous natives somewhere in the New Hebrides, and the skipper, the well-known Captain G. S. Kilgour, murdered out of hand. Brookes quickly saw in this the opportunity for a piece of propaganda. He managed to locate a photograph of Kilgour which he then pasted up in his Brisbane shop window above the simple caption, "Killed and Eaten". It was a gesture in questionable taste, seeing that the captain had relatives in Brisbane, and Brookes got no more than he deserved when the "dead man" turned up in Brisbane very much alive and very hostile and began an action against the ironmonger for bringing his name into public contempt. Brookes settled out of court.

However, these little brushes with the law, the day-to-day skirmish-ing with the various outposts of the Administration, had small bearing on the main issue. Brookes's major confrontation was with the Government, whose Polynesian Labourers Act he was determined to expose as a complete sham. The Immigration Office, said Brookes, had never raised a finger to put the law into effect. It was empowered, for instance, to approve or reject an application to employ, an application to recruit, purely at its own discretion. But who had ever heard of any application being refused? There was little barrier, it seemed, to anybody who wished setting out to recruit; little barrier after that, in the islands, to his recruiting how he liked. What about when he returned then?

Despite the Act, Brookes reported, having made it his business to find out, the procedure remained the same as ever. As the vessel came in sight of the Queensland coast, the supercargo or chief recruiter would be furiously coaching the recruits in the answers they were to give the agent. They, with heads all obediently bent, might appear to be listening attentively, though almost certainly they would not be, having already decided among themselves which plantation they wanted to go to and arranged to swap names with one another for that very purpose.

Then when the vessel dropped anchor and the agent was actually aboard, the bluffing began in earnest. To show how many years they believed themselves bound to serve, the recruit would be asked to hold up so many fingers. This was sure to cause some misunderstand-ings because the islander, when he wishes to express a figure, indicates it by the number of fingers he turns down, instead of by those left up. After this confusion had all been sorted out, most would be found turning down only one finger or two, trying to explain that they thought the period was for but one or two years or perhaps only months.

In any case nobody took any notice of them. The agent was probably only going through the motions anyway, while the employ-ers or their representatives were doing the real business—running an eye over the cargo to make sure they were neither too small and weedy on the one hand, nor too big and truculent-looking on the other, hurriedly negotiating with the skipper for the number re-quired. But whether sale was by auction or private agreement the terms were always the same, cash down on the table. When the *Syren* arrived in January 1868, Brookes had the opportunity to go aboard, whereupon he found, so he claimed, all sorts of irregularities: forms not signed; indentures witnessed by an illiterate seaman with the mark of a cross; the space reserved for a missionary's signature boldly signed by the mate.

It would fall to Brookes to spot any irregularities. He had a passion for exactitude in small things. However, one could hardly dispute his main point—that to regulate the trade as the Act purported to regulate it was really to kill it utterly, and this was not the intention of those who framed the Act nor of those who had to put it into execution. John Thurston, one-time Consul at Levuka, afterwards British Governor of Fiji, made his own recruiting cruise in the New Hebrides group in 1871 and discovered that if due regard were paid to all the requirements of Queensland's regulations then the cost of recruitment would amount to £12 to £13 a head. Yet the recruits were being sold in Queensland for as low as £7 each. The missionaries confirmed this, stating further that it was their invariable rule never to sign a recruiting form because it was impossible to explain to the recruit what it was all about.

So the Act of 1868 was a dead letter from the start: the planters ignored it; the shipowners ignored it; so did the Immigration Office. Writing to the *Courier* on one occasion a correspondent quoted a ship's manifest from the shipping columns of the Townsville *Northern Argus*: "From Maryborough, 1 horse, 35 bags of sugar, 2 bars of iron, 1,500 ft of pinewood, 13 Kanakas per Australian Joint Stock Bank, Townsville (Freight £27.12.6)." It was just as stated; the Kanakas were a job lot purchased by the bank in Maryborough on behalf of some pastoral clients in the far north, and consigned in the usual way. They were there for anyone to see, huddled together on deck amidst the rest of the cargo, with tin labels strung around their necks to say that their destination was the Norman River.

So squatters and sugar growers seemed to have survived the legislation that had threatened, once briefly, to ruin them, to render the costs of imported labour prohibitively high. Just as the recruiters, the contractors who supplied this labour, had so far survived the attempts of missionaries, anti-slavery societies, and certain naval officers to drive them completely out of business. However, there was one other important aspect of the Kanaka question that had not yet been satisfactorily disposed of—the behaviour of the islanders in Queensland.

For Queensland was not the Deep South in the "good old times" when slavery was a legalized institution and the planter was completely his own master. Neither was it, say, Mauritius, where the planters were virtually the Government and there was no such thing as public opinion to worry about. The Kanaka, neither as humble nor as absurd as he sometimes appeared, nervously setting foot in Queensland for the first time in his ill-fitting, hastily donned European shirt and trousers, could be a devil at times. The employer still had to find some way of keeping him in check without attracting the attention of people like William Brookes.

At first, particularly in the wild north, much discipline had not been necessary. For instance, when John Ewen Davidson took up Bellenden Plains station near Cardwell in 1866, the original party of pioneers had included twenty islanders, most of them Tannamen. Charles Eden, a partner in the venture at one stage, describes them as mostly tall, muscular, splendid-looking men, one of them, a Tannese called Sale, obviously being the leader. They worked hard during the day, clearing in the first few months, later ploughing, planting, trashing, weeding, even getting quite sunburnt as they hacked away, bare backs exposed between the stiflingly hot walls of cane. But every night they sang and smoked round the campfire before retiring to sleep in two large grass thatched huts with bunks rigged up all round the walls as though in a ship. They seemed well content. On Saturdays they tended their gardens, growing rather acrid taro with roots eighteen inches long and six inches in diameter in the swampy ground near the lagoon.

Their one real day, however, was Sunday, when they went hunting. They all had guns, provided by their employers to encourage them to hunt, together with a terrifying assortment of improvised weapons of their own. The most notable of these was the Tannaman's favourite foot-length bar of iron that he was capable of hurling with tremendous force. Every Sunday evening, says Eden, they came back with a great haul including wild duck, emu, kangaroo, even shark which they used to catch in the shallows of the Murray River by diving in and tackling them from underneath. Emu or cassowary, however, was evidently the most sought-after prey until one day Eden watched them return, shouting and screaming with laughter, obviously in a state of unusual elation. They had killed "big fella fowl", Sale told him triumphantly, and fought with "man o' bush".

This introduced a new element. The Englishman was intrigued and investigated the islanders' story with some care. It had soon become their regular practice, he claimed, to hunt "man o' bush" whenever they got the chance—both for sport and for food! Once, said Sale, the hunters had emerged out of a thick jungle of stinging-tree and wild raspberry bush and suddenly caught sight of their human quarry right in front of them beside a water-hole. The blacks all dived into the water as the islanders appeared, and for a long time managed to avoid the Tannamen's iron missiles by ducking deep out of the way. But the Tannese were only playing with them. When they tired of this, they took up various specially prepared weapons—shearing-blades bound to long poles—and waded in to harpoon their victims from the edge of the bank. The blacks were dragged out, and one after the other were finished off with the butt-end of muskets. The bodies were cut into strips to be carted home.

The story is impossible to verify. Cannibalism was certainly prevalent in the islands at the time, though primarily as a ritual practice kept in strict check by the village headmen. But as we have seen, the traditional measures of control in the islands themselves were already breaking down. And in Queensland they could have been quite lacking. Sale told Charles Eden, John Ewen Davidson's partner, that there was a young Banks Islander amongst them, hailing from a place where cannibalism was regarded with particular abhorrence. So in order to shock him they would make up outrageous tales of epic battles fought against their Aboriginal foes, always culminating in a glorious cannibal feast to bring the encounter to its proper conclusion. In the end, said Sale, the young islander had fashioned his own harpoon and insisted on accompanying the Tannamen on their next expedition.

Possibly this was a tall tale just to shock the Englishman, but the recruiters used to relate that a great joke among the recruits on board ship was to seize one of the young ones and pretend to prepare him for the pot. Even in Queensland today there are islanders living who can remember how their fathers used to boast of feasting upon the despised "man o' bush".

In any case it was inevitable that Kanaka and Aboriginal would clash. For the blacks would be lurking about from the day the strangers arrived, compulsively curious to know what the Kanakas were about, wanting to taste and handle anything new to them and, presumably, left lying about for their inspection. When the first cane sprouted at Bellenden Plains they were particularly destructive, and Davidson had to instruct his Kanakas to take their guns with them into the canefields and to fire on all trespassers. But keeping the Aborigines away was not easy. Placed between the scrub and the cane the islanders were an easy mark for spears. And in the canefields the Aborigines put themselves at an advantage by firing the cane before them and advancing behind a smoke-screen. The best tactic, the Kanakas found, was to seize their hoes at the first suspicious sound, form up shoulder to shoulder and charge.

R. A. Johnstone, an officer of Queensland Black Police stationed at Cardwell, relates that once a most sensational encounter was reported to him. For some months the better-armed Kanakas had been holding off the local Rockingham Bay natives without too much trouble. Then one midday Bellenden Plains was unexpectedly attacked by a mob of over a hundred Aboriginal warriors hailing from Hinchinbrook Island, more than thirty miles to the south and several miles offshore. They had apparently swum over to the mainland resting their chins on their wooden shields for support against the waves, and then crept silently overland through thick bush till they reached the lonely up-river plantation.

Bellenden Plains was taken completely by surprise. The twenty or so Europeans and islanders were at their midday meal, and their first indication of the attack came when a tongue of flame shot up out of the half-grown sugar cane. Slowly they discerned, through the heat and glare, a solid wall of men, crouched behind a barricade of locked shields edging towards them. There was never any real chance of Bellenden Plains being wiped out, for the defenders had an arsenal of guns, with plenty of hands to reload. And thus Englishmen and Tannamen together, nerved and calm, poured in volley after volley until the long line of invaders crumpled and gave way and it was all over.

Such moments of peril, endured together, tended to estabish a bond between master and servants—so much so in this case that when Bellenden Plains eventually collapsed under the pressure of accumulated misfortunes and Davidson moved his entire plant southwards to Mackay to start afresh, his twenty Kanakas went with him to begin the back-breaking task of clearing and grubbing all over again. Some at least stayed with him for a great many years. But in general it was not a good idea to arm the islanders, as this could only tempt them to be on the offensive against the Aboriginal population. They were mostly young, and whenever there was a temporary absence of supervision, some of them would be certain to wander away and run wild. Throughout 1867 and 1868 the *Port Denison Times* (Bowen) was constantly complaining of mobs of Kanakas camped on the outskirts of Bowen and Cardwell, a perpetual nuisance even to white residents.

Another mistake, perhaps no less unavoidable in the circumstances, was to send Kanakas inland. For in the great rush to take up and stock the expanses of new country being opened up all the way from the east coast to the Gulf, the squatters had had no time to worry about where they were going to find the labour. In September 1866 an association was hastily formed to import Chinese from Java, and when that failed they sought permission from the Government to use Kanakas. The first ten Kanakas were signed on as station hands in May 1867, and by March 1868 almost 700 out of the 1,539 islanders in the colony were in pastoral employment in the interior.

But the islanders fared no better than the local Aborigines, Scottish ploughboys, Rhineland peasants, or any of the other makeshift shepherds tried from time to time. It was too cold, too lonely, and they hated sheep. There were quite a few desertions during 1867, and then in 1868, when the sheep industry really began to suffer under the combined effects of dingo attack, footrot, and the terrible spreading spear grass, the pressure on the unfortunate shepherds became intolerable. During 1868 proceedings under the Masters and Servants' Act against delinquent shepherds and station hands increased so rapidly that one Police Magistrate at Bowen was no longer able to cope with all the work. There were stories of floggings and beatings, of managers having to fire into the Kanaka compound to get their men to work in the morning. There was nothing much the magistrate could do about it except to send the culprits to prison for a couple of weeks or make an order that they should forfeit their entire wages.

In June 1868 a particularly gruesome murder occurred on Conway station, inland from Bowen. When Gibbie and Bell, the two white men in charge, returned to the main station hut at midday they were suddenly set upon by four of their Kanaka hands—Efatese who had been brought to Queensland probably by the kidnapper, *King Oscar*, under Lewin. Gibbie might have wounded one of his assailants before he was fatally struck, but there was little resistance after that. The two bodies were dragged out of the hut down to a sandy creek bottom where they were afterwards found lying across one another, horribly mutilated. Sub-Inspector Isley, with his squad of native police, was camped only four miles away, and he was soon on their trail, easily able to follow the tracks of the fleeing islanders because one of them was obviously hurt and the others were trundling him along in a dray. But while the fugitives were easily trailed they were not to be so easily caught. They survived one sharp gun battle with police near Byerwon station, got clear away again, and were not finally rounded up until about a month later. Three were shot dead "while resisting arrest" or "attempting to escape" and one sixteen-year-old, Malutra, was taken to Rockhampton for trial. However, he was never prosecuted, and probably sent home by the next ship.

There was a rather wry sequel to the Conway murders. The *Port Denison Times* had been passionately concerned to avoid giving any impression that the northern squatters habitually ill-treated their Kanaka servants or used the ill-reputed Black Police to chase them when they escaped. It thought the cause of the north might be done irreparable harm if this sort of information got into the hands of William Brookes and his supporters. In fact, Brookes knew all about the conditions on the northern sheep stations, but at that time was much more concerned over a Polynesian station-hand who was actually suing his employer for wages at Bowen Police Court. In his journal he refers disgustedly to Kanakas who "gluttonize, get sick, run away, change masters at will"; calling them "useless mischief-making loafers, with elastic-sided boots and scarlet ties, making master look small at the Police Office". It was often forgotten that Brookes was not against the planters as much as against the Kanakas.

But the problem was not confined to the north; employers in the south were having their troubles too. Late in 1867 twelve islanders who had arrived by the *King Oscar* some weeks before wandered away from Ninds' plantation at Pimpama, to turn up finally at the Immigration Depot in Brisbane. Apparently they were looking for Ross Lewin, who had enticed them to Queensland with the story that their weekly rations would include ten pounds of meat and ten pounds of flour. They now wanted to tell him forcefully that all they were getting was one sweet potato a day among three, and one pumpkin among twelve.

There was no mistaking the correlation between those who had been kidnapped originally and those who behaved worst on the plantation. Other *King Oscar* recruits escaped from plantations along the Logan and Albert and were joined by eight recruits from the *Syren* who had dived overboard as the vessel was proceeding up the Brisbane River. They were recaptured during an intensive police hunt after a settler, James Preston, reported that his twelve-year-old daughter, while walking only two hundred yards away from her home, had been suddenly terrified by the sight of "a black man with a knife and a tremendous waddy" crawling towards her through tall grass.

This was a small incident among a number of others, but supported by the discovery of two or three bush camps littered with scythes, hoes, and shears, all fashioned into hunting weapons, was apparently enough for Parliament to decide on 14th May 1869 to appoint a Select Committee of the Legislative Assembly to investigate the whole question of Polynesian labour in Queensland. It was to consider whether the immigrants had been obtained by fraud; whether they were treated harshly by their employer, or with aversion by their fellow European employees; whether they were likely to prove injurious to the colonists at large, or whether, being Christians in many cases, the islanders were more likely to suffer through over-exposure to the colonists.

The proceedings of the Committee were of course a wonderful target for Brookes's satire. There was not the slightest prospect of it being impartial, he said, because there was hardly a politician in Queensland who did not have an interest in some large property or plantation. Nevertheless he was in his element when called on as a witness to answer various questions, having already prepared some rather damaging testimony concerning his erstwhile friend, George Raff, and his place on the Caboolture.

And yet, for all its presumed bias, the committee pursued its inquiries very diligently and managed to discover many interesting aspects of plantation life in the southern or more civilized portion of Queensland at the time. There was the sadist, for example, who loved to go to work on Kanakas, secretly behind the barn, with his long-lashed whip; who, knowing that they were terrified of the dark, had "fitted up an ingenious little dark room". There was also the brute, with a large stick always in his belt, who liked to knock them down sheerly for pleasure, striding into their camp and picking on somebody, to show he was master. But such people were the exception. More the rule on the average plantation, it seemed, was the petty, niggling, schoolmasterish type of discipline, not conceding anything in the way of time off and indulgences; work always had to begin on the dot. However, the islanders were not completely defenceless. When conditions grew intolerable they could desert and be brought before the Bench, when most probably their agreements would be cancelled, leaving them free to engage with some other employer. They had a fair idea of the relative advantages and disadvantages of various plantations, intriguing in many cases to get where they wanted. Where the white man behaved harshly and unsympathetically, it was usually because he distrusted them so much, and feared they would cheat him.

The Committee did not really come to any firm conclusions, though it thought, as Brookes had predicted it would, that the allegations of cruelty and kidnapping were grossly exaggerated. About all the abscondings and the fate of the absconders, it had nothing to say at all. It was of a piece with those discreet investigations conducted in Mauritius and in the West Indies from time to time. Just the merest hint of the dark practices, the turbulence beneath the surface was allowed to escape here and there. Then a smoke-screen of polite verbiage at the end, with one or two constructive little suggestions to help erase the impression that a real issue had been at stake in the first place. The average patriotic Queenslander, for instance, would be well content to accept the verdict of the eminent English novelist, Anthony Trollope, who visited several of their plantations in the early seventies.

On the planters' grounds they learn each other's languages, have to live as white men live, have to cook, sew, dig, plant, clothe themselves and be proud of clothes . . . lessons taken back to the islands, and then they send their friends and return themselves and so are gradually brought within the pale of civilization. . . . Happy the Polynesian who is allowed to escape from the savage slavery of his island to the plenty and protected taskwork of a Queensland sugar plantation.

Splendid, upright, British way of looking at it. William Brookes would have an uphill task battling against sentiments like these. Only he would attempt to.

There was to be another parliamentary inquiry in 1876 after Press reports had seemed to indicate the steady continuance of bad relations between recruiters and natives in the islands. It was suspected too that islanders were still arriving in the colony with little or no understanding of the real nature of their agreements. Brookes was to be an important witness at this inquiry also, going for the Committee in his usual head-on manner.

If we were told that husbands were separated from wives, thousands of children left without their natural protectors, homes desolated, villages ransacked and burned, drunkenness and fraud and every dishonest artifice employed in order to procure these men who have added so immensely to our comfort. . . .

But after that the level of discussion settled comfortably down again. The usual representative collection of witnesses were put through their paces and the Committee was finally able to report: "the evidence has been singularly corroborative of the willingness of the islanders to come to the colony, of the absence of anything to warrant the assumption . . . that they have been improperly obtained". Any blame attaching to the methods of recruitment, it said, could be attributed mainly to the operations of the Fijian and New Caledonian recruiters.

Still unwilling to concede defeat despite this latest rebuff, Brookes wrote in his journal of "certain businessmen in stock and station agencies who have withdrawn from the recruiting business, feeling it too delicate to be mixed up in". That was about all the progress he had made, however, after ten years; he or anybody else. The Navy, it is true, had its very impressive Pacific Islanders Protection Act, the famous anti-kidnapping legislation for the "prevention and punishment of criminal outrages anywhere within Her Majesty's Dominions", but as yet hardly any ships with which to operate. The missionaries, for their part, seemed not to have been heard from for some time. If a way was to be found to deal with the recruiters, it would have to come from the islanders themselves, independent of any outside assistance.

SIX

Changing Melanesia

ONE characteristic difference between Melanesian and European lies in their attitude towards human nature. The Melanesian takes it for granted that human beings tend to be selfish, greedy, jealous, quarrelsome, even cruel and bloodthirsty, just as they can also be loving and generous, capable of almost any kind of self-sacrifice for the sake of the community. That is Man, he says in effect. Why pretend otherwise? So he builds his society on the assumption that humans are very complex and variable creatures.

It is a realistic approach with many advantages, as the following story will illustrate. A group of men from another district have insulted the honour of a village by making lewd gestures before the village womenfolk on the occasion of a great feast. The hosts are angry. They regard the obscenities as an act of calculated disrespect to their village, reminding one another, after the offending visitors have departed, that those people have always been like that; that unless they are taught a sound lesson they will very soon transgress again. So several weeks later, after the auspices have been taken and the omens pronounced favourable, a war party sets out and a man belonging to the offending village is killed. The score is now even. The insult has been wiped out. Is it not common sense to punish one who betrays hospitality? the Melanesian argues. And if he is killed, is there need to feel guilty about it?

That evening, their anger spent, the warriors gather round to discuss the events of the day, like a victorious football team conducting a post-mortem on the match. The old men listen avidly, their eyes shining as they remember their own exploits; while the women, who are not supposed to know about men's matters but do, sit contentedly in the background, weaving mats.

However, the punished village has now become an enemy. For the victim, it happens, was a fighting man of great renown, the pride of the village he adorned, a deterrent to its enemies. In the excitement of the ambush, the avengers had had time only to see their arrows strike home before taking to their heels, not discovering until some days later that they had made an unfortunate mistake. Too late they seek to make amends by offering pigs in palliation. Already the machinery of vengeance, the eternal vendetta of tribe against tribe, clan against clan, has been set in motion once again and cannot be stopped until the debt is paid in blood.

Somewhere another war party is preparing. Somewhere death will come to someone round the corner of the trail. When it comes it will be a tragedy to those closest to the victim. But the community will have sustained no great loss. A younger brother possibly will step into the dead man's shoes and inherit the family. For the rest of the village there is only relief that a time of fear and uncertainty has come to an end. Nobody is shocked and horrified, and nobody demands an inquest into the crime.

There will always be violence and bloodshed, these people say. Just as there will always be feasting and dancing and the really great transcendent moments when a man is exalted to the highest; when the drums seem to beat out the message of life everlasting and indestructible, making the accidents of mere individual human lives seem irrelevant.

For generations the people of Melanesia had been at peace and war with one another, preoccupied by their own world, hardly disturbed by any other human world outside. For both the New Hebrides and Solomon Islands were situated in something of a cultural backwater, isolated from the great migrations and disruptions that streamed past them across the Pacific. Occasionally warlike peoples invaded them from Polynesia or from the west, introducing various new forms and customs to the places where they settled but making little impact on Melanesian life in general. The people were divided between hundreds of islands, with the largest of these divided into hundreds of tiny communities, self-sufficient in all the necessities of life, mutually suspicious and yet in many ways dependent on one another.

Most of the young men were incurably adventurous, seeking any excuse to set off by canoe for faraway places. Very often the canoe itself was the excuse. In parts of the Solomons an important canoe, decorated with as many as five thousand pieces of pearl-shell inset in various traditional patterns and hung with streamers of dyed palm leaves, represented the high point of Melanesian decorative art. The village would naturally want to show it off and the canoe might be away for months, making a triumphal tour of the islands. These distant communities which would never see these visitors in the

The Reverend Alfred Lombu—
Anglican native preacher.

A young recruit for the Church
at Vella Lavella.

Patteson's grave at Nukapu.

Bishop Cecil Wilson at steer oar.

normal course of events would compete with one another to provide the most lavish hospitality. The travellers of course brought presents and received them, and thus quite a considerable trade began.

Even in the New Hebrides where canoes tended to be smaller, less ornate, and not quite so much objects of admiration, there was much inter-island journeying. Islands many miles apart were linked in the most intricate trading relationships, even though the articles exchanged sometimes had a more ceremonial value than a strictly economic one. For example the hill people of north Malekula, the Big Nambas, liked to wear red, and in order to obtain the necessary dye, the reddening leaf *nese*, they would visit the sea-coast near the village of Matanavat, bringing with them certain pigs whose tusks had been trained to curve up and around in a complete circle, in a fashion which had a special significance for the coast-dwellers of Matanavat. The latter then would receive the pigs and set off for the island of Malo, which attached a particular value to the shell-bead money made so expertly by Matanavat. The Malo people in turn possessed mats that were always in great demand at Tangoa, the centre of the red leaf industry. So Malo would trade the mats for the leaf, transfer the leaf on to Matanavat and the Big Nambas would eventually receive the dye after it had passed through the hands of two separate groups of middlemen.

But *middlemen* is hardly the right word; trade for the Melanesians was a relationship of communities in a sort of competitive co-operation, each partner in the group striving to outdo the next, to put itself in the position of being able to hand on more than it could expect to get back.

Thus there was a constant tension even within groups, a need for every village to be ever on the alert lest its neighbour be at a competitive advantage. Not everybody competed, it is true, at least not at the beginning of the European period; there were villages or whole islands that would drop out of the race altogether, and, say, revert from using canoes to using rafts, and be universally despised as "rubbish people". In the course of evolutionary time, such communities would presumably disappear altogether. But the rest all had their place in the hierarchy—for example Tanna first, Eromanga second, Aneityum third. Wherever communities of roughly equal size and capacity were gathered together there was a pecking order.

This may appear fairly simple and straightforward, but in fact there were added complexities. Every island has two sides, one of which will for natural reasons be considered superior to the other. For example, off the north-east coast of Malekula are seven inhabited little islands known collectively as the Small Islands. To the out-

I

sider they appear to form one cultural whole. However, there is nothing united about them as a whole, or about any one of them as an individual unit. For each has climatically a markedly more favoured side, namely, that facing the mainland and protected from the weather. Thus, although the people of any one island might feel themselves to have a common home inasmuch as they have one name for their island and speak of themselves as belonging to it, the attitude of the two sides towards each other is one of irreconcilable opposition. In fact the two superior sides of any two adjacent islands will feel more closely allied in outlook and social background with each other than they can possibly feel with their own inferior halves. Thus no one island ever stands united in war against a common enemy. Though the islands are frequently at war with one another, invariably it is the superior side of one with the inferior side of another.

This sort of duality is latent all through Malekulan society. Take the average mainland village. It appears to the outsider as a single collection of huts, large and small, surrounded by gardens and fruit trees, with a common dancing ground, and perhaps a special children's playing area—a tiny unit of human civilization in the midst of the all-enveloping jungle. But it is actually split into two well-defined halves, perpetually antagonistic, ready at times to fly at one another, though in a more restrained way than if they were rival communities belonging to opposite sides of the same island. The meaning of it is best understood with reference to individuals. Every man must contrive to have his opposite, a rival of approximately equal stature against whom he is forever measuring himself in healthy competition. The hunter for instance stalks grimly after his prey, pursuing it for many tedious hours through the silent, unfriendly jungle, determined to capture the creature which he will then present to his counterpart as a sign that he is a huntsman of uncommon ability. It will then be up to his rival to match this with some gift equally hard-won and out of the way, to prove that he too is a force to be reckoned with. Each is helping to keep the other up to a mark of excellence and achievement.

To the Malekulan there is no point in living if he is not constantly striving to raise himself in another's estimation. It is to cater for this ambition that the institution of the graded society exists, providing the process whereby every male member of the community rises progressively in rank, grade by grade, every few years, until he is content to stop. Only the most ambitious keep going to the very top because every rise in grade (there may be twenty or more) means a larger expense, a larger outlay in the pigs that are the Malekulan's main symbol of wealth. It might seem strange that a man should want to give away all the wealth in pigs he has amassed over the years through the surplus food produced by his gardens, through payments for various services rendered to his kin and fellow villagers, all augmented by trade and much hard bargaining. Perhaps only the very dramatic nature of the ceremony that accompanies each ascent can help explain it.

People come from all over the place to the dancing ground. For a general truce has been declared; all the villages are momentarily at peace. Men, women, and children loaded with food and presents, even nursing mothers carrying their babies make their way along the winding jungle paths. It is a ceremonial occasion, so bangles adorn their arms and on other parts of their bodies are all sorts of personal ornaments made from sea shells, bunches of leaves, fern fronds, and the teeth and bones of birds, fish, and animals. Thus they arrive and divide into the sexes and stand or sit about, gossiping or minding the children or preparing the food. But there is a nervous, subdued quality to it all until quite suddenly the dancing begins.

It goes on all night. The dancing is superb because it is a competitive activity like everything else. Groups of dancers or individual performers have been practising new steps and new variations of old dances for months before. They dance whatever they feel, telling stories in ballet and pantomime of their everyday lives and adventures, love stories and war stories, fantasy and make-believe. They are putting their whole spirit into it, dancing away their frustrations and repressions, draining themselves of emotion, swaying, swinging, stamping, leaping, losing themselves in the confusion of whirling figures, of limbs bending and straightening, of columns advancing and retreating; allowing the gongs beating out their persistent rhythm in the background to dictate the movements of their bodies. The gongs command hypnotically, slowly increasing the tempo, faster and faster, then faltering, ebbing, then coming again faster and louder than ever before, until the pace seems to be unendurable and the body dies of the excitement of it.

For this is the meaning of the whole thing, to share with the man, in whose honour all have come, this experience of the body dying so as to be born anew. The owner of the pigs no longer exists. The following morning the tethered beasts are brought out struggling and squealing and lined up, row upon row, so that the newly born one can pass down the line killing them with one swinging blow, straight between the eyes, as he goes. The carcasses are then apportioned out between those present according to certain rules of reciprocity and kinship. And so the new man is free of all encumbering wealth, one further stage removed from the earthbound creature he started out as; ready if he desires to resume his upward journey towards the next goal.

This business of rising in grade is a terrible strain; at the topmost level a man is given thirty days to recover from it. Lower down the scale he might feel like sitting back and resting on his laurels. For his newly acquired status is permanent. His badges of rank, the feather in his hair, the special fence around his garden, his new place in the men's club house, are treated with the same kind of respect as are the badges of rank on a soldier's uniform. Unlike pigs these less tangible possessions do not have to be guarded and constantly tended. Nor do they generate as much envy and greed in his neighbours. What the man has done for himself, he has done also for the village, perhaps for the whole district. He has started off on the right foot so to speak, by providing everybody with a wonderful occasion for feasting and high excitement.

In a less material way, the people are grateful for having somebody to admire. The more eminent citizens the community can boast, the prouder it feels, and the more secure. The wives of the men of rank know exactly how they may behave in the women's camp, to whom they must be a little deferential and whom they can snub a little. The nightmare of not knowing where one fits in does not exist in Melanesian society. Nobody can pretend that you are just not there. The old men have their position based on the rank they have attained, and their widows are provided for when they die. The rules are not made by some remote authority and simply handed down. They are made locally by people in contact with the everyday needs of the community, with individual cases in mind. The mould which the average person must fit into is therefore adapted to realistic individual measurements. The parents are not disgraced because an unmarried daughter is got with child. The young mother is not obliged to hide her face from society. The bastard is immediately adopted by another member of the family. In fact in one part of Malekula, it is reserved for the very highest honour.

Here the highest grade in society is reached when a man takes the title of Man Hawk. This involves a rite of an exceptionally sacred character; symbolically, a man taking wings and soaring like the hawk far above the earth. The preparations for it might be fifteen years in the making. For this ultimate ascent a candidate might seize the opportunity of a bastard being born to adopt the child as his own, to rear him as a chief might rear a favourite son for the chieftainship. It is death for anyone to tell the boy his destined fate. For at the age of thirteen or fourteen, after a life in which every care and affection has been lavished upon him, he is conveyed to a secluded spot in the bush, this being the first stage of the supreme ceremony of all.

Finally, as the dancing comes to an end, the climactic moment is reached when the boy emerges from his seclusion and is led dancing, all unknowing and arrayed in his proudest finery, to the place where his loving father awaits him. Then the father strikes the boy dead with one sudden, murderous swing of his great club. Nothing more calculated to paralyse the hearts of all who behold it can be imagined.

The sacrifice of the beloved son was apparently very rare, bastards being so hard to procure. Much more common was the custom of buying a young man from some other district or bringing home the body of an enemy slain in battle, for the same purpose. If already dead, the victim would be ceremonially killed all over again on the sacrificial altar, the body cut up into tiny pieces and a morsel consumed by every male taking part in the ceremony. The comparison between Malekulan ritual cannibalism and the Christian communion rite where the partaker is held to consume the body of the sacrificed Christ was so striking that a Roman Catholic missionary investigating the subject is said to have torn up his notes lest his discovery become public. For the Malekulan was very like the primitive Christian, it seems, impelled by the same desire to escape the annihilation of the grave, seeking through the same sort of forms and ceremonies to consecrate himself for the life to come.

Viewed through modern eyes the world of Malekula may seem a narrow world, almost as if designed so that no man should ever be able to break out of the pattern. It is interesting to compare it with Malaita in the Solomons, which might be taken to represent human society at a slightly later stage of evolution. It is not hard to see why Malaita is different. There is a marked foreign strain in the make-up of Melanesian Malaita that can only be accounted for by an influx of invaders from outside, possibly from Polynesia, possibly from Indonesia, probably several centuries ago. The invaders may have arrived by deliberate intention or accidentally. The result, however, is clear: various characteristic features of Melanesian society ceased to exist in many parts of Malaita. No trace remained in the late nineteenth century of the double village, nor of the graded society. In their place appeared the hereditary chieftain, the undisputed first man of the village, surrounded by his courtiers, his bodyguard, his chosen bank of warriors whom he would reward from time to time with one of his surplus women. The village was still divided into two, but along quite different lines. On one side of the river (literally) lived the chief and the aristocracy; on the other, the commoners. Superficially, at least, the situation resembled England after the Norman Conquest. The chiefly families were in status like the Norman barons, without their castles. The commoners resembled the Anglo-Saxon elements, the older, now subjugated way of life.

It was not a strict caste system; a man could, for example, cross the river through his prowess in war or some related occupation. But the chief would tend to recruit his henchmen from elsewhere so that they would be more dependent on his favour alone and less likely to form alliances with any disaffected party in the village. The weakness of this kind of monarchical system is that the king always has brothers and relations jealous of his position, seeking always the chance to inspire the commons in a popular revolt against him, usually to subvert the succession to their own particular branch of the chiefly house. The king must be politic. In Malaita if he had no son to succeed him, he was allowed to adopt as heir and successor almost anybody he liked, perhaps a promising-looking boy from among the circle of his immediate relatives, or even a grown man and a comparative stranger from miles away.

Thus the invaders wrought great changes in the old way of life. For instance, it was a long-cherished custom in Melanesia and in all primitive societies to reckon descent purely through the mother. This is, after all, the more natural idea: the tie with the mother is indisputable, while paternity is sometimes more doubtful. So a child was regarded as belonging to the mother and her family and not to the father at all. At the age of puberty, therefore, a boy would ordinarily leave his father's household and go to live in the village where his mother had been born, which was thought of as being his real village. Here the task of bringing him up would be taken over by the mother's brother. The custom went against the natural affection and pride of the father deprived as he was of the opportunity of passing on to his sons everything he himself had learnt and built up during his own lifetime. He was left instead with the responsibility of looking after *his* sister's sons. However it was the custom and generally respected and obeyed for that reason, until the immigrant conquerors appeared upon the scene and simply ignored it in the case of their own families because it did not happen to suit them.

Exactly how the newcomers succeeded in imposing themselves and spreading their new ways upon the inhabitants is uncertain, but apparently a number of these chieftaincies were set up, some of which still endured very many generations later when the subject first attracted the attention of European anthropologists. Various chiefly houses had by this time gained enormous prestige throughout Malaita and even further afield; their fame expanded and perpetuated in the songs and legends. On the occasion of every big feast they would invoke the names of the great warrior chiefs of old and recall how their prowess had been handed down from father to son. The worship of ancestors had grown into nothing less than a religion, in fact. Mighty though he might have been on earth, a man was not half as much to be feared and propitiated, nor his assistance and protection so anxiously sought, as when after death he roved abroad in spirit form, a potent force for good or evil. Often it was the case that one branch of a Malaitan chiefly house supplied the reigning monarch, while another supplied the village high priest, responsible for celebrating the worship of their common ancestor.

Any attempt to reconstruct the past by hypothesis always has dangers, yet it is easy to understand how an ambitious man, inspired by the example of these immigrants, might seek to found his own family dynasty. And it is remarkable how easily even the most apparently cast-iron conventions will fracture and give way when they are suddenly challenged. Hereditary chieftainship was usually an older system, it appears, than the patrilineal one. One of these hereditary chiefs then, let us say, has resolved that the succession shall pass to his son though custom decrees that his powers, his rank, his land, his various possessions shall be inherited by his nephew. There is no point in merely hoping that others will respect his wishes in the matter after his death, so he dramatically steps down from his position, taking everybody unawares, and installs his son in his place. The community is thunderstruck, none more so than the nephew, the heir apparent, and his family. But they are powerless to do anything about it. The magic which they would normally call upon to work their enemy's undoing is sure to be overcome by the chief's counter-magic. Because of his wealth and prestige he will naturally have access to, probably be closely related to, the most effective sorcerer in the district. So the outraged family looks around for possible allies and finds none, because the others in the community have no precedents to guide them in a case like this and are cunningly waiting upon events. If the son then proves to be of the same stature as the father, no less capable of outfacing all opposition, the new way might well become entrenched.

Nothing like this can be definitely established as having happened in Malaita, because patriliny was firmly installed throughout the island before the time of its recorded history. But elsewhere in Melanesia in the early European period the process of change from matriliny to patriliny could be clearly observed, affecting one island after another, working at every level of society from top to bottom.

In such a fashion then a few all-powerful families broke up some of the traditional patterns and wrenched people's lives out of their accustomed courses. Drawn by the glamour of some particular chieftainship, for instance, young men journeyed from distant places, were caught by the spirit of the place and stayed, abandoning all the customary ties of kin and country. Or fugitives driven from their homes by war or black magic came and sought asylum. A village's proudest boast in Malaita was to be a haven and place of refuge; it was really this way, rather than by glory in war, that it became great. Other chiefs and their retainers would also come visiting, occasionally too, from about the middle of the nineteenth century, the crew of a European trader. All would be received in the same grave fashion, escorted through the village and settled down in a place of honour beside the chief's principal hut. Then the commoners would gather around and listen quietly to the talk, marvelling at the spectacle, all eyes on their chief as he sat in the midst of his guests dispensing the hospitality of the village.

There were various terms and phrases in the language to express what the chief stood for, what he was felt to do for his people. Thus he was said to be the "root of the land"; to "succour" the land; to "draw up" those who came to him for protection. He was looked to as the source of strength and comfort. Sometimes, out of sheer gratitude, a man would make him a spontaneous gift of pigs or foodstuffs; or a group of fishermen, after much labour in catching and carrying home a large turtle, would impulsively present it to their chief. In due course the great man, feeling that the time had come to acknowledge some of these favours, would announce a great feast in honour of some event. The messengers would go out into the countryside bearing invitations; the entire host village would labour for weeks beforehand preparing the food. Finally the dancers would rehearse their steps and the songmakers compose new songs describing the greatness of their chief, his wealth, his generosity, and the glory he had brought to the village, to the whole land.

The giving of feasts was primarily the chief's responsibility; from him everything good and gracious seemed to stem. What happened then when he died? The effect was a cataclysm. . . . Terror seizes the community, for the bottom of their world has fallen out. The gongs beat out the message: "The chief is dead. The water vessel is empty." The women wail their grief to the skies. Men hack savagely at a valuable fruit tree or rend a fishing net, as children in grief will suddenly destroy a favourite toy. Then after these wild outbursts of despair, grief and dismay turn to anger, to a sullen determination to be revenged. For unless the dead man was extremely aged, well past his life expectation, his death is put down to witchcraft contrived by some malicious rival.

Somebody, probably the son, undertakes to lead a war party, and young men prepare themselves for the grim business ahead, steel their bodies, avoid women, eat only sparingly of a restricted number of foods. Eventually the party sets out, and now all the villages in the district have reason to tremble. Nobody knows where the raiders will strike. Probably they have already settled on a victim, some known enemy of the dead man, but they will not scruple to slay anybody who gets in their way, if they are feeling in a particularly murderous mood. It is a very strained and tense time for everybody. But it does not last. Eventually the gongs proclaim that a victim has been provided, that the war party is on its way home, and all at once the tension that has made life barely tolerable begins to lift.

Once again in Melanesia the shedding of blood is seen to have a purgative effect. People are held to be unclean during the period of mourning; to be contaminated by that mysterious evil force that has suddenly brought death into their midst. A good, honest killing is felt to clean the air again. As the various taboos and constraints are taken off one by one, men go leaping round the village, symbolizing the fact that they are now free to resume their normal lives. By the time the war party have actually reached home, the gongs are sounding a new triumphant note: "The king is dead. Long live the king!" By this time too preparations are in full swing for the funeral festivities. The village is rapidly forgetting the dead chief. Their mood now is more to celebrate the installation of his successor. The root has sprouted, the Malaitans say, the ever-living root. . . .

A lesser village naturally might not be able to assuage its grief so grandly. For one thing it could not send its warriors rampaging round the district searching for some victim without inviting a more devastating response. Thus it might decide to kill somebody within the village; castaways and refugees were sometimes harboured for this very purpose. On the other hand it might arrange to buy a victim from elsewhere, or employ the services of a *ramo*, a professional fighting man who would undertake to perform the killing himself in order to earn what was called "blood money". The professional would then have to look out for his own life, which he usually did by keeping on the move from village to village, one step ahead of his latest band of pursuers.

In Malaita then, just the same as in Malekula, not every village headman nor every ordinary villager could live in the style he would have liked. But there could never be any excuse for weakness and the village that could not match the strength of its neighbours was open to recurrent humiliations. In times of crisis a raiding party might come storming through the place, causing the inhabitants to fly distractedly. They would be able to return safely later, however, for there was no intent to wipe them out, to do them permanent injury.

There were a dozen ways to prevent a war from getting out of hand once the balance was felt to have been restored and the warriors' fighting blood had cooled a little. After all, the combatants were primarily concerned with asserting their prestige as a group. Sometimes the fighting stopped during formal wars, or never actually started, while everybody listened, lost in admiration, to the splendid insults, the outrageous epithets the two sides were hurling at one another.

Perhaps one effect of foreign invasion was to make the Malaitans a fairly warlike people. When first encountering them in any numbers in the 1870s, Europeans found them a little more alert and aggressive, more sensitive of their personal honour, than most islanders. In Queensland the careful employer tried to segregate his Malaita men from the others, just as earlier he had segregated the Tannese. Put them in with another group and they would be sure to start a fight. But back in pre-European Malaita fighting played no bigger part in the lives of the people than it did anywhere else in the islands. With the rest of Melanesia their primary concern was not to destroy life but in their view to advance it.

The villages were constantly playing their war games; in which the individual, it seemed, was the sacrifice to secure the survival of the species. But it was not the dog-eat-dog existence as it appeared to the outside world. Warfare in fact did not keep the numbers in check; most islands overflowed with people. Malaita, one hundred miles long and on average thirty miles wide, had a population of about sixty-five thousand when the first official census was attempted. Almost certainly it was twice that earlier. In the north-east lagoon a number of tiny artificial islets, built out of coral rocks dredged from the bottom of the lagoon and no more than a few hundred yards around, had individual populations of up to three hundred.

The islands around the coast of Malekula were almost as crowded. Periodically, under the mounting pressure of population upon resources, a section of the inhabitants would break away and colonize part of some other island or an adjacent strip of mainland, or they would build another little island for themselves in the lagoon. This process was at work throughout Melanesia until the European invasion, when the rate of the population-growth first slowed down and then went into a rapid decline.

Malaita's first continuous contact with white people was through the Melanesian Mission in the early 1860s. Bishop Patteson called several times at the little island of Sa'a in the south and recruited three candidates for the mission training school in New Zealand from which Anglican interest in the area had originally come. Relations with the Malaitans were reported to be peaceful and happy. Then in 1868 the island of Manaoba off the north coast had a strange experience when the castaway crew of an American whale-boat was washed up on its shore. Four of the five survivors were so weak from hunger and exposure that they either died soon afterwards or had to be knocked on the head. But one, John Renton, an Orkney Islander of no more than eighteen or nineteen, recovered and went on to lead a remarkable life among the islanders. What happened to this young Scotsman was common enough in the nineteenth-century Pacific, but it was a rare adventure in Melanesia.

Renton remained only a short while on Manaoba before being bought and adopted by one Kabau, the powerful chief of the artificial islet of Sulu Vou. Possibly Kabau hoped that the white man should succeed him as chief; it would have been a great stroke for Sulu Vou. In the event he lived there as a privileged member of the aristocracy for the next six years, fished for turtle with fellow islanders, went to war with them, was initiated into their less sacred ceremonies, and was most useful to the community as a canoe-builder and net-mender.

It is helpful for the historian that Renton lived here at this vital period, for he experienced at first hand, and almost as a native, the effect of the labour traffic upon the island way of life. Reports of European ships in the vicinity were kept from him for quite a long while, but one day a deputation arrived from two islands south of Sulu Vou with the news that several of their people had been murdered and others abducted and carried off to Queensland. A party of men had been enticed out to the ship by a display of plane-blades. Bars of iron had then smashed down on their canoes as they reached the ship, and those not killed were seized in the water and hauled aboard by their hair. The final outrage was that the young son of the chief was shot dead as he swam back to warn the village.

The deputation's aim was to buy John Renton, for whom they were willing to give the remarkable sum of four hundred porpoise teeth, in order to kill him; to shed his white man's blood for the island blood his people had shed. This was the main reason, but it was also characteristic of Melanesian thinking that they should want to see their old enemy, and friend, lose also what they themselves had lost—the favoured one of the chief.

Kabau refused to give Renton up, swearing at the same time the oath, "You can have him if you cross my legs", that is, if you can commit adultery with my wife, whereupon I will have you killed. That was the end of that incident, but not very long afterwards three strange war canoes, paddles flying, crews straining furiously, bore down on Sulu Vou at a great pace. Renton, with a price upon his head, a standing temptation to every professional brave in Malaita, was terrified. But the visitors had only come to show off; a ship had piled up on their reef and they had looted it. One man had perforated his nose and ears with part of a clock movement; another was wearing a long trailing woman's dress and smoking a pipe, and so on. The population of Sulu Vou was envious and much impressed. For the first time in all those years, Renton recalled, they began to question him about his homeland, which they conceived to be an island called Queensland. Renton had never been in Queensland, but he described what he knew of Scotland and America to them, spoke of railway trains and factories and great cities and, naturally, was regarded as a monumental liar. Nonetheless, he had whetted their interest.

This was in 1873 or thereabouts. Then in 1875 he was most dramatically rescued. Captain Murray of the recruiter *Bobtail Nag*, while recruiting off neighbouring Isabel island had heard about a white man living on Malaita. Partly in the hope of finding him he had sailed for northern Malaita, a region which the recruiters were only just beginning to explore. However, he could see no sign of any white man on the morning of 8th August 1875, as he scanned Sulu Vou through the spyglass—only a lot of savages with fish-bones stuck through their noses, standing up in their canoes, ostentatiously demonstrating their lack of weapons as they drifted out towards the ship.

Actually a man *was* trying to attract Murray's attention, waving madly from the branch of a tree, but the ship was standing too far off for his antics to arouse any special notice. In despair Renton gave up and was walking away when he caught sight of a piece of plank and nearby a charred stick. He hastily scrawled out a message with the end of the stick (not wanting any of the islanders to know what he was doing) and found the chance to drop the plank in the bottom of the canoe going off to trade. Murray ultimately noticed this piece of wood with various black marks on it. He picked it up, found the marks indecipherable, turned it over and read, "For Christ's sake, save me."

The rescue of John Renton was the beginning of a fruitful period of relations between Sulu Vou and the white man. To pay for him a great quantity of axes, knives, and plane-blades were handed over (Kabau must have been a hard bargainer). And the tradition is that not a single flint tool was put to work upon the island after that day. The plane-blades were particularly useful, being attached to handles and used as adzes in the fashioning of canoes.

Meanwhile the *Bobtail Nag* had arrived back in Brisbane, where the castaway was treated as a celebrity and his amazing story, *Seven Years on a Cannibal Island*, serialized throughout Australia. Yet, despite the way he was lionized, he remained an exceptionally level-headed young man, not at all inclined to boast or romanticize, and he convinced people that his account of island life and his experiences, extraordinary though they might sound, were substantially accurate. In general his account cast the native in a favourable light. He had only good things it seemed to say of the islanders: they had never attempted to harm him; had looked after him as a youth; had taught him how to swim, to grow yams; had taken him away on long canoe trips, and offered him a wife—which he refused. They apparently liked white people, he said, and wanted to know more about them. Many, he felt sure, would like to visit Queensland.

The thought now occurred in certain quarters that perhaps the old-fashioned recruiting methods had been wrong; that they had succeeded only in antagonizing the very people whose friendship they should have cultivated. It needed only a little judicious flattery, Renton hinted, and the chiefs would not object to some of the young men leaving the village for a few years—provided they were properly paid for and their return guaranteed. It was important, however, that it was the chief with whom the understanding was reached, not the first impudent pretentious fellow to thrust himself forward. So the decision was made, only a few weeks after the young seaman's return to civilization, to send him back to Malaita in the role of Government Agent. Perhaps he would be able to build up a special relationship between Queensland and that teeming, eager corner of the recruiting world, to help avoid the mistakes that seemed to have been made everywhere else.

The following year Renton returned to Sulu Vou; everybody was overjoyed to see this old friend again, particularly as he appeared to be a figure of some authority among the white people. Once more a generous distribution of axes and iron tools was made, and ten recruits volunteered for Queensland, one of them an imposing young fellow called Kwaisulia, tall and glowering and square-jawed, whom Renton had known well on Sulu Vou and probably fired with the ambition to travel abroad.

Kwaisulia was not actually his real name; it was a nickname that, translated, meant "cut bits off" and referred to a custom of certain Malaitan hill tribes when they brought home the body of an enemy killed in battle. Kwaisulia's father was a hill-man, one who had left the hills and come down to the coast where life was much freer and fuller, less dominated by parochialism. He had then married into one of the chiefly families of Sulu Vou, being that type of restless adventurer who was regularly being recruited into the ranks of the aristocracy. The son had inherited the same free-ranging disposition: he was a pugnacious character, as it turned out, with a talent for kidnapping and killing people. However, for the moment he is out of the picture; gone off to Queensland where nothing more is heard of him for several years. By the time of his return the whole of Malaita, including that densely populated little piece of coastline with its thirty-three artificial islets enclosed by the north-east reef, had become engulfed in the labour trade. John Renton would have been a useful ally for both sides during this difficult period. But whatever influence he might have been able to bring to bear in preserving the balance between island and island was unfortunately lost when he was killed on Aoba in 1878. By this time various rivals of Sulu Vou, more accessible to the recruiters, had acquired a challenging array of weapons.

In order to maintain the island's traditional first place in warfare and ensure that Chief Kabau and his family might not be outgunned in the counsels of the lagoon, Sulu Vou was now constantly engaged with its neighbour in war—desperately concerned to capture whatever guns and ammunition it could lay its hands on. The casualties tended to be quite high—five or even ten men killed on both sides in one single raid.

The possession of fire-arms usually meant that islanders lost all sense of proportion. The gun itself was never particularly lethal in the hands of the islanders. Most natives had little idea of choosing a specific target and taking deliberate aim. They preferred to blast off from the waist in any direction. But its mere possession seemed to give the owner a feeling of invincibility; the noise it made, the smoke, its potential destructiveness exhilarated him. The main aim, it seemed, was to prime the weapon with as big a charge as it would bear and press the trigger. If the firer was knocked flat on his back so much the better. He would leap up again, said the recruiter William Waun of a Tanna acquaintance, shouting "*Remassan. Remassan.*" ("Good. Good.") For this reason the Tower musket was the most popular fire-arm, since it was known to take a very big charge. Long after the smooth-bore musket had been superseded by the latest Sniders and Martini-Henry breech-loading rifles, the demand for Towers continued unabated. The trader deftly met this by stamping the Tower brand on the locks of all his guns.

The gun then was the ultimate destroyer of life, not through its effectiveness as a weapon in the hands of the islanders, but through the number of wars it caused. Wars mean that, ultimately, people are killed. The firing went on for days, sometimes until all ammunition had been exhausted. On one occasion, at Nguna, when the two sides were separated by a wide stretch of water, it was sufficient for them to come regularly down to the water's edge and exchange shots even though they were well out of range of each other.

But it was rare that encounters were as harmless as that. Off north-east Malekula, where the islanders had been in regular contact with the recruiters since the visit of the *Syren* in 1867, wholesale massacres took place. The Europeans naturally made for the sheltered anchorages in the lee of the offshore islands, with the result that the "superior" sides got the fire-arms. The "inferior" sides were almost annihilated as a result. Then the island-dwellers made war against the adjacent mainlanders and went close to exterminating them too. There was no way of arresting this process of destruction, because it was no longer possible, as in traditional conflict, to equalize the number of dead. In the past, battle casualties had rarely exceeded two or three, so that when the winning side chose to break it off they could safely do so. For they knew that the losers would demand no more than one life from them in compensation. Now all the rules had gone by the board; the young men were being encouraged to kill indiscriminately; it wasn't a game any more. It was a matter of survival.

There is no point in dwelling on the terrible consequences of all this—the disruption to the ceremonial and hence the spiritual life of the people; the growing meaninglessness of the world they knew followed by the deterioration of valued relationships, and so on. One of the interesting, not quite so predictable, by-products of the time was the increase in cannibalism. The sacrificial aspect of the practice, the idea of a man becoming spiritually renewed through the absorption of a particle of flesh, scarcely existed any longer. Corpses were now plentiful, and many young warriors, having conquered distaste for human flesh, would eagerly "eat up", precisely because it had once been considered such a dreadful thing, and because it would give them the reputation of being afraid of nothing. Early in the twentieth century an east Malekulan chieftain established a new record of 120 men killed and eaten; his achievement proved by the skulls or other remains of his victims hung up outside his hut. He was a man with a prodigious contempt for his enemies.

Another feature of the changing scene at the turn of the century was the gradual disappearance of that characteristic phenomenon of Malekulan society, the double village. Once yoked together in a curious love-hate relationship, the two mutually opposed halves of what appeared on the surface to be a single entity had now sundered all formal connection with each other in many cases and were functioning as independent units. The reason, it seems, was that people sometimes felt safer living in smaller communities, in hamlets of perhaps a hundred or fewer, where each house would be guarded by a tall, bullet-proof fence and the jungle cleared back in a wide belt around the houses so that no attacker could approach unseen.

To huddle together thus against the outside world gave the villagers a stronger sense of group solidarity, a greater personal security. Even so, they did not seem to thrive in these circumstances but just continued to dwindle in numbers. One day, perhaps, some missionary body would discover them, most of the survivors appearing on their last legs, the old people badly undernourished, with some of the younger ones obviously the product of close inbreeding.

But whether or not they found missionary protection in the end, it did not much matter. A recruiter who landed on the island of Tongoa, near Epi, in 1879 found little difference in the outward situation of the two factions, missionary and heathen. He was approached by the leaders of both parties, seeking to trade recruits for guns. Each had long frizzy hair coiffured with lime and tied in a bunch on top. Each wore a pair of pig's tusks hanging from his neck; with a fish-bone employed as a nose ornament in one case, a small whale's tooth in the other. But the recruiter had no trouble distinguishing between them. The missionary chief was dressed in a white European suit and, perched precariously on top of his head, a yellow straw hat that was forever falling off and being replaced by an attendant. The heathen was naked, except for a piece of turkey twill hanging from a bark belt, and carried a short rifle. The missionary party, the latter explained urgently, were rapidly gaining the upper hand; several of their men had recently returned from Queensland with Snider rifles and many cartridges. His own village had only muskets and one double-barrelled breech-loader and had lost already twenty men in three years. His people desperately needed the recruiters' Martini-Henrys, and as a special inducement he offered two young girls.

It was small advantage to the community to have its young people go off to Queensland. The break-up of the old ties binding person to person, allotting to each his various duties and responsibilities, was never so acutely felt as at the moment of the traveller's arrival home again. A brother or some other person of his own kin and age group should have been looking after his garden, his fences, his canoe, his nets, fishing-baskets, pigs, dogs. But three years is a long time, and usually it was closer to three and a half before the recruit was actually home—or six and a half if he had signed on again. His kinsmen would probably hear he had died in Queensland, but if he was confidently expected and failed to turn up within a reasonable time (all kinds of delays and misadventures occurred while the recruit was in the process of being transported home), he would just as confidently be given up for lost. The Melanesian despairs easily sometimes, and is not the kind to keep a torch burning for the lost one.

Thus the gardens, which had been carefully tended in the owner's absence for perhaps three years, are suddenly neglected; the pigs, which he had once laboriously amassed with a view to buying his way up the social scale, are eaten; his other possessions appropriated. The returning islander, whom Trollope had once pictured as taking back with him the lessons of civilization, in fact often arrived home to discover himself not richer as the result of his experience, but completely destitute and wholly dependent upon the charity of others.

At the worst his whole village might have been destroyed in a raid by head-hunters and all his family and kin murdered. In either case there would be no question of his being "able to pass on his new skills to the village". He would very likely take the next recruiter back to Queensland and spend the rest of his life chasing one job after another. Even in the sandalwood era the process had begun of the islanders being permanently reduced to the status of migrant wage labourers.

Assume, however, that the traveller finds little changed in his absence, and all is ready for him to resume his rightful position in the community. Dressed, say, in a fashionable black coat, black silk topper with red pugaree, white shirt, red tie, white moleskin trousers, and yellow leggings, he is the object of universal admiration as he springs lightly out of the boat and stands on the beach. He waits to be greeted formally by all his kin. If he's a humorous fellow he might try to mimic the white man—by poking at things with his umbrella or pretending to consult his Waterbury watch and rushing back to the boat.

But he becomes bored with showing off after a day or two. The coat might be kept for the cold weather, but the other clothes and most of the knick-knacks will probably be passed on to his family and friends, until he is left wearing only a handkerchief around his neck and carrying the umbrella. On the island of Tanna one recently returned labourer was furious because the resident missionary refused to buy a pair of trousers that had cost him eight shillings in Queensland, even though they were, he claimed, the missionary's exact fit. He sold them to one of the native teachers for ninepenno'rth of tobacco.

It was usual for the returned recruits to become quickly bored and discontented again. Whatever their experience of Queensland, pleasant or unpleasant, they could not fail to be struck by how dull and slow the old ways were, where men waited on the sun, the moon, the flowering of plants, the coming of birds and so on. The man who had been to Queensland had developed tastes for new things—meat, tobacco, alcohol—and wanted these satisfied, not in the fullness of time, but urgently. But he found it impossible to explain this to

K

people whose outlook was so parochial and restricted, so steeped in custom. If, despite his impatience with them, he still had the good of the community at heart, he would want to change the people.

Thus, here and there, little churches and pulpits were set up and new voices began to be heard in the land. But if the outward form was Christian, the true character of the new religion was still basically Melanesian. The message quite simply was that the old gods, the various ghostly beings and spirits of the former living who were supposed to be looking after the welfare of the still living, had failed. They had failed before the much more potent spirits of the white people, spirits which could be invoked by a mere form of words and were not nearly so demanding in the matter of offerings and sacrifices.

It is impossible to follow here the fortunes of all these self-styled pastors and religious cultists. Nine out of ten of such "churches" were mere fly-by-night affairs, offering some cheap remedy for all kinds of spiritual ills. But it is interesting to notice how often they collapsed owing to the increasingly authoritarian behaviour of the preacher. It was characteristic of the returned islander to feel himself most like the white men when he was being bumptious and loud-mouthed, airing his knowledge of pidgin English, spouting some nonsense about Moses and Jesus Christ in order to dazzle the poor, ignorant stay-at-homes. Thus he would threaten his congregation with plague and pestilence, even with personal violence if it did not obey. Probably he would finish up by running off with somebody else's wife.

Yet at the beginning they might have been sincere. The problem was that the conscientious reformer got himself into the same position as the white man on the plantation. He would set the village cultivating some crop, for example, giving them this religion of work and prayer, trying to instil in them the virtues of self-discipline and self-denial, only to find after a promising start that they had lost interest. The only way then left to rescue the situation was to be ruthless.

Not many, of course, possessed any real reforming zeal; the majority were content to accept that almost everything they had once believed was rubbish, like seaweed on the beach. Some didn't even try to conceal their contempt from the moment they landed back home.

Government Agent Douglas Rannie spoke of one woman, an Amazon who had originally fled to Queensland with her lover, striding defiantly ashore, a rifle under her arm, making straight for the women's camp. After a few minutes she returned, climbed back into the boat and proceeded to address the crowd on the beach.

Haranguing them, partly in English, partly in the local dialect, she began by denouncing the men as cowards and bullies; the women as slaves. In Queensland, she told them, the white women did no work, but wore beautiful clothes and jewels while the men waited on them. For herself, she was going back to Queensland and she hoped that all the women on the island would follow her.

This was an outspoken woman's view; the men were rarely so outspoken. But what had chiefly impressed them about Queensland was quite obvious from the way they behaved. It was not the spectacle of a "people living in peace, unarmed and unafraid of each other" as conjured up by the moralists, but that of a master race, not needing to exert itself and living very comfortably on the labour of others. Sometimes a man was barely off the ship before taking to the bush with a handful of followers, setting up his kingdom in some unfrequented part, planning to emulate the recruiters by preying on the weak. Operating from tiny Lammen Island off Epi, from Marau Sound on Guadalcanal, and other well-known resorts, little groups of returned Queenslanders, joined by various other refugees and outcasts, led a bandit existence, robbing and firing villages, abducting women and stealing children to sell to the Malaita chiefs.

Undoubtedly the greatest pirate and kidnapper of these was Kwaisulia. It was mentioned earlier that he had gone to Queensland. He returned to Malaita and the artificial islands in the 1880s, eventually to establish a position as indisputably top man in the lagoon. This was no mean achievement; men who have built their homes by diving for pieces of coral rock in the lagoon-bed, breaking them up with nothing better than a sharpened stick, and making an island out of them are not easily subordinated.

Kwaisulia was not of chiefly rank. His mother was a chief's daughter certainly, but descent was reckoned only through the father in Malaita and his father had been a mere bushman. In some way or other, however, Kwaisulia became chief of Ada Gege, the little artificial island that his father had occupied and extended while he was living on Sulu Vou, and then proceeded to unite Ada Gege and Sulu Vou under his single rule.

He was able to do this first by taking advantage of the very unsettled state of the lagoon. Sulu Vou had become a very vulnerable little island since John Renton, the young Orkney castaway, had resided there in comparative security six to twelve years before. Not only was it being constantly harassed by more powerful, better-armed neighbours in the lagoon, it was also subject to raids by the Isabel head-hunters. Kwaisulia was able to promise the people complete protection, for on his return from Queensland he had entered into an understanding with the recruiters. It was a simple and obvious arrangement: in exchange for providing the white men with recruits, Kwaisulia was to be supplied with arms and ammunition and other things like dynamite, kerosene, powerful medicines such as arsenic or strychnine, axes, crowbars, fencing wire, iron spikes, and all sorts of building materials. He taught Queensland cattle dogs to give warning of an attack by night; anything that would help to render his position on Ada Gege virtually impregnable.

At one stage the outer fortifications of Ada Gege consisted of a very high wall composed partly of stone blocks, partly of tree-trunks that had been felled on the mainland, floated over, and upended side by side for five hundred yards all round the island, the whole being topped with barbed wire. The only entrance to the island was through two narrow passages, barely wide enough to admit a large canoe. Both were protected by a sort of iron portcullis, below which was a line of sharpened stakes planted inside the wall just under the surface of the soft mud.

Kwaisulia's first important victory was against Funaa Vou, Sulu Vou's oldest and bitterest and, latterly, more powerful enemy. In the year 1888, having prepared a grand alliance of four artificial islands, together with the very important village of Port Adam in the far south, Kwaisulia himself took charge of the strike force of canoes that headed the main assault. In the old days it would have been unthinkable for a great chief to expose himself in battle. The shock of perhaps losing him was too great for either side to contemplate. It would certainly have brought the immediate contest to a standstill, even if it were the cause of others later.

But Kwaisulia did not bother about tradition; he led the attack on Funaa Vou in person and his generalship proved decisive. Funaa Vou was completely smashed; many of the inhabitants were killed, and all the houses burnt. A little later, the survivors having fled to the mainland, the victorious general took possession in the name of Ada Gege and garrisoned the island under his eldest son, Jack.

He handed the island back, after the miserable remnants of its former population had been allowed to starve in the bush for several months. But it was all a betrayal of the old sense of balance. Normally questions of peace and war were decided by the elders of the community, the old shrewd men who had spent a lifetime in political skills and intrigue, prepared to spend weeks assessing the strength of the respective parties, calculating whether the village would be better served by war or a mere show of strength. Kwaisulia, on the other hand, would plunge heedlessly into war, arbitrarily setting one half of the lagoon against the other in defiance of most of the old family and island alliances, out of mere anger or vainglory.

Not long after the defeat of Funaa Vou, he set off in his famous white war-canoe at the head of three other Malaita canoes and a hundred men to take revenge on the people of Isabel. There are only vague details of what happened, but apparently a very large action was fought off the coast of Isabel, which by reports was almost like a Polynesian sea-battle. Great numbers of the enemy were destroyed, and the Malaitan fleet sailed triumphantly for home again. On the way however it stopped at the little island of Basakana, where the people of Ada Gege and Sulu Vou enjoyed special fishing rights, in order that Kwaisulia could annex the island. It was his, he claimed, by right of his victory over Isabel. Kwaisulia's style was like that of the modern nation-builder who has just united the people, having conquered various dissident elements, and is ready to treat on their behalf with the outside world.

Bishop Cecil Wilson of the Melanesian Mission, who met him aboard the *Southern Cross* several years later, described him as a tall, powerfully built man of formidable demeanour, wearing a peaked cap and three thousand porpoise teeth on a very elaborate necklace draped over his burly chest. His retinue had assisted him to rise from his place of state in the bow of the canoe and borne him ceremonially aboard, so that he could put a proposition to the bishop. He had heard that the British had recently appointed a "big fella Governor" at Ngela in the Floridas; that the "Governor" was planning to establish schools there. Well, he was "big fella Governor" over the northern half of Malaita and he would like to see schools established among his people too. He wished to say that if the Melanesian Mission provided the teachers, he would guarantee them protection.

Wilson unfortunately had to decline the offer, explaining that he did not have the resources. But he was most gratified to hear that Kwaisulia was now prepared to accept the *lotu* (the new teaching) and would see that at least one teacher was supplied, if only for the chief himself and his immediate family. At this, however, Kwaisulia burst into laughter. No, no, no, he roared. Not for himself. For his people. *He* didn't need a teacher.

Considered in a purely economic light and from the recruiters' point of view, to have one man with the authority to speak for the whole lagoon was undoubtedly the most efficient way of organizing the trade. It meant that recruiting could be carried on at all seasons in perfect safety, certainly with no risk of one set of trading partners being suddenly supplanted by another group less friendly to the white man. By comparison, in Malekula, where there was no Kwaisulia to rationalize the industry, a chaotic state of affairs prevailed. The recruiters never knew what to expect. Where Kwaisulia had used the support of the white man to unify the saltwater people and hold the hill tribes at bay, the offshore islanders of Malekula had gone on recklessly shooting up their saltwater kin of the adjacent mainland until, too late, they realized that they had left an entire stretch of coastline at the mercy of the hill-men.

The hill-men exploited this situation to the utmost. Until quite recently Malekula was one of the last places on earth where the anthropologist could wander at leisure and find so many of the old customs almost intact; where the old balance of tribe against tribe continued to be maintained to the grave danger of any villager careless enough to walk into an ambush; where people believed they had something too valuable to risk contaminating by exposure to the outside world.

In 1906, by which time resistance to the European invasion had virtually come to an end elsewhere in Melanesia (even New Georgia had succumbed), there were still tribes in the interior of Malekula that had never seen a white man's face, though they were all armed with the white man's rifle. That was the way they intended to keep it.

SEVEN

Recruiting, 1871-83

IT was a torrid morning in the 1880s. The heat of Ambrym was already overpowering; the glare almost painful as if the dazzling waters of Champion's Bay were alive with demons. To the crew of the little cutter *Constantine*, exhausted and bleary-eyed after the heavy binge of the night before, it was no time to be putting to sea, though they were somewhat cheered and encouraged to see the schooner *Dauphin* also in port. Jimmy Martin, the *Constantine*'s skipper, was more than cheered; in fact he was highly amused. Demoselle of the *Dauphin* was an old friend, an arch rival but a great drinking companion and just the kind of comic, volatile little Frenchman people like Martin could never resist playing jokes on. He decided to run up the French flag in mock salute—he had a good collection of foreign flags, never knowing in that uncertain part of the world which nation might not suddenly claim an authority over an island, what warship might come demanding to see his recruiting licence.

The Frenchman, however, had a spyglass trained on the *Constantine* and thus was forewarned. "So, so. Monsieur Martin is drunk again," Dick Henderson, the mate, heard him mutter in his abominable English. "I tell Buccaneer Martin he all same drunken pig. Dick," he called to the mate, "you watch, please. First, I take zis pig, zen zis bottle and so I tie ze bottle round ze neck of ze pig." By the time the *Constantine* was abreast, the pig was hanging upside down from the Frenchman's masthead, a bottle apparently stuck in its mouth and half-choking it, while Demoselle was stretched far out over the side, pointing up at the pig, screaming across to Martin, "Drunken swine." Suddenly, he had to dive for cover as the *Constantine*'s crew began pumping bullets into the wretched animal, causing those below to be bespattered by blood. Finally a shot smashed the bottle also and Martin bellowed back over the water, "Why don't you ask me aboard to eat sucking pig?"

The two were typical of the New Hebridean recruiter of that period—freelancers (perhaps freebooters is a better word), in that they recruited mainly for New Caledonia and the French and Australian plantations in the New Hebrides themselves, though also on occasions for Tahiti and Hawaii as well. The dozen or so English and Australian skippers who recruited almost exclusively for Queensland were much the same type. They needed this coarse, earthy sense of humour, this ability to remain cheerful in the face of the day-to-day beastliness of their job, simply in order to endure and earn a living. They were professionals. Since the revelations of the *Carl* affair in 1872 recruiting was no longer a business that many a decent God-fearing seaman cared to be mixed up in. No more outsiders had been attracted into the trade. The Sydney shipowners were sticking mainly to bêche-de-mer and copra, and the backbone of the industry was a handful of merchants in Brisbane and Maryborough; men who owned a few ships between them and were quite happy to put them to labour trading if the political winds were blowing in the right direction.

For the Queensland labour trade never slackened at any stage; in fact it could not always keep pace with sudden spurts in demand. Despite the mounting toll taken by shipwreck and native attack, there was never any shortage of vessels, for when the average South Seas trader was thoroughly worn out, and its seams began to gape open at the first hint of strain, it would be fit for nothing else but recruiting. The *Heron*, for instance, eighty tons, of Maryborough, was well-known to leak like a sieve. In a storm, said Government Agent Douglas Rannie, all hands would stand to the pumps and the entire shipload of returns or new recruits would be employed baling and filling the cracks. It was thus kept afloat for another eight profitable years in the labour trade until wrecked at Aneityum in October 1884.

One or two recruiters foundered at sea, like the *Sybil* with 150 recruits in 1902. But mostly they were lost on shore, like the *Heron*, when their ground tackle parted while at anchor. Apparently it was well worth patching them up repeatedly and sending them back to sea, even though they could be insured for only two-thirds of their market value, with premiums as high as 18 per cent, rising to 20½ in the hurricane months.

To take the instance of an earlier *Sybil* (not the ship lost in 1902), it was nearly twenty years old when it entered the labour trade in 1874, having been condemned some years before that. Once its Government Agent walked off at Havannah Harbour, claiming that it took in water at every seam, so it had to return to Maryborough with hardly any recruits. But apart from that the *Sybil* continued to do useful work, until eventually lost off Malekula in 1887. So, too, with another Maryborough vessel, the *Stormbird*. From 1871 to 1885 it was employed more or less continuously in the labour trade until the time when smoke-signals and the beating of drums began to precede its arrival everywhere, a sure sign that the islanders considered the ship unseaworthy and had placed a taboo on it. So the *Stormbird* was put up for sale in 1885, failed to find a buyer and was burned in the Mary River.

What of the crews who risked their lives in such vessels? Some of the Government Agents who had to endure their casual seamanship and brawling drunken ways for months on end called them the scum of the ocean. In his *Jock of the Islands*, the recruiter Jock Cromar claims that quite a few of the recruiting skippers had once belonged to reputable shipping companies and been dismissed, usually for drunkenness. Perhaps so, but the record shows that the majority of the ordinary seamen in the trade had been brought up on the Brisbane and Maryborough waterfronts and gone into recruiting as naturally as somebody born in a mining village goes down the mine. The habitual drunkenness, the consequent slackness and indiscipline were due more to the character of the life rather than any innate character of the men concerned; the labour vessels had to spend as much as five months sometimes between civilized ports and carried enormous amounts of liquor.

Visualize, for example, the voyage of the schooner *Ethel*, setting out from Maryborough in the early 1880s on a normal recruiting stint. According to Christopher Mills, its new G.A., the trade-room, which he had supposed was stocked with useful articles to exchange with the natives, served as the cellar. The women's compartment in the hold, which should have been separated from the men's by a partition and was in fact only blocked off by coils of rope, was being used as an armoury.

Under a proper method of port inspection, such illegalities would never have been permitted. However such inspection as existed was perfunctory, and at the time Mills was more concerned that several of the returns had been recently discharged from hospital suffering from incurable venereal disease and that no system existed, as it did in Fiji, to prevent them infecting their fellow passengers and ultimately fellow villagers back in the islands. He mentioned this to the captain, John Loutit, who laughed at him. Loutit was an old island hand who had been in the labour trade for fourteen years and suffered shipwreck and privation and every imaginable misadventure. He was more interested in his pigs than in Kanakas. A dozen or more of these creatures were allowed to run loose on deck, to the great annoyance of the passengers, but they were necessary, Loutit said, because they could be sold to the natives in trade, eaten when supplies ran low, or treated as pets. Certainly they provided infinite amusement and diversion for the skipper if no one else.

Loutit liked to stalk them around the deck, suddenly to surprise one and carry it off squealing to one of the wash-deck tubs where he might spend up to half an hour carefully scrubbing and grooming it. Then, having tied a piece of rope around its neck, he would allow the pig to bounce out of his arms, land on its head on the deck, so that, terrified, it scrambled to its feet again to go somersaulting over and over as it tried to run away. In an especially playful mood, he might fill the tub with boiling water, whereupon the pigs, sensing what was about to happen, would scatter madly in every direction, until Loutit, finally losing patience, would grab hold of a bucket full of boiling water to splash the pigs with it. Mills, after watching this almost daily performance, wondered if it were not really the Kanakas the captain would prefer to be tormenting, constrained from doing so only by the presence of the G.A. However, Loutit was not constrained for long. A little later, after he and crew had been playing cards all day and were growing bored, they decided to fire blank cartridges at a few of the Kanakas on deck for a diversion. When this too palled, Loutit had another idea. Going below to the women's compartment, he came back with some loose powder which he showed could be wound tightly in pieces of rag, a fuse inserted, and thrown down among the Kanakas in the hold. It was a hilarious way of passing the time.

Overgrown schoolboy viciousness like this could only have had the ultimate effect of causing the villagers to send on those drum-messages to one another, warning that the *Ethel* and its crazy commander were in the vicinity again; that it would behove their neighbours, friends or enemies, to keep clear. However, Loutit did not have to care what they thought: he had an agreement with various chiefs for a regular supply of boys, and that was that. Even before this, in the early period, he told Mills one day, he was "never short of a trick or two" as a means of getting his quota. At one stage he had an understanding with one of the Fijian recruiters. At first they had just stupidly competed with one another until Loutit had a brilliantly simple idea: "I take your returns," he told the Fijian, "you take mine." So for several voyages after that, the two of them would make for a certain rendezvous, an uninhabited island in the Banks Group, and exchange returns. The boys did not know what was happening and they were simply transferred from one set of plantations to another. The practice came to an end after Great Britain's annexation of the Fiji Islands in 1874.

But the idea of first calling at some deserted bay had remained a good one, Loutit maintained. Here he might put some of his more timid-looking returns ashore and hover around for a day or two. By that time they were terrified out of their wits by the ghosts of the place and would clamour to be taken back to Queensland. It was easier to get a more understanding G.A. in those days, he emphasized to Mills, the kind who mostly stayed in his cabin and saw nothing until the boys were brought to him for signature.

But John Loutit, who had so cunningly used his wits to survive in the trade for so long, made one fatal miscalculation in the end: to confide in Christopher Mills at all, for Mills had taken the job with the intention of writing down everything he saw and heard. His first voyage in the *Ethel* passed off fairly uneventfully. But the second was an unhappy affair that culminated with the agent's submitting to the Immigration Office a long list of charges against the master: of having ammunition unlawfully aboard; of being drunk and striking a native; of being drunk and shooting arrows at the boat-crew; of using foul and filthy language to a steward; of forcing his way into the women's compartment; of recruiting illegally around Tanna by buying boys from the chiefs. Ironically as it turned out it was Mills, the original complainant, who was brought to trial and convicted for having connived at illegal methods of recruitment. Loutit was also tried but acquitted. Nevertheless, it meant the finish of his career as a recruiter.

Not all the other skippers were as ingenious as John Loutit. Filling their vessels to their licensed capacity was mostly a matter of hard graft in this middle phase of the labour trade. When the voyage began to stretch into the fourth or fifth month, the profit to the owner and the amount of bonus to be divided among the men seemed hardly worth all the trouble. As early as June 1871, a G.A. aboard the *Stormbird* was inclined to be pessimistic about the future. He quoted one reluctant recruit: "Me, no go Brisbane. Me no fool. Work all day. Sometimes all night. White man get overtime; me nothing, only corn all same like horse, no, me no go; me get yam, coconut, taro. What for me work?"

Events however did not justify too much pessimism. It was impossible to generalize about the prevailing mood in the islands from one or two specific cases. Moreover, various pressures were already at work by 1871 which would cause some islands to be almost denuded of the young male population before there was any appreciable slackening off in the rate of the recruitment. Again, the islanders rarely spoke their true minds to the white man and thus rarely gave their real reasons for not enlisting. The real reason why the *Stormbird* was so often avoided was because of its reputation for being unseaworthy. Other vessels temporarily afflicted by an outbreak of fever aboard would have the name of being "sick-ships". "By'm by, he dead," William Wawn heard the knowing ones mutter when he recruited a Malaita boy on one occasion. On the other hand, sickness might be raging on an island and there would be a rush of men to recruit in the hope of being cured by the white man's medicines.

So business proceeded by fits and starts. The *Bobtail Nag* recruiting for Rockhampton in 1877 began by getting a good haul at Tanna near the beginning of the season. A number of old hands, returns deposited back at their village at the end of the previous season and already fed up with the place, jumped into the water and tried to scramble into the boat the moment they recognized the mate acting as ship's recruiter. He was an old friend apparently. There was no question of having to haggle with friends and relatives in terms of sticks of tobacco or rounds of ammunition. Inquiring what presents he should give in exchange, the mate was told, "Me no care. Me no belong this fellow place. Man here no good. Bloody rogue." A second man said, "Along island, me no get tobacco, grog. Me no get nothing. Rockhampton very good place."

Another recruiter was amazed when the vessel suddenly rounded a point of land and came across a group of boys aged about thirteen or fourteen sitting on some rocks. Send a boat urgently, the boys gestured. They wished to recruit. A few minutes later they were aboard. Where did they want to go, the white men asked with a grin, Queensland or Fiji? They did not care, they grinned back. Just so long as it was somewhere.

Naturally this sort of thing did not happen very often. Usually things went the other way: the boats would pull in towards a crowded beach, to find the natives eager enough to trade, but not to recruit. Next week, perhaps, but not just now. "By'm by. You wait a little bit. You catch plenty boy." Ordinarily the recruiter would never know the true reason for their reluctance, though in certain cases they did. Former labourers would genuinely wish to enlist again, but were put off because the Queensland destinations were unpopular. William Matson, G.A. of the *May Queen*, recruiting for the Brisbane district in 1874, found one group of islanders willing to work for such employers as Davy, Goodin, and Munro as he began to call off some of the names, but emphatically not for Louis Hope or George Raff of Caboolture.

What happened in Queensland, after the recruit had been sold, was beyond the recruiter's control. In Queensland, it seemed, the Kanaka was virtually the personal property of the master. He would put him to work in the field or about the house; move him from one district to another; sell him to a squatter in the far interior, if he wished. It was all in clear breach of the regulations, but the Immigration Office, whatever its reasons were, made little effort to intervene. However, it did not pay the recruiter not to keep faith. Recruits were hard enough to come by as it was.

Thus argued Carl Satini, a tough, ruthless Swede and one of the most experienced recruiters in the business, in a stormy scene with the manager of the Maryborough Sugar Co. late in 1876. Satini, called "Captain One-eye" by the islanders because of the strong cast in one of his eyes, was a man who would stop at nothing. When and where it was expedient to obtain recruits by force, he used force. But in the mid-seventies other methods were proving more profitable. If the natives did not believe he meant to return them after three years as agreed they just would not recruit any more, he shouted at Jamieson, the manager. But Jamieson refused to listen, arguing that the group of Tannese whom Satini was seeking to return at the expiration of their three-year contracts could not be spared in the middle of the crushing.

That evening Satini sent a party of seamen to entice the Tannese away from the plantation down to the wharf where the schooner *Chance* stood, all stowed and ready, waiting for the morning tide to take it away to the islands. But he was not quite quick enough. Jamieson followed them, marched his own men aboard the schooner and recaptured the runaways, attacking and knocking down Satini into the bargain. The manager was afterwards brought up before Maryborough's police magistrate and fined for assault. But there was no doubt where the sympathies of the Court lay. And it was not with the recruiters, judging from the magistrate's remarks. The business was seen as necessary but not popular. It had brought little credit to Maryborough ever since the *Jason* case in 1871.

William Wawn was another veteran recruiting skipper who was also conscious of this. Police magistrates, immigration agents, harbourmasters, all gave him trouble at one time or another. Legally as well as morally the recruiters could never be sure of where they stood. For example, in 1877 a Liberal Government passed regulations prohibiting the export of fire-arms to the islands. The shipowners were staggered; if such a law were ever to be enforced it meant that recruiting would be impossible and that they would have to find some other employment for their vessels. However, it soon appeared that the Government was not to be taken too literally on this particular point. Representations had been made by various responsible parties. In fact when the *Stormbird* sailed in June 1878, Wawn records that his G.A. had positive instructions to ignore the regulations. It would be sufficient merely to maintain a pretence of legality; to ensure that fire-arms were not exposed too openly, preferably packed in crates and manifested as containing axes. A survey of the seventy-three returns being taken home by the *Lavinia* in 1882, for instance, revealed that between them they owned 78 Sniders, 6 Spencers, 29 Enfields, 47 muskets, 9 shotguns, 2 revolvers, 1,861 lb. of powder, and 9,300 rounds of ammunition.

What were the recruiters to make of a situation where the Government legislated and then openly encouraged them to break the law? From start to finish, the whole trade bristled with anomalies and contradictions. To take another example, what were the relations between Government Agent and recruiter? According to the book of instructions, one of his responsibilities was to ride in the covering boat, to keep an eye on what was happening while the other boat was negotiating with potential recruits on the beach. Many agents in fact never left the ship and were content to be nothing more than rubber-stamps, signing their consent automatically when the recruits were brought to them. Others, more energetic, would thrust the ship's official recruiter into the background and take over the actual recruiting themselves. It depended very much on the calibre and integrity of the individual. For some were like William McMurdo, the son of a general, the relative of a prime minister and a governor-general, and had their own individual and very definite ideas about the proper mode of recruiting.

McMurdo did not, for instance, stick absolutely to the letter of the Recruiting Act. He thought a little coercion was sometimes good for the natives—providing the whole operation was conducted in a genuine spirit of British enterprise, in the interests of opening up the very backward South Seas generally to the benefits of civilization. With a G.A. such as McMurdo it was best to let him collect his own recruits and be totally responsible for their welfare and discipline thereafter. Thus aboard the schooner *Stanley* in 1883 he was forced to take action against six Kanakas caught stealing biscuits. He wrote in the log, "I then thrashed the whole six . . . and laid it on well this time. . . . They can stand pain wonderfully and their skins are thick." However, one of them died the next day, he had to admit. "I must have greatly overrated their powers of endurance."

Thus a recruiting skipper would sometimes have the vague indefinable suspicion that the G.A. represented some sort of higher interest than merely that of the colonial recruiting industry in general. Occasionally one might turn nasty and resign, like George de Lautour in 1883, or order the vessel home, like Government Agent Cheek did the *Madeleine* on another occasion, simply because skipper or recruiter had offended against some hitherto lightly regarded aspect of the regulations. Certain G.A.s did claim access to the Governor, over the heads of owners and members of Parliament.

Another mysterious higher power, another incalculable element in the situation, was the Navy, which was now much more active in the area than formerly. At the same time as the Imperial Parliament had been engaged in passing its Pacific Islanders' Protection Act of June 1872 (better known as the Kidnapping Act) the Admiralty had been drawing up plans for a fleet of fast schooners. These were specially designed to operate in the Melanesian waters and solely for the purpose of enforcing the provisions of the Act. A Sydney ship-builder eventually got the contract, and from 1873 onwards, one after the other, five of these little vessels were commissioned for service: H.M. ships *Alacrity*, *Beagle*, *Conflict*, *Renard*, and *Sandfly*, fifty tons each, each with a lieutenant, a sub-lieutenant, and a crew of thirty British Jack Tars; all kept spick-and-span and very Navy fashion down to the ship's band with concertina, triangles, and penny whistles.

Yet the anti-kidnapping squadron was not destined to achieve very much in maintaining law and order, for all the keenness of its youthful commanders. Primarily their duty was to "protect the islanders against ill-treatment by British subjects", when in fact the more pressing problem now was to protect British subjects against the islanders. But the instructions showed clearly how much public sentiment had swung round in favour of the native since the *Carl* affair in 1871, and the murder of Bishop Patteson in the same year.

It was symptomatic of this changing climate of opinion that Patteson's death had been thought of mainly in terms of the original provocation offered by one or other of the recruiting vessels. More directly it might have taught another lesson—that the islanders were learning to take care of themselves and quite capable of getting in first.

For instance in 1877 an English trader, William Easterbrook, was murdered on Tanna. H.M.S. *Conflict* arrived a short time later and established that Easterbrook had lived by selling gunpowder to the natives and been involved in a quarrel over payment. The lieutenant's duty in such circumstances was perfectly clear. He now demanded of the "ruling and responsible chiefs" that they deliver up the murderer or murderers within three days, and when they failed to do this he sent off to Sydney for further instructions. In due course two more warships turned up, H.M. ships *Beagle* and *Renard*, Lieutenant Caffin in the *Beagle* having strict orders that the affair was to be plumbed to the bottom and the culprits identified and duly punished.

Caffin therefore co-opted the services of the Reverend Thomas Neilson, and before long seventeen Tannese, including three persons of consequence, were brought in by a raiding party from H.M.S.

Renard and held aboard the *Beagle* as hostages. It was now only a matter of time before the guilty party would be handed over, and sure enough a great shout went up from the beach next day, proclaiming that the murderer had surrendered.

The man, Yumanga, who readily admitted to doing the deed, Neilson reported, was in fact in no mood to give himself up. So another expedition was sent ashore to bring Yumanga back. It is one matter to capture seventeen unresisting bystanders and quite another to nail down one dangerous and elusive quarry who has determined he is not going to be captured. The second expedition was a difficult, protracted business in which eight Tannese were killed and one seaman injured before the native reputed to be Yumanga was finally placed under arrest and escorted back to the *Beagle*. And then of course it turned out to be not Yumanga at all, but his brother.

However, as Neilson was quick to point out, though this brother was not the person who had fired the fatal shot, he had been present at the scene of the crime, prepared, indeed, to shoot the trader with his own gun if Yumanga's musket had misfired. Thus he was indisputably an accessory before the fact of murder. This was enough for Caffin, and Yumanga's brother was forthwith put on trial, found guilty and hanged at the yard-arm. There is nice irony in the fact that Yumanga ultimately escaped to Maryborough aboard a recruiter.

The Tannese were undoubtedly impressed: a life for a life was a fair exchange. The Reverend Mr Neilson returned to his good works ashore and the Navy departed, mission accomplished. Caffin settled down to write a lengthy dispatch for the Commodore that attempted not so much to justify or extenuate as to emphasize how at the end he had brought all the chiefs and their tribes together and given them a good lecture upon the awfulness of murder. Swift to punish, swift to bless, the Navy remained ever present in the background, he had solemnly reminded them, a mighty arm to protect right and redress wrong, be the perpetrators white or black.

Caffin's report apparently satisfied the Commodore as well as the Admiralty. But in the meantime another version had leaked out. Early in 1878 various English newspapers were making a lot of the way young naval officers were recklessly abusing their authority; questions were asked in the House about the extraordinary episode in the Pacific, where the wrong man had been hanged. As a result the Admiralty was forced to intervene once again and the discretion of naval commanders was even further restricted.

But there were some people in London, those professionally devoted to the interests of native races all over the world, who thought it should go even further than that. A new authority had recently been created in the Pacific, a legal device, largely a paper fiction called the Western Pacific High Commission, whereby the Governor of Fiji was granted a jurisdiction over all British subjects in the nearby Pacific. Why should the Navy be allowed any discretion at all in native matters? it was now asked. Would it not be better if naval commanders acted merely as servants of the Commission? It was against this background then, with Sir Arthur Gordon, the new Commissioner and a fierce upholder of the rights of the black man against the white, resident in Fiji and watching the Navy's every move with hostile suspicion, that Lieutenant de Houghton was sent to Batnapni Bay, Pentecost, to look into more trouble there.

This had begun with a French recruiter pulling down a native hut belonging to Chief Tabbiseisei. It was a thoroughly stupid action. Tabbiseisei had made no effort to help them find recruits, the French claimed, without having bothered to discover that the party they should have been dealing with was one Tabbisangwul, a returned labourer from Queensland. With some difficulty this man had placed himself at the head of a faction favourable to and dependent upon the recruiters, but it was only by guaranteeing the recruiters a steady supply of recruits and freedom from outside interference that he had been able to maintain his position. Now that freedom was destroyed.

The next visitor to the bay was the Brisbane recruiter *May Queen*. Having enjoyed friendly relations with Tabbisangwul for some years without cause to expect danger, the *May Queen*'s mate and recruiter jumped straight into a boat and headed for the shore without even thinking to take guns with him—very rash but very typical. The "welcoming" crowd of natives had waded out waist-deep into the water and now seized hold of the stern-post of the boat as if to guide it to the place where the white men always went for fresh water. But they were not Tabbisangwul's men but those of his enemy, Tabbiseisei.

Tabbiseisei had planned his attack very carefully in advance. He had anticipated that the white men's first need would be fresh water and so had arranged to have a line of axes planted under water along the route that led to a nearby beach spring. It all went off exactly to plan, the execution being all the neater and swifter because the recruiters were unarmed. The boat-crew, having formed a chain between the boat and the beach, were busy passing buckets to one another while the islanders all around them were surreptitiously searching for the axes with their feet, manoeuvring them along the bottom until each man was in a position to strike. Suddenly one man who had worked his way immediately behind the mate (who was still sitting in the boat) bent down, straightened again and drove his axe

L

deep into the white man's head. The Kanaka boat-crew were all
slaughtered in the same instant.

H.M.S. *Beagle*, now under the command of Lieutenant de
Houghton, was called upon to investigate the affair. What he would
have made of it, arriving out of the blue and finding only Chief
Tabbiseisei's party to instruct him as to what had occurred, is
problematical. As it happened Captain Satini in the *Sybil* was already
there and he made sure that it was Tabbisangwul who was present
with his version of the facts. Tabbisangwul prepared, said the crafty
Swede, to lead their combined forces against the scoundrel, Tabbiseisei, and destroy him for once and all. Satini must have assumed
that the young naval officer would be disposed to be guided by his
greater experience. He was not. If he harmed a single hair in their
heads, de Houghton told him grimly, he would lose his command.

Thus the punitive expedition which Satini had in mind turned
out to be a very tame effort, though it began belligerently enough.
De Houghton lined up the *Sybil*'s crew beside his own bluejackets
and the party headed off into the interior in the correct style, planning to take Tabbiseisei's village in the rear and cut off his means of
retreat. But by the time they arrived the village was deserted, and so
de Houghton ordered it to be burnt to the ground. He then
marched his men home again, presumably relieved at not having to
come to conclusions with the actual offenders. Only one person was
hurt on either side—Satini's bos'n—when a native suddenly sprang
out from behind some bushes and struck him on the back of the
head with a tomahawk. The attacker had then quickly disappeared
again, and de Houghton had forbidden his party to follow or attempt
any retaliation.

From the recruiter's point of view it was worse than useless to
have the Navy butting in like that. Before there had come to be so
many warships in the region, an old-fashioned recruiter like Satini
might have organized his own expedition and meted out some
weighty punishment in the right quarter. And when the Navy did
intervene, and failed to exact an appropriate revenge, it always
seemed to happen that the guilty party would emerge stronger than
ever, proclaiming that the man-o'-war was afraid to fight him. Before
this episode, trivial in itself, where Frenchmen idly destroyed one
small beach-hut and provoked the anti-European faction into a state
of open hostility, the pro-Europeans had been able to hold their
own. But after H.M.S. *Beagle* had come and gone and only added to
their irritation, Tabbiseisei had clearly gained the upper hand.
When William Wawn arrived at Batnapni Bay early in 1879 it was
to find that Tabbiseisei now controlled the whole district; that
Tabbisangwul had been obliged to return to Queensland aboard the

most recent recruiter. That was the end of Batnapni Bay as an important recruiting-centre. When finally the *Agnes Donald* of Fiji called there in July 1879 its boats were also attacked and ten of its men lost their lives.

Only ten miles to the north-west of Pentecost is the island of Oba. Oba had always been noted for its coconuts, and this was why several European traders had established copra-stations there at the beginning of the seventies. Yet for some reason the island was not greatly sought out by the recruiters until the late seventies when they had little choice but to go after recruits wherever they were to be found. So it was that on 4th November 1878 the Brisbane recruiter *Mystery* arrived. The crew, it seemed, knew little of Oba or its inhabitants; had no special contacts with any particular village and thus no means of discovering how it was that, only the day before, just a few miles down the coast, a Sydney trader, the *Heather Bell*, had become involved in a serious fracas with the islanders, losing one white seaman. However, John Renton, the *Mystery*'s celebrated Government Agent, had no fear of strange tribes and went boldly ashore where he immediately met a native, Aratuga, who had spent five years in Fiji and happened to be the only Oban in the neighbourhood who could speak English.

But it was not chance that had planted him there on the beach just at that moment. He was there by design as a decoy. Behind him, in the background, was Sikeri, the chief who had declared a war of extermination against the white man—evidently because the *Heather Bell* had been interfering with the island women. Aratuga leapt into the first recruiting-boat and offered to take Renton to a village in the next bay where he said recruits were to be had. Then, steering the boat out of sight of the ship straight into an ambush, Aratuga himself struck the fatal blow that accounted for the Government Agent.

He was eaten, it seems, along with Thomas Muir, the mate and the four islanders in the boat-crew. For Sikeri had promised the district a feast, concocting the preposterous excuse for holding one that he planned to dedicate a new taro bed for which a human sacrifice was required.

The Obans were not really regular cannibals, any more than the northern Malekulans to whom they were closely related. But on both islands the practice of "eating from the body of a murderer or detested enemy" was gradually increasing as the old ways steadily broke up.

Meanwhile Captain Kilgour in the *Mystery* (the same Kilgour whose likeness William Brookes had once pasted up in his shop-window wrongly supposing him to have been eaten) could discover no trace of the missing party and was forced to sail away again, none the wiser about what had become of them. However, he had no intention of forgetting the matter. In the following April he called again at Oba and discovered the lost boat, plainly visible from the sea, carefully hauled up above the high-water mark on the edge of the jungle. There could be no doubt about the fate of the two lost white men and the Kanaka boat-crew. Kilgour called for volunteers and a punitive expedition went ashore. It not only recovered the boat, but set fire to the village and all the crops, broke up every canoe in sight and carried off several pigs.

The recruiters had appeared to make it quits. The reality was that the wrong village had suffered—one which had merely bought the boat after being invited to Sikeri's cannibal feast. Thus when the affair came to be investigated, the case against Kilgour looked serious. A warship intercepted the *Mystery* in the course of a subsequent recruiting voyage in the Solomons and its unfortunate skipper was given the choice of going to Fiji as a prisoner aboard the man-o'-war or taking his own vessel there. He chose the latter course.

The trial could not have been more inopportune: Judge John Gorrie, Sir Arthur Gordon's Chief Judicial Commissioner in the High Commission, heard the case. A rather pedantic and narrow-minded lawyer, he was entrusted with the very wide task of bringing European law and order to formerly lawless Melanesia. For offences under the Pacific Islanders Protection Act (the Kidnapping Act of 1872), he had recently sentenced Captain John Daly of the *Heather Bell* to a fine and six months' imprisonment. And he now told Kilgour, referring to the captain's burning of the wrong village, "Until this private hostility is put down, we shall never be able to bring order out of the confusion or prevent the natives avenging the deeds of violence committed against them by our own countrymen." He then fined the accused £100, adding, "If I had proof of your having killed a native, I would have hanged you, sir, hanged you."

By now Oban affairs had become inextricably interwoven with those of the white man's world outside, with the game of high politics being played between the Admiralty and the Western Pacific High Commission. Quite independently of the inquiry into the Kilgour episode and the burning of the wrong village, another warship, H.M.S. *Wolverene* under Commodore John Wilson, had been investigating the murder of John Renton and the other white men from the *Mystery*. Wilson had no trouble finding Aratuga and establishing his complicity in the crime—the Obans were only too glad to give him up in the hope of averting a worse fate—and the question then arose of how to punish the prisoner, of what further punishment, if any, would be appropriate for the village as a whole.

At this stage, of course, Wilson had no idea that Aratuga was merely the scapegoat, and that the real culprits were sheltering in the background.

So far the sequence of events had followed a familiar pattern. Wilson was not the first British naval commander in the Pacific to find himself in the situation of holding, unwillingly in his hand, a man's life. Except that Wilson, being the Commodore and not a mere lieutenant, would be expected to act authoritatively without being able to pass the responsibility on to somebody else. The village, he decided, should suffer only a moderate fine of so many tusker pigs, but it should be responsible for the formal execution by hanging of the avowed murderer, Aratuga. Thus the people would see at first-hand the inevitable consequence of their actions and at the same time learn a valuable lesson in the way the white man administered justice.

This, then, was the plan, but fortunately for Aratuga it could not be put into action, because rising seas prevented his being returned to his village. Wilson was now obliged to do what he had been trying to avoid, send him on to Fiji for rival authorities to fight over the body. The High Commission won. And it was eighteen months finally before Judge Gorrie in the High Commissioner's Court decided that no single individual, such as Aratuga, could be held responsible for a crime in which the whole community had participated. The prisoner's position, Gorrie held, had been akin to that "of a common soldier obeying the orders of his superiors". "I cannot in such circumstances look upon the act of Aratuga who is not a chief . . . as separable from that of the hostile band . . . he must therefore be discharged."

Justice on Oba, by contrast, was swift and inexorable. In revenge for the white men's taking Aratuga away, Sikeri killed a resident American trader called Johnson. Johnson's partner, Chaffin, killed Sikeri. White and black were like two hostile villages in perpetual feud: nine men were killed from the visiting *May Queen*; H.M.S. *Miranda* retaliated by sending a party overland from coast to coast burning villages and laying waste. Oba became as dangerous as Malekula.

Thus everywhere, it seemed, the number of places open to the recruiters was shrinking: the smaller islands like the Banks Group had been pretty well depopulated; the larger islands, like mainland Malekula, Oba, Pentecost, and most of the Solomons, were too wild. Elsewhere at Aneityum, Eromanga, Efate, Nguna, Tongoa, the missionaries were firmly in occupation. Or were they? Were these "missionary" islands as effectively controlled by the missionaries as was commonly supposed? Hearing that a dozen or so recruits had been taken from Aneityum, Captain Joseph Vos of the *Lizzie*, a clever young Englishman new to the trade and looking for fresh angles, resolved to investigate the question at length.

Normally Aneityum was studiously avoided and, indeed, it was not a cheering prospect as the *Lizzie* coasted slowly along to windward keeping a sharp lookout for any signs of life. No streamers of smoke went up to denote that the natives were ready to trade. When a landing under recruiter Peter Dowell was eventually made well clear of the nearest mission settlement, a group of natives ostentatiously turned their backs and walked away. The recruiting party persisted. They were free to wander all over the place and finally they came across a boy who had obviously been in Queensland before and spoke fair English. Would he care to join the *Lizzie*'s boat-crew? He was invited, but he replied, "No, me no go boat-crew. Me too much lazy. [The work is too hard]".

Next, Dowell thought of the mission jailhouse. Perhaps he could bribe the jailer and persuade one or two of the convicts to escape to Queensland. But this tactic failed also. The prison population was interested, but the bribe offered must have been insufficient, or else they were too afraid of the missionaries to act.

Meanwhile, the recruiters had picked up a guide, Outon, a young man of about twenty, who spoke a little English and had pleasing manners, and was obviously fascinated by the idea of seeing Queensland; a friend, Nangaree, had already gone, it seemed. There was no real possibility of Outon's actually going; he made it clear to the recruiter that he was a mission boy. Yet he continued to loiter around the white men, and Julian Thomas, a journalist and writer who happened to be travelling in the *Lizzie* on this final stage of her voyage back to Queensland, recorded the following scene:

"Why don't you recruit him," I asked [Dowell], pointing to Outon, who was still with us in the boat. "Oh, he won't come. I tried him," was the reply. *Pour m'amuser*, I commenced the usual address, "Very good you go alonga Melbourne along me. Very good ki-ki. Pay very good. Pay money. Plenty shops. You buy what you like. You good fellow. I good fellow master."

But, Outon spurned my advances, giving an emphatic "No" to everything I said. "I go ashore," he said and once feinted as if he would jump overboard. "You foolish fellow, master no take you suppose you no like, me put you ashore at place belonga you," said Peter Dowell. . . . Outon hesitated and asked, "You go place Nangaree stop?" "Yes, I take you place where I leave Nangaree."

We passed the place where Outon met us; he looked at the shore; then Jack, our stroke oar, said, "You no be frightened; Peeta good fellow man. He no fight, no swear at you. You get plenty ki-ki, good fellow ship. Plenty boy belonga Efate aboard. All missionary boy. I missionary man. You stop along them you all right." "Ship he go Townsville?" asked Outon. "Ship he go Townsville." "You go alonga me to Melbourne?" I asked. A decisive "No" was the reply. "You go alonga me to Townsville?" asked Peter. A nod and then "Yes" and the boy was fairly recruited. I thought the arguments of our native boatman clinched the matter.

Outon represented one solitary recruit to add to the *Lizzie*'s total in exchange for a long exhausting day's work. But there was no other way of doing it. The successful professional recruiter like Peter Dowell, a person much prized by recruiting skippers, needed to be a little unscrupulous, it is true. But he also needed to have tact, patience and a fair understanding of the native mind. Carl Satini was another who liked to poke about the missionary islands. He too "hooked" a few at Aneityum on one occasion and again at Eromanga in September 1882 in the *Ceara*.

Satini was aware that the Eromangans had developed an almost unnatural craving for tobacco, having been accustomed to that luxury by the sandalwooders and then denied it by the missionaries. It was with the object of trading some sticks of tobacco for a recruit or two, that the *Ceara*'s boats were dispatched down the coast to the little inlet, south of the mission station at Dillon's Bay, which the Swede sometimes used as a secret rendezvous. The boat was in charge of a Tannese recruiter named Nomu (or George Turner, as he preferred to be known, after Tanna's first European missionary), a bloodthirsty villain, but a champion Kanaka-catcher who had been in the trade since the very early days of Ross Lewin. It was not the normal practice for a native recruiter to be allowed to take command of a boat out of the sight of captain or mate—natives were not supposed to be very trustworthy—and Satini would have been well advised to have followed the rule on this occasion. For as Nomu's boat entered the inlet well in advance of the second boat, he caught sight of a group of mission women and was suddenly overcome by desire.

Normally Nomu would have dallied with the Eromangans, bringing news of Queensland, judiciously displaying the tobacco, waiting for the hint of a significant look that told him he had found a potential recruit. But now he chatted, restless, as his eye roved wildly. This time he had only one particular recruit in mind, and suddenly he saw his opportunity and grabbed the girl and ran. Unfortunately one man had to be shot before he could bundle the girl into the boat and push off. So it was full speed back to the ship and heigh-ho and away up the coast before the incident could be reported to the Reverend Hugh Robertson at Dillon's Bay. But some time

later, eight miles further north, the two boats were close inshore
once again, seeking out the lay of the land, as predatory as before.

On this occasion Nomu spied two natives obviously following them
along the shore, one hanging behind as if he wished to speak to
them alone. So it proved. As the boat pulled in towards him, the
man waded out, holding up a hawk in one hand and a bow and
arrow in the other, to which Nomu responded by displaying five
sticks of tobacco. Badly as he wanted the tobacco, however, he had
no intention of going to Queensland in order to get it. For the man
was Umo, one of Robertson's most trusted native preachers and he
was horrified at the idea. Nomu, however, cut short his protestations
in mid-sentence by grabbing his hand and dragging him into the
boat. Umo resisted and was shot in the side, so Nomu flung him
back into the water and that appeared to end the incident.

For Satini, however, it was only the beginning. The wounded
Umo was rescued, but subsequently died, and when Robertson came
to hear that the recruiters had killed one of his favourite preachers
he was ready to move heaven and earth to see that the culprits were
punished. He rounded up dozens of witnesses, prepared a long
statement, and when he went home on leave in 1883 he was summoned to a meeting of the Western Pacific High Commissioner
where the affair was discussed at some length. Finally pressure was
brought to bear on the Queensland Government and Satini was
dismissed.

So another recruiter had come to grief, but not through an incurable addiction to violence as some people alleged, but merely because
he had been careless in allowing the violent Nomu to get out of
hand. The experienced recruiter was too anxious to keep on good
terms with the islanders to use force consistently or attempt to cozen
people. It paid better in the end to study their ways. Tannese, for
instance, liked to have all their purchases weighed even though
they did not understand the figures. So the thoughtful recruiter
might take a small set of scales ashore with him. Intending recruits
at the Maskelynes, off southern Malekula, liked to sleep aboard for
one night to see how they took to it. If they didn't take to it, says
Wawn, he would allow them to go home again the next day.

But what the natives liked most of all was some form of diversion.
They were normally a cheerful, high-spirited people who loved to
hold entertainments and go visiting. Now that the traditional inter-
island sea travel was more or less a thing of the past, they longed to
see new faces, hear new stories, have something fresh and different to
excite them. Dowell of the *Lizzie* had better success than most
because he had a talent for putting people at their ease, a gift for
presenting Queensland in an amusing, off-beat sort of way that some-

how conjured up a picture of the Kanaka sitting back in comfort, smoking himself green in the face, or off to the races on Saturday afternoon, togged up to the nines, flashing his money around like a white man.

The greatest recruiting salesman of all was supposed to be a Fiji recruiter, referred to as Jimmy R——. Jimmy was a natural-born entertainer with as many tricks as a professional conjurer, one of the few, apparently, who did not believe in just arriving in the bay, setting off a charge of dynamite and expecting natives to come running from all directions. Instead he would have himself rowed quietly ashore, send back the boats and become absorbed in some solitary occupation on the beach. . . .

Perhaps he is playing with a packet of wax vestas, affecting to start back in horror every time one bursts into flame. This is sure to claim a handful of spectators, whereupon he stoops down and begins unpacking a largish suitcase. He extracts a long black dress, a black mask, flasks, bags, balls, and other minor items of apparatus, a piece of folded cardboard that can be knocked up into the shape of a tall, conical hat. Finally, arrayed in his robes, he now tries to fix his audience's attention with feats of sleight-in-hand, before striding down to the water's edge to perform his most important trick of all.

First he fills various flasks with sea-water, carries them up the beach again and begins to drink—one flask after the other, pretending to find the flavour excessively agreeable, going back for another and another, until his stomach becomes visible, growing steadily more distended beneath his robes. At last he whips the costume aside to reveal a large waterproof bag underneath. The spectators are beside themselves with laughter, but before they can recover he suddenly bends down, kicks up his legs and begins to walk on his hands. He has completely won them over. Before long they are all laughing and talking together, fingering his things, treating him like a long-lost friend. All at once somebody inquires if he may recruit. The recruiter treats the offer as only a joke. "You too much gammon whitefellow. My word," he laughs. However, the question is put again more insistently and at length he consents. . . .

Another famous recruiter of the day, a man of very different stamp, was a hard-bitten American, James Proctor. Proctor would never have gone to any elaborate preparations for anyone. He was too much of an aristocrat, too forthright and direct in his methods, for that. Yet he too had this same capacity to share a joke with the natives; the ability to forget himself for the moment and see only the comical side of the situation—the ludicrous aspect of men's strivings —exactly as they did. Still only a young man when he first arrived in Fiji in the mid-sixties, he was a veteran nevertheless and a seasoned soldier who had lost a leg in the Civil War at the age of seventeen. His family had lost its Louisiana sugar estates and almost everything it owned, and now to recoup his fortunes, by any means at all, he had come to the savage South Seas. He was just the type to go recruiting in Melanesia in the 1870s, after his Fijian cotton plantation had gone bankrupt. The natives revered him.

Probably most of the tales about Proctor are apocryphal or grossly exaggerated, but they at least illustrate the swashbuckling style of approach that seemed to go down best with the natives, Europeans as well as Melanesian. Usually known as "Timber-toes" Proctor, the American had a variety of artificial legs designed for a wide range of activities—walking, riding, rowing, dancing! So when the recruiting-boat grounded on the beach he would sometimes affect to lean back in the stern-sheets, idly resting one foot on the gunwale. Then, very deliberately, having made sure that everybody was watching, he would reach for a revolver and shoot himself through his trousered leg.

If this produced the right effect, he would then take a sheath-knife and plunge it into what appeared to be the fleshy part of the calf. The object was both to impress them and at the same time make them laugh and forget their distrust of the white man—for the moment at least. Once, however, the outcome was almost low comedy. Refusing to believe that anybody could really be so insensible to pain, one native crept up behind and jabbed him in the buttocks with a pen-knife, causing the recruiter to leap high into the air, proving that he was human after all.

Another story, which sounds even more far-fetched, has Proctor and Satini working in unison. . . .

They have landed together on the island of Tanna and are exchanging greetings with one of the chiefs, and handing round presents. Suddenly Proctor becomes stern: he wants twenty recruits, and wants them that day. If he doesn't get them he will cause an eye to fall out of every native in the village. Everybody stares aghast, wondering if he really does possess this terrible power, when Satini, who has been rubbing away at his artificial eye suddenly lets it fall, to flop on the sand. Whereupon Proctor unscrews his wooden leg and lays it beside the eye. . . .

It does not really matter whether or not these things actually happened, though presumably there was some basis for them in fact. For the islanders it mattered that men like Proctor and Satini did exist, an awesome reality in their lives, having the power to cast some sort of spell upon them. These two were the most notably successful of all the recruiters—Proctor for German Samoa, Satini for Queensland. But there were plenty of others, prepared, it seems, to have gone on recruiting scornful of all the dangers, unmindful that their relations with the islanders were deteriorating year by year, continuing to devise means to winkle out recruits until none were left. Meanwhile in Malaita, as we have seen, through the recent alliance with Kwaisulia a whole new field, the prolific bushman populations of the interior, was just being tapped.

Thus it was not due to any faint-heartedness on the part of the recruiters that a crisis in the trade was developing. The Queensland planting community, or a large section of it at least, had been considering the question of South Sea Island recruiting and were, it seems, coming round to the view that their interests would be better served if it were soon to stop. Various reasons were advanced: the quality of recruits was falling off; too many died before completing their contracts; they were becoming too expensive.

But none of these things really explains it. Few planters paused to consider that the sources of supply might be nearing exhaustion, for they had been brought up to believe that the islands teemed with people and by bringing large numbers of the islanders to Queensland they were helping to stave off a serious Pacific crisis of pressure of population upon resources. But they were concerned that so many potential recruits were now so manifestly unwilling to come.

At one time the planters had had the idea that the time-expired labourer, arriving joyfully back at his island home, would be an enthusiastic missionary for the white man's way of life, inspiring the rest of the community to come flocking to Queensland after him. But it did not work out that way. Many of the returns were going home now in a highly resentful frame of mind, sometimes even turning and firing on the recruiting-boat the moment they were safely ashore. In March 1876, for instance, the crew of the Sydney schooner *Dancing Wave* was horribly massacred at Ngela in the Floridas at the instigation of a mob recently returned from Queensland. They had been just waiting for an opportunity like this after their Albert River employer had gone bankrupt and the mortgagees, refusing to become responsible for them, had sent them prematurely back home without payment.

After that every year brought its crop of murders and outrages. Mostly the victims were isolated European traders, killed for no obvious good reason, after living there for years in apparent security. By 1880 a crisis point was reached. That was a terrible year in the islands. It began with the looting and burning of another Sydney schooner, the *Esperanza*, at Kolombangara. Not a single member of the crew escaped. "Me take him altogether trade," Chief Hailey told Captain Ferguson of the *Ripple* a little while later, "musket, powder, tobacco, bread plenty, me take everything, me make big fire, ship he finish." Next month Ferguson, himself an old South Seas trading hand and quite a popular figure in the islands, was murdered at Bougainville. Only fierce resistance by other members of the crew prevented the *Ripple* suffering the same fate as the *Esperanza*.

Hitherto, assaulting whole ships had been confined largely to the head-hunters of New Georgia. Now the practice was extending to the entire Solomons. In September the New Zealand brigantine *Borealis*, temporarily engaged in the Fijian labour trade, was surprised in broad daylight at anchor at Kwai islet, Malaita. Five white men were brutally done to death one beautiful sea-green morning without having a chance to defend themselves. One of the boats, however, was away at the time and when the crew returned to find the vessel in the possession of howling savages they made off down the coast to Sa'a where three more labour vessels were recruiting.

The rescuers were too late to save anybody aboard except the cook, who had taken refuge in a half-empty water-tank, but they were in time to save the ship which had been thoroughly looted, but not yet burnt. A skeleton crew managed to sail it back to Fiji, where the public was free to inspect the damaged bulwarks, shrouds, and masts scored with the marks of innumerable axe-cuts, the deck-house completely shattered, every cabin ravaged. Here and there dark blotches of dried blood showed where one or another of the crew had been left to bleed to death.

The massacre caused a great stir in Fiji, as it did in New Zealand when the *Borealis* finally reached Auckland. Where was the Navy at the time? the newspapers asked. In Melbourne for the Cup? In Sydney or Adelaide or some other fashionable port of call? Playing cricket? Attending another garden party? And what was Sir Arthur Gordon, with his High Commissioners' Court, so high-minded in pronouncing judgment upon the actions of white men in the islands, so outraged when unfortunate natives suffered injury, what was he going to do about it? Except to repeat rather lamely that the Court had no jurisdiction over native offences, Gordon had no real answer. But the Navy was considering the question of establishing a permanent headquarters in the Solomons. Then, abruptly, the angry voices were silenced, all criticism suspended, by the tragedy that came to H.M.S. *Sandfly* at Mandoliana Island.

Lieutenant Bower, the *Sandfly*'s latest commander, was a large, cheerful Englishman with a magnificent physique, and exactly what one might have expected him to be—a first-class front-row forward and a first-class naval officer. Some time earlier at Duke of York Island, New Britain, the Reverend Benjamin Danks, the Wesleyan missionary, had watched him standing in the midst of a group of fellow officers, swinging a native club around his head, exclaiming, "I say, you fellows, just think of an Englishman among a crowd of these Johnnies armed with one of these." But Bower was not only a champion sportsman but a keen chart-maker and hydrographer as well, and it was mainly for the purpose of examining the island at close quarters in order to map it that he landed on little, uninhabited Mandoliana in the Florida group. It was the kind of work he loved and he was absorbed in making certain alterations to the outline while the four seamen who were with him bathed in a pool nearby. Suddenly five natives began firing on them from the surrounding jungle.

The Reverend Alfred Penny, the resident Anglican representative in the Floridas, claims that the attack was launched because one of the party, Vuria, son of the powerful chief Kalekona of Gaeta Island nearby, saw his chance to earn a head. He had not yet killed his man in battle and was anxious to do this and also to please his father. At that time Kalekona was a most awkward and disgruntled individual—not surprisingly as he was in the process of allowing himself to be converted to Christianity while at the same time cherishing a deep hatred of the missionaries, of the labour recruiters, and of the white men generally. Kalekona had also been threatening, as he had on numerous occasions in the past, to abandon his people and live elsewhere, though it was believed that he could be placated by a head.

According to Penny the fact that Bower had participated in a punitive expedition twelve months before against the village of Kalekona's brother on neighbouring Guadalcanal was pure coincidence. Quite by chance, apparently, Vuria just happened to see five white men go ashore at this lonely island well out of sight of their ship and realized he had them at his mercy. So he quickly got together a little war-party, landed on the far side of the island, and took the white men completely unawares.

Three of the bathers fell wounded and were finished off with clubs, but one sailor managed to flee into the jungle and get clear away. Bower raced madly down the beach and tried to launch the whaleboat. But it was too heavy for him, so he, too, plunged into the jungle. With his pursuers only about thirty to forty yards behind him, he somehow succeeded in giving them the slip. Finally, out of breath he took refuge in the hollow trunk of a huge banyan-tree and nestled down into it out of sight. Unfortunately it was a very obvious hiding-place and before long they found him, dragged him out and cut off his head.

Bower's murder had an effect above and beyond that of any ordinary trader or seaman. New orders from the Admiralty instructed commanders that henceforth it would not be sufficient

merely to investigate native aggression and then refer the matter to
the High Commissioner or some other higher authority for a
decision. The onus was upon them personally to deal out retribution
as promptly and as drastically as the circumstances appeared to
warrant, to take whatever action was necessary to prevent the recur-
rence of similar outrages.

The first fruits of the new policy were seen when Captain Bruce
in H.M.S. *Cormorant* arrived at Gaeta to punish the murderer of
Bower. Bruce wasted little time in fruitless questioning. No worthwhile information regarding the identity of the murderers seemed
to be forthcoming so he published the following proclamation: "In
consequence of an English officer and boat-crew being murdered by
Florida men, the Queen of England declares war with the whole
tribes of Floridas, unless the actual murderers are given up within
fourteen days." Fortunately, it did not come to that because the
missionaries intervened and persuaded the islanders to hand over
four out of the guilty five—each of whom was now tried and sum-
marily executed. Vuria, the chief's son, was the one who escaped, of
course, but the visit of the *Cormorant* must have had some salutary
effect even on Kalekona because, after having teetered on the brink
for what had seemed to the missionaries an eternity, he then
announced his surrender to Christianity. It was a great breakthrough
for the Church, and was ultimately beneficial to the recruiters, as
the Church of England officially approved the labour trade, under
proper supervision, and sometimes even encouraged it.

In Australia meanwhile the news of Bower's death had aroused
much anger and indignation, followed by a more or less general
sense of satisfaction when it was known that it had been fittingly
avenged. The stern action by the *Cormorant*, said the newspapers,
marked the return to an older, more realistic approach towards dealing with savages. The recruiters, too, appreciated the change, noting
how much readier the islanders were to recruit after the Navy had
arrived to administer a sharp dose of shot and shell. It was remarkable, judging from the number of hurried evacuations, how many
villages adjacent to those actually shelled or burnt evidently had
good reason to fear similar punishment also.

But the planters, taking a longer view, were less sanguine about
it; they were not yet convinced that the islanders were beginning
really to learn the lesson. In February 1882 the *Janet Stewart* of
Maryborough anchored off Kwai islet, Malaita, in almost exactly
the same spot as the *Borealis* eighteen months before. Although the
population of the little islet was supposed to have been bombarded
and thoroughly intimidated by a warship in the meantime, the
natives of Kwai by exactly the same stratagem decoyed two boat-

crews to a spot five miles down the coast so that they could take the ship at their leisure. William Lockhead, the G.A., was lying back in a deck chair on the poop reading a book when a group of natives stole up behind him, tilted back his head and split his face apart with one blow of a tomahawk. Lockhead was a frightful mess when Captain Ludford Thomas and the two boat-crews returned and found him.

But they had no time to get more than a glimpse of the horribly mutilated body before a dense cloud of smoke rising out of the fo'c'sle revealed that the ship had been fired. They rushed for'ard, past dismembered limbs scattered about the deck or lying in the scuppers, to put the flames out. But these had already taken too firm a hold and very soon they were forced to abandon ship, leaving the bodies of the G.A. and the rest of their murdered shipmates to be cremated on board.

Thomas and his men were rescued by a trader and taken safely back to Queensland, but there was heavy irony in the sequel to the story of the *Janet Stewart*. Its owner had gone bankrupt in the course of the last fatal voyage, and the creditors, refusing to believe that Thomas could have been so utterly witless as to succumb to the same lure that had destroyed the *Borealis*, had him arrested on a charge of deliberately setting fire to his own ship. For they were persuaded that he had conspired with the owner to defraud them. They, of course, did not know just how wild that particular stretch of coast was. They did not know that the villagers of the adjacent mainland would even club together to contribute blood-money for the taking of the next European vessel to come along. The point was that people were ready to believe almost anything of those engaged in the recruiting business.

To a meeting of the Mackay Farmers and Planters Association it was quite obvious that the current state of the labour trade in 1882 was a disgrace. What was to be done about it? Three possibilities seemed to present themselves: to abandon the Kanaka and try again to get coolies from India under an officially sponsored Government immigration scheme; to import gangs of Chinese from Hong Kong on a contract basis despite the additional expense; to reform the existing recruiting system. By this time Mackay had become the richest sugar-growing district in the colony, potentially by far the most important, and the local planters were very much disposed to blame faults of the labour trade, e.g., the multitude of small owners, the leaky, worn-out vessels, the poor quality of the crews, on the fact that the labour trade was based on Maryborough. They believed that some of the larger, more influential shipping firms should be attracted into the trade, companies with a fleet of small steamers that could scour the weather side of islands and seek out all the undiscovered little pockets of population in places ordinarily inaccessible to sail. It seemed a good idea, but how were they to get these big companies interested?

The Maryborough planters had also been very concerned about the problem, but they attributed the present demoralized state of the islands to the unscrupulous activities of the Sydney ship-owners and trading skippers. These people recruited in the islands as well, it was pointed out. Anybody in New South Wales could get a licence to employ islanders as crew, and Sydney had over a hundred vessels in the South Seas compared with Maryborough's nine or ten. In 1880 Sydney vessels had exported to the islands 125,000 gallons of rum and 223 cases of fire-arms. However, Maryborough's planters were as much divided as those of Mackay about the solution of the problem. Coolies, they thought, might be an avenue worth trying, together with a more vigorous prosecution of island recruiting.

Nobody was really very keen on the idea of Indian coolies. The Government was supposed to be contemplating another Coolie Act and not getting much further with it because of the certain storm of opposition it would arouse. However, by mid-1882 the labour situation was already pretty serious; with the prospects for 1883 really alarming. In the past eighteen months, £500,000 had been invested in the Mackay district alone, apart from what the Colonial Sugar Refining Co. had spent on its large new mill at Homebush. There were now twenty-five mills in the area, and as yet nobody could say where the labour was coming from to keep them all in production. At Bundaberg great strides had been taken, and the great Millaquin Refinery was about to start work. Plans were afoot to utilize white labour. Impossible, said the older hands; to introduce European labour into the industry would require them to sell sugar at less than the cost of producing it. However, by now the asking price of Kanakas at Maryborough had risen to £22 a head, cash down with the order, so with the support of a number of fellow planters, Frederick Nott of Bundaberg negotiated to import five hundred labourers direct from Ceylon. They were to be paid £20 a year with rations, the terms to be five years.

It was an attractive proposition—to go to Ceylon for labour. The south Indian Tamils, introduced into Ceylon by special arrangement with Madras and employed by the tea planters, were reputed to make the most docile, most amenable labour force in the world. But the Tamils, it was then discovered, were not available for export to Australia—the British governors of India had no wish to see them treated in the same way as the Aboriginal or Kanaka. Nott had to be satisfied with local Cingalese and not plantation labourers at that,

Residence of the Reverend J. Geddie at Aneityum.

The Reverend J. Goldie with his henchmen, former headhunters of the
Rubiana Lagoon, New Georgia.

Recruited. On the way to
Queensland *c*. 1890.

Three members of a
boat-crew.

but blacksmiths, carpenters, cooks, barbers, house servants, some elderly, one "quite decrepit", all unemployed townsmen fleeing from a period of depression.

None the less there must have been some contrivers and artful dodgers among them, for by the time the transport *Devonshire* reached the Australian coast in mid-November there was a conspiracy to defeat their agreements. Most of them had already decided to repudiate their contracts, claimed one of the immigrants, believing that these could not be enforced at law. However, the first batch of 250 were landed at Mackay without undue incident, but were heard to express horror at their first sight of the Australian bush: surely they would not be expected to work in country like that. The planters put this reaction down mainly to the strangeness of new surroundings. For they now had much more serious problems on their hands.

Anti-coolie organizations had sprung into existence with astonishing speed wherever one looked. It needed only a rumour that coolies were on the way, it seemed, for a mob to forgather at every local School of Arts to listen to some inflammatory speech on the subject. Back in the 1860s when the first Kanakas were arriving in Brisbane, William Brookes had been astounded and disgusted by his failure to get any worthwhile response from the working-class at all. Now it was the planters' turn to be astounded by the sudden violence of working-class reaction. The difference in attitude can only be accounted for by the fact that in the intervening years tens of thousands of Chinese had come flocking into Queensland after gold. This had enabled working men to see with their own eyes exactly what the presence of a large coloured population in their midst was going to mean to him. From the note of fear in so many urgent, excited voices one might have thought that the *Devonshire* was some Russian freebooter.

Evidently, the coolie was seen to pose some sort of threat that the Kanaka did not. Speaker after speaker cited the case of Mauritius, where indentured Indian labour had been originally introduced in 1834 and was now so tenaciously dug in as to be beyond all hope of removal. Or he spoke of Natal, where once again the Indian was becoming entrenched, buying allotments, starting businesses, ousting the white man in every direction. Indian coolies were not like Kanakas, it was pointed out. They were British subjects with recognizable legal and constitutional rights that could not be trifled with.

The Anti-Coolie League was weak in Mackay, and resistance to the Cingalese invasion was negligible. But at Bundaberg the League was all ready for them. Fifty-strong, it set out for Burnett Heads

M

with the intention of loudly opposing any landing. However, the planters had anticipated them and were already aboard the *Devonshire* warning the Cingalese of what to expect when the fifty men were sighted marching resolutely in the direction of the landing-place. Clearly the planters had exaggerated the physical danger of their situation. For when the Leaguers were almost upon them and beginning to shout out abuse and wave their fists in what was never to be anything more than a rowdy demonstration, the Cingalese drew knives as though prepared to sell their lives dearly. The demonstrators were quite taken by surprise; they had not bargained on a fight. Finally, after much argument among themselves, under cover of taunts at the planting party on deck, they withdrew.

The "Battle of the Burnett", as it was derisively called, had thus ended in the rout of the Leaguers. But, though they had been defeated in the field, they had won a great propaganda victory. As the incident appeared in most of the newspaper reports, the planters had been caught red-handed in the act of smuggling coolies into the country. Granted a little time and freedom from outside interference, the planters might have talked the Cingalese round to honouring their contracts. As a matter of fact, by agreeing to one or two changes in the original terms and other minor concessions, they had already done so in many cases. But the newspapers refused to leave the topic alone during the next few crucial days, and the Cingalese, encouraged to believe that public opinion was on their side, nearly all absconded. Unwilling to put their contracts to the test in a court of law and risk further publicity, the planters let them go and they drifted round the countryside in search of other work. In fact they found it much harder to get jobs than they had expected, since few Queenslanders were willing to make themselves unpopular by employing them. They were eventually absorbed somewhere or other, and mostly remained in Australia, where large numbers of their descendants are still living today.

That episode closed another possible avenue, and the labour outlook for the future was not merely serious but desperate. In the middle of all the publicity over the Cingalese, the schooner *Roderick Dhu*, under the command of Captain Turner, had returned to Maryborough after one of the most harrowing recruiting voyages on record. It had begun with one of the returns going insane, running amok with a knife, and having to be shot dead by the G.A. The next incident occurred at Paama, where the schooner's boats were repeatedly fired upon as they tried to land a batch of returns. They managed finally to get them safely landed, only to learn, from a canoe that drifted out to the ship the next day with the grisly remains, that they had been eaten. Another Maryborough recruiter, the *Helena*, met with shortly afterwards, reported having the same experience with its returns at Epi. By this time both the passengers who still had to be landed, as well as the Kanaka boat-crews who had to row them ashore, were starting to feel jittery. So Captain Turner decided to avoid Epi, a prolific but highly dangerous source of recruits, and try Tongoa instead. Tongoa, where a Presbyterian missionary, the Reverend Oscar Michelsen, wielded great influence, was supposed to be quieter.

But there seemed just no way of escaping disaster on this particular trip. The Tongoans might have been quieter, but they were not less treacherous apparently. A group of them came aboard while the boats were away, ostensibly to recruit, but in fact to urge those already recruited to seize the ship. It was very risky to commit the vessel to the charge of a single European seaman like this, but the recruiters had no choice at this stage. All their resources were devoted to the actual impressment of recruits. In the event, and fortunately for the absent white men, the Tongoans failed to stir the recruited Kanakas to any real sense of unity, so when the boats returned, less than half the islanders were actually in possession of the ship. They seemed determined to repulse any attempt by Captain Turner to reboard his vessel, but the majority were mere spectators. The white men quickly proved too strong; killing three of the mutineers after a sharp exchange of shots, they suppressed the mutiny with little difficulty. According to the ship's log that marked the end of the *Roderick Dhu*'s misfortunes. Apart from some minor trouble with gearing, it reached Maryborough on 29th October with a full complement of 103 recruits—a remarkable achievement considering all the trials it had undergone.

That was not the end and it was not the truth. It may seem strange that the circumstance was not noted by the Immigration Agent upon arrival at Maryborough; only after the recruits had been assigned to their various plantations did it become known that the great bulk of recruits were in fact the very same returns with whom it had started out. Turner admitted this readily when taxed with the question, but claimed that he had gathered all the returns together at a certain stage, explained to them that he would not be able to visit any more islands because of a fault in the ship's gearing, and asked them if they would be willing to recruit for another term. They had agreed and he had then sailed for home. Right or not, it was too late to do much about it. Turner escaped with a reprimand. But the authorities were very annoyed: Lynn, the G.A., was arrested and brought up on a manslaughter charge for shooting down the armed madman.

Recruiting was hopeless on this sort of basis. But coolies were out of the question and imported Chinese would be prohibitively expensive (namely, £18 a year in wages plus an initial £19 per head importation expenses, the planters had discovered). What was the answer then? To many people in Mackay at the end of 1882 one answer at least was Separation and the formation of a new State of North Queensland that would at least understand the basic economic realities and sympathize with their plight. Mackay was different from Brisbane and the big cities in the south; here the slogan, "Australia for the White Man" and other political catch-cries made little impression on the average citizen who was too conscious of how much his job depended on the sugar industry and how much the sugar industry depended on black labour. It was sheer hypocrisy, the planters told one another angrily, to pretend that God in his Providence had given this fertile country to the white man while the squatters were still in the process of systematically exterminating the Aboriginal population. However, the separation movement had not gained much ground when the news reached Mackay early in 1883 that the Fijian recruiter, *Lord of the Isles*, had paid a visit to the large island of New Britain and got 178 recruits in a matter of days. The solution seemed to have dropped from the skies.

EIGHT

Blackbirding in New Guinea

LOOKING at the map and seeing how close Queensland is to the large land mass of New Guinea and its numerous archipelagoes, one might wonder why the recruiters had not thought of New Guinea before. But in fact it was neither as close nor as inviting as it looked. There were navigational hazards: the southern coast, for instance, is protected by innumerable reefs and sand-banks. It was relatively easy to proceed directly north to the Louisiade Archipelago, off the eastern tail of the island, but beyond, the Bismarck Archipelago is a region of strong currents, narrow island passages, and dangerous tide-rips. It was possible, for example, to sail north through St George's Channel separating New Britain from New Ireland but not always possible to get back owing to the powerful current setting to the north-west. In fact the occasional trader from Sydney or Melbourne with business at these islands in the season of the south-east trades would continue northwards to round New Hanover, then beat six hundred miles to windward and so return to Australia via the Solomons and New Hebrides.

Thus from the recruiter's point of view the outward journey was quite perilous, while the homeward journey, with supplies of food and water usually running low, was too long. As for the main island itself, it was believed to be fever-ridden, and the ordinary South Seas sailor deliberately avoided it, fearful of contamination by its supposedly deadly, seaward-blowing malarial breezes.

There was really little inducement to go there at all. The Papuans, as the inhabitants of these islands were called, were a step or two ahead of the Melanesians in their progress towards civilization, with homes built up on stilts, canoes with very elaborate sails, and so on. But judging from the number of attacks made on passing white men over the years, they were apparently no less treacherous.

New Guinea thus possessed all the drawbacks of the older recruiting grounds and none of the compensations. Yet two classes of recruiter had been active in the Bismarcks and Louisiades in the seventies—the bêche-de-mer fishermen based on Cooktown and Thursday Island, and the Germans or their agents, like the American, Proctor, from Samoa. These newcomers seemed to the British to be a thrustful, unpleasantly aggressive people, whose right to be in the Pacific at all seemed highly questionable indeed. And yet persistently they had been pushing westwards from Samoa, skirting the British sphere of influence in the Solomons, alighting finally upon New Britain. In this region they had established no fewer than twenty-one trading stations by 1880—tiny outposts in this region of smoking volcanoes, in the charge usually of a single white man or half-caste. Every so often a schooner came to pick up copra and carry off recruits for the vast German coconut plantations in Samoa.

It was only a minor traffic compared with the Queensland labour trade, but these German recruiters too had fallen foul of the local missionaries—Wesleyans in this case, and very tough opponents. The Reverend Benjamin Danks on Duke of York Island in St George's Channel accused the recruiters of poaching. Working from their headquarters at Matupi on New Britain, they would make no effort, he said, to seek out their own sources of supply along the adjacent, heavily populated yet virtually untouched foreshores of that island. Instead they approached the Wesleyan outstations on New Ireland where the people were by this time partly civilized and the recruiting felt to be slightly safer. Danks countered by encouraging his teachers to invent horrific tales of what happened to the unfortunate recruit in Samoa.

One can at least sympathize with the missionaries' point of view, for the patient labour of years might be destroyed in one single day's recruiting. They taught that the white man had no designs upon the black and had come only to help him. But the evidence seemed otherwise. Before the people's eyes the recruiters were luring away the young, grabbing the women as they wanted them, with death to anybody who got in their way. Danks soon found they simply would not trust him.

A chief on New Ireland, for example, might solemnly assure Danks that there would be no repetition of say, an attack on a British ship, and that they would henceforth listen to the missionaries as men of God. But they never meant what they said. Two years changed nothing. The more influential chiefs continued to assure the missionary of their support; the recruiters went on recruiting, very often enthusiastically assisted by Danks's native teachers; more white men were murdered. By November of 1882, when the first Fijian recruiters appeared in the Bismarcks, the Wesleyans had lost

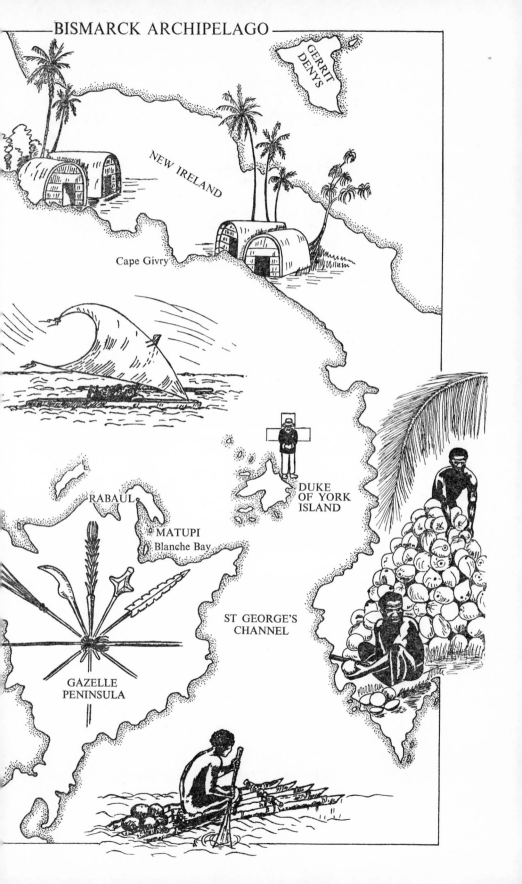

BISMARCK ARCHIPELAGO

GERRIT DENYS

NEW IRELAND

Cape Givry

RABAUL

MATUPI
Blanche Bay

DUKE
OF YORK
ISLAND

ST GEORGE'S
CHANNEL

GAZELLE
PENINSULA

eight native teachers in twelve months and were on the point of abandoning New Ireland altogether.

It was therefore hardly the right moment for the Queensland planters to approach the missionaries on the subject, but they were so excited at the news of the Fijians' success that they wrote immediately to every missionary organization in the New Guinea area, explaining their desperate need of labour, and seeking their co-operation. Benjamin Danks and Father Lannuzel of the nearby French Marist mission on New Britain both happened to be on furlough in Australia at the time. But replies were received from two members of the London Missionary Society, W. G. Lawes at Port Moresby and Samuel MacFarlane at Murray Island in Torres Strait, neither of them very favourable, though MacFarlane was inclined to be a little more sympathetic.

MacFarlane replied to the Wide Bay Farmers and Planters Association on 14th February 1883:

I have always maintained, I said so in Brisbane as long ago as 1863, that recruiting is to the benefit of planters and natives alike. But as to your immediate prospects in New Guinea, I fear the play will not be worth the candle. A vessel might sail along the New Guinea coastline for 1,000 miles without getting fifty volunteers. In the Papuan Gulf and along the banks of the Fly River there is a numerous population, but they are a wild and treacherous people. Those of the south-east peninsula are more tractable, but generally unwilling to leave home. Around the China Straits, however, where we have placed a few native evangelists, the natives have begun to manifest a disposition to see the white man's country. Some aboard bêche-de-mer vessels have visited Cooktown. Some from here might be induced to go and if treated kindly take a good report back to their friends. But I should not like to see the traffic carried on as it is in the South Seas. I cannot therefore advise you to risk any expenditure in attempting at present to get labour from New Guinea.

Andrew Goldie, the naturalist and explorer, another lonely white man in New Guinea at that time, said practically the same thing. He understood their problem, he told the planters, but "where should I be if anything went wrong. I have to live among them."

It seemed that the planters were as far from finding a solution as they had ever been. Repeating what he had already told the Mackay planters in private, Lawes, from Port Moresby, wrote a long letter to the weekly Queenslander. It was an appeal really addressed to the colony at large. "Please don't send any recruiting ships," he begged the colonists. "At the moment the natives are well disposed to the white man . . . and recruits can not be obtained except by the use of force and deceit." However, before this letter was actually published, another group of planters were already active. Forceful, enterprising new arrivals on the scene, they were less afraid of public opinion than the rather conservative planters' organizations of Maryborough and Mackay, and without waiting to knock, simply put their shoulders to the door and barged in. The way to New Guinea lay wide open.

In a few short years the sugar industry had emerged as the real growth sector in the Queensland economy. By 1880, capital was being attracted from Sydney and Melbourne and even from overseas. In its flamboyant way, big business ignored such minor considerations as the heavy initial costs, and the distance from established ports. It was concerned exclusively with the ultimate long-term prospects as evidenced by the rising world market. It had begun setting up operations in quite new parts of Queensland, in places like the Burdekin delta, where once only cattle had grazed; the lower Herbert, the south Johnstone River, and the Cairns-Mulgrave district where the country seemed to be nothing but jungle.

The Colonial Sugar Refining Co., for instance, was putting £200,000 into its great Victoria Mill near Ingham. This plant was supposed to have everything—electric light, automatic feeding into the rollers, conveyor belts, a weighbridge, and enormous Fowler steam ploughs for breaking up the virgin soil on the surrounding plantations. British shareholders invested another £200,000 in the Airdmillan Plantation on the Burdekin. They were taking a distinct risk in this region where the rainfall was lighter than in other places, but the company believed it would be able to solve the problem of water by pumping from the delta lagoons. This inspired others to follow its example. Neighbours of Airdmillan—Seaforth, Kalamia, and Pioneer—were also established in these years. Unlike Airdmillan, however, they were all privately owned though heavily indebted to a number of London and Scottish banks and mortgage companies.

North of Townsville it was mainly Melbourne money. On the Herbert a Victorian syndicate took over Gairloch and Bemersyde. The Melbourne Sugar Company opened up Hamleigh. Finally at Hambledon near Cairns, the biscuit manufacturers Swallow and Derham spent £180,000 on a vast estate of six thousand acres.

Naturally there was great local jealousy of these foreigners and many gleeful predictions that they would come a nasty crash. Some in fact did. But they had researched the ground pretty thoroughly and were unlikely to repeat the mistakes of the past. For one thing, they were determined to have as little as possible to do with the existing recruiting firms; instead they planned either to employ new firms or to charter their own vessels.

One big newcomer to the trade in 1881 was the Sydney and Townsville grocery, shipping, and general trading business of two Scotsmen, James Burns and Robert Philp. It was a good time to go recruiting: the demand for labour increasing by leaps and bounds and the partnership either owned or was able to lay its hands on a considerable fleet of elderly vessels suited to recruiting purposes. But success in business is not only a question of being in the right place at the right time, but also of putting these opportunities to an intelligent use. Thus Philp, the Townsville partner, would choose only the very best men.

One of his first skippers was the Swede Carl Satini. Satini in the *Ceara* pioneered the recruiting from the hitherto unexploited Aneityum, and created a Queensland labour trade record in 1882 by enlisting 438 recruits in the one season. He was, as we have seen, a crafty recruiter continually on the lookout for a new angle, so it was perhaps unfortunate for the partnership that he lasted so short a time as a Burns, Philp skipper. He was debarred from the trade after the Reverend Hugh Robertson had reported him for "stealing men" at Eromanga. But by this time Philp had discovered Joseph Vos, a young protégé of Satini's, destined in time to be as famous as his mentor.

Vos's first command came late in 1882 with the *Lizzie*, a large schooner converted into a barquentine to conform with the rig of other members of Philp's recruiting fleet. Philp made a point of keeping on excellent terms with the Immigration Office, and when the *Lizzie*'s G.A. left Brisbane to take up his appointment, he was warned by Sir Ralph Gore, the Chief Immigration Agent, to "see that you don't tread on the captain's toes too much". It turned out to be just as well for Vos that the agent had been so warned, for he got into a lot of trouble at Ambrym, where his recruiter, Peter Dowell, took a woman without paying for her, then took a man against his will, evidently with the intention of passing him off in Queensland as the woman's husband.

As a result of the ill-feeling created on this account, Captain Belbin of the *Borough Belle* was shot to death on Ambrym only a few weeks later. The Navy retaliated vigorously, and that was the end of Ambrym as a source of recruits for the time being. It was during this same voyage that Dowell managed to engage only one recruit after a full day's strenuous recruiting at Aneityum and was subsequently accused by the missionaries of kidnapping.

Unfortunately, while we do know something about the early voyages of these Burns, Philp recruiters, very little has come to light about the original recruiting voyage of the firm's later acquisition, the *Hopeful*. For it was the *Hopeful* that pioneered the route to

New Guinea and thus relieved the sugar industry at a point of acute shortage of labour. Exactly why the decision was made to send it to New Guinea, however, is a mystery. The owners themselves were so bent on keeping its destination a secret that they reported it clearing only for the South Seas generally.

We can only conjecture. We know that the *Lord of the Isles*, the Fijian recruiter whose phenomenal haul at New Britain had inspired all the recent interest in the New Guinea area, had been recruiting for the Colonial Sugar Refining Co.'s new Nausori Mill and surrounding plantations near Suva. Burns, Philp, we know, recruited for the C.S.R. in Queensland. Conceivably, then, Philp had heard through private sources that New Britain should not present too many recruiting problems despite the known obstacles, and that the Wesleyan mission authorities were in favour of the idea. Perhaps this would also explain why the general secretary of the Wesleyan Society had booked the return passage to New Britain for the Reverend Benjamin Danks and his wife in the *Hopeful* when nobody outside the initiated knew that the ship was bound for New Britain at all.

The Reverend Mr Danks sailing in a recruiter! Danks's views on the labour trade were simply that it was a creation of the devil. Surely he was not being asked to assist the recruiters in any way, guide them to the right spot, for instance, or use his influence with the natives to urge them to recruit. It's very strange indeed. None the less, Benjamin Danks and his wife and baby were the three passengers when the *Hopeful*, under Captain Briggs, sailed from Townsville on 7th February 1883, and very displeased he and his wife were about the accommodation provided for them.

The *Hopeful*, it seems, was another of Philp's bargains—an English schooner more or less abandoned in Townsville harbour at one stage after its owners had gone bankrupt. Danks complained that cockroaches and rats overran the whole ship; that for five weeks the three of them had to sleep on the floor of their unfurnished cabin with only a few trade blankets between them and the bare boards.

Danks, it should be remembered, was heavily prejudiced against the recruiters, so that the voyage may not have been so bad as he recorded it. But judging by extracts from his diary, it must have been pretty nasty just the same. On 14th February 1883, he writes, "Passed a wretched night. Tossed about most frightfully. Anchor chain got loose and broke away part of the foc's'le fittings. Bunks both wet. No sleep, miserable. . . . Cook seems to have an unlimited supply of rum. Intoxicated." 19th February: "A man fell overboard today. Threw him a lifebuoy. Immediately after his rescue a large shark appeared. The man was not thankful for his escape, but swore most horribly as soon as he reached the deck. Endured some fearful rolling today."

This clears up one point at least. If Captain Briggs had ever been counting on the missionaries' co-operation, he would surely never have subjected them to such treatment. Shortly before they reached Duke of York the Dankses were sitting alone in the saloon when a tremendous shock threw them to the deck. "Thinking she had struck a reef," said Danks, "I bounded up the companionway and there stood the captain in the midst of the men just as reckless as himself. He was laughing as over a good joke. He had deliberately attached a fuse to a piece of dynamite and dropped it among a school of fish right under the counter of the vessel where it exploded. I remonstrated with him but he simply laughed and uttered one of his favourite oaths."

A few days later they arrived safely at their missionary headquarters and thankfully bade the recruiters farewell—but not for very long. For the next three or four weeks the *Hopeful* just continued to cruise about, several times crossing over to New Ireland and back to Duke of York, evidently not meeting with much success in the vicinity of the mission outstations.

However, this was not the area where the Fijian *Lord of the Isles* had been so successful in the previous November. The Fijian had visited the northern end of New Ireland at a place called Neusa, where the German trading firm of Hernsheims had an outpost. Every so often when the Hernsheims schooner called at Neusa in the course of a round trip from Matupi there would be a great scramble by the local New Irelanders to take passages aboard. They were after tobacco mainly, and to earn this they would be happy enough to do odd jobs around the headquarters store at Matupi. Quite a few might also recruit from there for Samoa, but the majority would take the schooner back to Neusa at the end of three months. Not many were willing to leave home for periods of three years or more, as MacFarlane, the missionary at Murray Island, had warned the Queensland planters in his letter to them. But then along had come the wily recruiters from Fiji, and the New Irelanders' only thought was to see the world, not thinking to find out where they were going nor for how long.

Thus it was that the *Lord of the Isles* and three other Fijian recruiters could pick up 350 New Irelanders in no time, while the *Hopeful* cruising off southern New Ireland the following March got practically none. It is easy to see where the difference lay: the natives of the south were more worldly wise; the white man and his goods were no longer a novelty. And there was also a "coloured gentleman", a subsequent recruiter reported, "clad in a shirt and *sulu*, with a book in his hand . . . keeping abreast of the boats as they pulled along the beach. Every now and then, when any natives approached the water's edge and tried to communicate with us, he got in the way, and with a few words persuaded them to retire." Obviously he was one of Danks's Fijian or Samoan teachers religiously carrying out the missionary's instructions that none of the flock was to fraternize with the strange white men.

Nor is it difficult to believe, knowing their character, that the *Hopeful*'s crew would tolerate this sort of thing for very long. Soon they were grabbing the odd one or two wherever they could lay hands on them, grasping them by their woolly heads and pulling them into the boat. It was perhaps the first example, since the days of the *Carl* in 1871, of a Queensland recruiter wilfully and indiscriminately engaged in outright blackbirding.

Meanwhile, in Queensland, the secret about the *Hopeful*'s destination was out. It was hardly worth keeping any longer anyway. Father Lannuzel of the Marist mission in New Britain had stated quite openly to friends in Mackay, where he was then holidaying, that New Guinea would be an excellent place to recruit. Poor Lannuzel, the devoted, unworldly priest, could have had no idea what hope his innocent remark would inspire in the desperate planters. Messrs Rawson & Co. of Mackay, sugar planters turned private shipowners, and recently the purchasers of the brigantine *Fanny*, hastened to offer him a passage back to New Britain. The *Stanley*, of Maryborough, and the *Jessie Kelly*, chartered from Fiji by Bundaberg interests, were in the process of fitting out for the same place.

How touching it seems, how remarkable, really, that the little priest should have been so wrapped in his life's work as to have spent all those years in New Britain and remained in complete ignorance of what had been going on almost under his nose. But then he was better placed for this than the Wesleyans only twenty miles away on Duke of York. For at Nodup, near Matupi, he had been living quietly under the protection of Hernsheims, sheltered from the inroads of the German recruiters, and not even aware that Hernsheims themselves acted as recruiting agents for Samoa. Otherwise he could scarcely have spoken so indiscreetly and thus tempted the Australians to blunder into a domain which Germany was coming to regard as exclusively its own.

The Germans in fact had great plans for the region. At Mioko, a little island just south of Duke of York, the great new South Seas company, the Deutsche Handels und Plantagen Gesellschaft (known to most Britishers simply as the "Long-Handled Firm") was seeking to establish a central labour depot to serve the needs of its very many trading stations and plantations from Tonga in the south to distant Micronesia in the north-west. It had also proposed to its home Government that Mioko be a coaling station for the Navy, a base from which warships would patrol the northern coast of New Guinea, the Bismarcks, the Louisiades; in fact wherever it and other German commercial firms were in the process of setting up factories and stations.

These plans were still only on paper, however. Bismarck, the Chancellor, had given no definite promise of support. The Reichstag was plainly indifferent. Such was the position when William Wawn, commanding the *Fanny*, dropped anchor off Matupi on 14th April 1883. Father Lannuzel went off by canoe to his little native hut at Nodup and Wawn dropped in to see Edward Hernsheim at the store. He had always got on well with these German traders in the past and was therefore amazed when Hernsheim told him that it would be a waste of time recruiting in the New Britain area; that the natives were so prejudiced against recruiters that they were likely to kill him if he ventured to mention the subject.

Wawn naturally could not understand why Lannuzel should have so misled him. Puzzled and hurt, he returned to the ship wondering if the missionaries on Duke of York would prove more friendly. The Dankses did not prove to be, of course, and after a further few days frittered away to no purpose, dogged by the same frustrating experiences that had finally driven the *Hopeful* recruiters to open kidnapping, Wawn set a course northward for the west coast of New Ireland.

He had no particular objective in mind, except to get as far away from the missionaries as possible. He was drifting along a lee shore before a light south-easter, not realizing he was on the brink of discovering one of the richest single sources in recruiting history. The Cape Givry–Cape Strauch strip of coastline was located just beyond the range of the Wesleyan sphere of activities in the south and just beyond the main shipping routes used by the German traders and recruiters. Its inhabitants were like spectators who have caught the merest glimpse of the treat in store for them and are feverishly waiting for the curtain to be pulled completely aside so that they might be aware of all the wonders of the white man's world and thus on a par with everyone else. When the *Fanny* put in at a little bay, the majority of the people had scarcely even sighted a European vessel before. The scene is described by Wawn thus:

The boats were fairly rushed by men eager to get away, who tumbled in without waiting to be asked and fought and struggled with such of their friends as strove to detain them. Many who were afraid they might miss the opportunity paddled off to the ship in small canoes or on bamboo catamarans. Several swam off with the aid of dry logs of wood . . . all round the ship at least 50 canoes, carrying over 100 men, were paddling about, chasing or being chased. There was an uproar of shouting and laughing with prodigious splashing. Every now and then some young fellow who had been cut off from the ship by his friends would take a header. Diving down under the other canoes, he would not come up until close alongside when he would seize a rope conveniently hanging and so speedily clamber on deck. There was no waiting for "pay", nor yet for any agreement with regard to the term of service in Queensland or the remuneration at the end of it. All they wanted was to get away.

Wawn had to call it off by 3 p.m. on the third day, 28th April, by which time he had reached his licensed quota of 143.

The *Jessie Kelly* did almost as well. Operating in the same vicinity as the *Fanny*, it obtained 120 recruits in the same astonishingly quick time and was actually back in Queensland two weeks before her rival. Wawn had been delayed on the return journey after an encounter with the natives of New Britain in which he and his G.A. had been seriously wounded. Then came the *Stanley* of Maryborough and finally the *Lord of the Isles*, that large, handsome, three-masted schooner which the C.S.R. had swiftly transferred from the Fijian operation to supply the more urgent needs of its Victoria Mill and plantations on the Herbert.

Counting the *Hopeful*'s 102, obtained mainly by kidnapping, these five vessels recruited 528 labourers in the space of a month. This was in sharp contrast to the business currently being done on the Solomons and Hebrides recruiting-grounds. The next labour vessel to reach Queensland after the *Hopeful*'s return was the *Madeleine*, five months out of Brisbane in the old recruiting grounds for a grand total of 34! The ship had got one recruit at Epi, two at Ambrym, one at Malekula, none at Santo, one at Pentecost, three at Oba, two at Paama, and so on.

The effect of the successful New Guinea recruiting was already becoming apparent in the shipping trade generally. The Swedish barquentine *Fredericka Wilhelmina* arrived in Brisbane from Adelaide at the beginning of July, and its owner, genial, portly Captain Augustus Routch, immediately switched to recruiting. This vessel was easily the most splendid the trade had yet seen: 212 tons and licensed to carry 193, it had a splendidly spacious state-room for the Government Agent, as well as comfortable 'tween-deck accommodation for the recruits. By the time the *Fredericka Wilhelmina* arrived the cream had been skimmed from the shores of New Britain and New Ireland, but it was ideally placed to participate in the latest recruiting rush to several small groups of islands to the north and east of New Ireland—Fisher Island, Gerrit Denys, Abgarris, the Kaan Islands, and Sir Charles Hardy Island.

The statistics show how well business was picking up. In 1880, twelve Queensland recruiters made twenty-two voyages for a total of 1,995 recruits; in 1881, fourteen vessels travelled thirty-one times to the islands for 2,643; in 1882 there were eighteen ships, thirty-four voyages and 3,139 recruits. Then came 1883—twenty-six ships, fifty-eight voyages, 5,273 recruits, including 1,400 from the New Guinea region by only ten vessels in little over half the season.

It was noticeable also how this new spirit of optimism was giving an impetus to recruiting even in old directions. The *Emily*, for instance, visited the Santa Cruz Islands, where hardly any recruiter had been since the death of Bishop Patteson in 1871, and brought away 88. The *Emily* returned on its next voyage and got another 36. Even more daring, the *Alfred Vittery* of Maryborough, after a protracted, unprofitable tour of the main Solomons group, touched gingerly at the notorious head-hunting centres of Treasury and Vella Lavella and carried off 47 headhunters as to a tea party. Two other recruiters during 1883 successfully visited formidable Buka and Bougainville, the two islands associated in men's minds with the evil memory of the *Carl*.

But the most remarkable voyage of all was that of the *Stanley*. By a coincidence it happened to arrive at the Laughlan Islands to the south-east of the Bismarcks, where Hernsheims had recently established one of their more distant outposts, on the same day as William Wawn was having his most unsatisfactory interview with Edward Hernsheim at the firm's headquarters at Matupi. The Laughlans, a cluster of small coral islands, are not really very far from Matupi, though they belong geographically and linguistically to the Trobriands group. To Captain Joseph Davies of the *Stanley* and his masterful, military-looking Government Agent, William McMurdo, it must have seemed quite outrageous that Germany should be represented in the region at all—particularly when Hernsheims' agent appeared, a dirty, unkempt little man whom the natives called Charley and who lived with a native wife.

The fact was, however, that Hernsheims' schooner was several months overdue, and Charley, whose real name was Carl Tetzlaff, was not nearly so disreputable as he looked, merely suffering from a shortage of European food and clothes. Davies, however, chose to treat him as a beachcomber, pretending not to understand when Tetzlaff explained these circumstances and offered to exchange the captain a certain amount of copra in return for some provisions. "Don't talk Kanaka English to me," Davies snarled at him. "And get off my ship." Nevertheless the German contrived to linger on board for a while longer, and the crew, feeling sorry for him and

Samuel Griffith.

William Brookes.

A planter's home in the Bundaberg district.

The kind of communal dwelling-house plantation labourers in Queensland liked to build for themselves.

hoping that he might provide them with an introduction to some native women, invited him into the foc's'le for a proper meal.

In the meantime the G.A. had gone recruiting ashore. This was Davies's first experience of an agent like McMurdo, but so far he had had no trouble in adjusting himself to the situation. He understood that McMurdo was not a man to be baulked. From his cabin the Englishman would send him little formal notes addressed to "Mr J. Davies, master of the *Stanley*", informing him of their next port of call, the day they should expect to arrive, and so on. McMurdo, by taking over the recruiting in person, was helping to turn it into a more efficient operation.

Davies *en route* to New Britain had thus been instructed to call at the little-known Laughlans, where no white trader, apart from the occasional bêche-de-mer fisher, had ever been before, and McMurdo had gone ashore to open negotiations with King Tomuin. So far he had not deigned to acknowledge that any white man lived on the island at all. The interview with Tomuin was a great success; it was conducted in English, which Tomuin had learnt sketchily from his contact with the bêche-de-mer hunters. Twelve men were recruited in exchange for the usual variety of trade goods. They went aboard and were then allowed to go ashore again on condition they would return when required.

The exact terms of the engagements, however, were not fully understood, it seems, for when Tetzlaff heard of it and challenged Tomuin on the subject, he was told the recruits were going for the usual time, two months. They are not, Tetzlaff replied hotly, they're going for three years.

McMurdo reacted with characteristic choler. It did not matter, in his view, where they were. A gentleman's word was his bond anywhere. An agreement remained an agreement whether inscribed on parchment or concluded merely in the handshake of a naked savage. So when Tomuin eventually came aboard, protesting that three years (thirty-nine moons) was too long and that he had not understood the terms, McMurdo was obliged to be stern, to lecture the dismayed chief on the meaning of a contract. It usually happened like this. Sooner or later he would become so impatient with the "whining" ways of the islanders that he would lose control altogether. So, when the relatives of the twelve "recruits" arrived, seeking to return the presents previously handed over in exchange for their kinsmen, he refused to receive the visitors on deck and had them thrown into the hold and the hatches clamped down. They escaped in the night, however, and now the mood was truly upon him.

Next day fourteen or fifteen large canoes from the Woodlarks

N

arrived with yams to trade with the Laughlaners. But when they saw the shore strangely quiet and the big ship in the bay, a few of the braver ones came over to take a closer look at the white men. The visitors knew enough about the white men to be wary of them, but they had the confidence of numbers. There was not the slightest sign of actual danger until suddenly the whites made a rush and for a few seconds there was confusion on all sides—black men flying over the rails, diving into the hold, and one or two going for their lives up the mainmast. Eight were caught in the end and locked up in a cabin.

It was the crew's first experience of kidnapping and they were plainly unhappy about it, even though McMurdo had several times assured them that he would take full responsibility. The reaction of Davies, the skipper, was curious: the more he began to have doubts about these proceedings the more inclined he became to put the entire blame on the unfortunate German ashore. "If I catch hold of that white man, I'll leave him within an inch of his life," the crew heard him rage. "I'll flog him. I'll tie him with sand and coal tar."

Action was needed; something more stirring than chasing a few niggers who would not fight. And McMurdo made no effort to restrain Davies as he began to hand out Sniders, ordering all hands into the boats. They were going after Tetzlaff.

"I'm not going to stop you," the agent called out to him as they were rowed ashore. "Just remember, however, that this is a German copra station and this is your business which I as Government Agent do not enter into." Davies had no intention of being stopped by anyone. As they approached, Tetzlaff fired a single shot from a pocket pistol and then ran into the bush. The Laughlaners briefly debated whether they should stand and fight, and being overruled by Tomuin, fled with Tetzlaff.

There was virtually no opposition. The German's house stood defenceless—an ample structure built of logs and coconut-leaf thatch, surrounded by a native compound and various huts and outhouses. These held sixty tons of copra and several bags of pearl-shell, tortoise-shell, and a little bêche-de-mer. Davies strode from one to the other, putting each to the torch. Some copra was left unburned at the end, which they took back to the ship with them.

It is important to recognize that whereas the captain's quarrel was exclusively with the white man, McMurdo's was with the islanders. At sundown that same evening the agent went ashore again, arm-in-arm this time with one of his eight captives, and had a message sent to Tomuin: if the original twelve recruits were not aboard by sun-rise the following morning, the eight hostages would be hanged from the foreyard arm. Whether he would actually have hanged them is impossible to say. The twelve recruits duly failed to turn up, but in the meantime the hostages had managed to escape from the afterhold to which they had been transferred from the cabin.

Now it was McMurdo's turn to go on the rampage. They went off in the boats the next morning, heading for Tomuin's own island of Oberlark. It was laid waste—huts, coconut-trees, banana plantations, canoes. Then followed Fapetub, Washin, and Boodelun, where Gerrans, the second mate, also smashed up the canoes that the Woodlark Islanders had come over in—pointless to show mercy while the enemy remains obdurate; one cannot do business with a people who do not respect you. They had been warned what would happen; they had ignored that warning and they had now to be punished.

The following day, in perfect confidence that the islanders had thoroughly learned their lesson by this time and that all resistance would be at an end, McMurdo was rowed ashore, in a boat flying a white flag, to deliver his terms. A message went off to Tomuin that he had arrived and for some minutes he walked up and down the beach, his impressive military appearance accentuated by a slightly halting, stiff-legged gait—one solitary Englishman on a remote island, waiting to receive the savages' surrender. In time the dozen islanders arrived, urged by the terrified Tomuin. The little episode was over. The *Stanley* resumed its voyage to New Britain.

McMurdo was a man of unusual calibre, destined, one would have thought, for better things than the Queensland labour trade. However he would soon have the opportunity to demonstrate his real worth. But meanwhile at Matupi he made a point of contacting Hernsheim, to explain that a slight difference had arisen between Captain Davies and the German agent in the Laughlans, in the course of which a certain amount of German property had been damaged. He assured Hernsheim that Captain Davies would recoup the company for any losses it may have sustained. He intended to see to the matter personally.

After this the *Stanley* sailed for New Ireland, sighted the *Fanny* on its way south, and immediately their luck began to change. After their experiences in the Laughlans it was hard to believe, but the natives seemed to be completely without suspicion, cheerfully nodding at whatever the obviously incompetent interpreter was trying to explain to them and behaving as if the white men had come to bear them away to some charmed country beyond the seas. A week later, with a near-capacity cargo of ninety-one, the *Stanley* set sail for Queensland *via* the Solomon Islands, where McMurdo intended to buy yams and fill up their fresh-water tanks. Davies was prepared to have taken the risk of their supplies lasting until they reached

Queensland, but in the event they were able to get what they wanted at San Cristobal. They headed for home in high spirits.

On 30th June the weather turned foul, with heavy rain and an almost gale-force wind from the south-east. The next day it was worse, the wind developing into a regular gale that late in the afternoon in a driving downpour suddenly blew out the square-sail. The *Stanley* was already far off course, sweeping now towards disaster.

On 1st July McMurdo wrote in the log:

At a quarter to seven when sail was being taken in and the captain was going to wear ship, breakers by captain only were seen ahead; the helm was ordered to be put hard-up, but before it was hardly done she struck the reef; the yards were immediately thrown aback, though without effect, for the sea threw her up at each wave; the shocks were terrific, and the vessel rolled in a fearful manner; indeed, three rolls were so great that had the waves not been so great and caught her just in time, she would never have recovered and all would have been over; the booms were without guys and making great havoc; the after-hatch and a water-tank on deck were smashed adrift.

I was just making my way back from the braces and escaped being crushed by them; the confusion was dreadful; the recruits were swarming the decks and rigging, and to my unutterable horror some five or six jumped over on the weather side; I called to them to come back, to stop, and pulled all back that I could get at and so stopped more from going; none of them understood English; the poor fellows in the water were easily seen although the night was dark, as the white foam showed them up; they were trying to regain the vessel; each wave dashed them under the vessel's quarter out of my sight, and even now cannot understand how they came off clear; ultimately I got them to catch a rope and hauled in two and got the mate to help me with a third; others were so saved by their mates who followed my action.

The men were utterly exhausted; I imagined that night that many were lost; the vessel by this time was fully up on the reef, and receiving the full force of the waves on her port side, she laying on her starboard; every one was aft, white and black, and all asking me (calling from their different places) what was to be done; I was against the boats, but asked the captain, who also said "No", but I could not succeed in getting any suggestion from him; I proposed to cut away the masts and make a raft, but he said, "Not until morning".

I asked the men (who were about me) if they could work at a raft in the wash, and as they could not I abandoned all attempts at anything and awaited our fate; about this time, some twenty minutes or less after she struck, we discovered that the port boat was smashed and that the Laughlan men had lowered the other (we only carried two for 116 souls) and were making off; I threatened to shoot them if they did not return, and so, after a few minutes' yelling I succeeded in inducing them to return; the boat was half-full of water, and was being washed about dangerously; I threw a bucket to the men who got into her and suggested they should take her clear from the ship's side in case yards or masts fell; captain at first objected, but ultimately agreed, but the men could not succeed in reaching it although they were only knee deep; the boat was kept alongside all night in the wash.

At daybreak they were able to calculate their position—aground on Indispensable Reefs, more than a hundred miles from the nearest known land, with not a rock or foot of dry reef visible in any direction. The wind, however, had moderated, the ship was filling only very slowly, and there was apparently a lot of shallow water between it and the edge of the reef.

The next few days were spent building a raft and repairing the port boat, and in due course McMurdo had worked out how, in his view, they were going to be saved. All the whites with the exception of himself, the chief mate, and the cook would proceed to San Cristobal by boat to fetch help, while the other three remained behind with the recruits to supervise completion of a raft large enough to hold everybody.

It took a good deal of tact and persuasion to satisfy ninety fearful Kanakas that it was better for the white sailors to go first. But the boat party got safely away and McMurdo had a chance to tell them his plan. What he had in mind was something along the lines of the artificial islands of Malaita. Unfortunately there were no Malaitamen present to show them exactly how it was done; but he had given them the idea and it only needed one determined individual in authority to see that it was carried out.

To begin with, they were divided into gangs, working under a number of "boss-boys". One gang with knives and tomahawks waded out along the reef at a low tide to hew blocks out of the coral, constructing with them a kind of breakwater against the prevailing seas. Another gang laboured to raise a platform on top of the sunken coral to serve as the floor of a series of small cabins. The *Stanley*'s water-tanks were the cabins, rather dank and musty, perhaps, but absolutely weather-proof. Meanwhile yet a third group had been put to finishing the raft. This was now moored to the reef and rendered thoroughly watertight, ready in the last resort to provide them with a means of escape.

It was really a remarkable achievement, given that when they started a high tide had covered the reef completely. It was still cold, and at times the spray shooting over the breakwater beat down on them as they worked and bit into their bones like a rain of little soft bullets. Morale would suddenly falter and McMurdo and the mate would strap on their pistols and stride among them, kicking the sullen ones back to their tasks. He was like any plantation overseer, never certain whether they were sick or shamming sick, and always needing to drive them a little longer without being able to explain properly what he was doing since there was no common language. He was ill himself at one stage, but could not show it for fear of what would happen if he betrayed the slightest sign of weakness. In the end, after seven weeks, a trader rescued them in a cutter.

Surely if there was such a thing as compassion in the world, a means by which a man might be restored to grace, he had suffered for his misdeeds and made amends. It was a good omen, perhaps, that although thirteen of the islanders had already died of their sufferings or would eventually fail to recover, all the twelve Laughlaners managed to survive. But this was a matter which the gods would have to decide. On a more mundane level it was politics that would determine McMurdo's fate. For what the recruiters had done in the Laughlans, although sooner or later inevitable, was to involve the two nations, England and Germany, in a direct confrontation in New Guinea.

On 3rd April 1883, while the *Stanley* was still *en voyage* to the Laughlans and before the *Hopeful* had properly embarked upon its career of kidnapping, Queensland attempted to annex New Guinea. It seemed an outrageous thing; almost ludicrous in its presumption, this action by some publicly unknown official, a mere magistrate, turning up at Port Moresby in a tiny police cutter, hoisting the flag, taking formal possession in the name of the Queen. It was also beyond the colony's constitutional powers.

Yet not very long before, in the late seventies, there had been a section of the British Conservative Government urging the Queenslanders to do something like this. Sir Arthur Kennedy, the Governor at that time, said that the Colonial Office had hinted to him that if Queensland were to go ahead and annex, it might force the Imperial Government's hand. In the light of the expansionist movements of some of the world's major powers—for example, Russia in Manchuria, and France in Madagascar—the fears of Queenslanders for their exposed and vulnerable underpopulated north were not altogether unjustified.

To the north of them was the eastern half of the great island of New Guinea. In its present state, occupied only by savages, it stood as a potential menace to the colony's safety. It was unthinkable that it should fall into the hands of any foreign power; that eventually it could ever be anything else but British. Yet successive Queensland governments, weighing the possible advantages against the costs, had been reluctant to take decisive action in the matter.

In the eighties the issue became much sharper. While Queens-landers, alarmed at France's designs on the New Hebrides, were urgently demanding that Britain do something, Gladstone was playing his hand more coolly, affecting to make gentle mock of their fears. It appears that a large new company, the Compagnie Caledonienne des Nouvelles-Hébrides, founded by a very masterful New Caledonian businessman, John Higginson, had been busily engaged buying up large portions of Malekula and Santo and other islands. And Higginson was known to be closely associated with the French Administration in New Caledonia and strongly suspected of acting on confidential information that France intended to annex the New Hebrides.

It was obvious: there were already 22,000 French convicts in New Caledonia, as well as 4,000 soldiers, and great debates were taking place in the French Press and Parliament about the propriety of ridding the country of its recidivist (habitual criminal) population altogether and sending it out to some remote part of the Pacific. Putting two and two together, Queenslanders had decided that this latest wave of convicts, possibly 10,000 in all, was about to descend on the New Hebrides.

Then, quite suddenly, the French "menace" was completely for-gotten and Germany emerged as the real enemy. Early in 1883 an article that had appeared originally in an obscure German news-paper, the Augsburg *Allgemeine Zeitung*, fourteen months before was reprinted in translation in newspapers throughout Australia. The article said in part:

If we fix our eyes upon this large island according to its physical geo-graphy and possible developing characteristics only from the standpoint of the colonial politician and cultivator, it appears to us . . . not in the least a contemptible object of possession. And in case the German Government make attempts, as many wish, to acquire the island we might, perhaps, in the interests of the nation, congratulate ourselves on the acquisition. According to our opinion it might be possible to create out of this island a German Java, a great trade and plantation colony which would form a stately foundation stone for a German colonial kingdom of the future.

German colonization! Even New South Wales, least of all the Australian colonies inclined to disturb the *status quo* in the South Seas, thought something should be done. And something was being done. Thomas McIlwraith, Premier of Queensland in 1883, was a big, bluff Scot who would prove in this emergency to be the ideal man for the occasion.

He was not only Premier, wrote an unkind Englishman of the time, "he is the entire Government, and a pushing tradesman to

boot, to say nothing of his being a Scotchman endowed with all the
vulgar forces of the Glasgow school . . . how very objectionable it is
to have for Premier one who does a roaring trade in shipping, steel
rails, and general merchandise, besides having an interest in the
printing line and not above doing a stroke of business in land".

But the fact that he was a successful businessman with substantial
private interests to safeguard surely did not establish his unfitness
to handle the affairs of the colony at large. Perhaps the contrary. On
26th February he drew up a long memorandum for the Governor,
setting out half a dozen important reasons why New Guinea should
be immediately annexed on behalf of Great Britain. He was prepared to concede that Queensland now agreed to defray the costs
of governing the area. At the same time he wired his Agent-General
in London to press for annexation at the earliest possible moment.
Then, after waiting for three more weeks and receiving no reply, he
wired Henry Chester, the police magistrate at Thursday Island, to
proceed urgently to New Guinea to take possession.

It was immediately assumed by all those hostile to the Government
—that dubious alliance of squatters and planters—that New Guinea
was being acquired for the sake of its swarming multitudes—cheap
labour for their canefields and outback station properties. And undoubtedly there were reasonable grounds for such an assumption,
if for no other reason than the number of labour vessels that had
cleared for New Guinea waters since the annexation had been
announced. Even more sinister was the circumstance that at least
three vessels—the *Hopeful, Fanny*, and *Stanley*—had departed before
the announcement, that is, in the period when the plot had presumably been developing.

Had the owners of the *Hopeful*, for instance, been less secretive
about the vessel's destination, and had Thomas McIlwraith not
happened to be an influential partner in the North Australian
Pastoral Co., the situation would not have looked half so furtive and
underhand. For this company was in the middle of buying up
various large cattle holdings and subdividing them into estates
suitable for growing cane. As it was, it appeared like a deal between
the Premier, Burns, Philp, and the large overseas interests apparently
bent on acquiring most of north Queensland.

Yet, despite all that was rumoured in Brisbane at the time, it is
unlikely seen from this distance of time. There were too many
conflicting interests involved; the situation in the Pacific was too
complicated for one to presuppose a conspiracy. In the first place it
was unclear for some time what extent of territory Chester had
actually laid claim to. Was "all that portion of New Guinea and the
islands and islets adjacent thereto, lying between the 141st and 155th

meridians of longitude" intended to include the Bismarcks? Nobody seemed to be sure. And would it be more advantageous, from the recruiting point of view, if they were? If, as appeared likely, Great Britain were to take charge of the territory itself and run it as a Crown Colony, there was a distinct possibility of a total ban being placed on the export of labour to Queensland. The Indian Government was even now planning to do this with regard to its coolies.

To the older generation of planters, the established communities of Mackay, Maryborough, and the Moreton Bay district, the idea that they had been contemplating some gigantic coup with respect to New Guinea was quite fantastic. In fact so sensitive were they about public opinion, and so nervous about further antagonizing the electorate with general elections in the offing at the end of the year, that they were still grimly working on the details of one far-fetched recruiting scheme after another—Chinese, Japanese, Javanese, Maltese—right up to the moment when the *Hopeful* arrived back in Townsville with its cargo of strange-looking Kanakas and immediately turned all minds towards New Guinea. Fortunately, it was not yet known that they had been kidnapped.

But the monstrous rumours continued to grow, and at the end of June, when the British Cabinet could no longer defer a decision about New Guinea, it was this belief that the colony only wanted the additional territory to secure its labour supply that caused the Imperial Government to repudiate Queensland's action altogether. Moreover, the British Cabinet was not yet convinced that Germany had serious intentions in New Guinea, nor prepared, on behalf of Great Britain, to undertake the expense of acquiring more, simply for the sake of keeping a watchful eye on the Queensland labour trade.

Recruiting was meanwhile still continuing at a merry pace in the New Britain–New Ireland region. Nothing quite like it had been seen since Ross Lewin and his band of cutthroats had cleaned up the coasts of Tanna and Epi in the sixties.

It is interesting therefore, in the face of this onslaught, to see how the German recruiters were faring. Judging from a report which the German consul at Samoa forwarded to Berlin about that time they were not faring very well. British policy, he began rather dramatically, aimed at monopolizing the entire trade of the South Seas with the ultimate object of proclaiming wholesale annexations. Subsequently, on 9th September 1883, Baron Plessen of the German Embassy in London sent a Note to Lord Granville, British Secretary of State for Foreign Affairs. In it he itemized the various "abuses and excesses committed by English labour recruiting expeditions to the grave detriment of the hitherto good relations subsisting between

German traders and natives of these localities [New Britain and New Ireland]".

There was, first, the case of the *Hopeful*, which had been openly kidnapping; secondly, of the *Fanny*, which had contrived to set two rival villages at loggerheads and thus provoked a general war in which the mission of Father Lannuzel had been destroyed and the two white men belonging to the recruiter, the captain and Government Agent, badly hurt. Finally there was the *Stanley* at the Laughlans, where German property had been wilfully plundered, German lives threatened, for absolutely no reason at all. The note concluded by calling for co-ordinated efforts by Britain and Germany to "prevent any transaction at the limit which divides the lawful trade in Polynesian labour from slave trading".

Officially the Queensland Government knew nothing of the German protest before receiving a copy of this Note from London in March 1884. In fact it knew the whole story of the Laughlan affair by the previous September. Tetzlaff's long-awaited schooner having finally arrived and borne the much-injured agent back to Matupi, Hernsheim immediately laid his agent's complaints before a British deputy-commissioner of the Western Pacific, whose report on the matter was read by McIlwraith in Brisbane only six weeks later. The Premier immediately recommended that McMurdo be dismissed, his extraordinary heroism in saving the lives of the ninety-one recruits marooned on the reef notwithstanding.

No more than a hint of the affray at the Laughlans, however, had leaked out to the general public. Neither the Government nor the labour trade seemed in any way compromised. Yet the feeling remained that the recruiters had been trespassing on forbidden territory; that steps should be taken before something disastrous occurred. But it was not to be left to McIlwraith to decide what steps, for at that point his Government was decisively defeated at the November elections. A Liberal administration took office in its place, and the planters and shipowners quickly received a foretaste of what they could expect from the incoming premier, Samuel Griffith. The entire New Britain–New Ireland recruiting field, they learned unofficially, was henceforth to be considered out of bounds. Likewise the New Guinea mainland. At the same time new regulations were published forbidding labour vessels to carry fire-arms either for trade or for their own use in recruiting. This edict appeared so preposterous to the recruiters that they took it to be just the usual administration window-dressing, not realizing at this stage how serious the change of Government was going to be for them.

Nothing, it was noted, had been said about the Louisiade Archipelago, the D'Entrecasteaux Group, the Trobriands, and all the little islets and coral atolls stretching away to the south-east of New Guinea, many of them so small and off the beaten track as to be unmarked on the Admiralty charts. Presumably the Government had never even considered the possibility of recruiters being attracted to such a region. For navigation within the barrier reef enclosing the Louisiades and other similarly dangerous localities was so intricate that European vessels would ordinarily seek to anchor before nightfall.

This then was Philp's opportunity to pull off another of his small master-strokes. He now secured the services of William Wawn, formerly of the *Fanny*, who was just out of hospital after his recruiting accident at New Britain and thus temporarily without a ship. An outstanding navigator with an especial knowledge of the New Guinea area where he had once lived as a trader, Wawn was appointed to command the *Lizzie* and given the task of opening up the Louisiades. He replaced young Joseph Vos, who was transferred to the *Hopeful*. Wawn would thus blaze the trail in one direction, to be followed up by Captain William Inman in the *Ceara*, while the other two Burns, Philp recruiters, the *Heath* and *Hopeful*, would return to the recruiting grounds north of New Ireland, Gerrit Denys and the Kaan Islands, which Inman had so successfully exploited during his last voyage in the *Ceara*.

It was immediately obvious why Vos had been so anxious to give up the *Lizzie*. It was "the worst old ballahoe for sailing", says Wawn, "that I ever put my foot aboard of. On a wind she was nowhere, especially with a strong sea when she would pitch up into the wind and then tumble off two or three points, enough to drive the helmsman mad." Hardly the ideal type for the Louisiades. However, the work began quite promisingly in this entirely new field, Wawn proceeding cautiously from atoll to atoll, steadily filling the ship with recruits as he went. They were certainly not impressive in physique—not to be compared with the sturdy inhabitants of the Solomons and New Hebrides—and they suffered also from some sort of skin complaint. But it was now January 1884, and the planters could not afford to be choosy.

At Teste Island, the recruiters met a rather remarkable individual, a Captain Nicholas Minister, who was introduced to them as being in the bêche-de-mer business. He was also known as Nicholas the Greek and Monsieur Ministere of France. He was actually an Austrian and a fascinating character of many depths and many disguises, hard as flint to look at, but a fluent diplomat who managed to remain on good terms simultaneously with the missionaries at Port Moresby, the German trading companies, and the Queensland authorities at Cooktown where he traded his bêche-de-mer.

Many stories were current about Nicholas; that he robbed the caches of fellow traders; drove his native divers relentlessly; had built up a huge personal fortune by sheer roguery. But one which the Navy could vouch for with embarrassment concerned a man-o'-war which was sent to interview him. Believing Minister's headquarters to be on Joannet Island, the captain had called first at Redlich Atoll to inquire the way. Minister had nicely anticipated them, and met the naval party himself on the beach there. He listened politely to their story without in any way disclosing his identity. He could not believe his old friend, Nicholas, capable of behaving harshly towards his Kanakas, he told the lieutenant at last. However, they would *all* go and find him and see for themselves. From the Redlichs, then, he proceeded to guide them through a maze of channels until the young lieutenant was completely lost off the north side of Joannet. At this point their guide disappeared quietly ashore and left them to their own devices. It took the sailors more than a week to extricate themselves.

Alas for honest William Wawn—completely unsuspicious, with no conception of what a slippery, treacherous little man he had to deal with. When his visitor came aboard smiling to dine in the captain's cabin, he assured Wawn that if it was labour he was looking for, he could expect his warmest co-operation and support. What were Wawn's plans? Of course he achieved exactly what he wanted, namely, to find out which islands Wawn intended to visit so that he could be there first to give the inhabitants warning.

It proved not so easy to thwart the recruiters as Minister had hoped. Admittedly, at several places the islanders refused to go near the ship's boats, while quite a few of those already recruited escaped again when the vessel chanced to call at their island a second time. But Wawn was a bold and skilful navigator as well as a great explorer of uncharted islands and little-known passages. Very delicately he threaded a path between innumerable reefs, managing to reach many out-of-the-way places where the Austrian had not thought to forestall him. In the event, then, it only took longer than it might otherwise have done, had Minister not gone in front to spread the word that a tribe of white head-hunters was on the warpath. Even so, at the end of only five weeks 126 had been recruited and Wawn decided to press his luck no further and head for home.

Meanwhile the *Ceara* had done even better. Unknown to Minister until too late, it had arrived at the eastern end of the Louisiades ten days after the *Lizzie*, spent less than three weeks recruiting 107, mainly from the two large islands of Sudest and Rossel, and got back to Townsville three days before the *Lizzie*. The passage of thirty-eight days out and home established a record for the Queens-

land labour trade. It was never to be equalled or even approached—
except by the *Ceara* itself returning to the Louisiades on the next
voyage.

How was it managed in the face of the missionaries' confident
predictions that recruiting New Guineans for periods of longer than
a few months would be impossible? It seems that the recruiting was
done exclusively by mission natives belonging to the London
Missionary Society outstations whom the recruiters would employ
ostensibly as interpreters, but in fact as artful fishers of men. "You
come and look out bêche-de-mer?" the "interpreter" would ask. Or,
"You go work on ship. Sail about. See white man's island?"

And the islanders would answer "I think you gammon us".

"I no gammon. I missionary boy."

"Orright."

A knife or tomahawk or some beads were then handed to the
recruit's friends and he climbed into the boat, content that he was
in good hands. It would have needed a recruiter of stern principle to
intervene at this stage to point out that the contract was for thirty-
nine moons.

So the partnership of Burns and Philp which had lately been
transformed into a limited company (incorporated April 1883) was
doing rather well out of its recruiting sideline. Two voyages by the
Ceara, one by the *Lizzie*, one by the *Hopeful*, all in the first four
months of 1884, netted a total of 501 recruits. At an average selling
price of £23 a head, this amounted to a gross profit of more than
£11,500. In addition the *Heath* was still out, so also the *Lizzie* which
had had to put into land somewhere near Cairns to repair a leak
(Wawn had just discovered that cockroaches had eaten a hole clean
through the white pine casing of the outer hull in the region of the
rudder).

It was not surprising then that the partners were in an aggressive
mood, even casting a speculative eye at the Australian Steam
Navigation Co., their principal shipping rival, reputed to be in a
shakier condition than its monopoly of the north Queensland coastal
traffic would imply. However, for the time being the firm was to
have its hands full with the affairs of the *Heath*.

It is not remarkable, given the very odd collection of people
employed as Government Agents from time to time, that A. J.
Duffield should be the G.A. attached to the *Heath*. He was a
peregrinating Englishman with rather eccentric ideas, who just
happened to be passing through Brisbane at a time when a great
debate was going on in the Press about the ethics of the labour
trade. He was inquisitive enough to want to find out something
about it for himself at first hand. In much the same fashion two

years before, a young man destined to be famous as "Chinese" Morrison had taken passage aboard the recruiter *Lavinia* masquerading as an ordinary seaman, for the specific purpose of writing on the labour trade for the Melbourne *Leader*. But whereas Morrison had been prepared to keep an open mind about his subject, Duffield went determined to denounce it.

He had travelled recently through South America and had at first been fascinated, then dismayed, and later plunged into a state of sickened revulsion at the corruption of this "new" world, by the spectacle of this decaying legacy of Catholic Spain, by the "tinsel crosses and plaster images, objects of veneration that were only the sweepings of any junk-shop in Seville, all passed on to the wretched Indians by the local parish priest as the price of remission of last week's sins".

Later, *en route* across the Pacific, observing the flag of England waving rather absurdly, he thought, over some distant clump of coconut-palms, he had been struck by further horrible doubts. This great thing, Imperial Trade, he had pondered. Lofty abstraction. Life-blood of the nation, and so on. What was it in reality? Had not the British themselves warred against China, not many decades past, to force the Chinese authorities to agree to the wholesale importation of cheap opium from British India? Surely, like the wealth of Spain, it was nothing more than a "traffic passing through gorgeous toll-bars kept by painted beadles in the pay of secular potentates". Thus obsessed by the notion of the rottenness beneath the outward show, seeking everywhere the evidence of the sordid trafficking by which men grow rich and holy, he had arrived in Brisbane and met Samuel Griffith.

It was a genuine meeting of minds: the shrewd lawyer-politician with literary tastes, secretly at work on his translation of Dante, and the wealthy amateur, the disillusioned world traveller who happened to have published a translation of Cervantes. Presumably they were also at one on the subject of recruiting, for it was Griffith who procured Duffield's appointment as Government Agent, thus provoking questions in the House whether this man, Duffield, was not being sent out to the South Seas expressly to expose the labour trade.

The planters would have been even more suspicious had they known that almost his first act upon going aboard the *Heath* was to measure the vessel. Its true carrying capacity, Duffield noted with great satisfaction, was nowhere near the licensed 156, but more like about 80. However, he kept his calculations to himself for the time being, thinking it would be more effective to compile a long list of further irregularities as they occurred and then to present it to the shocked owners at the end of the trip.

However, nothing further of a seriously irregular nature came to Duffield's notice. The *Heath*'s skipper, a peppery little man who swore frightful oaths and evidently suffered from an internal disorder, had nevertheless very strict ideas on the matter of kidnapping and also kept his men under an iron discipline. Apart from this, the *Heath* was recruiting just to the north of New Ireland where the islanders were still well disposed towards the recruiters. It would have been plainly stupid to have used violence. Fearlessly the islanders scrambled aboard to buy tobacco, fish-hooks, glass beads, handkerchiefs, jews' harps, sometimes leaving behind a boy or girl of about fifteen or sixteen.

Duffield set himself to working out the approximate cash value of such transactions. The wholesale price of ten thousand Birmingham moulded glass beads, he surmised, would be somewhere in the region of 2s. 3d. Thus a single recruit or a canoe full of yams might cost the recruiter 6d. The largest amount he saw paid for a recruit, two pipes, three fish-hooks and several figs of tobacco, he calculated at 7s. 5d. Striking an average then, allowing for insurance of the vessel, depreciation, fees to the Government, etc., the total costs per recruit might be about £8 per head. A largish vessel like the *Heath* would be able to get in three trips a season. And this should return its owners an annual net profit of over £6,000. Not bad, Duffield thought, considering the *Heath* had cost only £1,500.

This was *not* allowing, however, for prying interlopers like Duffield himself or a Government of southern politicians, seemingly determined to reduce ship-owners and planters and the whole sugar industry to utter ruin. The *Heath* had managed to secure only eighty-seven recruits after four months—poor going indeed compared with what the *Lizzie* and *Ceara* had been achieving in the Louisiades. The sole reason for this pitiful performance, raged Captain Samuel Finlay, was the Government's ridiculous ban on the sale of fire-arms to the islanders.

But the worst was not known until the *Heath* arrived back at Townsville on 27th May, and Duffield reported to the local Immigration Agent that every one of the eighty-seven had been illegally recruited. They had been induced to sign or put their marks to a form of agreement, he claimed, without the slightest attempt being made to tell them what they were signing and for how long they would be required to serve.

The recruiting trade was convinced that Griffith and Duffield had concocted it between them. They pointed out that the agent had made no attempt to warn Finlay at the time, and had not even accompanied the boats to supervise any of the actual recruiting. He had not dared, Duffield replied, to trust himself to Finlay's ruffianly boat-crews after the skipper had been constantly ridiculing and belittling him in front of the men since the voyage began. A Government Agent, he claimed, was completely at the captain's mercy the moment the vessel was out of Queensland waters.

Duffield's charges, repeated at a public meeting and again subsequently in a pamphlet circulated throughout Australia, had turned the voyage of the *Heath* into an open scandal. This was not at all what Griffith had really intended in appointing the Englishman as his confidential source of genuine information about the labour trade. It meant now that a magisterial inquiry had to be held at Mackay, in the course of which, naturally, further scandalous happenings came to light. It became known that the man who had originally measured the *Heath* was not a qualified shipwright surveyor but merely the Townsville harbour pilot. He had calculated the vessel to have accommodation for 156 recruits, but now, on being remeasured, it was found to have a licensed capacity of no more than 108. The recruits themselves also had been re-examined and, again on a more searching assessment, a bare twenty per cent were judged either old enough or strong enough for plantation labour.

The only possible conclusion for the two magistrates to arrive at was that the entire shipload should be immediately returned to the islands, with Burns, Philp to receive a modest compensation for their trouble. But Duffield did not escape severe censure either: his failure to carry out his prescribed duties caused the two magistrates strongly to recommend that he never again be employed by the Government in any capacity whatsoever.

It was evidently difficult for Griffith's enemies to understand that he was not trying to destroy the labour trade at this stage, but merely to make it more respectable, to remove the suspicion that the responsible authorities more or less condoned all the notorious illegalities associated with it. For example, in April 1884, the law eventually caught up with Davies and McMurdo of the *Stanley* and they were brought up before the Brisbane police-court on charges of kidnapping at the Laughlan Islands. Griffith had shrewdly intervened, assisted by his Chief Justice, to have the offenders extradited and the case heard by the High Commissioner's Court at Fiji instead. Thus the colony was spared the spectacle of a jury listening solemnly to a long recital of recruiting misdeeds, only to come to the conclusion that the accused had acted in self-defence.

Then, no sooner had he managed to get this tricky affair out of the way, than he had been confronted first with the case of the

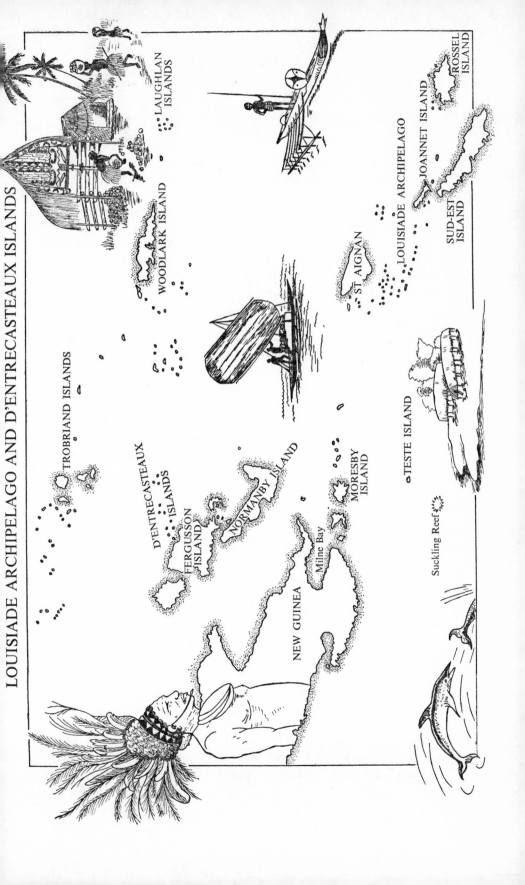

LOUISIADE ARCHIPELAGO AND D'ENTRECASTEAUX ISLANDS

LAUGHLAN ISLANDS

WOODLARK ISLAND

ROSSEL ISLAND

JOANNET ISLAND

LOUISIADE ARCHIPELAGO

SUD-EST ISLAND

ST AIGNAN

TROBRIAND ISLANDS

D'ENTRECASTEAUX ISLANDS

FERGUSSON ISLAND

NORMANBY ISLAND

TESTE ISLAND

MORESBY ISLAND

Milne Bay

NEW GUINEA

Suckling Reef

Heath, then with those of the *Lizzie* and *Ceara*, accused by the L.M.S. missionaries at Port Moresby of having virtually depopulated a large section of the Louisiades.

Nicholas Minister was this time the mischief-maker. After failing to prevent the recruiters ravaging his domains at will, pirating over two hundred islanders in one sweep and then immediately returning for more, he had gone to Cooktown to lay charges of kidnapping against the two skippers. As he had no real evidence on which to base the charges, the authorities were unimpressed, so he passed the information on to a newspaper reporter. The result was that a rather saucy little paragraph appeared in the gossip columns of the Queensland *Figaro*: "Where in thunder, you will ask, did the *Ceara* go to obtain over 100 Kanakas and back to Townsville in 38 days. Well, dear boy, I don't mind telling you. The recruits were got from the south-east corner of New Guinea. Houp-la."

It was cunningly misleading, this wicked little innuendo: that the Griffith Government which had come to power with the promise of taking action against the labour trade was in fact secretly abetting it. The records reveal that the Government was quite embarrassed by the suggestion.

That was on 23rd February. A few days later Minister sailed for Port Moresby to lay the story before the missionaries, to whom perhaps he should have gone in the first place. For where questions of right and wrong were concerned, what the missionaries had to say in those days carried no little weight. Thus, when the Reverend James Chalmers of L.M.S. wrote a strong letter of protest to the Brisbane *Courier*, it seemed to be only a matter of time before the Government on this occasion actually did something about it. Concurrently with the inquiry at Mackay into the affairs of the *Heath*, the police magistrate at Townsville was instructed to investigate allegations that two more Burns, Philp vessels, the *Lizzie* and *Ceara*, had been illegally recruiting in the Louisiades. The firm's troubles had all come at once, it seemed.

Ironically, more than fourteen months earlier, in April 1883, James Burns in Sydney had written to Philp in Townsville: "I think we should retract back into bona fide business but no doubt the labour traffic is a temptation, though very risky." In October he had written again: "I don't think we should go further into the nigger business. It would be better if we could sell or charter vessels to others for that purpose." By the following June they were still in it, with the *Lizzie-Ceara* inquiry now on, and Burns was again insisting that they withdraw. "It [the labour trade] is not worth troubling ourselves about" he complained on 4th July, "just for the sake of making a little more money." But the time had passed when they could retire gracefully. On 3rd May the *Hopeful* had sailed for New Guinea, and no power on earth could retract what had already been done.

For its fourth voyage in the labour trade, the *Hopeful* was commanded by Captain Louis Shaw, who had previously been mate in the *Ceara*. Thomas Freeman, the chief mate, was also new, but Neil McNeil, the second mate and recruiter, was the same second mate and recruiter who had started the kidnapping at New Britain on the *Hopeful*'s first voyage. As for Harry Scholfield, the G.A., he was simply a hopeless drunkard.

Kidnapping, like drink and other bad habits, is too easy to acquire and too hard to break off, and once having lapsed, one is all to liable to lapse again. Originally at New Britain McNeil had been tempted to snatch islanders by force because the Germans and the missionaries between them had made it almost impossible to obtain recruits by any other means. The situation was something the same when the *Hopeful* arrived off the eastern tip of New Guinea, the region where William Wawn, on his second voyage in the *Lizzie* only five weeks before, had eventually given it up as pointless and returned to Townsville with only sixty-seven recruits.

At Moresby, Basilisk, and Hayter Islands, north to Normanby and Fergusson, east to the Woodlarks, and finally south again to St Aignan and the Louisiades proper, Minister and his agents had covered the ground pretty thoroughly by this time. Thus, wherever the vessel stood-to to anchor, a watch was posted ashore. And when the ship's boats started around the coast, canoes were seen to precede them and the beaches and villages would be invariably deserted. The result was that only two recruits were shipped at Moresby Island; two or three at Basilisk; none after crossing over to Milne Bay on the mainland. Finally McNeil tried cunning; with judicious gifts and flattery he managed to seduce from their allegiance two Loyalty Island native teachers, Diene and Eponisa, attached to the London Missionary Society. With the aid of these two, then, recruits began to offer freely, being told only that they were going to the white man's country for two moons. Finally, with a tally of forty or more, they parted from the teachers and headed over towards Normanby. But with them they took one, Cago, an English-speaking New Guinean who was to prove invaluable. If he got "plenty boys", Shaw had promised him, he would be given "anything belonging white man down at Townsville".

The rest of the voyage proved to be nothing but a long record of kidnapping and enticement, as the following excerpts from a subsequent Royal Commission of inquiry into the *Hopeful*'s proceedings will show:

About the 24th Wararai was visited, and here numerous canoes came out to the ship, and thirty recruits were taken on board. Some declared that they wished to buy tobacco, and that in stretching up the side of the ship from their canoes to obtain the tobacco in exchange for their fruits, they were dragged on board by McNeil against their will, and told they were going to work for two or three moons. . . . The *Hopeful* then stood over to Fergusson Island, or Hilliwow. Several canoes came out to trade with the ship. Two boats were lowered. In the first was McNeil (coxswain), Preston, Harry, Jack, and Alec; and in the second, Barney Williams at the helm, Rogers, Charley, and two Teste Island boys. When the boats were lowered the canoes were turned shorewards, upon which chase was given, McNeil directing his attention to one containing eight natives, and Williams to another with six or seven in it. McNeil was unable to overtake that which he was pursuing, and he stood up in his boat and fired at the canoe. The native who was steering was struck at the back of the neck; the bullet came out at his throat, and, striking the man next to him on the right shoulder, the latter fell overboard and sank. The steersman fell in the canoe, dead. All the other occupants of the canoe leapt into the water, the canoe was overtaken, caught hold of by Jack and cut with a tomahawk by McNeil, who then directed his crew to pick up the natives who were swimming about in the water. Four were so rescued, and, to prevent escape, placed beneath the thwarts of the boat, while two were believed to have reached the shore by swimming.

In the meantime Williams had been encouraging his crew to pull smartly so as to catch up with the canoe containing the six or seven natives. The latter made for a reef which had only a foot or two of water on it, but before reaching it the canoe was cut by Williams, and the natives, as usual, took to the sea. A rifle was fired and one islander shot; five and a small boy were picked up by the boat. One of the rescued islanders jumped overboard from the boat, whereupon Williams followed him with a large knife in his hand. As the islander was coming up on the reef Williams cut the poor wretch's throat, and he sank into deep water. The boat was then pulled up to the reef, from which Williams leapt into it. The two boats then joined company, and the little boy, being of no use as a recruit, was cast adrift on two coconuts, which were tied together and placed under his arms. The little fellow was seen to slip from the coconuts and was drowned in the surf. The canoe cut by McNeil had not sunk. It contained the body of the steersman. Williams cut the head off, and the mutilated remains were thrown overboard.

There were now four natives in each boat, placed under the thwarts to prevent escape, and in this fashion they were brought to the *Hopeful*, from which the shots fired had been heard and the smoke of the rifles seen. Williams, it was also observed, changed his trousers as soon as he came on board, and hung those he had taken off in the rigging. As the *Hopeful* was bearing away from Hilliwow a woman in a canoe paddled out to the ship and cried after it, but no heed was given to her. The eight natives thus "recruited" were not permitted to go on deck for two days.

Though a digression, it may here be stated that when brought to Queensland and sent to Victoria plantation on the Herbert River, they effected their escape, wandered about in the bush for two months, made their way northwards, and were at last found at the mouth of the Johnstone River, whence they were reconveyed to Ingham. . . .

On 2nd July near Teste Island, the *Hopeful* was boarded by officers of H.M.S. *Swinger*, who overhauled both logs, the G.A.'s and the captain's, and found all correct. On 17th July the *Hopeful* reached Queensland with 123 recruits, 28 having dived overboard and escaped in the course of the journey home. Even more curiously, Captain Pennefather, Polynesian Inspector for the Herbert and Johnstone River districts, noticed nothing amiss either, though he examined them at some length. But Mr E. Cowley, the C.S.R.'s manager at Victoria, certainly did, absolutely refusing at first to have anything to do with such a sickly, intimidated-looking group. He then reported the matter to Sydney, and before long the cat was out of the bag.

But it was not the *Hopeful*'s exploits that precipitated Germany's move to annex New Guinea so much as those of the *Stanley* some time before. On 2nd August, the Berlin Foreign Office conveyed a note to the British Foreign Secretary, referring to various points of difference between England and Germany in the Pacific, placing at the top of the list, "the unsatisfactory state of negotiations about compensation for the depredations against German property committed by Queensland labour trade vessels".

Basically, it was not the labour trade that had caused Germany to become so agitated so much as the fear of Perfidious Albion's long-term intentions, and the current activities of its colonies. In the event, it was virtually the end of New Guinea as a recruiting-ground, for on 19th August 1884, the German consul-general in Sydney received a telegram from Berlin: INFORM IMPERIAL COMMISSIONER VON OERTZEN IN NEW BRITAIN IT IS INTENDED TO HOIST THE GERMAN FLAG IN THE ARCHIPELAGO OF NEW BRITAIN AND ALONG THAT PART OF THE NORTH-EAST COAST OF NEW GUINEA WHICH LIES OUTSIDE THE SPHERE OF INTEREST OF HOLLAND AND ENGLAND. In the face of this, Britain virtually had to follow suit and proclaim a protectorate over the southern coast.

And what of the man most responsible for these sudden developments, William McMurdo? On 6th August, he and Davies were tried before the High Commissioner's Court at Suva as engineered by Griffith, found guilty of kidnapping and sentenced to three months' imprisonment. They were released after only one week by order of the High Commissioner, Sir William Des Voeux, Arthur Gordon's recent successor. McMurdo was afterwards publicly congratulated by the Commissioner for his energy in saving the islanders wrecked on the reef and presented with a large subscription. So the case of William McMurdo had been weighed in the scales of justice, and he was reckoned to have paid his debt for what had happened at the Laughlans after all. Nor was it the end of his career in the Queensland labour trade. He managed to rejoin the Immigration Department after a long interval and actually died in that employment on 4th July 1903.

NINE

The Reaction in Queensland

UNFAIR or not to Queensland, the impression created in Fiji by the McMurdo case was that the Queensland labour trade was a vile traffic which one upright Englishman had been striving to clean up almost single-handed. Indeed, to read McMurdo's G.A. journals with their recurring references to the agent's dramatic intervention on the side of islanders illegally recruited, one might easily imagine McMurdo as a kind of Saint George against the Dragon Queensland. Governor Des Voeux, as a matter of fact, was so moved by these stirring narratives, that he wrote to London deploring the attitude of the Queensland Government in deliberately shutting its eyes to abuses that people had been pointing to for years.

It was unfair then. It was sheer prejudice. But such sentiments were all too common abroad. For instance in May–June 1883, when the question was whether Britain should support the colony's annexation of New Guinea, the colonists had been very hurt and genuinely amazed by the nasty things said about them in the British Press. "A nation of slaveholders", they were described in *The Times*, "a blot on the Empire".

It needed someone like bluff Sir Thomas McIlwraith, who had been knighted in 1882, to say "bosh" to these opinions, which he did with all his usual fervour and forthrightness. But then in November 1883 he was succeeded as Premier by Samuel Griffith, the lawyer. And Griffith was neither so intolerant by nature nor so single-minded in outlook that he was not capable of seeing the other side of the argument.

All round, in fact, his intellect was markedly superior to Sir Thomas's, possibly to any other in Queensland, and it is no disparagement of the man to say that he knew this and thought himself best qualified to lead the colony in consequence. For he was one who regarded the great public issues with the utmost seriousness, who liked to ponder them in solitude and eventually to arrive, carefully, logically, precisely at the correct solution. Having thus decided what was in the best interests of the colony, it was then merely a question of persuading his fellow colonists to see it in the same light. And in this respect he was unbeatable. As a presenter of cases he was quite tireless, and it frequently happened, after he had put the argument for his client or introduced a bill into Parliament and was quietly gathering up his notes and preparing to resume his seat, that there seemed for the moment no possible rejoinder. It was no wonder that his party tended to hero-worship him, and that those who disagreed with him would loathe him passionately for being so unshakeable in his convictions, so certain that he was in the right.

In fact, he was not so infallible, as we shall see. But about the sugar industry he was unquestionably right. He saw, when he really began to apply his mind to the subject in the early eighties, that the plantation system with its dependence upon imported Kanaka labour would simply have to learn to live without its Kanakas or be replaced by a better system. The two races were like milk and vinegar; they would not mix. Even in the islands it was not possible for the recruiters to have even casual acquaintance with the inhabitants without a series of bloody clashes that had blackened the fair name of Queensland throughout the civilized world. To compel them to live permanently side by side with white Queenslanders was plainly to create a state of permanent tension that would eventually make the task of governing them wellnigh impossible.

There had been no sign that the Government of Thomas McIlwraith was ever going to recognize this. In 1880, for instance, a new Pacific Island Labourers' Bill had been introduced into Parliament, mainly in consequence of the rather alarming mortality of Kanakas on the Maryborough plantations of Messrs Tooth & Cran and Robert Cran & Co. Two doctors, John Thomson and C. J. Hill-Wray, had been sent by the Government to make a report following complaints by the local Inspector of Polynesians. And the state of affairs they discovered, while not particularly surprising by the standards of plantation life all over the world, was still sufficiently serious to call for fresh legislation on the subject.

All the plantations, in terms of scrupulous concern for their employees' needs, were bad, they reported. But the really large plantations were the worst. Where the contact between employer and employee was minimal, the manager was under strict instructions, in the name of maximum efficiency, to be as economical as possible with his operating costs. Most of the deaths on the plantations owned by the Crans could be traced to this determination of the management to save money. Thus, on Yarra Yarra and Irrawarra, the two big out-plantations of Yengarie, the amount of bread provided was in accord with the prescribed ration, except that it was not really bread at all but "irregular lumps of dough partially baked". Neither could the tea properly be called tea, being only two and a half handfuls to fifteen gallons of water—not exactly a sustaining brew for men who performed ten to twelve hours manual labour a day, six days a week.

These hours that they were obliged to work raised another point. They were too long; particularly when some of the labourers were only boys of fifteen or sixteen. On plantations like Yarra Yarra the labourers were distributed too thinly to the acre, and one man or boy was expected to do the work of one and a half men elsewhere. There were 750 acres under cultivation at Yarra Yarra with fewer than a hundred field-hands employed, compared with an average ratio for the area of four acres per man. Here they were simply overworked, and when an epidemic struck and the weaker ones succumbed there was usually no doctor to see them, no hospital for them to go to—nothing but a strong dose of castor oil to be administered, less as a cure than as a stern reminder of what would happen if they permitted themselves to fall sick again.

Dysentery was the great killer on all the plantations, caused largely by the islanders' drinking habits. In the fields they would throw themselves on the ground to quench their thirst from the nearest puddle or water-hole just as they did in the islands. Unfortunately the plantation waterholes, unlike those on the islands, were fed by surface drainage from fields often covered in manure. The only way of overcoming this problem was to send water-carts into the field with them. But water-carts were a distraction, many employers felt, tending to divert labour from the more essential tasks, and most plantations had dispensed with them.

Again, the islanders preferred to live in grass huts of their own manufacture instead of the plantation's neat little weatherboard huts with iron roofs that provided the simplest means of collecting water. At Yengarie and Irrawarra the water-supply came from a stagnant water-hole with a greasy-looking surface. Samples of it were put under a microscope by the investigator and found to be teeming with bacteria. In 1879 the mortality rate of the Kanaka population in the Maryborough district was 74 per thousand compared with 107 per thousand on the three plantations of Robert Cran & Co., Yengarie, Yarra Yarra, and Irrawarra. It was 180 per thousand among the new arrivals—startling figures for a community composed largely of young males between the ages of fourteen and thirty-five. "Poor feeding, bad water, over-work and the absence of proper care when sick" were the causes, Thomson and Wray reported. Quite a scandal in Maryborough was provoked by their revelations.

But it was too simple to blame only the planters. There were Tannese on the Cran plantations, easily distinguishable from the other islanders because they were taller, blacker, stronger-looking, who did not seem to suffer nearly to the same extent though they lived under exactly the same conditions. Evidently they had the constitution to withstand the severe diarrhoea that attacked all newcomers to the plantations. But then it was hard to imagine the Tannese putting up with conditions not to their liking. In fact, how a Kanaka lived was in good measure up to the individual. On Magnolia plantation, for instance, all hands suffered severely from the cold on winter nights and there was also an unusually high incidence of consumption on the plantation. But as they were allowed to visit Maryborough for week-ends where they traded all their blankets for drink, this was not surprising.

The new Act, while it increased the plantation ration allowance, limited the age of recruits, and required employers and recruiters to provide proper medical supplies, and so on, did not really affect conditions on the plantations or labour vessels, since it could not ensure responsible behaviour among the Kanakas. But then as the Postmaster-General explained when introducing the Bill into the Upper House, the legislation had been made necessary primarily because the Imperial Government was worried about certain aspects of the labour trade. The Thomson-Wray report was another reason, naturally, but he did not want the opinions of honourable Members to be unduly swayed by a couple of doctors, because medical men were frequently wrong.

Thus the legislators aimed at clearing up some of the obvious abuses, giving their legislation a progressive up-to-date look, embodying the latest humane ideas, without at any time imposing any impossible burdens on the employing class. All it amounted to, argued Griffith, leader of the Opposition, was a slight scratching of the surface. Take, for example, Clause 7 of the Bill which proposed that licences to import islanders be restricted exclusively to those engaged in tropical or semi-tropical agriculture, such as sugar-growing, cotton, coffee, and so on. A very necessary measure all would agree, long overdue. But it hardly went to the root of the problem. It did not prevent employers engaging any who had completed their three-year contracts, the time-expired islanders who now constituted more than a quarter of the total Kanaka population. Of course not; it would have created hardship for the pastoral element, who found the acclimatized Kanaka very useful in droving and various types of contract work.

But the whole point about this class of labour, one of the reasons why such a clause had been inserted in the bill, was that the Kanaka was not always engaged in employment but preferred to drift round the countryside or congregate in the large towns "making the week-end hideous with his drunken orgies", as the Member for Mary-borough complained.

To have included all Kanakas within the scope of the bill, to have made it illegal for any to be employed in towns at all, as Griffith now moved in amendment, would have been a step towards curing the nuisance. However the amendment was defeated, the Government disingenuously claiming that it would be an unwarrantable interference with the right of a free man to seek work where he chose.

It was an interesting point: evidently Griffith had recognized by this time that what the anti-Kanaka party chiefly objected to in the Kanaka was not the threat to the working-man's job, but the spectacle of him, dressed up in livery driving his master's coach or trundling the baby along some fashionable thoroughfare, serving behind the counter, behaving for all the world as if he were part of the place. At sawing, splitting, fencing, bullock-driving, and so on, in the manly environment of the outback, the white man would work cheerfully beside him and not really resent the colour of his skin. But in the towns, in the closely settled districts, it was a different matter. Here his allegedly loose ways of living were a perpetual source of embarrassment, a contamination from which the working-man would have to break away permanently if he were ever to bring up his kids decently, achieve some sort of dignity in the world. Griffith, alone of all the politicians, seemed to understand this.

The working-class vote had become very important to the Liberal Party. Once it had been predominantly middle-class in outlook, drawing its support chiefly from the ranks of business and pro-fessional people, tradespeople, smallholders—all in fact who went in fear of the power of the squatter or planter. But a party in the course of time can come to mean different things to different people, and to the Working Men's League and kindred organizations it was now first and foremost the party of anti-Kanaka. With this thought largely in mind, Griffith invited William Brookes to stand for Parliament again. It was for North Brisbane in the by-election of 1881 in the Liberal interest, and he handsomely defeated John Sinclair, an ironfounder and former Lord Mayor of Brisbane. "You have administered a powerful vermifuge to the army of adventurers, carpetbaggers, and parasites who have made this colony a favoured financial resort," Brookes told the electors.

With rhetoric such as this, by constantly harping on his favourite theme, Brookes was to prove a useful tool and ally in the campaign against the squatters, even if he was hardly Griffith's kind of politician. It was not within Griffith's conception of responsible leadership to desire to see the whole sugar industry ruined for the sake of getting rid of the Kanaka, as Brookes claimed *he* did. But then Griffith lacked the other's capacity to feel passionately about some particular topic, the same impulse to tear down, to destroy the thing he hated. He would seek instead the constructive approach, intent on steering a passage around the impediment and avoiding any head-on collision, as a lawyer will bend his mind to working out a settlement acceptable to both parties. If it were necessary that the planters should suffer so that the community should benefit, he would have no compunction ultimately in making them suffer. But for the time being he was convinced that the money the planters were bringing into the industry was essential to its development and that the plantations could not exist without black labour.

So, in the period 1880–3, in the days before he would take office, he went very cagily. He was adamantly opposed to the introduction of coolies, he assured the Anti-Coolie League, and looked anxiously to the day when the Kanaka too would no more darken the land. Yet he had no real objection to the islanders, he told the planters when he visited Mackay, provided the labour trade was properly conducted, provided they were well cared for on the plantations and there was no alternative source of supply. The betting in financial circles, among the speculators in northern sugar lands, was that no drastic changes would be made when Griffith came to power; he was simply using the Kanaka bogy as a vote-catcher and would let it lie once he got in.

Granted, he had to be careful what he said. But underneath all these ambiguous utterances did he have any genuinely positive ideas, aside, naturally, from becoming Premier? In the debate on the Pacific Island Labourers' Act of 1880 he had spoken of men living on their own northern farms, growing their own sugar, making not large fortunes but fair incomes, bringing up their families respectably and well and selling their produce to the mills. Were the small-holders, the settlers who had taken up properties in the sugar districts in considerable numbers since the Land Act of 1876, to be his means of salvation for the sugar industry? They were a rather depressed class at this stage, utterly dependent on the nearest mill-owner to mill their sugar, too busy on their selections to have time to study the labour situation or to be aware of how the market was behaving. And some were predicting that they could not last much longer but would be absorbed into the larger plantations around them. However, they held on like terriers in many cases, and thus disproved the theory, which to the northern plantation-owner had become nothing less than an article of faith, that the white man could not manage heavy manual labour in the tropical canefields.

God, it was argued, had made the tropics for the black people to live in. The European who remained there too long would inevitably degenerate. True, white men were chopping down trees and splitting sleepers, digging post-holes and gouging mines all over north Queensland without suffering any apparent ill-effect. And in south Queensland there were cane-growers who ran their own successful small plantations dispensing utterly with Kanakas, using mostly the labour of wife and children. True, the planter retorted, but stand in the middle of a cane-field on a hot day, where the leaves met over-head and there was no fresh air and no relief from the steamy exhalations rising out of the ground, and see how you got on. The argument, to the planter mind, was unanswerable, since hardly a white man throughout the length and breadth of North Queensland could be found to undertake "nigger work" in the fields. Moreover, what small proprietor in the south didn't start using Kanakas as soon as he made a little money?

But times were beginning to change, and now the planters had the case of the small proprietors around Mackay and on the Herbert to contend with. In 1882 for instance, the Herbert River Farmers' Association was formed, which very soon declared: "We small settlers can explode the belief that the district only can be developed by gangs of black labour with a few white bosses. We are six who have been in the district continuously for upward of ten years. We have done hard work from fencing to scrub-clearing, and in spite of having no trips to the south we can physically measure ourselves with those fortunate ones who have had the advantage of recuper-ative trips."

These small proprietors were a useful class of people for Griffith to set up against the southern tycoons with their splendid new estates and evident determination to dictate the trend of events. In some of his election addresses during 1883 he spoke of introducing European immigrants who would start off as labourers on the plantations and later become small growers themselves. But he really could not see how they were going to survive economically against the plantations—at least, not until a certain engineer, Angus Mackay, returned to Queensland in 1883, an enthusiastic advocate of the central factory system.

The Queensland Government had sent him to study sugar pro-duction in the West Indies, where he had discovered the industry booming in the French islands and languishing in the British and Spanish islands. This state of affairs he attributed wholly to the fact that the French firmly separated the operations of cane-farming and sugar manufacture while the others did not. It was simple enough. The mill, independently organized, concentrated all its resources on increasing the yield of sugar extracted from the cane. The plantation concentrated on increasing the yield of cane per acre. The result was that both miller and planter tended to get a higher return on his investment.

Mackay's recommendation that the central mill idea be generally applied to Australia had a great impact. On 23rd February 1884, twenty selectors on the lower Burdekin advertised in the *Port Denison Times* (Bowen) that they were seeking capital to set up their own Central Mill Company. They had discovered the ideal site—a central point surrounded by a score of thriving selections within a radius of one and a half miles, which should be able to guarantee the mill six hundred to a thousand acres of cane ready for crushing by mid-1885. All they needed was £12,000 they estimated, "for the buildings, a set of double-crushing rollers, a six-ton vacuum pan, three open batteries, four Weston's centrifugals, three 50 h.p. boilers".

Not only the selectors were interested. So, from a different angle, were some of the big companies. For Angus Mackay had also postulated of the central-mill system that it was "one of the most certain solutions of the labour difficulties which beset sugar production all over the world".

Oddly enough, this was nothing more or less than the same system which the C.S.R. Co. had itself introduced to the northern rivers of New South Wales when it first moved into the region in the late 1860s. Of course, conditions in New South Wales were very different; established communities of small farmers were already in existence when the company arrived. And there was never at any stage the slightest possibility of Kanakas being legally imported into New South Wales. Quite a number had in fact drifted over the border from southern Queensland and no attempt was ever made to get rid of them despite the boast that the Kanaka would never be tolerated in New South Wales.

But it turned out then that it was not after all a question of the management having a decided preference for one system over the other, for when the company transferred the bulk of its operations to Queensland it immediately followed what was economically the most viable line and became the largest estate owner and importer of Kanakas in the colony, watching with jaundiced eye the efforts of a few small-holders to establish themselves.

Then quite suddenly the central factory idea reappeared in a new light—as a possible answer to the growing labour problem—and the company underwent a swift change of heart and reversed its attitude to the selector altogether. Early in 1884 it entered into a seven-year agreement with the small growers of the lower Herbert under which the company paid ten shillings a ton for their cane and undertook to do the harvesting.

This was a very different business from the vague, uncertain arrangements, the verbal promises so often unfulfilled, that had existed in the past. This gave the farmer some security. He could be confident now that all his cane would be crushed; that no message would come to him at the last minute that there was no labour available or that the mill had broken down; that he would have to look for some other planter further down the river to buy his crop.

However Griffith had no time to consider the full import of all this just then, for in November 1883 he had been swept into power by an overwhelming majority, proclaimed the champion of "White Australia", of the little man, and of much besides. He had things to attend to: there were important administrative reforms to be instituted; the long business of tidying up to do after a Government that had devoted most of its time to the business of making money, or development as it was called, and too little to the business of government. He had had no chance to do much about the labour question when it cropped up again in quite another form through a rather ugly incident that occurred at Mackay Racecourse on Boxing Day 1883.

It began in the Kanaka enclosure when an old Tannaman named Boslem went up to his usual refreshment-booth and asked for a bottle of beer. Unexpectedly he was refused, the proprietor having been warned recently by the planters to cease sly-grog selling to the Kanakas or be prosecuted. But to be able to buy a bottle of beer in a public place was the right of every time-expired Kanaka, and Boslem was angry, shouting taunts at the booth-keeper as he walked away, which quickly attracted a crowd. Before long a mob of forty islanders, mostly Tannese and Loyalty Island men and nearly all old hands, began throwing bottles in the general direction of the line of booths, causing some of the occupants to retreat to the grandstand.

At this stage, claimed a spectator, the disturbance could easily have been held within bounds, except for the activities of a gang of larrikins in the European quarter who now seized hold of sticks and palings and surged into the native section, driving the Kanakas out of the enclosure, through a fence and onto the road. Then came a mob of horsemen, urging their horses furiously and swinging stirrup-irons in their hands as they rode hell-bent, it seemed, on slaughter. Through them and over them they trampled, across prostrate bodies, until there seemed to be not a living Kanaka left in sight.

Only one of the islanders, in fact, was killed outright, but it looked very serious with so many bodies on the ground, so many bleeding and battered figures to be picked up and taken into hospital. That night Mackay was deserted, hardly a soul in the streets. The next day, out on the plantations, the European hands huddled in their quarters and refused to stir when called upon to go to work. The two races did not mix, Griffith had said. Was Australia to have the heritage of Europe or the heritage of Asia?

Griffith was determined that the whole system should cease. It was not yet possible to separate the two peoples entirely, but in January 1884 he was hard at work upon his Pacific Island Labourers' Amendment Bill, upon a new set of rules and regulations designed to reduce the friction to a minimum. There was first the question of the time-expired Kanaka, the situation whereby the man who had served his time was free to accept employment in any part of the colony while the still-indentured labourer was restricted to tropical agriculture. His bill would propose that the restriction be applied to all; that only those should be exempt who could prove that they had been resident in the colony for at least five years before a date to be proclaimed (subsequently fixed as 1st September 1884).

Furthermore, the term "tropical agriculture" was to be understood purely as field-work in connection with the cultivation of certain crops and not such diverse occupations as sugar-boiling, engine-driving, carpentering, fencing, looking after the horses, driving the master to Church, being nursemaid to the children, or domestic or household work of any kind.

This much for the Kanaka, now for the unscrupulous white man who never hesitated to take advantage of their native ignorance, of their incorrigible disposition to be led astray. By a further clause it was to be decreed that no person was to be employed on a recruiting vessel, as master, mate or recruiting agent, unless personally approved by the responsible Minister.

The bill when it was finally drawn up, debated, and duly passed into law on 10th March 1884, with only some minor amendments at the committee stage, contained only a dozen or so clauses in all. It seemed not a very formidable piece of legislation, yet when it came to be applied it proved to be devastating, bearing down with unrelenting severity on all who had dealings with the Kanaka, but especially so, it seemed, on the recruiters.

By regulations, under the Act, labour vessels were to be painted "a dull slate colour", with a black ribbon painted round their topsides, and would be required to hoist a black ball to the main-mast while actually recruiting. By these presents ye shall know them! But why black! It was probably the least of all the inconveniences the recruiters would now have to suffer, simply to repaint themselves, but it was the regulation that the recruiters resented most. Why should they have to appear in so sombre a light? Was black their badge of shame?

The recruiting trade was never quite the same again after the "cast-iron" regulations of 1884. In the past ship-owners and skippers had largely ignored the recruiting laws, encouraged as they were by the half-hearted efforts of G.A.s, medical officers, and immigration inspectors to enforce them. The Government itself did not seem to take them seriously. But a number of fresh appointments had been made under the new régime and there was now quite a different atmosphere abroad.

Section 9 of the latest Act declared it unlawful to offer fire-arms to any islanders, and Government Agent Kessack of the *Madeleine*, for example, meant to see the law obeyed to the letter. There was uproar on the beach at Tanna when the schooner arrived in October 1884, when the boats landed empty of guns. The returns had none; the boat-crew had none to exchange for more recruits.

If the Tannese had not been so completely flabbergasted they would have grasped the situation quicker than they did and seen that they had the recruiters at their mercy. As it was the visitors escaped with their lives, and Kessack had no intention of making the same mistake a second time. At the next stop the returns were hustled ashore in early morning light and the boats already on their way back to the ship before any of the villagers awoke to what was happening. It made the recruiting very difficult indeed. The *Madeleine* had a wretched trip, and took only fifteen recruits in four and a half months.

It was strange, but the recruiters felt much more nervous now that their returns were deprived of their usual weapons than in the days when they had gone home armed to the teeth. The *Ceara*, for instance, was very unfortunate. The new regulations had come into force before its departure from Townsville in June 1884, with the result that its returns came aboard seething with anger, having just been told that it was illegal for them to be in possession of fire-arms. After having saved up most of their three years wages for this very purpose, they naturally felt not a little cheated. They were on the point of seizing the ship, the *Ceara*'s skipper reported, when, providentially, they fell in with H.M.S. *Miranda*, whose captain agreed to convoy them until all their returns were landed. Many of the recruiting skippers said the same thing: they did not feel happy until they had landed their last return. And so the practice developed to quite alarming extent in the late 1880s of not returning the recruit to his home island but of bundling him ashore at the first opportunity on the pretext that the vessel was going no further.

P

The intent of the legislation, to reduce the amount of armed violence in the islands, fell hopelessly short of realization. By mutual arrangement, in the majority of cases, the recruiter made straight for Port Resolution, on Tanna, or Vila harbour, in Efate, or some other convenient centre where the return could buy everything he wanted from the local European, usually French, trader. It was the shopkeeper in Queensland who was the main loser. They were reduced to pleading, increasingly to no effect. For the returning islander, looking longingly at all the goods on display, jingling his coins in a little bag, could only shake his head and answer "Me fellow keep him. By'm by me fellow buyem gun along island man." In 1884, 2,033 islanders were taken home; in 1885, 1,857; in 1886, 2,611. Quite a few were time-expired labourers who had re-engaged for a second or even a third time at a figure much higher than the original £18 a year, so in terms of money being taken out of the country, the loss was considerable.

The ship-owners, however, were the principal sufferers. Between January and June 1884, twenty-one ships recruited 2,330 Kanakas; in the second half of the year, eighteen ships in thirty voyages recruited only 935. A Burns, Philp schooner, the *Juventa*, 152 tons, had the honour of making the most unproductive voyage on record. After six months it returned with only one recruit, having spent much of that time vainly seeking to engage a competent interpreter. For, under the new regulations this was the recruiter's first responsibility. What James Burns was moved to comment on hearing of this is not recorded, which is unfortunate, because he had some strong remarks to address to Philp on a previous occasion, after the *Hopeful* had returned with only about 90 out of a possible 132.

In the event the *Juventa* was soon after sold off to the Queensland Government to finish its career as a coal lighter on the Fitzroy River. And this sort of thing was happening in practically every port along the coast. River work was about the only thing left for the old recruiter after being forced out of the trade by the newer, larger vessels. Burns, Philp in fact had quit the trade altogether by the end of 1885. Only about fifteen or sixteen vessels were left, recruiting something fewer than two thousand islanders a year.

Griffith was not finished with the trade yet, however, though for the moment his attention was diverted by fresh troubles on the plantations at home. It seemed that of the 2,700 natives recruited in the New Guinea region since the *Hopeful's* original voyage in May 1883, scarcely one of them was fitted for plantation labour. It should be remembered that many of them had been kidnapped and would arrive in Queensland sweating with fear in imminent expectation of being eaten. And even if by now they had been convinced otherwise, they rarely made a good impression when first introduced to the older hands on the plantation. Though in some cases they were sturdy, they were generally undersized, timid, and unable to converse. In many other islanders they inspired disgust. "You got spear?" the Tannese would challenge them. Or a whole mob would come up to them in the cane-breaks, fondling tomahawks and long gleaming cane-knives with which they made sudden, frightening, throat-cutting motions. "You fella sleep. Sleep good," they would mutter and make off, grinning, to scare the next group.

Scores of New Guineans deserted within only a day or two of arriving and were never seen again, unless to be caught prowling about the plantation buildings in search of food and warm clothing. In September 1883, planter John Bird of Coomera hired ten Kaan Islanders, part of a consignment recently arrived in the *Jessie Kelly* at Brisbane. He could see that they were inclined to be edgy, needing delicate handling, and went to some trouble to make them feel at home. But one day a gun exploded behind a standing group of them and they took off like startled rabbits to find some burrow in the distant scrub. By the time they were retaken many weeks later a higher authority had decided that they should forthwith be returned to the islands, though Bird was still without labour to do his trashing.

It was months before the authorities in Brisbane grasped the fact that this sort of thing had been happening on almost every plantation in Queensland. Isolated instances came to their attention, like that of the ten escapees from Coomera only thirty-six miles away. But in most cases the problem was one which the planters had determined to deal with themselves, not even admitting that it existed, lest the Government should use it as another argument for abolishing the labour trade. For instance, early in June 1884, a group of twenty-three Moresby Islanders were delivered to the Mourilyan Sugar Company on the South Johnstone. They were not the first New Guineans whom the manager, Langdon, had had to cope with, but they were by far the most troublesome. They refused to work. They tore up their blankets. They stole things. They fell ill. They deserted. They even deserted from the little plantation hospital and lay outside shivering in the wet cane and contracted fatal chills.

When the first group of five or six disappeared, Langdon took a squad of four Tanna boys, trailed them through the scrub and brought them all back except one who crawled away, naked, on all fours, into a patch of thick jungle undergrowth and refused to come out. There were several more desertions after that, but as often as they escaped the Tannese would recapture them. Finally on 14th August 1884 ten got clear away, managed to steal a Chinese fishing-boat at the mouth of the Johnstone River, and sailed it to the L.M.S. mission station at Murray Island in Torres Strait. From there they were taken to Port Moresby, happening to arrive on 5th November just as Commander James Erskine arrived to proclaim a British Protectorate over the south-eastern portion of New Guinea and adjacent islands. The Reverend Mr Lawes of the L.M.S. and Erskine interviewed them together and discovered that they had been recruited by the *Lizzie* on the understanding that they were to work on a Queensland sugar plantation for two moons. Only at Townsville had they learnt that the period was actually three years or thirty-nine moons "whereupon all wept bitterly".

But it was not the number who deserted that brought the whole question out into the open, but the number who died: 1,469 islanders died in Queensland in 1884, or 14.75 per cent of the total Kanaka population of the time. This compared with 7.5 per cent in 1883—an increase that can only be accounted for by the exceptionally high death-rate of 24 per cent among the New Guineans employed mainly on the new company estates in the north.

Why was it that the big plantations always seemed to suffer the high death rates? The reason for the poor living conditions, and the deaths, at Yengarie was according to Thomson and Wray sheer meanness. But the C.S.R. at its Victoria plantation on the Herbert did not begrudge money spent on the health and well-being of its employees and yet they died just the same. The water-supply was irreproachable. The accommodation included weatherboard dormitories with verandas and glass windows. It was not the fault of management that the islanders kept asking if they could break up the dormitories and use the timber for the upright poles in the little grass huts that they preferred to sleep in. The food was mostly grown on the estate and should have been nutritious.

A hostile critic of the planters who visited the Herbert a few years later alleged that it was a common practice for the local plantations to buy "scallawags", i.e., diseased cattle, to feed their Kanakas on. He did not state whether Victoria was one of them, but in any case the point is irrelevant. The New Hebrideans and Solomon boys thrived on whatever the fare provided, enjoying much better health in general than the 150 Europeans employed at Victoria.

But the New Guineans for the most part continued to languish and decline. Cowley, the C.S.R.'s manager at Victoria, complained that half his New Guinea hands should never have been allowed through by the port health authorities in the first place; instancing one with a half-foot, another with a contracted hand, a third who told him he had only come to Queensland to get medical treatment.

A worse pest than grub in the cane, stated another planter, was the labour agent who signed on behalf of the employer when the vessel arrived and then sent on boys who were plainly sick.

Irregularities certainly occurred at Ingham, the little port for the Herbert, but the death-rate among the New Guineans seems to have been fairly uniform throughout the north. In mid-January 1884 A. R. MacDonald, the very efficient Polynesian Inspector at Mackay, visited the C.S.R.'s Homebush plantation where twenty-five New Irelanders were reported to have died of dysentery. He could find no reason for this heavy mortality, unless, as he said, it was that "their constitutions were not adapted to changes in the climate". But perhaps MacDonald, zealous though he was, knew less, or was less inclined to be outspoken in his opinions, than certain officials in Fiji.

The casualties in Fiji after the C.S.R. had bought its first lands there in 1880 and began clearing were truly frightful, and Henry Anson, the Agent-General for Immigration in 1883, did not hesitate to say so. Of various estates belonging to the C.S.R. Co. he remarked, "Appalling numbers of actual deaths . . . have taken place thereon and examples of a grave nature have been observed by myself and the Inspectors upon the estates of Navusa and Nausori which very nearly amount to manslaughter." According to Dr B. G. Corney, Fiji's Chief Medical Officer, the C.S.R. had apparently been using newly imported islanders, hard driven by overseers, to do the heavy initial clearing, and they had proved simply unequal to the tasks. He also thought opening up new jungle land for sugar cultivation was "the source of the *materies morbi* and epidemic dysentery, often attended with sloughing ulcerations of the mouth, gums and rectum".

Queensland was not Fiji, certainly, but the conditions were broadly similar: new land, big companies, large-scale clearing, large numbers of new recruits, mainly young and very strange to it, treated like so many impersonal units, filing anonymously past the kitchen-window, then sent out into the fields to work beside better-muscled, bigger men, who naturally jeered them, mocked them, urged them on to do the impossible; played practical jokes on them by making them pick up the sack of meat of their midday meal, and take it to the overseer to whom they were to say, "Bag, he stink."

On 6th October 1884 MacDonald reported the arrival of the *Sybil*—almost the last labour vessel to reach Queensland from the shores of New Guinea. It brought forty-eight recruits, rather small in size, said MacDonald, but healthy and apparently content. Three weeks later, however, "many of them were coughing badly, several showing signs of having been assaulted". They told MacDonald that

some Chinese had frightened them. Then came the very last recruiter
to arrive from New Guinea, the *Heath*, and it looked as if gods, bent
on destroying the recruiters, had first made them mad. For the
Heath returned from a highly unsatisfactory voyage at a disastrous
time—when the whole colony was being assaulted with the details of
the *Hopeful* kidnapping case.

The *Heath*'s was a futile expedition. A week out of Mackay, with
the prospect of squally weather, Wawn decided to replace his worn-
out mainsail, only to discover that the spare canvas was rotten. He
set the crew to covering the old sail with large overall patches and
hoped somehow to be able to keep out of the path of the north-west
monsoon. Thus restricted in his movements, he spent a couple of
months working the Laughlans, the Woodlarks, the Trobriands,
Normanby and Fergusson, finding it impossible to get even an
interpreter at most places, let alone a recruit. Minister and the
missionaries seemed to hold sway in the region.

At Moresby Island one of the mission teachers did come aboard
to offer his services as an interpreter, but his real purpose, it turned
out, was to lure ashore some of the recruits already aboard and
steal the ship's stores of tobacco. However, a final total of nineteen
recruits was secured in the end, and after further adventures, during
which the vessel was becalmed and almost wrecked on the Great
Barrier Reef, it reached Townsville.

The immigration authorities in Townsville, like most public
servants in the north in those days, had the reputation of being
fairly easygoing, that is, towards the northerners against the arbitrary
interference in their affairs on unfeeling Administration in Brisbane.
But there was no sign of that now; their inspection of the *Heath*
was the sharpest Wawn had ever encountered. He was told none of
the recruits could be accepted, as there was no interpreter aboard to
assure the immigration inspector that they understood the terms of
the contracts. Three, moreover, were ill and would be placed in
hospital at the expense of the shipowner.

As it turned out, the decision to reject the islanders was reversed
after the local office had been in touch with Brisbane, and the sixteen
fit Kanakas went off to the Drysdale Brothers' Pioneer plantation on
the Burdekin. They immediately absconded: one was drowned
crossing a creek; two died in the bush, the rest managed to find their
way back to Townsville. They told an interpreter that the Kanakas
at Pioneer kept too many knives; they feared they would be murdered in their sleep. This was harmful publicity for the recruiter
and for the planters, and certainly of no help to the crew of the other
Burns, Philp vessel, miscalled the *Hopeful*, now on trial for their
lives before the Brisbane Supreme Court.

The case had opened on 24th November 1884 and was still in progress when the *Heath* recruits absconded about a week later. Great numbers of witnesses were being called for both sides, but there was never, at any stage, the chance that the accused would escape, as so many in their situation before them had escaped. In the end all were found guilty. The two first-degree killers—McNeil, the recruiter, and Williams, the bos'n—were sentenced to death. The two principal accessories—Shaw, the skipper, and Scholfield, the Government Agent—were given life imprisonment. Other members of the crew got ten years and seven years.

The sentences were savage, but, as Griffith told a deputation of petitioners seeking commutation of the two sentences of death, he had never heard of a voyage of such murderous atrocity as that of the *Hopeful*: at least thirty-eight natives had been shot by different members of the crew. He would prefer to have seen every one of them hanged from their own yard-arm. However, there were no executions: the death sentences were commuted, and eventually in 1890 all the prisoners were released by order of the Government, except for Scholfield, the drunken G.A., who had died in irons on 17th January 1886.

Evidently Griffith had been waiting to get these criminal cases dealt with first, for immediately afterwards he appointed a Royal Commission charged with the task of finding out just how it was that all those other New Guinea recruits had been brought to Queensland. There were seven other voyages, Griffith thought, that particularly required investigation—two by the *Ceara*, two by the *Lizzie*, one each by the *Heath*, the *Sybil*, and the *Forest King*.

Nobody seems to have been surprised by this latest development. The wildest rumours had been flying: that the Government was going to outlaw the labour trade altogether; that every Kanaka in the colony was to be sent home immediately; that north Queensland would then secede from the rest of the colony and obtain all the labour it needed from the German colony of New Guinea. Up in the sugar towns they were carrying Griffith's effigy through the streets and ceremonially sending it up in flames. It was a time of great excitement in North Queensland, when some breakdown in the established order seemed at hand, a time when a prudent man like Robert Philp would withdraw from the labour trade for the time being and a fool would rush in.

Captain Augustus Routch was not exactly a fool when it came to scenting an opportunity, but he was an impulsive, emotional man who sometimes behaved foolishly. He was upset, to begin with, by the wreck of his own proud command, the fine brig barquentine *Fredericka Wilhelmina,* in Empress Augusta Bay, Bougainville. Even

before that, Rowe, his G.A., had been involved in a murderous affray
with the natives in which the top of his skull had been sliced off and
the brain exposed. The second mate, too, had been severely tomahawked. Another labour vessel, the *Lochiel*, had happened to arrive
just at that moment, having aboard the crew of the wrecked *Alfred
Vittery*. The *Fredericka* was thus able to continue recruiting with
the *Alfred Vittery*'s G.A.—until it came to be wrecked and in return
its crew rescued by Captain James Howie in the *Ariel*. Rowe,
remarkably enough, was still alive when the *Lochiel* reached Queensland, but he never properly recovered and afterwards died in a
lunatic asylum.

Different men respond in different ways to such experiences.
Routch's reaction was to return as soon as possible to the scene of
these harrowing adventures and endeavour to make good his losses
(the planters were offering £25/10/- a head at Cairns), and perhaps
to inflict a few losses on the islanders also by way of revenge. He
firmly intended to continue after recruits, but for the moment he
was too pressed by business matters to go personally and had no
vessel fitted out for recruiting. So he persuaded Captain Howie of
the *Ariel* to take command of his little 100-ton copra trader, the
Elibank Castle, and sent it off in the labour trade. The fact that the
schooner held no recruiting licence and lacked any proper accommodation for recruits did not deter him. He even told several people
quite openly that he had various scores to settle with the islanders,
so that when the *Elibank Castle* sailed from Cooktown on 6th
November 1884, a few weeks before the *Heath* case opened, it was
described in the local paper as being "bound on a purely kidnapping
voyage to the Solomons".

Routch and Howie evidently had decided that the ship make for
the western Solomons, which Howie knew well from his trading
days. Here the risk of meeting a patrolling man-o'-war would be
very slight, since the ordinary recruiter rarely went there. The real
risk, however, which both of them seemed to have forgotten, lay in
attempting to recruit from a region of head-hunters. The natives of
Rubiana Lagoon, Gizo, Kolombangara, Vella Lavella, and so on
were just as curious about Queensland, no doubt, as the rest of the
Solomon Islanders. But they could not simply recruit and submit to
being carried off to the white man's country with a lot of other
recruits. They were head-hunters; beyond the pale. They would
have been killed.

There were times when a particular recruiter had received word
from some local trader that it would be safe to visit a particular
island, had gone there and done well. There were as well places like
the Shortlands where one could treat with King Ghorai, who was

still active in the area until Germany announced the annexation of the Shortlands in 1886. But the recruits obtained on these occasions had been in reality merely slaves, victims of some raid, whom the head-hunters were now willing to exchange for some other commodity. It was all right to go there and trade on the islanders' own terms, but on 12th January 1885, when Captain James Howie dropped anchor off Rendova Island, only six miles to the west of New Georgia and the Rubiana Lagoon, it was in the crazy belief apparently that he was going to dictate the terms. He would outsmart them, he thought, pretend to be collecting copra, and, under cover of this, tempt a few of the younger ones to desert.

So for a couple of days the two parties traded peacefully with one another and Howie found it even easier than he had expected. Not only was he able to sound out numerous potential recruits, several of whom could speak a little English, but also to concert arrangements for them to escape without danger of recapture. The plan was that the boats would go ashore on the morning of 15th January, ostensibly to load copra, but in fact to enable all those intending to recruit to swim out and jump in. They could thus be out to the ship and safe before any pursuer had a chance to overtake them—a very necessary precaution since the islanders could very swiftly launch their great war-canoes and give chase.

It was quite a clever, well-conceived stratagem, seeming to entail small risk for the recruiters even if it failed to come off. Unhappily the local chief, Poogey, had known of it from the beginning and prepared his own counter-stratagem. Five chosen warriors visited the schooner early that next morning and insisted on accompanying Howie and his boat-crew back to the beach where the copra was supposed to be waiting. The skipper could only agree to have them go with him and got into the boat, calling out to the mate, Banks, on deck, that he was only going to get the copra and would be back within the hour.

Banks never saw what actually happened. He was watching intently through an eye-glass when a sudden squall swept across the bay, blotting the boat from view. When it lifted after about ten minutes, all he could make out was the boat being hauled towards the beach by a crowd of islanders while others, up to their waists in water, were handing overhead, from one pair of arms to the next, three rather bulky looking objects that could have been bodies.

This was always a desperately difficult decision to make—whether to stay and try to discover definitely the fate of one's shipmates, to establish that they were beyond all human aid, or to flee, before the islanders got the ship. Banks was in a quandary; he could see nothing more happening ashore, no other suspicious circumstances.

Then all at once bullets began to whistle through the rigging and he knew with dreadful certainty what must have happened.

There remained now only three white men aboard with three more Kanaka deck-hands. They stayed for several hours longer, said Banks, exchanging fire with their attackers, until some chance shot brought a spar crashing down at his feet and he decided it was time to run for it. Two of the crew bravely offered to go aloft and loosen topsails, and they managed to ease the schooner out of the bay and stand away to sea. Three weeks later the steamer *City of Melbourne* rounded Double Point, just south of Port Douglas on the Queensland coast, and was not surprised to see, having itself just endured a severe buffeting, a small schooner drifting disabled and helpless. The disabled ship was flying a distress pennant and signalling "In want of assistance. Lost anchor and cable. Sails blown away." This rescue, not far from Port Douglas, ended part one in the saga of the little *Elibank Castle*.

Routch must have been a remarkable man; hearing of this disaster to a second of his ships, he sailed at once from Cooktown to Port Douglas to take command. A magisterial enquiry into the cause of death at Rendova caused some delay, but it still took less than seven weeks for him to have the little schooner repaired, refitted, and back to sea, bound for the Solomons. Was it business or war; recruiting or retaliation? His real intentions are not known. There was at this time a rush to take up land in the islands. It seemed, for the knowledgeable, that ever since Germany and Britain had begun carving up New Guinea, further annexations would follow. The New Hebrides and Solomons were reputedly next on the list, so this was the time to get in, before prices became prohibitive. Howie, as a matter of fact, had delayed some weeks in the Louisiades during the *Elibank Castle*'s previous voyage, to negotiate the purchase of a piece of Bentley Island.

What Routch was up to exactly can never be known, but on 17th May he put in at an unidentified island in the Solomons group and invited the islanders on board to trade. Among these people! According to David Brown, the bos'n, they "went completely off their heads" at the sight of "trade" spread out on the deck—knives, tomahawks, axes, sharp and blunt instruments of every size and description. He had been just coming up the companionway, the bos'n remembered, when a naked savage jumped down and swung a tomahawk at his head. Somehow he managed to evade the full force of the blow and ran blindly into the hold, stumbling and bumping into pieces of cargo, until he found a hiding-place, a dark corner of the foc's'le, and lay there out of breath. He could hear pandemonium on deck and then silence. He knew nothing more until he found seaman Hugh Gildie beside him, sobbing and moaning, clutching a face covered in blood. He had been attracted to this hiding place by the sound of heavy breathing. They were the only members of the crew left alive.

The pair did what they could to dress one another's wounds by the light of a bull's-eye lantern, and finally, well after dark, ventured on deck and stood for a while listening, guns in hand. There was no sound, and they began picking their way aft through the bodies until suddenly frozen at the sight of a light in the captain's cabin. A moment later a native emerged from the top of the companionway, saw them in the same instant as they saw him and dived into the cabin, shouting a warning to another man already inside. All four men had guns, and both sides now began taking pot-shots at each other. But the white men had the advantage, for the natives did not grasp the fact that they were easy marks silhouetted against the light; the two seamen were able to edge closer and closer until near enough to shoot their opponents dead.

The *Elibank Castle* now began its last adventure. It was ten days before the wounded pair felt strong enough to do anything, but finally they desperately summoned up the strength to get the ship under way. Neither had any knowledge of navigation so they just steered in the general direction of New Guinea until they piled the schooner up on a reef and took to one of the boats. Mercifully Gildie was drowned when the rudder became unshipped during a gale— and knocked him overboard. But Brown, delirious by this time and almost blind, was eventually washed up on some beach on the north coast of New Guinea to be rescued by friendly natives and handed over to the crew of a Dutch brig who returned him to Queensland.

That finally was the end of the story of the *Elibank Castle*. But the natives of Rendova Island did not forget readily. Some years later a white visitor carrying a camera landed at the same fatal beach intending to photograph some of the native flora and fauna. But one of the natives told him if he were going to take pictures, he ought to take him, for he was the man who had killed the captain of the *Elibank Castle*.

Howie was dead. Routch was dead. The ranks of the recruiting skippers were thinning. And during this time between January and April 1885, while the *Elibank Castle* had been *en route* to and from the Solomons, Griffith's three Royal Commissioners had been journeying from plantation to plantation throughout North Queensland interviewing their 480-odd native witnesses, preparing their report. They had been asked to concentrate on the voyages of six particular vessels, including the *Hopeful*. They found that scarcely a single one of these several hundred recruits, none certainly of those examined, had been fairly and legitimately recruited.

Perhaps there had been little actual physical kidnapping, except in the case of the *Hopeful*, yet the methods of the other vessels, said the commissioners, were so patently dishonest as to be almost as bad: for instance, the pantomime of gesturing with the fingers to explain the conditions of service. Three fingers held up were supposed to denote three yam seasons. But some of the islanders did not grow yams or even know what they were. Again, vague motions by the arms were thought to indicate the cutting or trashing of cane. To the islanders the only suggestion this conveyed was of those cheerful working-bees when groups of them would get together to slash the long grass. Nobody tried to explain to them what the cane-fields were actually like. They certainly did not know it was going to mean work, work, all day, until they were too tired to eat their pannikins of rice in the evening.

Such things the commissioners had brought to light by careful probing. Yet it is a remarkable fact and a fair commentary, perhaps, on the Queensland labour trade at the same time that out of 462 recruits whom they recommended to be returned instantly to New Guinea at the expense of the colony 58 refused to go and duly completed their three-year terms of service. Eight years later a newspaper correspondent discovered one of the *Hopeful* recruits still employed on Seaforth plantation on the Burdekin. He had no desire to return home, apparently never had had from the day of his arrival. "You makem plenty fella pound?" the newspaperman asked. "No," the man replied. "Me too much run about. Spendem money." Perverse human nature that will not do what an enlightened Government has found best for it.

However, the main points of the report concerned the recruiters themselves. They had been exposed to all the world as unprincipled scoundrels. The *Hopeful*'s crew had already been dealt with at law. So Griffith now had every justification in proclaiming, with respect to the remaining five vessels, that all those masters, crews, and Government Agents and any others guilty of bringing recruits from New Guinea or its environs during the period under review should be barred from all further employment in the labour trade.

The year 1885 was turning out to be even worse for the recruiters than 1884—likewise for the planters. World sugar prices had been steadily declining all through 1884, but in January 1885 came a really sharp drop. Compared with an average of £25 a ton the planter had received for all grades of sugar in 1883, he was now getting less than £15. The rapidly expanding Government-protected beet sugar industries of France and Germany contributed heavily to the problem, forcing Javan and Mauritius sugar out of the free English market and on to the Australian. How, asked the planter, could he be expected to produce sugar as cheaply as it was produced in Mauritius, where the coolie got a shilling a day without rations, or in Java, where he got only sixpence. The total cost of maintaining one Kanaka, reckoning the expense of importing him, paying his passage home again and everything else, was well over two shillings a day.

More than that, Queensland's biggest market was Victoria with its jam and biscuit factories, distilleries, breweries, soft drink factories, and so on. Before Queensland sugars could even begin to compete with their overseas rivals, they had to pay an intercolonial impost of £3 per ton. Did their own Government, then, help them at all? Did it subsidize them as, say, the German Government subsidized the sugar beet producers in Germany? Not a bit. It made them pay an importation fee of thirty shillings per islander on top of the astronomical fee already charged by the recruiter. Surely, the planters argued, if Griffith really had their interests at heart, he would legislate not merely to cure a few abuses in the labour trade, but to enable the Government to take it over altogether, control it from end to end, just as Britain superintended the coolie traffic from India to Mauritius. If he had the interests of the sugar industry at heart. Frankly they wondered about him; he seemed not their sort of person at all.

There was thus much debate among the planters in 1885 about what they were going to do. Take the industry to the Northern Territory or Western Australia, said some; secede, said others. On 14th January 1885 John Ewen Davidson, *doyen* of the planters, happening to be in London, addressed a letter to Lord Derby, the Colonial Secretary. In view of the remoteness of Queensland's tropical north, the letter suggested, its inadequate representation in the Legislative Assembly, the difficulty of administering it at long range, the diversity of interests between the inhabitants of tropical and temperate Queensland on the subject of coloured labour, would it not be more convenient if a line were to be drawn horizontally from Cape Palmerston to the South Australian border, and the colony divided in two.

There was no likelihood of the British Government being interested in this proposal—not with Queensland bonds standing so well on the London market. But more important, the Imperial Government had imperial problems elsewhere. It was trying to consolidate an Empire, and a Separatist movement anywhere could set up reverberations in quite a number of other places, for example, Ireland. But the letter was duly passed on from the Colonial Office to Sir Anthony Musgrave, the Queensland Governor, and ultimately from Musgrave to Griffith, who naturally would have none of it—neither of this treacherous talk of secession, nor of these allegations that he was out to destroy the sugar industry.

Griffith was normally very concise. In his speeches, official letter writing, necessary public pronouncements, or when answering a question in Parliament or introducing a bill, he would never utter a word more than necessary. Words were too important to him, too charged with precise meaning, to waste on the empty air. But when roused, when some impudent heckler or irresponsible critic needed to be thoroughly squashed, he would launch into a harangue and go on and on until his anger was all spent.

So it was on this occasion in his reply to the Governor: he found not just one or two reasons but many why the question of North Queensland separation was simply not to be entertained. It was a mere catch-cry; one heard it from time to time, but dismissed it contemptuously. Whenever there was discontent over the allocation of development funds, or whenever the inhabitants of Bowen, Townsville, Rockhampton, and other towns thought there was a chance of theirs becoming the northern capital voices were raised. Now it was Mackay, where the planters were furious because of their failure to obtain coolies from India. What it all meant in the end, accused Griffith, was simply that a handful of people in the north wanted to have their own way on the coloured labour question. He knew their basic and endlessly repeated argument—that white labour was unsuited to tropical agriculture. As he had pointed out on numerous occasions in the past, however, this still had to be proved.

The separationists were clearly not making much progress then: the British Government was characteristically non-committal; their own Government uncompromisingly opposed. Throughout 1885, however, they continued to agitate; to bombard the Governor with petitions and to start a vigorous campaign in the British Press. But nothing they attempted could shake Griffith from his purpose. And so, finally, he brought down his famous Pacific Island Labourers' Amendment Act of 1885, a model of compression as usual, just the bare eleven clauses, the sting being in the tail: "After the thirty-first day of December 1890, no licence to introduce islanders shall be granted." The end of the recruiting trade was thus announced in sixteen words, with an explanation that summed up everything that needed to be said in explanation in two brief sentences: "Five years would give the planters ample time to make new arrangements. If they wished to exist, it would be their business to work with the rest of the community."

TEN

Recruiting—the Last Phase

THERE were times when Griffith must have been profoundly disappointed by his failures to carry out what he had set his heart on. He was so right in principle, and yet so often wrong in practice. Nobody it seems could tell him where he had gone wrong. He was a shy man, and being on a different intellectual plane from most of his fellows he found it difficult to communicate with them, to discover their real feelings. Perhaps it was the people he was trying to help, like the farmers, who did not understand what he was trying to do for them, or perhaps the administrators responsible for making the ideas work who did not understand and thus caused something to be lost in the execution. There was no saying exactly, but loss there was.

He seemed, too, to be cursed with ill-luck. The riot at Mackay racecourse, for example, had occurred only six weeks after he had taken office, almost simultaneously, that is, with Queensland's first genuine attempt to make the labour trade look respectable. This single event did as much to bedevil the relations between the two races as any other in the history of the trade. Within weeks the news was all over the islands with the result that at Tanna, Epi, Malaita, and all the main recruiting grounds it was impossible to sign on recruits for Mackay for months afterwards. Mackay, as we know, had once been highly unpopular but had gradually risen in native estimation to oust Maryborough from favouritism. Now, dramatically, it declined in popularity again, while Bundaberg, where all the building and fresh activity was going on, became the new favourite. It made the task very difficult for some of the newly created G.A.s and inspectors who had recently been appointed especially to administer the 1884 regulations. Griffith must have asked himself why could not this thing have happened during the five years McIlwraith had been in power?

Again he was strikingly unlucky with his scheme for establishing communities of small farmers growing and milling their own sugar. After Angus Mackay's enthusiastic proposals for setting up a system of central mills in Australia, the C.S.R. Co. had applied something very much along the same lines on the Herbert and by the end of 1885 there was no doubt that the system was efficient. The Herbert farmers had encountered plenty of other troubles, but they were pleased with their central mill. So on 4th November 1885 Griffith moved in the House that "the sum of £50,000 be granted in loans in aid of the establishment of central sugar mills". He had been approached by a group of farmers in the Mackay district, he said, who would be prepared to mortgage the whole of their land to the Government as security if it would lend them the money, subsidize them on a pound-for-pound basis, to build and equip their own mill. It seemed a pretty fair proposition, and Griffith thought the Government ought to agree to it, with the stipulation that all cane supplied to the mill should be grown solely by white labour.

In the event two enterprises did start up at Mackay under the Griffith plan, the North Eton Central Mill and the Racecourse Mill, both of which came a disastrous flop. When they eventually got into production, after numerous false starts, it was found to be impossible to keep them going without depending overwhelmingly on Kanaka-grown cane. The farmer-shareholders in the mill co-operative just could not find the white labour to work their farms. Being mostly young men who had only recently taken up their selections, they had no large families to help them, like some of the successful small planters in the south. Nor could they get any outside help. There was a tremendous amount of boring, back-breaking toil involved in starting a cane-farm. It had been estimated that to plant only one acre as many as 5,600 pieces of cane had to be separately cut, loaded on to a cart, off-loaded, planted, buried. Then there was the cultivation, trashing, weeding. Not many white men could stand or would offer for such work.

But a mob of youngsters from the islands would accept it if they were allowed to go their own pace, in spurts, with time off now and then for a bit of skylarking among themselves. The islanders were usually manageable if kept together in their own naturally formed groups. But a system was coming into practice on the Herbert and in the Bundaberg district whereby some of the bigger planters had begun to subdivide their estates, leasing off portions to a settled community of smaller growers around them, and then to hire out the plantation's own work-force, a squad at a time, to each individual tenant in turn. This was the only way the average farmer could get established. Without Kanakas he could barely begin.

There had in fact been one plantation in Queensland in 1885 that employed exclusively white labour, and continued to be conscientiously opposed to the use of Kanakas. This was Spring Hill, at Bundaberg, and it was the example that is said to have persuaded Griffith that his plan was feasible. But a year or two later, inevitably, it seemed, even Spring Hill had reverted to Kanakas. Only the Government-subsidized mills had to struggle along without them.

There was nothing wrong with the basic conception. History would justify Griffith's claim that the white man could labour in the tropics without ill-effect, could grow his own sugar with his own hands. But for the time being he had to accept the fact that another of his favourite schemes had betrayed him. Perhaps if he had studied the problem in greater detail, been more aware of what the man on the spot would actually have to contend with, he might have seen that the experiment was premature at that stage. Looking back from this point of history, we can see that he miscalculated the willingness of the white Australian hired labourer to undertake what was called "nigger work".

But then he had never understood what we would now call "industrial relations". For example, he expected no trouble in introducing an immigration scheme for various classes of European—Germans, Danes, Piedmontese, and Lombards—in the hopes that these thriving, industrious peoples would one day develop a sort of peasant economy in North Queensland. He did not see, presumably, that the local trade-union movement would interpret it as an attempt to reduce wages for the European working man. The unions would fight him bitterly on this, irrespective of his protests that he only intended to use the white immigrant to help drive out the coloured.

But the group he had misjudged most were the planters. Now with their backs to the economic wall, they were infinitely more dangerous opponents than in the past. Then they had been flush, spending gaily, buying up more land than they could possibly need, and never bothering their heads about making the most economical use of what they had. The abrupt fall in the price of sugar; the sudden awareness that the beet sugar industry in Europe was far more efficient and better organized than their own, woke them up painfully and abruptly. There were too many mills for one thing; too much money invested in the latest American machinery without the technical skills to accompany them so as to extract from the cane the largest possible quantity of sugar at the least possible expense.

Great technological advances had been made in the 1880s, mainly by the C.S.R. Co. It had discovered, for instance, that double crushing in conjunction with the soaking of the megass (crushed cane fibres) in hot water after it had passed the first set of rollers yielded

Q

about 15 per cent more cane juice, with an overall higher sugar content, than a single crushing. But this sort of technical knowledge came too late to save a mighty enterprise like Airdmillan; the mill would have needed to make further investments in equipment to take advantage of the technique when by 1886 it had already spent £200,000 and never at any stage looked like paying a dividend. Airdmillan was to be a complete disaster. It had bought fifteen thousand acres of valuable sugar land when the market was at the top, built a wharf and four miles of permanent track, and had crushed for only two seasons. In 1893 a visitor to the Burdekin came across a pile of expensive equipment, vacuum pans, filter presses, steam-ploughs, locomotives, long lines of trucks, rusting away in the sun and the mill building in the centre of it all, standing empty.

It was much the same story throughout the north. Hamleigh on the Herbert, the property of the Melbourne Sugar Co., cost £120,000 and was sold a few years later for £13,000. Its neighbour, Gairloch, upon which another £120,000 had been expended, realized £11,000. In the Cairns district, Swallow and Derham's Hambledon was £180,000 in debt. Mulgrave was in the hands of the Bank of Australasia with an overdraft of £140,000. The boom had started in the McIlwraith era and collapsed in the Griffith era. And it was Griffith of course who received all the blame; Griffith had closed the New Guinea trade and sent home those already recruited, and was now going to cut off the supply altogether.

But it was not the shortage of Kanakas or any contemplated shortage that had brought about the industry's plight. If anything, the planters had been suffering from too many Kanakas in 1885 rather than too few. Having to part prematurely with their New Guinea labour was in fact a great relief to many plantations. For they were already in the position of having to cut back their acreages quite drastically as a result of the fall in sugar prices some months before. When, after 1886, so many of the larger plantations began to go under, the labour position became easier still. In a way it was the law of survival of the economically fittest beginning to operate. Those plantations that used their resources the most intelligently survived, scooped in the remains of their competitors and emerged from the period of crisis stronger, more resilient, better adapted to survive in the harsher economic conditions of the time than before.

One small example of how wasteful the planters could be with their island labour was connected with the use of the megass as a fuel for the furnaces. It contained more heat than firewood, and being constantly available in endless quantity it was obviously the fuel to use. Yet the technique of "tedding" the megass, as it was called, was highly wasteful. It was spread out in the sun to dry, then raked over, raked up and carted under shelter whenever it looked like rain. It was a tedious, long drawn-out operation that might keep as many as twenty-four Kanakas busy for most of the crushing season. No big profit-minded company, no class of planters like the shrewd French in the West Indies, would have tolerated the system for a minute. But it was the way in Queensland, where there always seemed plenty of labour to spare, until the mid-eighties when Henry Braby, a consulting engineer employed by Drysdale Brothers at Pioneer plantation, invented his patent megass drier. This was a process whereby the megass was dried while on its way from the rollers to the furnaces by using the waste heat from the boiler flues. It reduced the number of hands needed from twenty-four to four.

Yet while acknowledging that he might have used this Kanaka labour extravagantly in the past, the planter did not mean to give the impression that he could do without it now. Whatever they did in the south, no northerner was prepared to budge an inch from the proposition that the European was physically incapable of labour in the canefields, and during the electoral contest in 1888 Griffith had even accused the planters of inserting articles in German and Danish newspapers, and sending emissaries to spread the doctrine that Queensland plantation conditions were for the white labourer tantamount to slavery.

So the planters fought back, using means that were evidently not always too scrupulous, and seemed to be much more sanguine about their prospects in 1888—despite the continuing depression in the industry and a serious drought—than they had been when Griffith came to power five years before. Of course, they were counting on McIlwraith turning him out in the June general elections and reversing his decision to end the labour trade. And if that failed, there was still separation.

The planters were managing to survive Griffith, but what of the recruiters? By the time the legislators had finished with them, by the year 1892 when control of the labour trade was thought to have reached a state of legislative perfection, the recruiters were bound by seven Acts of Parliament, colonial and Imperial, together with eighteen schedules, fifty-four regulations and a list of thirty-eight instructions for Government Agents.

The G.A.s referred to these latter as the thirty-eight commandments, and perhaps they were a bit primly ridiculous, like that which obliged the agent, in accordance with Regulation 35, to see that "recruiting was not proceeded with on Sunday", or its fellow that insisted that "married persons are not to be allowed to recruit singly, and then, husband and wife together, only with the consent of their chief". Of course, from the recruiter's point of view, it did not matter what the regulations said so much as what the agent said and did. And in this respect there were signs that the recruiting was getting more difficult. To replace all those who had lost their billets as a result of the Royal Commission of 1885, half a dozen more appointments were made in 1885–6, and the latest breed of G.A., it seemed, was both inclined to be more officious than his predecessor and more liable to have notice taken of his complaints in Brisbane.

For example, the *Eliza Mary* arrived back at Bundaberg on 22nd December 1886, having been ordered home by its G.A., Major Howitt, because of the "grossly insulting behaviour of her master, Henry Blaxell, and his son, John, the carpenter". Blaxell was not accused of any offence against the natives, it should be noted, only of "failing to place himself under the orders of the Government Agent while recruiting". What had happened, in fact, was that the *Eliza Mary* had come upon the copra trader and grog peddler *Mary Anderson* at Malo Pass, Santo, and Blaxell had gone aboard to renew his supplies of liquor. He could just as easily have dealt with one of the French traders ashore.

He was not to know that Howitt would now feel compelled to intervene, to go aboard the trader himself to warn its commander not to sell the *Eliza Mary* anything more; the skipper drank too much already. Blaxell was already waiting for him when he returned, in a furious rage, shouting that if he ever attempted to leave the ship again without his, the captain's, permission, he would have him thrown into irons. Then young John Blaxell chipped in with a few impertinent remarks of his own. He had no alternative, said Howitt, but to order the schooner back to port. His action was subsequently upheld by a departmental enquiry in Brisbane and the two Blaxells were debarred from any further participation in the trade.

In June the following year there was an even more remarkable case—a complete reversal in fact. This time it was the recruiter *Ariel*, which returned prematurely to Bundaberg, not even having reached the New Hebrides at all. Drink again was the cause, but this time it was the agent, W. J. Murray, who was involved. He had committed suicide at sea while in a state of delirium tremens, reported Captain Lewis. So another enquiry was held and Lewis was dismissed from the trade for allowing his G.A. to drink to excess!

The recruiter could not win, it seemed; not under Griffith certainly. But in fact the conditions of recruiting did not change very much in the period after 1885—vessels were shipwrecked, shot at by natives, reported by their G.A.s to be totally unseaworthy, their crews consumed by drink, drowned and more than once dead by their own hand. But there were no more reported kidnapping incidents of the kind that had brought disgrace to the trade in 1883–4, even if this were due as much to good luck as good management. For there were still a few skippers and recruiters around who had survived the purge of 1885, and who would not stop at a little kidnapping—if they had the right kind of G.A. Captain Rogers, for instance, skipper and part-owner of the *Young Dick* in 1885–6 had formerly been mate and recruiter aboard the *Heron*. A big burly man, boisterous and red-headed, Rogers was a great bluffer of the unfortunate natives.

In 1883, to quote a typical example, he turned up in the *Heron* on the east coast of Malaita shortly after H.M.S. *Dart* had been sent there to inflict reprisals on the inhabitants for an earlier attack on the *Janet Stewart*. The *Dart* had been more severe than was usual in such cases and had burned and destroyed villages over a wide area. Rogers found many old friends and contacts in a state of great trepidation about further such visits, so he deliberately decided to play on these fears. They would be given the chance of signing on voluntarily, he told one group of saltwater men, otherwise, he would sail off and inform the nearest warship that they had made an unprovoked attack upon his ship. By these and other shameless tricks, the *Heron* was extremely successful off Malaita during the early part of 1883. Then Rogers learned that blood-money had been put out for his head and he did not venture in the direction of Malaita again until after the wreck of the *Heron* in December 1884, when he was offered a share in and command of the *Young Dick*.

He could not afford to avoid Malaita indefinitely because, from about 1885 onwards, that island had come to supply overwhelmingly the largest number of recruits to Queensland out of all Melanesia. Though neither Kwaisulia in the north-east lagoon, nor Powlanga, his great ally and colleague at Port Adam in the south of Malaita, had yet attained the high point of their power, they had already established such firm relations with the recruiters as to be able to provide them with almost unlimited access to the teeming hill-tribes of the interior.

The New Hebrides and Solomons at this time were not fast running out of people, as reports, particularly from the missionaries, seemed to suggest. Though some of the smaller islands and the shores of the larger ones were heavily depopulated there remained places like Malekula, Santo, Guadalcanal, and Bougainville, whose inland populations were still pretty well untouched. However, where no channels existed for regular communication with the bush tribes, the recruiters could only cruise round certain well-known localities, Big Bay, Santo, for example, on the chance of picking them up during one of their occasional voyages to the coast. Then they were quite

likely to recruit in large numbers, for the young bushmen were as
eager and as keen to see the outside world as anyone else.

This was the situation which Kwaisulia and Powlanga were able
to exploit in Malaita. Thus skipper Rogers, putting in with the
Young Dick at Port Adam in October 1885, immediately sent word
to the influential Powlanga, who eventually arrived alongside in his
canoe and was entertained to lunch. This was the sort of treatment
Powlanga evidently expected, and he set off the next day with the
ship's boats to guide them up an arm of the harbour to where, he
predicted, various bands of bushmen would be waiting.

It proved to be just as he promised. At this place and that he
would ask to be put ashore, and natives, invisible at first to the
watching recruiters, would suddenly materialize out of the bush and
begin to parley with him. Usually he was able to return with one or
more recruits. His powers seemed almost magical. But how did he
manage it, the recruiters wondered. Did he put any pressure on
them? Evidently not. The recruits came forward quite willingly
once they felt sure Powlanga would protect them from injury at the
hands of the saltwater people.

If there were any pressure applied, it was probably by their own
bush chiefs or those professional killers or *ramos* as they were called,
now beginning to flourish in the islands, since almost any man
could gain the title simply by ownership of a good rifle. From killing
in order to gain blood-money, it was obviously but a short step to
blackmail and abduction. Such people would constrain men to
recruit, it seems, merely by going up to them and saying, "I can't
stand your face. Get out or I will kill you." One very sickly recruit
explained to the health officer at Townsville how he had come to
volunteer for Queensland in the first place: "Big chief blonga island
[Malaita] blonga me tellem 'You sick. You no good me. S'posem you
go alonga ship. Me gettem axe. Me gettem 'bacca. S'posem you no
go, me killem you'."

It was calculated that 90 per cent of the recruits engaged for
Queensland in this period were bushmen. And so it was on this
voyage. With the assistance, first of Powlanga, later of one or two
other saltwater chiefs, similarly engaged as middlemen, Rogers was
able to return to Maryborough with a full complement of 120
Solomon Islanders and have ample time to have the schooner refitted
before setting out again for the same destination as soon as the
hurricane season was ended.

They reached Malaita again on 1st May 1886, and John Hornidge,
Rogers' recruiter, went ashore at Mabo, a village previously pointed
out by Powlanga, where a native called Rady offered to act as
interpreter. It would have well paid recruiters to have refused the

services of every islander who came forward with an offer to interpret, particularly on Malaita. In fact, it was a common practice on parting with such a person to supply him with a "reference", in reality an instruction to the next European to read it to give the holder an almighty kick in the pants for being an unmitigated scoundrel. For the interpreter belonged to a footloose tribe, well enough qualified for the role no doubt by his previous experience of Queensland or Fiji or some island mission station, yet rarely to be trusted. If, like this Rady, he was also a refugee from some other district, and thus especially anxious to be of some service to his hosts, he would be the ideal person to act as a decoy if the village happened to be on the lookout for some white man's head.

However, they did not get Hornidge, though they tried. After being lured away by Rady out of reach of the boats and, out of sight of the ship around the corner of a little inlet, he was suddenly set upon by natives armed with tomahawks. He managed to escape by running for his life through the jungle undergrowth, bleeding as much from the brambles that tore at his face as from the deep wounds in his scalp, and he was lucky enough to come out on the beach quite near where the boats were waiting. Such incidents were only in the day's work; back aboard the *Young Dick* they soon had Hornidge patched up and Rogers proceeded on to Port Adam, where he found chief Powlanga being currently employed by the Fijian recruiter, *Meg Merrilees*.

Just at that time H.M.S. *Opal* also arrived, carrying in it a passenger, Richard Comins, an Anglican missionary. He was seeking a new outlet for the Church—his man at Sa'a down the coast having been placed under a curse by the powerful chief, Doraweewee. Some days later, then, following a conference between Comins, Powlanga, and the three ships' commanders, the *Young Dick* was towed round to Mabo behind the warship. Later, having been displayed to the villagers as a reminder of their treachery, it was manoeuvred into the background while nineteen shells were fired into the village—after which a native mission teacher was landed.

The *Young Dick* resumed its voyage northward along Malaita's eastern shore where, again, members of the boat-crew were lucky to escape death when arrows fell all round them as they pulled past a rocky point. But the recruiting just went on, day after day, and by 20th May, when the schooner rounded a large headland and sailed into Sinerago Bay, they had already about fourteen or fifteen aboard. They were largely bushmen obtained in the usual way, through the intermediacy of some shore tribes. But Sinerago, a huge land-locked harbour capable of sheltering a whole fleet, was a different proposition.

The people here belonged not to the shore and the saltwater, but essentially to the hills behind. Thus, although they possessed an assortment of rafts, dug-out canoes, and even a few crudely made outriggers for moving about the harbour and passages in the mangroves, they were exclusively fine-weather sailors who never went to sea. According to some of their saltwater enemies they could not even swim, and were liable to be so scared in the water once it reached as high as their waists as to become quite giddy and fall over.

Despite this alleged disability, however, they did not seem to be at any great disadvantage when dealing with European ships. They had already accounted for at least one ship's crew before—by the same old device, used up and down the coast, of luring part of the crew away on a ruse and then overwhelming those who were left.

But certain bone-headed seamen like Rogers never learn as long as they live. The morning after anchoring he was off down the coast with two boats, leaving back on board the mate, Charles Marr, in command, the G.A., Home Popham, and four members of the crew, including able seaman Thomas Crittenden. Before long a canoe with six men came alongside calling up to the white men to send a boat ashore as they had a recruit.

The G.A., however, told them to go back and fetch the man themselves. This they did, and all then climbed on board to examine the ship's trade and discuss the price. Home Popham was in his cabin signing on the recruit, while Marr and the spokesman for the bushman party were haggling over terms in the adjoining trade-room, when a score of canoes and catamarans came jostling round the ship. Each sitting occupant had a short-handled tomahawk concealed in a dilly-bag or green leaf wrapper.

The man talking to Marr actually gave the signal to attack, shouting out something which caused the men in the canoe to jump to their feet and come swarming up the ropes to the assistance of those already aboard. Marr managed to hurl his fellow out of the cabin and lock himself inside. Crittenden, asleep in the foc's'le, woke up and seized hold of a couple of guns. But the rest had no chance. Home Popham died with a pen poised over his G.A.'s log-book and still clutched in his hand. He was apparently the first to be dispatched, the others quickly following, after which the natives went yelling round the deck hacking viciously at corpses they chanced to stumble over but more intent on grabbing what they could get before Rogers should return with the boats.

They had Marr and Crittenden yet to reckon with. And these were formidable. The mate had a collection of fire-arms to choose from in the trade-room, and every so often he could get one of the natives in his sights and press the trigger. He would grow quite light-headed and jump for joy as if he was playing a game and had scored a point. Crittenden was sitting, straddle-legged high up in the yards by this time, so he could enjoy a strange feeling of detachment as he sat, shooting down through the rigging, picking them off very coolly, one after another, apparently with no sense of personal danger. Only one of the natives attempted to come up after him and Crittenden got him straight away, causing him to scream out in agony and go slithering back to the deck. After that they left Crittenden in peace. Suddenly they all disappeared over the side, some message having reached them from the shore evidently, for a few minutes later the two boats reappeared round the point rowing strongly towards the ship.

There was no need for this reckless waste of human lives. With proper thought it was possible to deal quite safely with the islanders —as the *Flora* proved by sailing unconcernedly into the bay at the same moment as the *Young Dick* was on its way out. The two recruiting vessels did not recognize one another in the westering sun or communicate, but Douglas Rannie, the *Flora's* G.A. and unofficial chief recruiter, had heard of the massacre of the previous day and planned to take advantage of it. Rannie, a Scots soldier of fortune, was a very experienced man with the natives who conducted the recruiting like a military operation and left nothing to chance. He had calculated that the islanders would be in a nervous, apprehensive mood if they had done murder, waiting for the other side to hit back, and all the more likely to recruit and get safely away to Queensland before the warship arrived. Nevertheless he was taking no risks. Both boats were heavily manned and heavily armed. And to guard the *Flora* he had left aboard a squad of thirty Santa Cruz recruits—islanders of whom the Malaitaman went in great fear, as their arrows were supposed to be poisoned.

It seemed for a while as if Rannie had misjudged the situation. For the shore was quite silent except for a few shots fired at the boats, so the *Flora* continued on after a few days to Nongosila and Kwai, two tiny islands connected at low tide by a sand-ridge, whose twin populations had combined to achieve the destruction of the *Janet Stewart* in 1882. Its charred ribs were still visible near the entrance to the harbour as a reminder of their great victory. However, the Kwai people were now in a more friendly mood and handed over twenty recruits, all bushmen and none other than the men who had played a leading part in the raid on the *Young Dick* and then fled north to take refuge at Kwai. Rannie had been right about them after all.

He was not always so lucky. At Ada Gege he had been counting on Kwaisulia to supply them with the bulk of their Malaita recruits, but

Kwaisulia was preoccupied at the time with his impending attack upon Manaoba and could not spare a single man. He suggested instead that they try Manaoba. They went there only to get the same reaction from the Manaobans: they were friendly and polite, but needed every man they had to repel an expected attack by Kwaisulia. The *Flora* none the less was able to recruit a fairly full cargo, without the recruiters at any stage having to expose themselves to serious danger. The *Young Dick* meanwhile had been forced to put back to Queensland, with only fifteen recruits, with its G.A. dead.

The two vessels happened to strike one another again when the *Flora* arrived home in July 1886 and came to anchor at Dungeness, near the mouth of the Herbert, waiting to be inspected. The *Young Dick* also lay at anchor nearby, about to depart with a group of New Ireland returns from the C.S.R.'s Victoria plantation. These, incidentally, were almost the last batch of New Irelanders to return. Rogers and Marr had come aboard to pay no more than a friendly visit when suddenly there was a shout and a scurry as Marr recognized one of the Sineragans and charged towards him. The man escaped, however, to find a secure hiding-place somewhere below, and some hours later the *Young Dick* sailed out of the river, never to be seen again, lost with all hands in the region of the Great Barrier Reef.

Rogers had been strongly warned by the pilot to delay his departure as a storm was imminent. But always slow to learn, he just sailed anyway and thus accounted for himself and his crew, including Charles Marr and Thomas Crittenden, the heroic survivors of the previous voyage; for his G.A., Jim Fowles, the first native-born Queenslander to be appointed to the post, and finally for about ninety New Irelanders who had arrived in the colony expecting perhaps to be eaten but instead were drowned.

So the recruiting went on; naturally there were some new faces in the trade after the wholesale debarrings of 1885, as well as several new vessels, the *Fearless, Para, Archimedes*, together with various others with brief careers like the *Young Dick*. Yet, though the newcomers were larger and able to make longer journeys, they fared on the whole neither better nor worse than their predecessors. On the one hand they had to contend with much stricter Government regulations that undoubtedly restricted their freedom of action. On the other, owing to the greatly increased naval activities in the area they could be freer in their dealings with the islanders, having generally less to fear from their sudden attacks. In 1886, 1,595 recruits were obtained; in 1887, 1,988; in 1888, 2,291; with a drop to 2,032 in 1889 owing to effects of the previous year's drought. Then numbers jumped back to 2,459 in 1890, the year in which recruiting was scheduled to stop. So there was no tapering off towards the end, in fact the recruiting carried over well into 1890 as a result of the great eleventh-hour rush by planters to obtain labour by getting ships away before the last recruiting vessel could be sent on 31st December 1890.

Few people really expected the trade to end even then. Particularly not since Griffith had gone out of office in 1888 and been succeeded as Premier by his rivals McIlwraith (June–November 1888) and Boyd Morehead (Acting Premier, December 1888–August 1890) during the temporary retirement of McIlwraith through illness. The planters must have been confident that it could be now only a matter of time before the veto was lifted and the trade resumed. And yet the new Government, though pledged to support the sugar interests in whatever way possible, was surprisingly slow to act.

In 1889 a Royal Commission appointed to investigate every aspect of the industry found conditions desperate indeed, and urged by a majority of two to one that the end could not be long delayed unless measures were adopted "to permit the continuation of indentured Kanaka labour for some time at least". The position at present, the majority report stated, was this: "The effects of the existing depression of the industry have already been felt in the timber trade and in the iron foundries of the colony, and the prosperity of the important towns of Mackay and Bundaberg is already, to some extent, affected by it. The shipping trade . . . is also interested in the sugar industry and it must also be borne in mind that sugar is the only article of agricultural produce of which any appreciable quantity is exported." This last point was the key to the Commission's findings: the value of the colony's sugar exports was estimated at £800,000 in a normal year, and they had found not a single item of evidence to suggest that there was any other agricultural industry in the colony capable of replacing sugar.

There it was in a nutshell: Queensland was dependent on sugar; sugar, apparently, on the Kanaka. And yet for more than twelve months, until their Government finally collapsed in August 1890, McIlwraith and Morehead managed to dodge the issue. It was not really so surprising however—if one recalled how soundly they had been defeated on that very issue in the elections of 1883. In view of the present doubtful state of the electorate, their most prudent course was obviously to do nothing. Morehead thus managed to remain at the helm, his reputation not enhanced but still intact, when quite suddenly, after several weeks of tense back-room lobbying, a certain amount of shuffling took place among the top cards in the deck and a new political combination emerged—a rather strange-looking animal, a Coalition Government of Griffith and McIlwraith, nicknamed the "Griffilwraith". But as always where Griffith was concerned there would be no shelving of the ultimate responsibility. He was Premier and would make the final decisions.

He was certainly a brave man, a very resolute and high-principled man. And if his actions now lacked quite the same assurance as of old, he still believed that he was needed, in these uncertain times, to do what was right, irrespective of what people thought. Undoubtedly, as a politician he had made many mistakes. He had tried to establish the farmers with his central mills and failed, many of them turning in their despair to his worst enemies, the northern separatists. He had tried to do the right thing in the *Hopeful* case and had spoken of wanting to see the murderers hanged at the yard-arm. He seemed unaware that there was a substantial body of opinion throughout Australia, including newspapers like the Protestant *Evangelical Standard*, for whom the black people represented the evil and animal side of man. To them the idea of white men having to suffer for some offence against natives was enough to drive them into the streets, screaming that they had never known "a black race yet which was not treacherous from infancy up to grey-headedness", hurling obscenities at the "smooth-tongued, oily wretches that those high in power in Queensland wanted to sacrifice two of our white men for".

It caused much distress to Griffith then to learn that there were still Queenslanders capable of feeling this way. He wanted to believe that such people did not exist, even ceasing at one stage to reply to their numerous petitions on the subject. But it was a very hot issue indeed and provided a great talking-point for his opponents, who went to the polls in 1888 committed to the release of the *Hopeful* prisoners.

In the event Griffith lost the elections; Morehead kept his party's promise to release the men, and by the time Griffith was back in power again in August 1890, the matter was over and forgotten. The great question now was the outcome of the massive struggle which had been building up between capital and labour. From that August, when the great maritime strike began, to the following July, when the great shearing strike finally came to an end, Griffith had hardly time for anything else. Queensland threatened to become a battle-field. But then as the threat of civil war gradually disappeared and society returned to normal, he could turn once more to consider the sugar industry.

The situation in the industry seemed as serious as ever. More and more mills were closing down. Even the C.S.R., which had already invested huge sums in Queensland, was rumoured to be on the point of cutting its losses, selling out altogether, and transferring the bulk of its operations to Fiji. However, Griffith saw one gleam of hope. The planters had, given the circumstances, changed their views on the question of importing white labour from Europe. For during 1891 various plantation owners on the Herbert and Burdekin had been making arrangements to bring out about 350 northern Italians. They would be obliged to labour for two years in the service of the planter after which they would be able to set up on their own, having an assured contract to supply the mill with a quota of cane per season. This was exactly what Griffith had been urging the planters to accept all along, and thus on his approaching Cabinet tour of North Queensland at Christmas 1891, he looked forward eagerly to seeing something of the experiment at first hand.

It was an utter failure. The "new unions", as they were called, saw to that. They had taken a beating in their first round with the capitalists, but they still stood in good heart, and in no mood to tolerate any capitalist attempt to undercut the existing European wage structure through this so-called indenture system or any other dubious subterfuge. This was something they could hit back on. So they hounded the unfortunate Italians from the moment of their arrival, causing most of them to break their engagements and go tramping from town to town in search of work, much as the indentured Cingalese had been compelled to do at Bundaberg in 1882. The unionists treated these Italians with the utmost suspicion until convinced beyond all question that they had become transformed into Australian democrats, prepared to stand up to the employer at the drop of a hat.

Griffith might have expected this reaction from the labour movement. The unions were still licking old wounds and were blind to everything but their own immediate needs. Still they had helped him to face up to the vital question, and on 12th February 1892, within a month of his return to Brisbane, he issued his famous manifesto to the people of Queensland: "You are aware that for many years I was the most determined opponent to the introduction of coloured or servile labour into Queensland. My objection was not on account of the colour of men's skins but because the employment of such labour under the conditions to which we had become accustomed was injurious to the best interests of the colony regarded as a home for the British race."

It was not in his best style, the short, sharp sentences that cut to the bone. It rambled considerably, to explain the straitened economic circumstances that had obliged him to change his mind, the implacable attitude of the unions "which would not allow any work except under conditions unknown in any other part of the world and for three times the wages". But it got there in the end, to announce that he favoured extension of the Kanaka traffic for at least another ten years. "By that time I have no doubt such further developments will have taken place as will enable the sugar industry to be carried on without fear of our reverting to the former system."

Not many politicians are prepared to admit having made a thundering great mistake about the foremost political question of the day. And the decision was Griffith's alone, the Cabinet knowing nothing of the impending announcement until just beforehand. He was apologizing really for failing to see how far the Kanaka had become an essential part of the system. The Kanaka was much cheaper (costing about £26 a year to maintain compared with £75 for one European), but it was not only that. In any case he was still capable of negotiating for better wages and conditions, even without a formal trade-union organization. For the islanders kept constantly in touch with one another and were well aware, probably more so than the average planter, of the latest developments in every part of the colony.

If wages were inclined to fall away in the off season, say, those waiting to re-engage would hang off for a while, quite able to live off the land in the meantime if necessary, until the consequent scarcity of labour should oblige the employer to accede to their terms. But there was one thing the planter could be sure of, once those terms had been agreed to and accepted—there was little likelihood of the Kanaka going on strike, unlike the white mill worker whose favourite tactic was to walk off the job at the height of the crushing.

The impression of one newspaperman, a correspondent of the *Sydney Mail* wandering at large through the sugar districts in the latter part of 1892, was that the Kanaka tended to take almost the same proprietorial interest in the plantation as the planter himself. Thus he noted the difference between the white hands, holding themselves indifferently aloof, gathered in their quarters by night to drink and play cards, and the islanders, relaxed outside their huts, smoking and gossiping, one man practising some dance steps, another strumming a banjo and breaking into a song, behaving as if they owned the place.

The proportion of old hands serving their second or third terms at a negotiated wage to new recruits freshly indentured from the islands was now by 1892 well over half and rapidly approaching a ratio of three to one. The possibility that recruiting really would end in 1890 and never be resumed was a factor in helping them to strike a better bargain. The wages of time-expired Kanakas rose steadily from approximately £12 a year before 1886 to an average of

£18 a year in 1892, as the numbers re-engaging rose also. Thus when recruiting actually ceased altogether for a time during 1891-2 the total number of islanders in Queensland dropped only very slightly. In 1894, the lowest point of the nineties, the figure stood at 7,489 compared with the 7,580 of 1889.

Many of these had been in Queensland fifteen to twenty years; it had become their adopted home. At the end of the initial three-year period, groups of them would go off together, via bush paths known only to themselves, in order to meet and discuss with friends in other parts of the colony before deciding whether to return to the islands or re-engage. In very many cases they would book a passage home and then cancel it at the last minute. If they did return, however, the chances were about even that they would then recruit a second time, probably complaining to the recruiter of having had to wait months for a ship. If not, they would quite possibly never return home.

For the pull of home was not as strong as it had once been. If, as was often the case, their village had been destroyed and the wider society of neighbouring villages related by blood and marriage dispersed and broken up, they would not be missing very much. Wives were in short supply in Queensland, the proportion of women to men growing less as time went on (only 379 to 8,049 in 1898). But so they were in the islands, where the old men monopolized them. In Queensland, moreover, women could be more easily shared or bought and sold. And then there were also the Chinese and Japanese-kept brothels. There were not a great number, in these circumstances, who seemed to want to settle down with one woman and raise a family. And it never happened, as the planters had originally hoped, that the children born on the plantations would be the nucleus of a never-ending supply of future labour. Kanaka births on the plantations were relatively few.

The important thing was that they were still able to retain their sense of belonging to a community, of having an assured place in the world. On one occasion a certain islander, accused by a white cook of being only a "blackfella", walked ten miles to lodge a complaint with the local district inspector; "Me no blackfella," he protested indignantly. "Me boy blonga islands. Fella blongs longa-here, he bloomin' blackfella."

Every so often to nourish this feeling of community and local superiority the islanders held a great feast. Pigs were bought from the local farmers for about ten shillings each, and people came on foot, on horseback, in traps, from the surrounding plantations, from the nearby township, even from other districts. The owner of Pleystowe plantation, Mackay, said that eighteen of his boys owned their own hacks so that they could travel freely at week-ends; that he had known others to ring up Mackay and order a drag and four horses for the evening. Not that he approved of such "corroborees", for this was a time when everybody got full of liquor and one of those terrible inter-island affrays was likely to break out. Even if there were no bloody battles planters would have a hard time getting their boys to work on Monday morning.

Actually neither Griffith nor many of the planters appreciated the relief that the islanders must have felt at the re-opening of the recruiting. For the islanders could regard it in an important sense as a sort of testimonial to their services, a recognition of what they meant to the colony. The figures perhaps bear witness; the number of re-engagements were more than ever after 1892, despite a slight lowering of wages on the whole and the decline in the availability of the right jobs.

Griffith had in fact inspired confidence all round. Except for some of the newspapers, which spoke of his "amazing volte-face", and the usual collection of cynics and detractors who sneered that the C.S.R. had forced his hand by threatening to remove to Fiji, most people actually appeared to be pleased with him for a change. Even the vociferous northern unionists seemed not too displeased, calculating apparently that they were now sufficiently strong to take care of the question in North Queensland once Separation was achieved. Only in England, which one might have expected to remain neutral in such a purely colonial concern, was there a great outcry made, and that could be traced very largely to the work of one man.

The Reverend John Paton, former senior Presbyterian missionary in the New Hebrides, had written so many letters to Griffith on the subject of the labour trade that Griffith was heartily sick of him. Apart from the staggering verbosity, what especially irritated the Premier about the reverend gentleman was his utter disregard for fact. He just wrote, apparently, without bothering to check details, trusting that his conscience and overcharged heart would tell him what to say. Some of his statements were quite outrageous. Thus he had in his time accused the Queensland Government of supporting slavery; the planters, of allowing their boys to die off like flies in their first year so that they could pocket a year's wages; the recruiters, of having caused the virtual depopulation of the islands by carrying off willy-nilly, men, women, even little children.

For most of the time he harmed his own cause more than those he opposed. The recruiters for their part could retort that "the population of Aneityum has decreased much more sensibly than that of any other island in the New Hebrides although it has been under the sole control of the Presbyterian mission for about thirty years

The C.S.R.'s Childers mill in the Bundaberg district.

Time-expired labourers, having decided to remain in Queensland, built homes like this one.

The overseer with a chipping gang in Queensland.

Kanakas cutting cane on a Queensland plantation.

The recruiter *Fearless* with recruits on their way home.

and has been almost unvisited by traders or labour vessels".

There was another unfortunate consequence of his attacks in that they put a device into the hands of a few crafty men who would simply use him for their own particular ends. The Melbourne *Argus* at one stage had been in the habit of regularly publishing his charges against the recruiters, but selecting especially those which referred to the activities of Queensland vessels. There were certain parties in Melbourne who had invested heavily in Fiji, and were anxious for it to appear that it was predominantly the deeds of the Queenslanders that had earned the trade its bad name. Then a particular letter of Paton's was published—a lurid document, a catalogue of child-snatchings and violence and sudden death, yet sufficiently circumstantial when it came to specific cases to make some sort of action clearly necessary. The Navy therefore made an investigation and found the particular allegations to be quite baseless, denied even by Paton's own colleagues in the islands. As a result the *Argus* was obliged to drop him altogether.

What was concerning Griffith in 1892 was that immediately after his manifesto Paton began writing furiously to everyone he knew in England—Members of Parliament, the Colonial Office, the Anti-Slavery Society, all the Protestant missionary societies—throwing out the most reckless accusations, making it sound as if the trade were every bit as bad as it had ever been. In fact not a single kidnapping incident had been reliably reported in all the years between 1885 and 1892. Not only that, but numerous masters and recruiters and one or two G.A.s had been debarred for minor breaches of the Act, while as the result of a rigid inspection by the Department in Queensland the mortality rate on the plantations had dropped markedly.

Nevertheless Paton managed to create a tremendous furore: church meetings were held on the question all over the country; petitions went to Parliament urging Britain to intervene "in the name of humanity"; a prolonged controversy raged in the letter columns of the national Press over the essential morality of the traffic. John Selwyn, retired Bishop of Melanesia, writing from Godalming in Surrey, had one or two interesting points to make in rebuttal of Paton. The Church of England, stated Selwyn, had been in favour of the trade, with certain qualifications naturally, since the days of Bishop Patteson. Surely, he argued, the poor, heathen islanders could not be harmed by being taken to a Christian country. If they were, it suggested there was something wrong with Christianity as much as with the labour trade. But, as a matter of fact, experience in Queensland and Fiji had made innumerable converts of the islanders. He had seen with his own eyes the changes wrought in them upon their return and thought these people by far the best instruments for

R

making future conversions. He felt sure Paton had exaggerated the evils of the trade. As for the Church of England, it would prefer to adapt a useful migration to its own innocent ends than to present a jealous opposition!

Of course, the two churches rarely saw eye to eye on any subject. More surprising, however, and rather more forcefully expressed was the opposition of Paton's own Presbyterian Church in Queensland. It was not widely known at the time, but some years before, in 1888, a small local mission had been formed, yet another missionary arm of the Church, devoted specifically to the welfare of the Kanaka in Queensland. And yet energetic and enthusiastic as the work had been, especially in the Mackay district under the direction of the Reverend John McIntyre, it had received only tepid support from fellow missionaries in the New Hebrides. Judging from the manner of some of the returns on their arrival home, the activities in Queensland were rather a waste of time and money, their letters implied. Nevertheless McIntyre had persisted and established no fewer than twenty-one little mission outstations around Mackay, with hopes of carrying the work even farther afield when the recruiting was resumed. Now here was the great John Paton hurling his thunderbolts from on high, alleging that the Church had been condoning slavery on the plantations, charging his hearers to beware that by renewing the labour trade they would be making war on God's work in the islands.

So the Foreign Missions Committee of the Presbyterian Church which had been encouraging McIntyre in a mild way added its voice to the mounting chorus of protest, confirming the growing impression in England as well as in Australia that John Paton was altogether too much of a zealot to be taken at his word. He had in fact succeeded in prejudicing his own case and winning some sympathy for his victims. In the end nothing emerged out of all the controversy apart from what Griffith had already known. If genuine abuses continued to exist he would have been glad to hear of them, with a view to clamping the regulations even tighter about those recruiters. Thus, following his decision to reopen the trade, he had written to the High Commissioner for the Western Pacific and other authorities, seeking possible suggestions for further ways of improving it. And only then, after failing to receive anything particularly worthwhile or constructive by way of reply, had he enacted his Pacific Islanders Extension Bill along practically the same lines as the older legislation. What more could he do? Not only had he suppressed all, or almost all, of the undesirable features of the traffic, but there were now definite grounds for believing it to be the means of achieving positive good for the island people.

Even the most earnest and well-meaning of the missionaries had not sufficiently recognized at first that the Melanesians had minds craving to be instructed, as well as souls to be saved. They tended to assume that learning would have to start from scratch, or behind scratch, really, since the poor natives had so much to unlearn to begin with. Reason, it was assumed, had been overlaid in their minds by superstition and various dark heathen beliefs. Thus the missionaries concentrated on bringing them to a knowledge of the love of God, on filling them with the Holy Spirit, hoping that the darkness would thereby be washed away and they might then be able to reach them. Meanwhile the natives hungered for knowledge.

As far back as 1881 there was a case at Tanna where a Christian native teacher boarded one of the recruiters and, finding the conditions aboard reasonably satisfactory had then sent word to his pupils ashore that they should recruit also. In Paton's subsequent letter to the *Argus*, however, it was made to appear as if a trap had been laid by these devilish recruiters to decoy the teacher aboard and then use him to inveigle the rest of the flock. "So soon as 100 [?] were collected," said Paton, "the vessel sailed away."

But there was nothing really remarkable about a whole congregation suddenly deserting. It began to happen all over the New Hebrides after 1882 when Florence Young started her Sunday School classes for the Kanakas on her brothers' Fairymead plantation, Bundaberg.

Florence Young was a very capable organizer; before long she had most of the plantation staff attending and was in the process of founding the Queensland Kanaka Mission for the purpose of extending the work to the whole Bundaberg district. The fame of "Missy Young" spread through the islands. Admittedly the instruction she gave was little different in the long run from what the islanders were accustomed to in the New Hebridean mission schools. But they *were* learning to read and write, and learning much faster in Queensland than they did in the islands, where there seemed little point to this.

When George Da-te-man, for instance, returned to Ambrym from Fairymead in 1888 he was not content until he had persuaded his friend, Albert Lisa, to go also, and enjoy the same advantages as himself. George also started building his own little school on Ambrym, and when a recruiter finally appeared he told Albert, "Now you go along Queensland along Miss Young and learn this what I tell you." Then, giving him some books, "Suppose you no find 'im true, when you come back I all same you. I wait, no build 'im school till you come back." So Albert Lisa went—and others also. No doubt the recruiters were only too pleased to assist in such a spontaneous spreading of the Gospel, but it cannot be said that the official missionary organizations approved. The tendency for the Church to fragment into sects and to lack a firm centralized control were weaknesses inherent in the situation in Melanesia already. The multitude of independent operators springing up all over the place only made matters worse—as the case of Peter Amboo-oba of Malaita would prove.

Amboo-oba was a product of Miss Young's undenominational Queensland Kanaka Mission at Kalkie, Bundaberg, and being a man of exceptional, almost messianic gifts and great strength of character, he had thrust himself upon the Mission's attention as a likely person to establish its first outpost in the islands. However, not only Amboo-oba and the Mission were involved. Henry St George Caulfield, Polynesian Inspector at Bundaberg, a stern, devout, former Ceylon tea planter was also closely associated with the Youngs, and arrangements were made to launch Amboo-oba on his mission with a certain amount of ceremony. He was to depart in the recruiter *William Manson*, and the Youngs, as well as members of Parliament, representatives of the Immigration Department, the Press and others, would all be there to give the occasion their blessing.

Here then was not only an unlikely conjunction of missionary and recruiter setting out together under the aegis of the Government, but the master-owner of the *William Manson*, 360-ton barque, the largest and best equipped ever to enter the trade, was none other than that well-known blackbirder of former days, Captain Joseph Vos.

Nine years before, in 1885, it may be remembered, Vos had been disbarred from the trade together with all those who had gone recruiting in the neighbourhood of New Guinea. Then in 1888, with Griffith ousted from office, certain names had been quietly removed from the black list and Vos had been able to re-enter the trade. He had always been one of the most resourceful of the recruiters and was now exploiting a new device—the phonograph.

His plan was to visit certain Queensland plantations, take photographs of various well known individuals, and then ask them to record mechanically whatever message they might have for their friends back home. Vos perfected it and it grew to be quite an effective performance. With the aid of glass slides and the limelight he would enlarge the pictures to approximately life-size on a large screen in the background and grind out these messages praising this or that aspect of plantation life. To his astonished audience it would eerily appear as if their own sons and brothers were talking directly to them. No wonder the natives still believed in ghosts. Trick it might have been, but the phonograph attracted a lot of respectful attention. Things like that combined to give the impression that the *William Manson* was the glamour vessel of the moment.

In the event the Youngs' choice to conduct Amboo-oba and his two young assistants to their station in the islands fell upon Captain Vos, and on 27th April 1894 his ship sailed down the Brisbane River to begin what was actually only the second recruiting voyage of its career, though the name *William Manson* was already one of the best known in the trade generally.

The barque's immediate destination was Malaita's north-east lagoon, since most of its returns came from that neighbourhood. And Vos intended to waste no time trying different localities, but to deal exclusively through his friend Kwaisulia.

For the coast of Malaita was as dangerous as ever, probably more dangerous than in the days of the *Young Dick* in 1886, as German recruiters had discovered the area in the meantime and been buying up recruits at the impressive rate of one Snider and so many boxes of ammunition per head. Further south numbers of villages had formed a regular Navy, a war fleet of about a dozen canoes, which could assemble at short notice for the purpose of attacking any recruiter foolish enough to anchor within range. But in the lagoon itself Kwaisulia was paramount. He had conquered all his saltwater enemies or succeeded by diplomacy in bending them to his will, and here the recruiter could be safe.

As the *William Manson* sailed into the lagoon and came within sight of Ada Gege, a canoe came quickly off, and Vos, recognizing Kwaisulia in it, immediately hove to. He received his visitor at the head of the gangway and the usual palaver went on: Vos pretended that he had called only to land some returns and was not interested in recruits; Kwaisulia agreed to this, pointing out that in any case recruits were particularly hard to come by just at that time of year.

Before long, however, they had settled on terms, and over and above the beads, axes, and tomahawks per recruit, Kwaisulia was to receive one large whaleboat, exactly of the type of the *William Manson*'s own boats, only covered in fore and aft. That afternoon, the two men went off together in the barque's steam launch to take the soundings and inspect the lay of the land.

It was not until that evening, while the ship was standing to an inshore anchorage, that the captain remembered his commission to establish the three missionaries. According to Vos, the following conversation then ensued. "I have some missionary boys on board who wish to form a school here", he told Kwaisulia. "Where do they belong to?" the chief replied. "Let me see them." Vos produced his three Malaitamen, Peter Amboo-oba, Billy Try, and Koby.

Kwaisulia thereupon took them aside, spoke to them for a few minutes in the native language, and then turned to Vos, exclaiming angrily: "I do not want those bloody black missionaries here. By'm by they will be bigger than I am. Suppose'm white man, he wantem stop, me look after him. Pay 'im ground. He put 'im up house." In other words, if a *white* missionary came, he would then sell him land and protect him from injury. But otherwise . . . no.

In that case, said Vos, the would-be missionaries, not being able to settle, had no option except to re-engage for another three years in Queensland in the hope of then being able to return to Malaita again under the charge of a white missionary.

However, this was not what the three missionary boys themselves said when they eventually arrived back in Bundaberg. Their story was one of having quarrelled violently with the captain on the voyage out, being treated no better than the ordinary returns, in consequence of which Vos had told Kwaisulia not to accept them under any circumstances. They maintained that, having arranged this with Kwaisulia secretly, the captain had then staged the little scene on the poop to make it appear as if Kwaisulia was really the one responsible.

Actual recruiting then began on Monday, 21st May 1894. The ship's recruiter, Michael Curry, was in charge of one boat; George Olver, the G.A., of the other. Kwaisulia, with two stalwart henchmen, Gwaliasi and Kowa, were with them also, in Curry's boat, and it was now under the direction of Kwaisulia that they headed for the fish market, a strip of beach where the saltwater people would bring their fish to exchange for the yams and taro brought down by the bushmen. The market being then in progress, the bushmen could see Kwaisulia with the recruiters and watched his approach with some alarm.

They had good reason to be afraid. Their most usual experience of Kwaisulia was seeing him hovering about in a canoe, waiting to pounce on the boxes of some recently returned batch of recruits. Still, on this occasion they should have been in no danger. They were in comfortably superior numbers, well-armed, and in the presence of their own powerful chief, Sooba. So pretending to be not particularly aware of his arrival, they went on with their marketing, when suddenly Kwaisulia seized one boy bodily and began to drag him off to the boat. Gwaliasi and Kowa each had another in the same fashion, except that Kowa's man had one arm partly free and was striking feebly back with a tomahawk, making Kowa bleed. Sooba had evidently betrayed them. Some of the bushmen half-heartedly raised their rifles, but they were leaderless for the moment and too bewildered to know how to act on their own initiative, and when Kwaisulia, wading off with his victim, turned round and commanded them in English, "Don't shoot the boats", they obediently lowered them again.

The three "recruits" were now thrust under the thwarts in the two boats, and Olver ran up a small flag, a signal to the ship to send the launch as they had some recruits. By this time they were in deep water, and when the launch arrived the three scrambled into it of their own accord, there being no need to hold them in further restraint since they were bushmen and could not swim. Kwaisulia called out to the agent as they were departing, "Government, you are not cross with me. Captain told me to pull boys." And Olver replied, "No that's all right."

Actually it was not all right, not quite. For in the excitement of the moment Kowa had seized the wrong boy—a certain Zeelotta, the son of an influential bush chieftain whom Kwaisulia had no desire to antagonize unnecessarily. The mistake, however, was not discovered until the ceremony of signing on later in the day.

Billy Try was very useful at this stage. After the evident failure of the missionary enterprise he had entered enthusiastically into the kidnapping, acting as the agent's interpreter and general right-hand man in the boats. "Tell him three year," Olver now ordered him, indicating Erringa, the first to be signed. Erringa was now supposed to touch the pen which Try was holding out to him, in token of his willingness to have a cross marked alongside his name in the agent's log. But Erringa was inconsolable, having done practically nothing else but weep from the moment of coming aboard, and he refused to touch anything. So Try had to catch his hand and hold it while Olver wrote "three year" and put Erringa's cross beside it.

Sooquow, the next candidate, did what he was bidden without complaint, but the third man, Zeelotta, looked very upset and resentful about something. Vos, who had been standing in the background watching, took Try aside and told him, "You talk along Zeelotta there and get him sign." Thus his identity was disclosed and all further attempts to compel him were forthwith abandoned by urgent request of Kwaisulia. Two days later he was returned to his father.

It is impossible to say how many recruits in all Kwaisulia helped them obtain, since the entries in the G.A.'s log, specifying times and places, are not to be believed. But according to an enquiry held at Bundaberg upon the barque's return the following took place:

Two women, Zoung warra and Tow allie, were forcibly taken here; they were both single women, not belonging to Quisoolia's [Kwaisulia] salt-water tribe. The first named, when she saw what was going to happen, ran away and took refuge in a place reserved for women only. Her pursuers could not follow her in there, but called the assistance of two

women, who went in, caught her, and placed her in a canoe, in which
she was brought to the boats. The second woman was cooking in a
house, dragged out, and as she came she seized hold of a post and held
on until it broke. A woman she was living with, named Funghi, came to
her assistance, and tried to hold her, but Quisoolia picked up a club or
big stick, and beat Funghi until she let go or fell down. Tow allie was
then taken to the boats, being put into the recruiter's boat first, and then
passed on to the Government Agent's boat, that officer handing her in
and supplying her with a piece of calico.

Zoung warra subsequently died in Brisbane Hospital from "in-
flammation of the brain"; Tow allie became the wife of Billy Try.
There was the case of Basseah Carlo and his wife, Gualomy.

Living some distance out of their village, at daylight on the morning
they were caught they found their house surrounded by a chief called
Ettica and his fighting men. The house was smashed open and they were
dragged out and carried to the beach where the *William Manson*'s boats
were waiting. A baby "at the breast" and another child were left behind
in the house. None of the force used on this occasion could be seen from
the boats, the couple walked into the recruiter's boat because they dared
not do otherwise, and it was only after they arrived that they made known
the manner in which they were recruited.

A husband and wife was an unusual catch. In earlier times it had
sometimes been possible to secure women, since there were cases of
couples eloping. But in these days when the recruiting was more
than ever under the control of the chiefs, desirable young females,
whom they monopolized, were almost unprocurable. The planters,
though, were paying top prices for females, and this explains why
Kwaisulia was concerned to abduct the wives of the saltwater people,
having to raid his own larder so to speak, when men were much more
readily obtainable by dealing with the bush chiefs. Even so he was
not particularly successful, arriving mainly with the not-so-young and
not-well-favoured, whom Vos would have to refuse or reluctantly
accept in the hope of marrying them off to male recruits as the voyage
proceeded. (This was made necessary by the regulation which forbade
the recruiting of single women or married women without their
husbands.) However, such tactics did not always work, and in this
case a number of "unattachable" females were carried around at
some expense for several weeks until finally they had to be put
ashore.

So the recruiters finally parted with Kwaisulia, not specially
pleased with his efforts on this occasion, and set out for the New
Hebrides. At Epi on 25th September another incident occurred.

The boats went to a small island, La Menu [Lammen], close to Api [Epi], recruiting, and returned with three islanders, two men and a woman; the latter (Oooloomorrie) was obtained from a canoe and claimed to be the wife of one of the men, Koolooah. It is now pretty certain that she was not his wife and the taking of her by the *William Manson*'s people led to a very serious disturbance next day. It appears that both boats were at Api, where they had gone to pay for some stores, and while there the La Menu people came and demanded the return of the woman. This demand must have been made in real earnest, as the Government Agent sent at once to the ship for the woman and handed her back to the people claiming her. Thus the matter might have ended satisfactorily, but the *William Manson*'s people became intoxicated and in that condition set out for La Menu. Upon arrival there some firing took place; accounts differ as to who commenced it, but eventually the recruiter Curry, and part of the boat-crew (coloured and white) rushed the village and set fire to some of the houses close to the beach, four of which were destroyed.

Perhaps it was just as well that Griffith had retired from active politics in 1893, before these events took place. "Adequate provisions must of course be made, and they can be made, for preventing abuses in the introduction of labourers," he had proclaimed in re-opening the trade. Paton and the Presbyterians, for all their wilful over-colouring of the case, had retorted, "It cannot be carried on with justice to the natives, nor with honour to the British nation."

For the recruiters could not change their spots, nor the islanders their skins and deep-rooted objections to having control of their destinies taken out of their hands by the white man or anyone else. In fact they had never thought of themselves as having been ex-ploited at all, rather of having adapted their lives after the fashion that suited them best to meet the circumstance of a widespread invasion of their islands by the recruiting ships. There was no other means of recruiting, except to abide by the conditions laid down by men like Kwaisulia. All the successful recruiters acknowledged this, including Vos himself, and took the appropriate precautions to ensure that not a hint of the real situation ever reached the ears of the Department back in Brisbane. However, Vos had been out of the trade for eight or nine years and may not have fully understood how the temper of the times had changed since the comparatively free and easy days of 1882–4. Otherwise he would surely have gone to more trouble to cover up his tracks.

And yet, on the other hand, he had always been a bit like this, a rather superior kind of Englishman, noted for his sang-froid, for his preference for playing the violin rather than, say, playing cards with the men. It hardly occurred to him that he might have anything to explain or hide away where savages were concerned. And so the frustrated teachers duly arrived back in Brisbane, where Peter Amboo-oba immediately informed the authorities of all that had taken place.

The Department of Immigration, Pacific Island Labour Branch, was genuinely shocked that such things were still possible in this day and age, and even more shocked by Vos's bland assertion that the *William Manson* had done "no more than was common to all labour vessels". "Such an assertion," wrote O'Neil Brenan, the Immigration Agent, to the Colonial Secretary's Office, "is untrue and most unjust to the respectable staff of Government Agents in the service. People who know anything of the trade nowadays are well aware that irregularities cannot take place and remain undiscovered and the *William Manson* case, I submit, proves it."

Brenan examined the recruits in person in Brisbane, as did Caulfield, the Polynesian Inspector, subsequently in Bundaberg, and both being satisfied that Amboo-oba's story was substantially correct, kidnapping charges under the Imperial Kidnapping Act of 1872 were laid against Captain Joseph Vos, George Olver, the agent, and five other members of the crew (later withdrawn in the case of the seaman Nash, who had turned Queen's evidence). They were committed for trial at the next sessions of the Queensland Supreme Court.

It was a most regrettable scandal from every point of view, but particularly from the Queensland Government's; about the worst thing that could have happened to its ambition to be granted a share in the administration of that portion of the Solomons recently annexed by Great Britain. It looked as though some malign fate had intervened again, and that Queensland was to be thwarted of its hopes in the Solomons just as it had been cheated in the case of New Guinea.

However the case was still far from over. The evidence against the *William Manson* may have looked pretty black, at least as black as that against the *Hopeful*. But in the box Vos and his men had a very good story to tell, and they stuck to it with remarkable unanimity, from skipper down to cabin boy. Kwaisulia had offered to supply him with recruits, said Vos. He did not always inquire how the chief obtained them. But he had seen none who had not climbed willingly aboard nor enjoyed listening to his phonograph whenever it pleased them to demand it. To use force in the circumstances was unnecessary. As a matter of fact, in the case of the two recruited at the market, he *had* pursued some inquiries but had learnt that Kwaisulia and his men had been only a handful in the midst of 150 armed bushmen. And apart from that the bush chief, Sooba, had agreed to their going.

It was the evidence of a man whom the Court could respect; whom his loyal crew obviously did respect. How different was the impression created by Nash, the informer, their former shipmate; or by the pious, smirking Billy Try, the "missionary" boy who glibly told how the captain would invite him into his cabin for a cigar. Later he had openly joined the kidnappers and been rewarded, he boasted, with one of the kidnapped women. He had certainly duped the good folk at Fairymead. Finally there was Amboo-oba. Well, he might have been a man of different stamp from the other two, Try and Koby. But the reason he had quarrelled with Vos on the voyage out, which had caused the captain to threaten to put him in irons, was that he had been after the women all the time. A missionary fornicator no less!

There were thus two quite conflicting stories before the Court—one put forward by the native witnesses, the other by the white. It was impossible apparently for the jury to choose between them. Its only possible course was to find the prisoners not guilty. That was the end to the *William Manson* case and the last occasion of any Queensland recruiter's having to answer for his conduct before a Court. Never again, until the end of the labour trade in 1906, would the department be obliged to endure such scandal. As for Vos and his associates, they were promptly debarred from taking part in the trade ever again. Even if they had not kidnapped, they had broken just about every other rule in the book.

In retrospect it seems strange that Vos should have taken Amboo-oba so lightly and been blind to his extraordinary qualities. "Amboo" in Malaita means sacred, a person touched by the sacred spirits, and it seems that Peter Amboo-oba regarded himself not only as a holy person, but one divinely appointed to carry the message of Everlasting Life to his people, to rescue them from that state of mental, moral, and spiritual destitution which the kindly, good-hearted missionaries in Queensland had been at great pains to point out was assuredly theirs. It was blindly foolish of Vos to attempt to sign him on again after Kwaisulia had refused Amboo-oba permission to land. Vos had been stupid not to let him go perhaps somewhere else. As it was, the missionary was back to Malaita aboard the next labour vessel, the *Para*, together with Try, Koby, and all those who had been carried off by the *William Manson* against their will.

Try and Koby proved to be the kind of Christians whose "conversion" is merely to impress their friends and relations in the islands, and who quickly revert to heathenism when they find the locals much less inclined to be impressed than they had imagined. But nothing could shake Peter Amboo-oba from his faith.

He had entrusted himself this time not to Kwaisulia, but to another saltwater chief nearby, whose treatment of him even so was hardly respectful: he was given a place to live underneath a hut with the pigs. This did not bother him, he later told Florence Young; he had just said to himself: "My Jesus He been come down along place belong stable me all right, thank you. I pull'im out rubbish I sleep there." But after a while the locals grew tired of him, and told him to go.

Eventually he came to his own people, bushmen who inhabited the extreme northern district of Malaita. Nor did they think much of him, returning home after so many years, with no box, with no presents to share out among all the kin. He had, to all appearance then, done the community little honour during his travels abroad. But they did not utterly reject him. His relatives still had an obligation to look after him. Thus he was allowed a patch of land down by the sea-shore where he lived alone for the next four years, 1896–1900, a hermit in his little hut, an object of derision to one and all who passed on their way to market. On a nearby tree he had fastened a text from John 3:16. It was in English, which nobody could read in that neighbourhood, but "God, he might see," thought Peter. "And Devil might see and say to himself, 'Eh, man belong God here, more better I clear out'."

But he persevered and broke through his isolation finally. How, exactly, it is impossible to say, but according to Miss Young it was through a miracle wrought in the year 1900: the gardens in the hills behind failed because of drought, but Peter's alone continued to flourish as before. People began to think that perhaps there was some special power protecting him. Parents would let their children go and visit him, the women would also come and listen, as well as some of the men, and in time quite a few were converted and came to settle on the shore so that eventually a whole new village, Irombule, grew into being.

Certain factors operated to draw them there in the first place: the chance to get a wife without having to pay bride-price, or to get away from the domination of the old men. Or perhaps there was something greater altogether, the promise of immortality, the possibility that some part of their own individual selves was too precious ever to be entirely extinguished.

But it was not easy to be a Christian in the early days of the village when it was liable to be raided from the hills at any time. And those who believed, believed fiercely, not like so many of the Queensland-converted boys whose Christianity was mainly a matter of convenience. In the end the Christian community created by Peter Amboo-oba out of his own sheer will and imagination endured as long and sturdily as any in Melanesia. It still flourishes today.

In many ways therefore it was a pity when the Queensland Kanaka

Mission took over Irombule officially and placed their own white missionary in residence. It was almost inevitable where one man had laboured so long alone that two would sooner or later fall out. So it proved. Amboo-oba's old weakness, adultery, was the immediate cause that led to his being suspended by the mission authorities some years later. Thereupon in rage and bitter disappointment he tried to wreck the whole organization and openly boasted that he would take it with him to hell. In time he repented of such thoughts and was readmitted to membership, but with all his old powers and prestige gone. It is characteristic of the white man, however, that he should wish to run everything himself. After all, it was *his* Christianity presumably. Just as it was *his* sugar industry. And already he had decided to dispense with the Kanaka's services in that field too.

ELEVEN

Deportation

THE statistics published by the various Churches, showing the number of islanders converted, the number baptised, the number of regular attenders at chapel and so on, are impressive, but the fact remained that not a great proportion of the islanders in Queensland had time or will to worry about the state of their souls. They were a pretty healthy and active crowd generally, and at the end of a hard week's work they would be off to where the action was. At their disposal were the Chinese gambling dens, which in many cases also supplied opium and various potent brews, like "hell fire" and "chain lightning" to really get them hopping, as well as prostitutes, black, half-caste, and coloured.

Naturally there were incidents from time to time, where mobs of Kanakas, roving the back streets, out to raise Cain in Chinatown on a mixture of cheap gin and opium, would battle it out with the police with bottles and sticks. As part of the New Year celebrations in Cairns in 1901, a band of these roisterers were on the spree in the European section of town when they were stopped by two constables; two opposed to fifty or more. The police were chased back to the station, to issue forth in large numbers a little while later to carry the fight into the Kanaka quarter, where the islanders had retired to barricade themselves into two boarding houses. A ding-dong struggle ensued, the police trying to force a way in, the defenders resisting desperately until one of these flimsy structures gave way like a pack of cards and seventeen Kanakas were carried off under arrest.

They were mainly young men, it should be remembered, sowing their wild oats, behaving much like any other army of young men stationed on foreign soil—like white Queenslanders in Cairo in 1916 for example. But they were not white, they were black, and they were expected somehow to have more sense of how to behave in the presence of Europeans.

It was a difficult problem, though. There were so many different races in Queensland: Chinese, Japanese, Cingalese, Javanese, Malays, Indians, Manilamen, South Sea Islanders, Aborigines. Mostly they were tolerated, these lesser breeds, provided they kept their inter-racial brawling to themselves. But every so often an explosion would occur. Their numbers would reach a point where their presence all at once appeared overpowering, and the local white population would suddenly rise in wrath, almost as one man, and lash out, scattering them in all directions.

It had happened on the goldfields against the Chinese in Victoria in the 1850s, in New South Wales in the 1860s, and later, in the 1870s, on the Palmer River diggings in Queensland. It happened at Mackay racecourse in 1883, against the Kanakas. There seemed always to be this underlying antipathy, this apprehension that the coloured person, or almost any foreigner for that matter, represented a point of weakness, a spot of infection upon the moral fabric of the nation. In the late eighties and nineties, with the *Bulletin* in Sydney never ceasing to have a good laugh and a sneer at the expense of "Chows", "Japs", "niggers", "Tommy Tannas", and all the other "mongrelized races", and with William Lane in Brisbane doing the same in the *Boomerang*, it grew worse. It was becoming a national obsession.

In 1896 the Parliament of New South Wales passed a bill designed to extend the provisions of the anti-Chinese Act of 1888 to "all persons belonging to any coloured race inhabiting the Continent of Asia, or the Continent of Africa, or any island in the Pacific or Indian oceans". New Zealand passed a similar bill. Yet no sudden influx of coloured peoples had occurred or seemed imminent. In Queensland the numbers of Kanakas remained steady. The rise of Japan in the Pacific might have contributed to the reason for it. Or the rise of the Labor Party within Australia.

All that George Reid, the Free Trade Premier of New South Wales, was able to explain in introducing the bill, was that it was part of an Australia-wide plan to complete the country's defences against coloured immigration. As Federation plans evolved, so did the concept of "White Australia".

The planters, then, knew exactly what to expect when Queensland joined the Commonwealth. Three parties contested the first federal elections in March 1901, and not one of them was prepared to yield the first place to its rivals in its advocacy of a White Australia. And thus in due course, upon the formation of a national Government, a certain Dr Walter Maxwell, employed by the Queensland Government as its Director of Sugar Experiment Stations, was commissioned to make a comprehensive report on the sugar industry;

to consider whether it would not now be carried on without the use of Kanaka labour.

Maxwell was very fair, whatever pressure he may have been under to take a particular line. There were now no fewer than 2,610 cane-growers in Queensland, he pointed out, the great majority small ones, while the total acreage had practically doubled in the nine years since Griffith had permitted the reintroduction of Pacific Island labour, from 23,623 to over 45,000 acres. It was not, however, the resumption of the labour trade that had been mainly responsible for this, but Thomas McIlwraith's Sugar Works Guarantee Act of 1893. This had authorized the financing of a large number of central mills through Government debentures and thus given a terrific impetus to the growth of small holdings by creating a sudden demand for more cane. Wily old Sir Thomas had thus been able to make political capital out of Griffith's pioneering mistakes.

The brisk building of all these new mills had brought into the industry large numbers of progressively minded young farmers and their families. "It is apparent," said Maxwell, "that the maintenance of the sugar industry and the settlement of the country is to be very chiefly in their hands. . . . As labourers working for hire, many of these settlers would never have been found on the soil, but as free men, with a personal interest in the occupancy of the lands, they are the hardest performers of given kinds of work in the field, and by their labour they have already modified the exclusive employment of subject labour and in localities where hitherto white labour had hardly been found." The small holders were themselves also dependent on black labour, at certain seasons of the year, almost as much as the large plantations were. But the fact remains that in fifteen years from 1885 to 1900 the Kanaka population had fallen from 11,745 to 8,795 while the acreages of cane crushed had more than doubled.

The Maxwell report was quite sufficient for the Government to go ahead with its plans. There was little real debate on the subject, and on 17th December 1901 a Commonwealth Act was assented to, to provide for the "Regulation, Restriction and Prohibition of the Introduction of Labourers from the Pacific Islands".

There were three principal provisions: "No Pacific Islander shall enter Australia after 31st March 1904"; "No agreement shall be made or remain in force after 31st December 1906"; finally, power was to be granted to the Minister, or "officer authorized in that behalf" through the courts, to deport back to the islands every Kanaka still remaining in Queensland at the end of 1906, or, in the case of those whose agreements would not terminate until that date, in the period immediately following. The only exceptions were to

The returns with boxes are not likely to keep their possessions for long.

A victim of the Deportation Act.

Aoban girls were renowned for their looks. *Left*, before recruiting; *right*, after recruiting.

be those statutorily exempt by the Queensland Act of 1885—about
seven hundred.

Again the planter had been served notice; again he had five years
in which to do what he was told or get out. It seemed that he had
become something of an anachronism in the reinvigorated, confidently forward-looking Queensland of the new twentieth century.
Could he be afforded, with his rather spendthrift habits, his energetic
but erratic pursuits—horse-racing, exploring, botanizing, and so on?
The gracious old homestead at the end of some long, jacaranda-lined
avenue, the wide rambling tropical gardens, shrubberies, conserva-
tories, lagoons of water-lilies, tall clumps of bamboo, tennis-courts,
were surely the sort of thing that one associated with a more
leisurely, self-indulgent age. What a blatant waste of good cane-land
for instance, all these were. The small holder would cultivate right
up to his front door. The planter would have been better employed
in his botany studying the life-cycle of the cane-grub and experi-
menting with new varieties of grub-resistant cane. Either that or
turn the property over to some large company run by engineers,
scientists, economists who knew something about orderly marketing
procedures that would do away with the crazy business of the
planters' cutting one another's throats in their anxiety to get their
product on the market first.

The hard times of the eighties and nineties had certainly thinned
them out. But there were still a handful of old-style planters remaining at the end of the century, British-born mostly, younger sons
and connections of the nobility, retired Army men with ample
private incomes, former tea-planters from India and Ceylon, sugar-
planters from the West Indies. Now they were engaged in furious
lobbying about Parliament House, Brisbane, in one last, desperate
attempt to stave off the inevitable.

They could not have had a better man than Robert Philp, Premier
of Queensland at this critical juncture, to put their case. But not
even Philp, patient, far-seeing tactician, shrewd judge of political
opportunity that he was, could see any way out now.

Before the federal elections he had obtained assurances from
Barton and Reid, the leaders of the two main Federal parties, that
no sudden violence would be offered a "great national possession"
through the immediate withdrawal of all its black labour. But then
had come the elections, with its overwhelming vote for Labor
throughout Queensland, especially in North Queensland. And this
could only be read as an unmistakable sign that the people were not
going to tolerate the retention of the Kanaka for very much longer.
All that Philp could promise at this stage was a protest to the Prime

s

Minister urging that his Pacific Island Labourers Act was an un-warranted intrusion upon States' rights.

The planters finally had recourse to London again, petitioning the British Government, through a document purporting to have been signed by three thousand Kanakas, to disallow the Act on the grounds of the hardship caused to those islanders already long resident in Queensland.

It was all quite fruitless. The Commonwealth Government re-mained adamant that the Kanaka should go, and accordingly in 1901 and 1902 passed measures to hasten his departure. These made imported sugar subject to a duty of £6 a ton and provided for an excise of £3 per ton on manufactured sugar, less a rebate of approxi-mately £2 per ton for cane grown and cut by white labour alone. This rebate, or bounty as it came to be called after a modification of the system in 1903, undoubtedly had a great effect, for by 1905, when the total number of growers had increased to 3,422, 78 per cent of them employed solely white labour. Hundreds of Kanakas moving from one district to another complained to the local inspector that they were no longer able to find jobs.

The statistics, however, are slightly misleading. The larger growers still relied principally on Kanaka labour, and an analysis of com-parative figures shows that *in terms of cane produced* only 37 per cent of the total crop was grown by white labour, and 63 per cent by black, even though the rebate had now been operating for three years. Moreover, in the far north, the latter figure was as high as 88 per cent, suggesting perhaps that the planter had been right: white men could not sustain the heavy manual labour in the extreme tropics, or at any rate not to a point where it was economi-cally significant. They might be prepared to give it a go, but would very soon find it beyond them.

Maxwell in his 1901 report had cited the case of Mulgrave central mill near Cairns, where maintaining a staff of eighty-eight during the crushing season, the mill required a labour turnover of 409 employees for short periods only. Many of the growers complained also. They would, for example, contract out a particular task to a white gang of say, fifteen, to discover probably that while they could work faster and harder than the average Kanaka, something or other would cause them to go sour on the job. A gang of fifteen might turn over fifty to sixty men in only a few weeks.

It was strange indeed, for they would complain, it seemed, about everything under the sun, except the heat of the sun itself. A planter in the Bundaberg district, to give one example, had hired a gang of strapping young white men, just down from mining in the north, to do some chipping for him. It was monotonous work, though not particularly exacting. The Kanakas' style was to chip away, ten hours a day, singing, more or less contentedly, as they worked. They were also about one-third as expensive, but this planter was anxious to register as a grower of white-grown cane only and he had given the job to the ex-miners. After only a few days, however, they came to him asking to be paid off. But he couldn't pay them yet, the planter expostulated, the job was only half done. And they had done less than a gang of Kanakas would have done in the same time. "You're not saying we can't work better than niggers," one of them snarled. "A white man can beat two Kanakas any day." The trouble, it seemed, was due to the time of year; there was too much dew on the cane.

There may have been outstanding exceptions, but the older-fashioned type of planter would not believe that white labour wasn't hopelessly unreliable. And he was not going to be changed by argument. He would rather pin his faith in getting the law changed in acknowledgment of the fact that he was still right. And in that respect there were signs, indeed, by the end of 1905, with only twelve months to go, that he might be making some progress in this direction.

From the beginning, the Commonwealth had been concerned that the whole deportation proceedings should go off without mishap. "The Commonwealth Government," Alfred Deakin, the Federal Attorney-General, had written in 1902, "will endeavour so to provide that whenever the closing scenes in the Kanaka employment on the plantations in Queensland arrive, they shall be accompanied by none of the cruelties and barbarities with which it was initiated."

Since then, reports had come to the Government that grave injustices *would* occur unless particular regard were paid to individual cases. It was thus decided, after consultation with the local State Government, its partner in the enterprise, that Queensland should hold yet another Royal Commission, this time to inquire into the most efficient and humane means of carrying out their joint task; whether any of the islanders should be exempt from deportation; how the gap created by the departures could best be filled.

There seemed now some hint that not all the Kanakas might have to go; that there was still room for negotiation on this point. So it was very important that the Commission should go into the matter as minutely as possible. In fact it interviewed more than three hundred witnesses, European and Kanaka, from Nerang in the south to Port Douglas in the extreme north, before eventually concluding:

Our inquiries leave no doubt that there are in the State certain Pacific Islanders who by reason of extreme age and bodily infirmity would be unable to procure a livelihood if returned to their native islands. There are also individuals who have resided in Queensland for such a lengthened period as to render it highly probable that they would, upon return, find themselves complete strangers; . . . In many cases a prolonged subsistence upon a European diet would be found to have completely unfitted islanders for the vegetable food which constitutes for the most part the sustenance of natives in the South Seas. . . .

Some of the islanders now in Queensland have, without doubt, resorted hither for the purpose of escaping the death punishment to which they had in their native islands rendered themselves liable consequent upon breaches of tribal laws; whilst others have fled from their homes to escape from a vendetta originating in a prevalent belief in witchcraft. According to the evidence, the compulsory deportation of such individuals to their own "passages" would be, in effect, their death warrant.

This was a remarkable conclusion, no doubt about it! The business of repatriation had been going on, vessel by vessel, for close on forty years, and for most of that time under the supposed superintendence of the Immigration Department. Never before had responsible Queenslanders shown themselves so concerned about the welfare of the unfortunate returns once they had departed! One wouldn't have suspected them capable. Indeed, if some of the missionaries located in the islands were to be believed there had been occasions when sickly and diseased returns had been simply hustled onto a ship for home before they infected anybody else, without the slightest attempt being made to cure them while there were still doctors and medical facilities available.

There was, for instance, the case of the recruiter *Empreza*, which left Brisbane on 12th January 1893 with 153 returns, some already ill with dysentery, and duly delivered them to their homes in the New Hebrides. The result, alas, was that two hundred people eventually died, including a missionary wife together with all her children. Yet the G.A.'s report on the health of the returns was that it had been "generally good".

The Royal Commission presented an unarguable case for the exemption of certain categories of islanders, and its recommendations were duly embodied in a second Act of Parliament passed just in time on 12th October 1906. It would now be possible under this amending legislation for a man to claim exemption from the Act if he could fulfil one of the following conditions: he had come to Australia before 1st September 1879; he was of extreme age, or suffered from any bodily infirmity which would prevent his earning a living in the islands; he had married a woman with whom he could not return to the islands without risking the life of himself or his family; he had married a woman who was not a native of the Pacific

Islands; he was registered as the beneficial owner of freehold land in Queensland; he had been continuously resident in Australia for a period of not less than twenty years prior to 31st December 1906.

The planters, farmers, shipowners, captains, Government Agents and their supporters who gave evidence before the Commission were still fighting hard to keep the trade going. There were stern arguments: terrible starvation would result, they predicted, if thousands of deportees were simply dumped back on their islands all at once; food resources would be strained beyond endurance; they doubted, however, if it could ever come to that—most of the returns would surely fall victim to the fierce bushmen, particularly as they were being sent back unarmed.

The Queenslanders had hoped right up till the last minute that a reprieve would come, an extension of the traffic for perhaps a few more years at least. But it was just not possible. Queensland was now part of Australia; the interests of Queensland did not carry the necessary weight, when put in the balance with those of the rest of the Commonwealth. In fact preparations for deportation, the initial rounding up, had been steadily proceeding even while the Commission was in session.

Queensland's Immigration Agent, O'Neil Brenan, and his chief deputy, Henry Caulfield, assisted by the entire staff of the Immigration Department, Pacific Islands Branch, had been especially seconded to the Commonwealth for the purpose, and were already set out on their mammoth task. They began with all the "walkabouts" or those not currently engaged under any agreement, together with the professionally unemployed, the opium addicts and other street-corner nuisances, the inmates of jails, asylums, and so on.

It has been generally assumed that the Kanakas bitterly resented their dismissal. Some fled away to the bush and managed to escape the great dragnet. Others were caught and marched sullenly to the ships. One islander on the Herbert harangued his fellow countrymen and was reported thus:

He vigorously claimed they had built up the white man's sugar industry and illustrated his arguments by drawing attention to the surrounding canefields which were the result of Kanaka labour. In a final burst of tearful indignation, he declared, "White man no more want black man, use him up altogether, chase him away, plenty Kanaka no money go back poor", and with a gesture of supreme contempt broadcasted through the crowd a handful of coppers.

It will be discernible, however, from these remarks, that the insult to his race was not his primary concern: he was having to go home broke. Presumably he was one of the many who had spent all he had earned or somehow got rid of it and was now confronted with the prospect of having to return without a "box" and thus endure a very painful loss of face.

For the traveller in Melanesia was traditionally the bearer of gifts. Every Kanaka interviewed by the Royal Commission had, in fact, been asked if he did not fear to go home lest he be killed. Without exception they had scoffed at the notion, for no one was likely to admit that his island was so "wild" that a man was liable to be murdered there out of hand. But there were many who said, "Countrymen make a row alonga me if I have no box."

It was the islanders at home who felt insulted: "White man he go along Queensland, he take'im country belong blackfellow, now by'm by he say 'Altogether coloured man, you clear out. This country belong white man.'" They were becoming quite sophisticated in their knowledge of the world. The Melanesian Mission had taken some of its converts on an educational visit to New Zealand and they had returned full of information of how the Maoris had had their land taken away from them but later managed to get some of it back. Nor was it merely the expulsion of their people from Queensland that was making them so aware. In the New Hebrides Britain and France were in the process of going beyond their Joint Naval Agreement of 1887 to the point of establishing a form of Government there. Thus an English lady journalist visiting Tanna in 1906 was rather taken aback to find the island in the grip of a sort of "Tanna for the Tannese" movement. And it was recently repatriated labourers from Queensland who were in control of the movement. It was they who were trying to work the population up to the point of "getting rid of every white on the island" in revenge for their own deportation from the canefields.

As for the younger men in Queensland, who were, after all, those mainly affected, they had pretty well made up their minds to it by the end of 1906. If there was work back in the islands (and a great increase in planting both in the Solomons and New Hebrides had taken place during the previous ten years), and none in Queensland they were just as happy to go home. In fact very few had definite opinions of their own on the subject, most being content to follow the example of the more forceful and articulate ones among them. It was known, however, that the money was poor in Fiji in comparison, so the efforts made by the C.S.R. to approach them individually, to get them to agree to go directly to Fiji instead of back to their own group, fell completely flat.

It was the older people chiefly who suffered the most. For despite the various escape clauses in the new Act, quite a number apparently did not know they were eligible for exemption till too late—

married couples, for instance, from different islands, with their Queensland-born children.

The children would be objects of great admiration as they came aboard the returning ship, babes in arms booted and bonneted, being giggled over by their adoring mamas; little scholars with their school satchels and shining morning faces, immaculately scrubbed for this most momentous occasion. But they would have a rough time of it in the islands, even when taken straight under the wing of the missionaries. Their fine clothes, meaningless now, would be shed upon landing; their feet unused to running over coral would be horribly lacerated. A missionary on Malaita calculated that in the regions with which he was familiar only about one in ten survived, most succumbing to fever after a few weeks.

Actually it is very hard to estimate how many of those technically exempt were in fact deported, just as the number of those who were meant to go and did not is likewise uncertain. It is little wonder that the Department's books failed to balance. There were those who escaped the clutches of the Act and got safely away, perhaps to mingle unobtrusively with the populations pearl-shelling on Thursday Island and elsewhere, who did not have to go anyway. There were numbers of Loyalty Islanders and alleged Loyalty Islanders who could not be deported in any case because they were supposedly French subjects and did not come within the definition of "Pacific Islander" as set out in the Act. And there were those, and God knows how many, who had died unrecorded deaths or were yet alive and skulking in some hole-in-the-corner retreat on the outskirts of town.

One authority gives 3,642 as the number deported, apparently based on the costs incurred by Queensland under the repatriation scheme operated by the Commonwealth. Another gives 4,391, which probably includes those gathered in by Brenan and his men and booked aboard one of the regular Queensland-licensed recruiters before the Commonwealth took over in October 1906. Whatever the exact figure, the main exodus began in that October. The New Hebrideans were shipped to Brisbane; the Solomon Islanders, in approximately equal numbers, to Cairns, so that these two groups of mortal enemies should be the maximum distance apart during this critical period.

Generally, however, it was a much better-tempered leave-taking than Brenan and Caulfield had counted upon. Burns, Philp had won the contract to carry them back, its line of steamers, the *Moresby*, *Malaita*, *Tambo*, and others having accommodation for several hundreds at a time. There were often quite gay scenes in Brisbane as the repatriates poured noisily aboard, dressed to the hilt, with silk dresses and flowered hats and smart suits, waving umbrellas and shouting jokes at the small crowd of friends, missionary folk and fellow islanders who had come down to see them off. They had an astonishingly incongruous assortment of baggage with them—sewing machines, kitchen stoves, kerosene lamps, phonographs, bicycles, cricketing gear, boxing gloves, spades, hoes, and various implements for clearing the jungle and breaking up the virgin soil when they got home. For many had fanciful ideas about what they were going to do: one wanted to see his island split up into tiny parcels of land, where each man could be his own sugar planter, coffee grower, corn farmer, with the right to live on his own ground as he liked. Another had quite a sporting air about him, rakish Panama hat, small leather bag slung over one shoulder, but was found to be carrying under another arm a board with some multi-coloured scriptural text inscribed, which quite ruined the effect.

Many of them had ambition to open a school and start teaching— something, anything, the ABC, farming, religion, cricket, foot-drilling. It did not necessarily mean they had any deep sense of vocation, the inspiration of a Peter Amboo-oba, for instance. They just fancied themselves in some position of eminence or authority, standing in front of the class waving their arms in exhortation, leading the procession to the altar, being responsible for the uplifting and inspiriting of all the timid ones who had not gone.

Aboard ship they might sit about for hours gambling in quiet, intent, little groups, only to be suddenly quite transformed and place a saucer over the dice, put away their money, and bring out their Bibles and hymn-books for the daily church service. They were not to be divided into the usual white man's categories of the strict and the loose-living. They thought of themselves more as an *élite*, with those they had left behind regarded as the ignorant, "bush Kanakas"—their contemptuous term—non-starters in the race, not entitled to the same privileges.

However, some of these very self-assured New Hebrideans now returning after so many years away may have been underestimating the quality of the opposition. It was the Solomon Islanders departing from Cairns who seemed more aware of the true situation in the islands. Two-thirds of them would be going back to Malaita, an island torn by fighting from end to end, where there were still a hundred old scores to pay off.

Take the situation of Ohnonee, for instance: "Unmarried, Ex *Lady Norman*, 3/9/1900. Employed by James Reynolds, Port Douglas. Brother had returned to Malaita previous year and since written saying their father killed by bushmen. Ohnonee thought to be also on their list." The Minister could use his discretion in a case like this to allow him to stay. But it is not known what actually did happen to him. If news of his reprieve did not reach him till the last minute, as sometimes occurred, he might still have decided to go, with friends, possibly to Ngela in the Floridas, where there was a mission station and plenty of work; possibly to Malaita, to some passage other than his own where there would be a brother to look after him; possibly to home and risk it. In any case he would want to be armed if possible.

Inspections of the islanders' baggage took place at the depot in Cairns, again on board ship after they had embarked, and again before they finally landed. Still they managed to smuggle guns ashore with them. A roll of fabric was just as likely to conceal a sawn-off Martini-Henry rifle. An umbrella might be the hiding place of a dismantled shot-gun. A woman, seemingly a little stiff in the stride as she ascended the gangplank, lacking the familiar easy swing of the hips, was a certain object of suspicion. She would assuredly be wearing a gun, strapped to one leg, under her long petticoats. The fashionable-looking, high-heeled boots would have to come off too. Such dainty steps were a certain indication that the wearer was having an uncomfortable time treading down little cardboard boxes of .303 ammunition.

And the Malaitaman could be a difficult, slippery person to handle when he had a grievance. During those final few weeks in Queensland some could only be brought to go by being summoned before a J.P. and sentenced. Thereafter they were conveyed in chains directly to the ship. A young bystander recalling the scene in later years gives this impression:

Two by two they came through a passage made in the crowd from a gateway in the fence to the foot of the gangplank, black shoulders topped by black curly-tufted hair, with bare chests and torn trousers. Their sweaty bodies gleamed in the thick yellow light and the iron shackles on their wrists and ankles clinked and clanked as they shuffled forward, breathing heavily and without a word. In the background the wails of their womenfolk persisted. The human stream pushed forward . . . up the gangplank they stumbled. . . . "Thank Christ that's over and that's the last of the black bastards" he heard a voice. . . .

The last of them! Packed off after 43½ years with a shove and a curse. But at that time, and even now in places, to put white men and black men together would mean an end like this. It took an unusually perceptive black man to see that what was known as white civilization called for a special sort of effort by the individual, if he were to get anything much out of it, more than most whites in fact are capable of making. Nor did the average white person see it; he imagined simply that he occupied a privileged position in the world and did not see how anyone "less than himself" could ever occupy it also. If Queensland had ever represented freedom to the islander, or easy riches or any other apparent avenue of escape from everyday reality, he had been under a great delusion, now being dispelled.

If, on the other hand, he had come and observed with a shrewd eye that there were various advantages to be gained by steady, hard work and a certain amount of self-denial, then he was unquestionably the gainer. He was in a position to choose which kind of life suited him best.

About 1,600 islanders remained in Australia after the last of the deportees had gone, some illegally, most of them members of a closely knit little community, notably at North Rockhampton, Nambour, and Cudgen over the border in New South Wales but with other small pockets in almost all the main sugar districts.

A total of 317 in Queensland were farming on leaseholds; another 13 owned virtually their own freeholds, with the land actually being held in trust for them by white men. They were farmers, fishermen, fencers, footballers, surfers, and great sportsmen, keen participants in everything, sending their sons north for the cane-cutting during the season exactly as the white farmers did. Quite suddenly it seemed that the problem of where the labour for the canefields would come from after the Kanakas were gone did not exist any more.

Once it had been the New South Wales border which marked the limit of where European labourers would be able to stand the climate. Then it was the line passing through Rockhampton; later still, that through Townsville. But in fact, as has been shown, white labour will go anywhere in the world if the wages are right. The solution was simple: take away the stigma of the work being "Kanaka work" by taking away the Kanakas, and young miners, for example, would no longer complain about the headaches the job gave them.

The work could be very tough, but certainly not beyond endurance. White men would not usually sing as they worked in the way the Kanakas did, but they tackled it in a very purposeful, thoroughly businesslike manner, in gangs, almost as if determined to prove that one European was worth two Kanakas any day.

In fact he was worth three, judging by the amount of work he got through in an equivalent period of time. In cane-cutting, for instance, the production of Kanakas had been reckoned at less than two tons per man per ten-to-twelve-hour day; in the post-Kanaka period it was found to average four and a half tons for a strictly eight-hour day. Calculating the cost of white labour at three to four times greater than that of black, it meant that the employer was hardly worse off than before.

Actually, as the figures of 1911 proved, 8 per cent of this "white" labour was in fact black, but by this time the distinction between white and black hardly mattered, the remaining islanders had been so thoroughly assimilated. The 1911 Census also showed the total Pacific Islander population in Queensland to be 1,704, of whom 86 per cent were classed as breadwinners. In 1921, however, by which time this figure had risen to 1,869, no fewer than 518 were female; of the men 822 were wage-earners, 275 self-employed, and 25 employers of labour. Another 228 were resident in New South Wales.

So the islanders permitted to remain in Australia generally prospered. It would be interesting for purposes of comparison therefore to discover what became of those compulsorily returned to the islands. But it is hard to find out very much. The odds were certainly stacked against them at the beginning. The islands were in a chaotic state in the early years of this century, even if certain favourite old customs such as head-hunting had been abolished.

In 1899 A. W. Mahaffy, a fierce Irishman, Assistant British Resident Commissioner in the Solomons, began touring the western part of the group in the Government ketch, systematically smashing every war canoe he came across. And in a very few years that was the end of that particular pastime. In 1902 the Methodists were finally able to establish themselves on New Georgia, right by the entrance to the once-dreaded Rubiana Lagoon.

And behind the terrible Mahaffy and his squad of twenty-five Fijian and Solomon Island police boys; behind too the warships of the Anglo-French Joint Naval Commission in the New Hebrides, all the missionary organizations were on the march. It denoted progress of a sort, no doubt. The mission stations with their devoted staffs were havens of peace, it sometimes seemed, when all around was ravaged by fighting. But they harboured all kinds, the gentle and the God-fearing, as well as the criminal, the fugitive from justice, and the treacherous ones who had guided the warships to the destruction of their enemies.

Still it was undoubtedly better from the returning labourers' point of view that there should be some areas of neutrality rather than none at all. On mainland Malekula, which by contrast had very few missionaries in relation to its population, there was simply no countervailing influence to hold back the rampaging hill tribes. In 1900 they had delivered a sort of ultimatum to the handful of European settlers at Sou'west Bay, more or less to the effect that they would not tolerate their presence any longer but intended to purge their island of the white man altogether. A group of disembarked Queensland returns on one occasion were marched straight back to the ship at gun-point.

In 1905 they issued another challenge. After "making themselves strong" by eating those white people who still remained they then proposed to take on the whole British Empire. In retaliation a party of officers and men from the warships *Pegasus* and *Meurthe* in a combined Anglo-French operation marched eleven miles inland from Bushman's Bay and destroyed a village, though without effecting the capture of certain wanted individuals. "Big fellow ship no catch me," they continued to boast. "Man-o'-war allasame old woman."

In these circumstances the deportees could not be landed at their own villages. The few Malekulans amongst them had to go instead to one or two different mission stations where they were very soon a confounded nuisance, as they were hardly likely to find the routine of mission life very exciting after the wicked delights of Bundaberg and Mackay. The missionaries would be obliged to get rid of them eventually, when they would take to the bush to begin a campaign of harassment of the mission that could only end fatally for themselves.

Those who did best in the long run were men who were to strike out for themselves, attacking the virgin forest like selectors on a pioneering cane-farm. They founded their own villages, as Peter Amboo-oba had, at Malu'u on the north end of Malaita. In fact it might have been partly Peter's example which inspired them, since most of such settlements were in that region. Here also they were not very far from Tulagi in the Floridas, the headquarters of the British Resident Commissioner. His friendly interest in them ensured that they were safe from *ramos* like Kwaisulia.

The decline of the labour trade was a great blow to Kwaisulia and others like him. He grew much less aggressive in his later years, relying more on his exceptional skill as a diplomatist than on force to maintain his authority. His end was an unlikely one; one day at Basakana Island, which he had once claimed as his own on the strength of a successful raid upon Isabel, he blew himself up with dynamite while fishing.

But how the pioneers fared would depend ultimately upon the personality of their leaders. And given competent ones, there was no reason why they should not succeed. For it was in this way that most of the artificial islets had begun—by a group of young men going off together to build their own place. Perhaps at first some important personage could be persuaded to come down from the hills and live with them, to give the village status. But sooner or later their own "ngwane inoto", literally, man of importance, would emerge, probably through his power to make the land flourish with the aid of all the new tools and techniques.

In due time, and in proportion to his ability to provide feasts and entertainments and make handsome presents, to shed lustre on all about him, he would be accepted beyond the village, which would then gain a name for itself. Most, if not all, the new settlements founded in 1907 are still there today, so some of the returns at least made a solid achievement.

All things considered, the massive deportation went off moderately well. A Queensland Government Agent watching one small party disembark remarked on the undemonstrative nature of the reunion with old island friends. Yes. The relatives were all no doubt wondering whatever had happened to the returned men's boxes, to the new pipe, to the twist of tobacco they had been looking forward to in exchange for helping to carry those boxes up the hill to the village. The returns equally would be wondering also how to explain the absence of boxes to carry.

But there was at this stage none of the dumping of defenceless bushmen on a deserted beach, such as had characterized the final stages of the recruiting trade.

In the Solomons, Charles Woodford, the British Resident Commissioner, had insisted that one of his own officers supervise the actual landing, not trusting the Queenslanders to do the job properly by themselves. Thus most of the Solomon Islanders were at least landed safely, but what happened to individual ones after that is mainly hearsay. A few are alleged to have been killed in payment of old grudges, but there were no wholesale massacres, and no great hardship suffered from shortage of food.

Only one known tragedy marred the mass return. A certain Alamemea, a giant of a man by all accounts, had been serving a jail sentence in Queensland for murder when he was suddenly packed off home, actually landing back on Oba in September before the full-scale deportation proceedings of October 1906 had really begun. He was still in a murderous frame of mind some weeks later, vowing to kill the first white man he saw in revenge for his treatment in prison, when Charles Godden of the Melanesian Mission arrived at Alamemea's little village in the hills to dedicate the newly completed Church.

The service was over, a feast had been eaten, says one account, and a party was proceeding down a steep slope in single file. Godden, in the leading division, was talking and joking with those about him, not realizing that Alamemea with a rifle and axe had joined on behind the group. Gradually he made his way towards the front. All at once Godden stopped to remove a pebble from his shoe, and as the people with him continued, unnoticing, to move on, Alamemea, right behind him, had him completely at his mercy. At point-blank range he shot him in the thigh, severing the main artery Then as

Godden fell to the ground, blood spurting from the wound, Alamemea jumped in with the axe.

The murderer was not caught until several days later. Two of his brothers came across him in hiding, and having persuaded him to drink a little kava with them, managed to overpower him. He was later handed over to a warship, taken to Fiji, and sentenced to prison again.

Bishop Patteson had been the Church's first great missionary martyr to die for the sins of the labour trade. Young Godden, from Euroa in Victoria, was the last. And, perhaps, in some symbolic way, as they had devoted their lives to the service of mankind, they were making atonement. For Melanesia was now only a shadow of what it had been. Its population, once estimated at millions, had come to be counted in thousands. The Queensland blackbirders alone were not responsible for this, but they had been one of the chief contributory causes. They had taken about 61,000 recruits and returned fewer than 45,000. But it was not just the lives lost or men left in Queensland, or even the villages they had destroyed in Melanesia. That was only a small part. The destruction came with the guns they had brought, the hatreds they had produced, to the point where every man's hand was now raised against his neighbour.

The recruiting still went on, to Fiji (until 1911), and to New Caledonia and other places, but 1907 is the date from which the islanders began very slowly to rebuild, with a certain amount of outside help, after the devastation of the previous forty-odd years. In Santo they have a fable. There was a bird, the little green warbler, who once sang most beautifully all day long until one day he lent his voice to the fruit-dove, so that the latter might sing with this lovely musical voice at a concert of the birds. The dove however was such a success at the concert, liked his new voice so much, that he would not give it back, and to this day the little green warbler has no voice to speak of. He has lost his song. But he flies about still and thrives more abundantly than ever.

TWELVE

Epilogue

WELL, we ask at the end of it all, was it slavery or was it not? Slavery or merely some variety of immigrant labour scheme, perhaps only slightly less repugnant in character, but altogether different in moral category? How did the Queensland trade compare with similar practices in other parts of the world, for example? Slavery and slave-trading had been abolished by law in every part of Europe and its colonies and in South America by the end of the nineteenth century. But there were other very anomalous forms of labour traffic still in existence.

While the Kanaka era in Queensland was being gradually brought to a close under pressure from the other States in the Commonwealth, the South African mine-owners of the Rand were petitioning the Conservative Government in Britain to permit them to import Chinese for underground work in the mines. The Tories agreed to consider their petition, even making some tentative inquiries that suggested that they might quite heartily approve the idea. Boer opinion in South Africa did not seem particularly revolted at the thought. Coolie immigration into Natal had been in existence for forty years and more, and the local sugar industry had never been in a more flourishing condition. Only a few miles away in Angola, the Portuguese were busily shuttling "voluntary" labourers over to their cocoa plantations on Sao Thome at the rate of three thousand a year. The mine-owners only wanted a hundred thousand altogether; it seemed a not unreasonable request. Balfour at length consented.

However, it soon appeared that the Conservative Prime Minister had made a serious miscalculation. None would have dreamt it two years before, but the issue that came to dominate the 1906 general elections was the issue of "Chinese slavery" in South Africa. The popular Press ran stories of pigtailed foreigners breaking out of their horde compounds in Johannesburg, running riot on the veld. Billboards in the streets pictured Chinese in chains, Chinese being flogged, Chinese rising up to murder their white masters. A very effective cartoon showed a coolie in a wide straw hat above the caption "Tory British workingman".

There was no mistaking the strength of the British working-class sentiment in the matter. The Conservatives lost the elections by a wide margin, and the succeeding Liberal Government never hesitated for a minute to direct that the recruiting stop immediately. The following year it appointed a Commission under Lord Sanderson to enquire into the emigration of Indians to the British crown colonies and protectorates. The twentieth century had arrived, it appeared. The whole question of taking cheap imported labour from one poor country to supply the industrial needs of some altogether richer country was very much under review.

In the long run it does not really matter whether the hapless creature we hold in the palm of our hand, whom circumstances have placed in the position of being entirely dependent on our charity as employer, has any legal rights or not. The question of whether he is in fact a slave in these circumstances is purely academic. The question of whether he is being outrageously exploited is one which anybody with common sense can very simply decide for himself. It was the ordinary Australian in Sydney and Bourke, in Hobart and Hall's Creek, not from self-interest, not even perhaps as a member of any organized labour movement, without ever having seen a Kanaka in his life, who decided that the modern Australia was not going to flourish on cheap coloured labour—just as the ordinary Briton had made the same decision about the trafficking in slaves early in the nineteenth century. In 1908 the last Kanaka was deported to the islands; in 1909 the last Angolan was dispatched to Sao Thome; in 1910 the last Chinese left the Rand. No more islanders were taken to Fiji after 1911 or to New Caledonia a little later. The Indian coolie trade to Natal stopped also in 1911; to Trinidad in 1917; to the other West Indian Islands in 1920. . . .

Select Bibliography

CHAPTER 1

British Parliamentary Papers. Papers relative to affairs of the colony of Queensland, 1861, XL [2890]; Correspondence relating to the importation of South Sea Islanders into Queensland 1867-8, XLVIII [391, 496].

Campbell, P. *Chinese Coolie Immigration.* London, 1928.

Chesson, F. W. *Coloured Labour in British Colonies.* London, 1872.

Harris, J. *A Century of Emancipation.* London, 1933.

Mellor, G. R. *British Imperial Trusteeship, 1783-1850.* London, 1951.

Parnaby, O. W. *Britain and the Labor Trade in the Southwest Pacific.* Durham, N.C., 1964.

Queensland Legislative Assembly, Votes and Proceedings, 1860-7.

Queensland Parliamentary Debates, 1864-7.

Short, R. *The Slave Trade in the Pacific.* London, 1870.

Stevens, E. V. "Blackbirding". *Queensland Hist. Soc. Journal,* 1950.

Towns, R. *South Sea Island Immigration for Cotton Culture.* Brisbane, 1863.

Towns, R. Papers: private and business collection. Mitchell Library.

CHAPTER 2

Armstrong, E. S. *The History of the Melanesian Mission.* London, 1900.

Brenchley, J. L. *Jottings During the Cruise of H.M.S.* Curacoa *among the South Sea Islands in 1865.* London, 1873.

Cheyne, A. *A Description of Islands in the Western Pacific Ocean.* London, 1852.

Erskine, J. E. *Journal of a Cruise among the Islands of the Western Pacific . . . in H.M.S.* Havannah. London, 1853.

Fox, C. E. *Lord of the Southern Isles.* London, 1958.

Gaggin, J. *Among the Man-Eaters.* London, 1900.

Guppy, H. B. *The Solomon Islands and Their Natives.* London, 1887.

Inglis, J. *In the New Hebrides.* London, 1877.

MacDonald, D. *The Labour Traffic versus Christianity in the South Sea Islands.* Melbourne, 1878.

Paton, J. G. *An Autobiography.* London, 1889.

Patterson, G. *Missionary Life among the Cannibals.* Toronto, 1882.

Rivers, W. H. R. *Essays on the Depopulation of Melanesia.* Cambridge, 1922.

Robertson, H. A. *Erromanga, the Martyrs Isle.* London, 1902.

Shineberg, D. *They Came for Sandalwood.* Melbourne, 1967.

T

Steel, R. *The New Hebrides and Christian Missions*. London, 1880.
Tippett, A. R. *Solomon Islands Christianity*. London, 1967.
Tucker, H. W. *Memoir of the Life and Episcopate of George Augustus Selwyn*. London, 1875.
Woodford, C. M. *A Naturalist Among the Headhunters . . . Solomon Islands*. London, 1890.

CHAPTER 3

British Parliamentary Papers. Correspondence respecting the deportation of South Sea Islanders, 1868-9, XLIII [408]; Further Correspondence relating to the importation of South Sea Islanders into Queensland, 1871, XLVIII [468]; Further Correspondence respecting deportation of South Sea Islanders, 1872, XLIII, [c. 496].
Dunbabin, T. *Slavers of the South Seas*. Sydney, 1935.
Hope, J. L. A. *In Quest of Coolies*. London, 1872.
Markham, A. H. *The Cruise of the* Rosario. London, 1873.
Palmer, G. *Kidnapping in the South Seas*. Edinburgh, 1871.
Wood, C. T. *Sugar Country*. Brisbane, 1965.

CHAPTER 4

Brewster, A. B. *King of the Cannibal Isles*. London, 1937.
British Official Printed Papers. Great Britain and Ireland: Colonial Office: Copies or Extracts of any communications . . . regarding outrages committed upon natives of South Sea Islands. . . . London, 1873.
British Parliamentary Papers. Correspondence relative to the introduction of Polynesian Labourers into Queensland, 1873, L [c. 793].
Derrick, R. A. *A History of Fiji*. Suva, 1946.
Forbes, L. *Two Years in Fiji*. London, 1875.
Moresby, J. *New Guinea and Polynesia*. London, 1876.
Rhodes, F. *Pageant of the Pacific*. Sydney, 1936.
Searle, G. *Mount and Morris Exonerated. A Narrative of the Voyage of the Brig* Carl. Melbourne, 1875.
Yonge, C. M. *Life of John Coleridge Patteson*. London, 1874.

CHAPTER 5

Bernays, C. A. *Queensland Politics during Sixty Years*. Brisbane, 1919.
Bolton, G. *A Thousand Miles Away: A History of North Queensland to 1920*. Brisbane, 1963.
Brookes, W. Papers in Mitchell Library. Family Archives. Journal, 1867-8. Diary, 1885-91.
Easterby, H. T. *History of the Queensland Sugar Industry*. Brisbane, 1931.

Eden, C. H. *My Wife and I in Queensland*. London, 1872.

Jones, D. *Cardwell Shire Story*. Brisbane, 1961.

Lilley, W. O. *Life of the Hon. William Brookes*. Brisbane, 1902.

Report of N.S.W. Royal Commission Appointed to Enquire into Certain Alleged Cases of Kidnapping. . . . Sydney, 1869.

Report of Select Committee of Queensland Legislative Assembly into the Operation of the Polynesian Labourers Act of 1868. Brisbane, 1869.

Report of Select Committee of Q.L.A. on General Question of Polynesian Labour. Brisbane, 1876.

Roth, H. L. *The Discovery and Settlement of Port Mackey*. Halifax, 1908.

Trollope, A. *Australia and New Zealand*. London, 1873.

CHAPTER 6

Cheesman, L. E. *Backwaters of the Savage South Seas*. London, 1933.

Codrington, R. H. *The Melanesians*. Oxford, 1891.

Cromar, J. *Jock of the Islands*. London, 1935.

Deacon, A. B. *Malekula: A Vanishing People in the New Hebrides*. London, 1934.

Harrisson, T. H. *Savage Civilisation*. London, 1937.

Hopkins, A. I. *In the Isles of King Solomon*. London, 1928.

Ivens, W. G. *Island Builders of the Pacific*. London, 1930.

Ivens, W. G. *Melanesians of the South-east Solomon Islands*. London, 1927.

Layard, J. W. *Stone Men of Malekula*. London, 1942.

Marshall, A. J. *Black Musketeers*. London, 1937.

Penny, A. *Ten Years in Melanesia*. London, 1886.

Penny, A. Diary, 1876-86, Mitchell Library.

Rannie, D. *My Adventures Among South Sea Cannibals*. London, 1912.

Speiser, F. *Two Years with Natives in the Western Pacific*. London, 1913.

Wilson, C. *The Wake of the Southern Cross*. London, 1932.

CHAPTER 7

British Parliamentary Papers. Correspondence respecting the natives of the Western Pacific and the Labour Traffic, 1883, XLVII [c. 3641].

Deane, W. *In Wild New Britain: The Story of Benjamin Danks, Pioneer Missionary*. Sydney, 1933.

Giles, W. E. *A Cruise in a Queensland Labour Vessel to the South Seas*. Canberra, 1968.

Melanesian Mission, Annual Reports, 1857-1906.

Michelsen, O. *Cannibals Won for Christ*. London, 1893.

Moles, Ian. "The Indian Coolie Labour Issue in Queensland". *Queensland Hist. Soc. Journal*. Vol. 5.

Queensland State Archives. Accession 36/3686. Regina *v.* Mills, Loutit, and Burton re kidnapping by the *Ethel*, 1884.

Royal Navy Records. Australia Station. Records of the Commander-in-Chief, Pacific Islands, vols. 14-19.

Scarr, D. *Fragments of Empire: A History of the Western Pacific High Commission 1877-1914*. Canberra, 1967.

Thomas, J. *Cannibals and Convicts*. London, 1886.

Wawn, W. T. *The South Sea Islands and the Queensland Labour Trade*. London, 1893.

CHAPTER 8

Birch, A. & MacMillan, D. S. *Wealth and Progress: Studies in Australian Business History*. Sydney, 1967.

Brown, G. *Autobiography of a Pioneer Missionary*. London, 1908.

Connolly, R. *John Drysdale and the Burdekin*. Sydney, 1964.

Corris, P. "Blackbirding in New Guinea Waters". *Journal of Pacific History*, vol. 3, 1968.

Duffield, A. J. *Recollections of Travels Abroad*. London, 1889.

Duffield, A. J. *What I Know of the Labour Traffic*. Brisbane, 1884.

Fowler, W. *McMurdo of the Schooner* Stanley. Queensland Heritage, 1968.

Gordon, D. C. *The Australian Frontier in New Guinea, 1870-1885*. New York, 1951.

Griffith, S. W. Pocket diaries, 1862-1915, and other papers. Dixson Library, Sydney.

Jacobs, M. G. "The Colonial Office and New Guinea 1874-1884". *Historical Studies, Aust. and New Zealand*, vol. v, 1952.

Lawes, W. G. Journal, 1876-84. Mitchell Library.

MacFarlane, S. *Among the Cannibals of New Guinea*. London, 1888.

Powell, W. *Wanderings in a Wild Country*. London, 1883.

Queensland Legislative Assembly, Votes and Proceedings, 1883-5.

Queensland Parliamentary Debates, 1883-5.

Romilly, H. H. *The Western Pacific and New Guinea*. London, 1887.

Romilly, H. H. *From My Veranda in New Guinea*. London, 1889.

Vockler, J. *Sir Samuel Walker Griffith*. MS., Mitchell Library.

CHAPTER 9

Queensland Legislative Assembly, Further Correspondence on the Subject of Separation of the Northern Portion of Queensland, Votes and Proceedings, 1886.

Queensland Parliamentary Debates, 1880, 1886-92.

Shann, E. *An Economic History of Australia*. Cambridge, 1930.

Stephens, A. G. *Why North Queensland Wants Separation*. London, 1893.

Wawn, W. T. Private logs, 1888-90. Mitchell Library.

Willard, M. *The White Australia Policy*. Melbourne, 1923.

CHAPTER 10

British Parliamentary Papers. Correspondence relating to Polynesian Labour in Queensland: 1892, LVI [c. 6686]; 1893-4, LXI [c. 7000]; 1895, LXX [c. 7912].
Department of Pacific Island Immigration, Annual Reports, 1889-1906.
Hogbin, H. I. *Experiments in Civilisation*. London, 1939.
Paton, J. G. *The Kanaka Labor Traffic*. London, 1894.
Report of Royal Commission into General Conditions of Sugar Industry in Queensland. Brisbane, 1889.
Shaw, F. *Letters from Queensland*. London, 1893.
Young, F. *Pearls from the Pacific*. London, 1923.

CHAPTER 11

Commonwealth Parliamentary Debates, 1901-7.
Commonwealth Parliamentary Papers, 1901-7.
Godden, R. *Lolowai*. Sydney, 1967.
Grimshaw, B. *From Fiji to the Cannibal Islands*. London, 1907.
MacLaren, J. *My Odyssey*. London, 1923.
Queensland State Archives, Accession 36/3654-60. Papers relating to deportation proceedings and other matters.
Report of the Royal Commission on Sugar Industry Labour in Queensland. Brisbane, 1906.

In addition to the above, the newspapers of the day are a valuable source of references to the labour trade. In particular the *Moreton Bay Courier*, later the Brisbane *Courier*, is important. But it requires to be supplemented by the other capital city dailies, e.g., the *Sydney Morning Herald* or the Melbourne *Argus*, as its approach tends to be somewhat partisan. The weekly *Queenslander* (1866-) is also useful, together with the *Fiji Times* (1869-) and such other local newspapers as the *Mackay Daily Mercury* (1866-) and the *Port Denison Times* (1864-).

Index

Aborigines. *See* Australian Aborigines
Aborigines Protection Society, 67
Ada Gege islet, 136-7
Admiralty. *See* Royal Navy
Airdmillan Plantation, 173, 230
Alamemea, of Oba, 273
Albert River, 44, 95
Amboo-oba, Peter, 248-57, 272
Ambrym, 139, 174, 247
Aneityum, 25, 29-34, 154-5
Aniwa, 46-7
Anti-coolie movement, 165-6, 208
Aratuga, of Oba, 151-3
Austin, *Captain* John, 59-60
Australian Aborigines, 108-10, 168

Banks Group, 38, 48, 50-1, 153
Bartlett, *Captain*, 75-7
Belbin, *Captain*, 174
Bellenden Plains station, 108-9, 110
Bemersyde plantation, 173
Berry, "King", of Isabel, 23-4
Bird, John, 215
Black Dog. See under Ships
Blackbirding. *See* Kidnapping
Blake, *Captain* William, 46
Blaxell, Henry, 232
Blaxell, John, 232
Bobtail Nag. See under Ships
Bougainville, 25, 180, 233
Bowen (Queensland), 110
Bowen, *Sir* George, 6, 7, 12-13, 53
Bower, *Lieutenant*, 160-1
Boyd, Benjamin, 8
Braby, Henry, 231
Bramston, John, 93
Brenan, O'Neil, 254-65, 267
Brenchley, J. L., 40-1
Briggs, *Captain*, 175
British and Foreign Anti-Slavery Society, 12, 42, 53, 103
British Government, and labour trade, 6, 156, 225, 262, 275-6; and New Guinea protectorate, 201, 216
Brooke, *Rev.* Charles, 66
Brookes, William, 74, 151; denounces labour trade, 100; career and character of, 100-1; enters Queensland politics, 102; loses seat, 102; con-

Brookes—*continued*
ducts press campaign, 102-5, 107; supports abolition movement, 103; attacks Government, 105; intervenes in *Syren* case, 106-7; criticizes islanders, 111-2; satirizes Select Committee, 1869, 112; and 1876 Committee, 114; fails to win public response, 165; returns to Parliament, 207-8
Brown, David, 222-3
Bruce, *Captain*, 162
Buckingham, *Duke* of, 53
Buhot, John, 43
Buka, 25, 82, 180
Bundaberg, 164, 227
Burdekin River, 173, 210
Burnett River, 86, 99
Burns, *Captain* Henry, 29
Burns, James, 174, 198, 214
Burns, Philp & Co., 174; character of recruiting vessels of, 175; close relations of with Queensland Government, 1880, 185; finds recruiting profitable, 193; vessels of accused of illegal recruiting, 198; quits trade, 214; wins contract to return deportees, 267
Bwaxat, chief, of New Caledonia, 9

Caboolture River, 7, 44, 113
Caffin, *Lieutenant*, 147
Cago, of New Guinea, 199
Cairns, 173, 258
Cannibalism, 108-9, 131
Cardwell, 108, 110
Carl. See under Ships
Caulfield, Henry, 248, 254, 265, 269
Ceara. See under Ships
Chalmers, *Rev.* James, 198
Chester, Henry, 188
Cheyne, Captain Andrew, 20
Chinese labour, 167-8
Choiseul, 19, 23, 25
Cingalese labour, 165-6
Coath, John, 48, 69, 93, 105
Colonial Office, 13, 53, 91, 186, 225, 245
Colonial Sugar Refining Co., goes to Queensland, 99; invests at Mackay,

Colonial Sugar Refining Co.—*continued*
    164; at Ingham, 173; in Fiji, 175; in
    N.S.W. 210; turns to central factory
    system, 210; expenditure of on
    Kanaka health, 216; death-rate on
    Fijian plantations of, 217; techno-
    logical advances of, 229-30; rumour-
    ed intention of to quit Queensland,
    244
Comins, *Rev.* Richard, 235
Convict transportation, 5
Conway station, 111
Cooktown, 170-2
Coolie trade, 5-6, 12; to Mauritius, 5,
    165; to Natal, 6, 165, 275-6; to
    West Indies, 5, 13, 276; to Queens-
    land, 164-6
Coomera River, 95
Copeland, *Rev.* Joseph, 36
Corney, *Dr* B. G., 217
Cotton industry, 1-7, 13, 95
Courier, Brisbane, 12, 105, 107, 198
Cowley, E., 201, 216
Cran, Robert, 97, 99, 204
Crittenden, Thomas, 236-7
Cromar, John, 141
Crossley, John, 45, 52
C.S.R. *See* Colonial Sugar Refining Co.
Curry, Michael, 250

Daly, *Captain* John, 152
Danks, *Rev.* Benjamin, 160, 170, 175-6
Davidson, John Ewen, 108-9, 225
Davies, *Captain* Joseph, 180-6, 196, 201
Deakin, Alfred, 263
Demoselle, *Captain*, 139
D'Entrecasteaux group, 190
Deportation, authorized by Common-
    wealth Restriction Acts 1901-6,
    260, 264; Government supervision
    of, 263, 265; begins, 265-6; uncer-
    tainties concerning, 266-7; scenes
    associated with, 267-8; effects of in
    Queensland, 270-1; effects of in
    islands, 271-4. *See also* Legislation
Des Voeux, *Sir* William, 201, 203
Deutsche Handels und Plantagen Gesell-
    schaft, 177
Don Juan. See under Ships
Dowell, Peter, 154-6, 174
Drysdale Bros., 218, 231
Duffield, A. J., 193-6
Duke of York island, 176-8

Easterbrook, William, 147
Eden, Charles, 108-9
Efate, 36, 46, 55
Epi, 46, 135
Eromanga, 25-9, 155-6

Erskine, *Commander* James, 216
European immigration, 209, 229, 241

Fairymead Plantation, 99, 247
Fanny. See under Ships
Fenwick, John & Co., 49
Ferguson, *Captain*, 24, 160
Fiji, labour conditions in, 69, 217; annex-
    ed by Great Britain, 142; expan-
    sion of sugar industry in, 175
Fiji Times, 68
Fijian labour trade, 68, 69-70, 74, 142,
    175, 217
Finlay, *Captain* Samuel, 195
Florida Islands, 19, 22-3
Fowles, James, 238
France, in the Pacific, 50, 52, 187
Freeman, Thomas, 199-200
Funaa Vou, 136-7

Gairloch plantation, 173, 230
Geddie, *Rev.* John, 11, 30-4, 36, 88
German recruiting, 158, 177
Germany, expansion of in Pacific, 170,
    177-8; confronts Britain in New
    Guinea, 186-7; protests over Queens-
    land action, 190; moves to annex
    New Guinea, 201; annexes portion
    of Solomons, 221
Gerrit Denys island, 179, 191
Ghorai, "King", 24-5, 41, 66, 220-1
Gibbins, *Captain*, 44, 47
Gildie, Hugh, 223
Godden, *Rev.* Charles, 273-4
Goldie, Andrew, 172
Goodenough, *Commodore* James, 98
Gordon, *Sir* Arthur, 149, 160
Gordon, *Rev.* George, 33, 37
Gordon, *Rev.* James, 38
Gore, *Sir* Ralph, 174
Gorrie, *Judge* John, 152-3
Government Agents, position created 1870,
    71; virtual impotence of, 143; duties
    of, 146; attitude of, to regulations,
    231
Greuber, *Captain*, 10
Griffith, *Sir* Samuel, becomes Queensland
    Premier, 190, 211; meets Duffield,
    194; intervenes in *Heath* and *Stan-
    ley* cases, 196; accused of abetting
    the recruiters, 198; association with
    Brookes, 207; considers European
    immigration, 209; promotes legis-
    lation to control labour trade, 212-
    13; appoints Royal Commission, 219;
    bars certain recruiters, 224; pro-
    motes central factory system, 228;
    opposed by unions, 229; loses general
    elections, 1888, 239; record of failures

Griffith—*continued*
  of, 240; tours North, 241; permits resumption of labour trade, 241-2; retirement from politics, 253
Guadalcanal, 135, 233

Hailey, Chief, of Kolombangara, 24, 159
Hambledon plantation, 173, 230
Hamleigh plantation, 173, 230
Hawaiian recruiting, 140
Hayes, "Bully", 66
Head-hunting, 19-23, 35, 67
Heath. See under Ships
Herbert, Robert, 13
Herbert River, 96, 173, 216
Hernsheims & Co., 176-7, 180, 190
Higginson, John, 187
Hill-Wray, C. J., 204-6
Homebush plantation, 164, 217
Hope, *Captain* Louis, 43, 44, 47, 95, 144
Hopeful case, 219, 223-4, 240. *See also under* Ships
Hornidge, John, 234-5
Houghton, *Lieutenant* de, 149-50
Hovell, *Captain* Albert, 55-8
Howie, *Captain* James, 220-2
Howitt, *Major*, 232

Immigration Dept., inspection of labour vessels by, 48; fails to condemn labour trade, 49, 145, 213; duties of, under 1868 Act, 53-4; and care of islanders in Queensland, 69; relations with leading recruiters, 174; character of, in north Queensland, 218; and reaction to *William Manson* case, 254; and superintendence of deportation, 264. *See also* European immigration *and* Queensland Government
Immigration Office. *See* Immigration Dept.
Indian Government, 5, 7, 12, 164
Indispensable Reef, 185
Ingham, 173, 217
Inglis, *Rev.* John, 11
Irving, J. C., 70
Isabel, 19, 128

Jason. See under Ships
Johnstone, *Sub-Inspector* R. A., 109

Kaan Islands, 179, 191, 215
Kabau, chief, of Malaita, 127-8, 130
Kalamia plantation, 173
Kalekona, chief, of Ngela, 161-2
Kava, 31
Kennedy, *Sir* Arthur, 186
Kidnapping, accusations of against *Uncle Tom*, 43, 46; variations of, 47-8, 70,

Kidnapping—*continued*
  224; by *King Oscar*, 48; by *Syren*, 50; by *Young Australian* 56-8; by *Jason*, 70-3; by *Carl*, 80-4; by *Hopeful*, 177, 199-201, 224; by *Stanley*, 181-2; by *William Manson*, 250-3. *See also* Recruiters
Kilgour, *Captain* G. S., 105, 151-2
King Oscar. See under Ships
Kolombangara, 19, 23, 24
Kwaisulia, chief, of Malaita, social origins of, 129-30, 135; recruits for Queensland, 130; returns to Malaita, 135; becomes overlord of lagoon, 135; attacks Funaa Vou, 136; attacks Isabel, 137; meets Bishop Wilson, 137; alliance of with recruiters, 159, 234, 237-8; attacks Manaoba, 238; assists Vos in recruiting, 249-51, 254; death of, 272

Labour vessels. *See* Ships
Lannuzel, *Father*, 172, 177-8, 190
Laughlan Islands, 180
Lautour, George de, 146
Law Courts, 58, 60, 63-5, 91, 93-4, 105, 152, 201, 218-19, 254
Lawes, *Rev.* W. G., 172, 216
Legislation: Queensland Coolie Act, 1862, 7, 12; Polynesian Labourers Act, 1868, 53-4, 71, 106-7; Pacific Islanders Protection Act, 1872 (Kidnapping Act), 92-3, 114, 152; Pacific Island Labourers Act, 1880, 204-8; Pacific Island Labourers' Amendment Acts, 212-13, 226, 261; Pacific Islanders Extension Act, 1892, 246, 260; Commonwealth Restriction Acts, 1901-6, 260, 264. *See also* Queensland Government
Lennie, Robert, 55-8
Levinger, Hugo, 55-7
Lewin, Ross, 10-11; early career of, 42-3; character of, 43-5, sets up own business 45-6, 49; begins kidnapping, 46, 69, 111-12; buys the *Daphne*, 58-9; settles on Tanna, 60-1; death of, 94
Lisa, Albert, of Ambrym, 247-8
Lizzie. See under Ships
L.M.S. *See* London Missionary Society
Lockhead, William, 163
Logan River, 1, 44, 95
London Missionary Society, 172, 198, 199, 216
Lord of the Isles. See under Ships
Louisiade Archipelago, 190
Loutit, *Captain* John, 141-3
Loyalty Islands, 45-6, 50, 55, 211, 267

McDonald, A. R., 217
McEachern, *Captain* R., 49-51, 105
MacFarlane, *Rev.* Samuel, 172, 176
McIlwraith, *Sir* Thomas, 187, 188; plans annexation of New Guinea, 188; his Government defeated, 190, 203; replies to British criticism, 203; becomes Premier for second term, 1888, 239-40
McIntyre, *Rev.* John, 246
Mackay (Queensland), 95, 99, 239; native attitudes towards, 98, 227; importance of, in sugar industry, 163; and separation movement, 168; Racecourse incident, 211-12
Mackay, Angus, 209-10, 228
McKenzie, Robert, 49
McLeod, Donald, 36
McMurdo, William, 146; travels in *Stanley*, 180-6; charged with kidnapping, 196; found guilty, 201; journals of, 203
McNeil, Neil, 199-200, 219
Magnolia plantation, 206
Mahaffy, A. W., 271
Malaita, 23; patrilineal system, 122; chieftainship, 124; funeral ceremonies, 125; wars, 125-6; first relations with Europeans, 126-7; artificial islands, 126-7; religion, 134; importance of, in Queensland recruiting, 233; danger of, to recruiters, 249
Malekula, 36, 43, 50; social life in 115-16; trading relationships of, 116; ceremonial life of, 119; graded society in, 120; relations of, with Europeans, 131, 137-8, 271-2; general decline of, 131-2; religion of, 134
Mandoliana island, 180-1
Marist mission, 31, 172
Markham, *Captain* Albert, 84
Marr, Charles, 236, 238
Martin, *Captain* James, 139
Maryborough, 44, 68, 74, 99, 105; native attitudes towards, 98, 227; opposes Sydney influence, 164
Mathieson, *Rev.*, 36-7
Matson, William, 144
Mauritius, 5, 7
Maxwell, Walter, 259-60, 262
Meiklejohn, John, 71-4
Melanesian Mission, 38, 50, 88, 126, 245
Melbourne Sugar Co., 173, 230
Michelsen, *Rev.* Oscar, 167
Millaquin refinery, 99, 164
Mills, Christopher, 141-3
Milne, *Rev.* Peter, 70, 72-3
Minister, Nicholas, 191-2, 198, 199, 218
Missionaries, control of Aneityum, 29-34, 154; oppose recruiting, 46; character

Missionaries—*continued*
of, 74; attitudes of, to labour trade, 77, 154; protests of, to Queensland Govt. 198; their influence in islands, 244-5, 245-8. *See also* London Missionary Society, Marist mission, Melanesian Mission, Native teachers, Presbyterian mission
Morehead, Boyd, 239, 240
Moresby, *Captain* John, 87
Moresby Island, 218
Morris, William, 80-4, 93
Morrison, George, 194
Mount, Henry, 80-4, 93
Mourilyan Sugar Co., 215
Muir, Thomas, 151
Mulgrave plantation, 230; central mill, 262
Murray, *Dr* James, 78-85, 93-4
Murray, W. J., 232
Musgrave, *Sir* Anthony, 225

Native teachers, 70, 74, 76
Nausori mill, 175, 217
Navusa plantation, 217
Neilson, *Rev.* Thomas, 56, 147-8
Neusa, 176
New Britain, 169-70, 177, 190
New Caledonia, 9, 45, 49-50, 52, 187
New Caledonian recruiting, 140, 274, 276
Newcastle, *Duke* of, 7
New Georgia, 18, 20
New Guinea, 169-70, 172, 186; character of natives, 169, 215-16; recruiting begins in, 175; annexation of, 186-9, 201; end of, as recruiting area, 201; death rate among islanders from, 216
New Hebrides, 45, 187, 233, 266
New Ireland, 169, 170, 176-8, 190
New South Wales, 39, 65, 187, 210, 259, 270
Nguna, 70, 74-5, 77, 130
Niuta people, 76-8
Nomu, of Tanna, 155-6
North Australian Pastoral Co., 188
North Eton Central Mill, 228
North Queensland separatism, 168, 225

Oba, 15, 153, 273
Olver, George, 250-1
Outon, of Aneityum, 154

Paama, 56-8
Paddon, James, 29, 31, 34
Palmer, Arthur Hunter, 52
Palmer, *Captain* George, 61-6, 84, 91
Parliamentary investigations into labour trade: Queensland Select Committee, 1869, 71, 112; Select Committee,

Parliamentary Investigations—*continued*
1876, 114; Royal Commission, 1885,
219, 223-4, 232; Royal Commission,
1889, 239; Royal Commission, 1906,
263-4. *See also* Queensland Government

Paton, *Rev.* John, 36-40; at Aniwa, 46;
world-wide contacts of, 56; attacks
recruiting trade, 58; writes to Griffith, 244; accused of exaggerating
labour trade evils, 244; support of
by Melbourne *Argus*, 245; influence
of, in Britain, 245; opposition to in
Australia, 246

Patteson, *Bishop* John, 48, 88-90, 126, 147

Pearl-shelling, 45

Pease, *Captain* Ben, 66

Pennefather, *Captain*, 201

Penny, *Rev.* Alfred, 161

Pentecost Island, 149

Philp, Robert, 43, 174-5, 191, 219, 261

Pioneer plantation, 173, 218

Plantations, 15; crushing methods of, 97-8;
great expansion of after 1880, 173;
conditions on, 204-5; death-rate
upon, 216; economic crisis of, 230;
wages on, 242-3; numbers of labour
employed by, 243

Plessen, *Baron*, 189

Pleystowe plantation, 243

Poogey, chief, of Rendova, 221

Popham, Home, 236

Port Adam, 233

Port Denison Times, 110-11

Port Douglas, 222

Port Moresby, 172, 186

Powlanga, chief, of Malaita, 233-4

Presbyterian Church, 246

Presbyterian Mission, 30, 39, 55-6, 58, 63

Preston, James, 112

Pritchard, Thomas, 59, 62

Proctor, James, 157-8

Queensland, 6, 12, 14, 67, 69, 107, 204; as
field for free emigration, 7, 104; interest of islanders in, 17, 128; pro-
gresses in tropical agriculture, 43,
95; large-scale introduction of island
labour into, 48; expansion of pastoral industry in, 48; expansion of
sugar industry in, 43-4, 164, 173;
relations with Melanesia, 129; reputation affected by labour trade, 204,
254; dependence of, on sugar, 240

Queensland Figaro, 198

Queensland Government, passes Coolie
Act 1862, 7, 12; passes Polynesian
Labourers Act, 1868, 53-4; appoints
1869 Select Committee into labour

Queensland Government—*continued*
trade, 112-13; appoints second Committee, 1876, 114; issues regulations
re firearms, 145; contemplates new
Coolie Act, 164; attempts annexation of New Guinea, 186; reaction
of, to German protests, 190; bans
New Guinea recruiting, 190; accused
of failing to suppress abuses, 203;
enacts legislation controlling labour
trade, 1880-5, 204, 206-8, 212, 226;
investigates sugar industry overseas,
209; appoints Royal Commission,
1885, 219, 223-4, 232; appoints Royal
Commission, 1889, 239; ambitions of
regarding Solomons, 254; appoints
Royal Commission, 1906, 263-4

Queensland Kanaka Mission, 247-8

Queenslander, 172

Racecourse Mill, 228

Raff, George, 49, 104, 113, 144

Rannie, Douglas, 134, 140, 237-8

Rawson & Co., 177

Recruiters, 75; character of, 140-1; attitude
of to G.A.s, 141, 146; find difficulty
in getting recruits, 144; official hostility towards, 145, 147; relations
with Navy, 150; tricks of, 156-8, 224;
problems of after 1885, 232-3. *See
also* Kidnapping

Reef Islands, 89

Reid, George, 259

Rendova, 23, 221-2

Renton, John, 127-30, 135, 151

Riots, 211-12, 258

Robertson, *Rev.* Hugh, 155-6, 174

Rockhampton, 144

Rogers, *Captain*, 233-6, 238

Rossel Island, 192

Routch, *Captain* Augustus, 219-23

Royal Navy, 39-40, 63, 65, 68, 87; views on
labour trade, 53; character of commanders of, 61; inability of to control labour trade, 84, 91; legislation
assists work of, 114; attitude of towards certain recruiters, 147; co-
operation with Western Pacific
High Commission, 148-9; with
missionaries, 162

Rubiana Lagoon, 18, 19, 26: association of,
with head-hunting, 22-3; generally
avoided by recruiters, 220; capitu-
lation of, to missionaries, 271

San Christobal, 89

Sandalwooding, 8-9, 26, 28, 34, 43

Santa Cruz Island, 89, 180

Satini, Carl, 145, 150, 155-6, 174

Scholfield, Henry, 199, 219
Seaforth plantation, 172, 224
Selwyn, *Bishop* George, 88
Selwyn, *Bishop* John Richardson, 88, 245
Shaw, *Captain* Louis, 199-200, 219
Sheridan, R. B., 98
Ships
  Labour Vessels:
    Agnes Donald, 151
    Alfred Vitter, 180, 220
    Archimedes, 238
    Ariel, 220, 232
    Black Dog, 44-9
    Bobtail Nag, 128, 144
    Borealis, 160
    Borough Belle, 174
    Carl, 79-84
    Ceara, 155, 191-3, 213, 219
    Chance, 145
    Daphne, 59-65
    Don Juan, 10, 11, 13, 44, 46
    Elibank Castle, 220-3
    Eliza Mary, 232
    Emily, 180
    Emma Bell, 89
    Empreza, 264
    Ethel, 141-3
    Fanny, 74-8, 177-9
    Fanny Nicholson, 52
    Fearless, 238
    Flora, 237-8
    Forest King, 219
    Fredericka Wilhelmina, 179, 219
    Heath, 193-6, 198, 219
    Heather Bell, 45, 151
    Helena, 167
    Heron, 140, 233
    Hopeful, 174-8, 189, 199-201, 214
    Janet Stewart, 162-3
    Jason, 68-9, 71-4
    Jessie Kelly, 177, 179, 215
    Juventa, 217
    King Oscar, 46-8, 111-12
    Lavinia, 146, 193
    Lizzie, 154, 174, 191, 219
    Lochiel, 220
    Lord of the Isles, 168, 175-6, 179
    Lyttona, 104
    Madeleine, 146, 179, 213
    Margaret Chessel, 70, 89
    May Queen, 105, 144, 149
    Meg Merrilees, 235
    Mystery, 85, 151
    Nukulau, 85
    Para, 238
    Percy, 45
    Reliance, 59-60
    Roderic Dhu, 166-7

Labour Vessels—*continued*
    Spec, 45, 46
    Spunkie, 47-8
    Stanley, 48, 179, 180-6, 190
    Stormbird, 85, 141, 143, 145
    Sybil, 140, 150, 217
    Syren, 49-51, 112, 131
    Uncle Tom, 42-3, 44, 54, 55
    William Manson, 248-55
    Young Australian, 55-8
    Young Dick, 233-6

  Naval Vessels:
    H.M.S. *Alacrity*, 147
    H.M.S. *Basilisk*, 87, 91
    H.M.S. *Beagle*, 147, 150
    H.M.S. *Conflict*, 147
    H.M.S. *Cormorant*, 162
    H.M.S. *Curacoa*, 39, 40
    H.M.S. *Dart*, 233
    H.M.S. *Falcon*, 46
    H.M.S. *Miranda*, 153, 213
    H.M.S. *Opal*, 235
    H.M.S. *Pegasus*, 272
    H.M.S. *Pelorus*, 9
    H.M.S. *Renard*, 147
    H.M.S. *Rosario*, 81, 84
    H.M.S. *Sandfly*, 147, 160
    H.M.S. *Swinger*, 201
    H.M.S. *Wolverene*, 152

  Others:
    Brothers, 8
    City of Melbourne, 222
    Constantine, 139
    Dancing Wave, 159
    Daniel Watson, 28
    Dauphin, 139
    Dayspring, 77
    Devonshire, 165
    Elizabeth, 26
    Esperanza, 159
    Isabella Anna, 26
    John Williams, 32
    Malaita, 267
    Mary Anderson, 232
    Moresby, 267
    Peri, 86-8
    Ripple, 24
    Southern Cross, 38, 47
    Tambo, 267
    Telegraph, 45
Short, Robert, 54
Shortland Islands, 18
Sikeri, chief, of Oba, 151, 153
Simbo, 18, 19, 23
Sinclair, John, 207
Sinerago Bay, 235-6

Slavery, in Africa, 5, 52, 275-6; in Mauritius, 5, 44; in Peru, 42; in West Indies, 5, 44; attempts by Royal Navy to suppress, 63
Solomon Islands, 18, 233
South Johnstone River, 215
South Seas Trading Co., 55
Spiller, John, 95-6
Spring Hill plantation, 229
Stanley. See under Ships
Steel, *Rev.* Robert, 58
Stormbird. See under Ships
Sudest island, 192
Sugar industry, beginnings of, in Queensland, 43-4, 67; problems of cane-growing, 96; in N.S.W., 96, 210; extends to Maryborough district, 97; production figures of, 99; extends to Mackay and Bundaberg, 164; large investment in, 164; labour problems of, 164, 168; on the Herbert, 209; decline in, 224; markets, 225; in European countries, 225. *See also* Colonial Sugar Refining Co. *and* Plantations
Sugar mills, 96-7, 209-11. *See also* Homebush plantation, Millaquin refinery, Victoria plantation, Yengarie mill
Sulu Vou, 127-30, 135-7
Swallow and Derham, 173
Sydney Mail, 242
Sydney Morning Herald, 64
Syren. See under Ships

Tabbisangwul, chief, of Pentecost, 149
Tabbiseisei, chief, of Pentecost, 149-50
Tahitian recruiting, 140
Tanna, 28, 35-40, 144, 266
Tannese, character of, 4, 16, 25, 35, 108; employment of, in Queensland, 16-17, 215-16
Teste island, 191
Tetzlaff, Carl, 180-2, 190
Thomas, Julian, 154
Thomas, *Captain* Ludford, 165
Thomson, *Dr* John, 204-6
Thursday Island, 170
Thurston, *Sir* John, 58
Times, The, 203
Tomuin, Chief, of Laughlans, 181-3

Tongoa, 132, 167
Tooth, Robert, 97, 204
Towns, *Captain* Robert, 1, 4, 7, 34, 95; career of, 8-9, 26, 29; character, 8, 11, 26, 42; inaugurates labour trade, 10-17, 42; defends conduct, 63
Townsvale, 1, 7, 13-14, 43, 45
Townsville, 16, 218
Trade-unions, 229, 241
Treasury Island, 18, 23, 180
Trobriand Islands, 180, 190
Trollope, Anthony, 115, 133
Try, Billy, of Malaita, 249-51
Turner, *Rev.* George, 28

Umo, of Eromanga, 156
Uncle Tom. See under Ships

Vella Lavella, 19, 23, 180
Victoria plantation, 173, 216
Vos, *Captain* Joseph, 154; chosen as Burns Philp recruiter, 174; debarred from trade, 224; master-owner of *William Manson*, 248; alliance of with Kwaisulia, 249; trial and acquittal, 254-5
Vuria, of Ngela, 161-2

Walsh, William, 49, 73-4
Wawn, *Captain* William, 98, 130, 144, 150; finds regulations oppressive, 145; begins New Guinea recruiting, 178; becomes Burns Philp recruiter, 191; recruits in *Heath*, 218-19
Wesleyan mission, 170, 175
Western Pacific High Commission, 149
Whish, *Captain* Claudius, 44
White Australia Policy, 259
Wide Bay Farmers & Planters Association, 172
William Manson. See under Ships
Williamson, Ishmael, 49-50, 105
Wilson, *Bishop* Cecil, 88, 137
Wilson, *Commodore* John, 152-3
Winchester, *Captain*, 36
Wiseman, *Sir* William, 39, 91
Woodford, Charles, 273
Woodlark islands, 181-3

Yengarie mill, 98-9; plantation, 204-5
Young Australian. See under Ships
Young Bros., 99
Young, Florence, 247, 256
Yumanga, of Tanna, 148